SAYYEDAT NESĀ' AL-ᶜĀLAMĒN

Chief of the Women of the World

Moṣṭafa Ḥosayni

First published in England in 2003 by
Islamic Propagation Center

www
real-islam.org.uk

A cataloge record for this book is vailable from the British Library

ISBN 0-9539260-3-6

﴾IN THE NAME OF ALLĀH, THE MOST COMPASSIONATE, THE MOST MERCIFUL﴿
﴾ALL PRAISE IS DUE TO ALLĀH, THE LORD OF THE WORLDS﴿
﴾THE MOST COMPASSIONATE, THE MOST MERCIFUL﴿
﴾MASTER OF THE DAY OF JUDGMENT﴿
﴾THEE DO WE WORSHIP AND THEE DO WE BESEECH FOR HELP﴿
﴾KEEP US ON THE RIGHT PATH﴿
﴾THE PATH OF THOSE UPON WHOM THOU HAST BESTOWED FAVORS﴿
﴾NOT (THE PATH) OF THOSE UPON WHOM THY WRATH IS BROUGHT DOWN, NOR OF THOSE WHO GO ASTRAY[1]﴿

Dedication

For Islam's youngest sacrifice,

the Martyred Fetus,

the Third Sebṭ,

the first offering of the Rightful Khelāfah,

the first victim of the Bakri party,

for Moḥassin;

I dedicate this humble work, hoping that it would prove a useful provision on "The day on which property will not avail, nor sons[2]".

---

[1] Holy Qor'ān = sōrah 1.
[2] Holy Qor'ān = sōrah 26, āyah 88.

CONTENTS

ARABIC TRANSLITERATION 7

INTRODUCTION ***11***

GRIEVANCE **16**

SAYYEDAT NESĀ' AL-ᶜĀLAMĒN BEFORE MARRIAGE ***24***

Fāṭimah's creation 24
Heavenly child 25
The pregnancy 27
Her birth 28
Human Houri 30
Naming the newly born 30
Date of birth 31
Khadējah dies 32
Fāṭimah and the Idolaters 33

SAYYEDAT NESĀ' AL-ᶜĀLAMĒN'S MARRIAGE ***35***

Abō Bakr and ᶜOmar ask for her hand in marriage 35
Amēr al-Mo'menēn asks for her hand in marriage 37
Marriage in the sky 38
Fāṭimah takes ᶜAli as her husband 39
The marriage gift 40

The wedding 41
The wedding banquet 42

SAYYEDAT NESĀ' AL-ᶜĀLAMĒN'S CHILDREN ***43***
Birth of Imām Ḥasan 43
Birth of Imām Ḥosayn 44
Birth of Sayyedah Zaynab 45
Moḥassin, the Martyred Fetus 46

SAYYEDAT NESĀ' AL-ᶜĀLAMĒN'S MORALS ***48***
Altruism 49
Contentment 53
Courage 55
Equality 56
Excessive generosity 57
Honor for knowledge 60
Love for teaching 62
Patience 64
Simplicity 66
Zohd 67

SAYYEDAT NESĀ' AL-ᶜĀLAMĒN'S MISSION ***69***

HER DOᶜĀ' **73**
A- Secret Adᶜeyah: 75
B- Private Adᶜeyah: 75
C- Public Adᶜeyah: 76

HER POLITICS **84**
Complete Endorsement For Amēr al-Mo'menēn 85
Importance of a pledge of allegiance 85
Importance of Fāṭimah's endorsement 87
Fāṭimah's pledge of allegiance 89
Complete Rejection Of Abō Bakr's Party 92
Open confrontation with the Bakri party 92
Total condemnation 95
Severe protests 98
Labeling The Bakri Party As Non-Moslem 99

Calling for uprising 101
Fāṭimah ignores her injuries 101
Completion of proof 103
Why did she not ask for uprising publicly 104
Who did she ask? 105
Fāṭimah calls for uprising 106
Feeble excuses 107
Mo°āwiyah admits 108
Continuous Mourning 109
Mourning on Rasōlollāh 109
Why so much mourning? 110
"What" and "Who"? 111
The Bakri party bans Fāṭimah from mourning 113
Reasons behind the ban 114
°Omar's view about mourning the dead 115
Fāṭimah's persistence 119
Fāṭimah's perseverance 119
The House of Grief 119
The Bakri party demolishes the House of Grief 120
Her Political Legacy 120
Secret burial ceremonies 121
Endless opposition to the Bakri party 122

HER TEACHINGS **124**
1- Narrating from Rasōlollāh 126
2- Teaching from her own 131
Actions Before Words 134
The Book of Fāṭimah 137
Her Students 141
1- Asmā' bint °Omays 142
2- Feḍḍah 143
3- Jābir ibn °Abdollāh al-Anṣāri 148
4- Omm Ayman 152
5- Omm Salamah 154
6- Salmā 156
7- Salmān 157

SAYYEDAT NESĀ' AL-ᶜĀLAMĒN IN THE HOLY QOR'ĀN ***163***

1- The Āyah of Taṭ-heṛ (purification) 163
2- The Āyah of Mobāhalah 174
3- The Āyah of Qorbā 178
4- The Āyah of Ahl al-Dhekr 182
5- Sōrah of al-Kawthar 189

SAYYEDAT NESĀ' AL-ᶜĀLAMĒN IN THE HOLY HADEETH ***195***

1- Fāṭimah's Satisfaction and Anger 196
2- Fāṭimah and Rasōlollāh 198
3- At war with your enemies and in peace with your friends 203
4- Sayyedat Nesā' al-ᶜĀlamēn 204
5- Human Houri 208

SAYYEDAT NESĀ' AL-ᶜĀLAMĒN'S KARĀMĀT AND MOᶜJEZĀT ***211***

1- The light of Fāṭimah's face 211
2- Fire does not burn Fāṭimah 212
3- The light of Fāṭimah's wrapper 213
4- When Fāṭimah threatens to curse 214
5- Angels serve Fāṭimah 215

SAYYEDAT NESĀ' AL-ᶜĀLAMĒN AND RASŌLOLLĀH'S MARTYRDOM ***217***

SAYYEDAT NESĀ' AL-ᶜĀLAMĒN AND THE BAKRI PARTY ***229***

ᶜAli and Fāṭimah's options 236
Fāṭimah's role in the defense of ᶜAli 237
Several attacks on Fāṭimah's home 239

MOḤASSIN, THE MARTYRED FETUS **248**

A revealing comparison 249
Who took part in the attacks? 250
Abō Bakr orders the attacks 252

Rasōlollāh prophesizes Fāṭimah's sufferings 255
Ahl al-Bayt Speak About Fāṭimah's Suffering 260
Fāṭimah speaks about her suffering 260
ᶜAli speaks about Fāṭimah's sufferings 262
Imām Ḥasan speaks about Fāṭimah's suffering 264
Imām Sajjād refers to Fāṭimah's suffering 265
Imām Bāqir points to Fāṭimah's suffering 265
Imām Ṣādiq speaks about Fāṭimah's suffering 266
Imām Kāẓim speaks about Fāṭimah's suffering 268
Imām Reḍa mentions some of Fāṭimah's suffering 269
Imām Jawād refers to Fāṭimah's suffering 270
Imām ᶜAskari refers to Fāṭimah's suffering 271
Bakri Leaders Confess To Their Crimes Against Fāṭimah 271
Abō Bakr's confession 271
ᶜOmar's confession 272
Fāṭimah Rejects Abō Bakr And ᶜOmar 277
Were Abō Bakr and ᶜOmar truthful in their apology? 281
Whoever dies without knowing his imām… 282

THE BAKRI PARTY USURPS SAYYEDAT NESĀ' AL-ᶜĀLAMĒN'S POSITIONS ***284***

What Were These Positions? 284
Fadak 284
The Seven Farms 285
The Khoms of Khaybar 286
Rasōlollāh's inheritance 286
Khoms 287
Usurpation of Fāṭimah's positions and her demand for them in Bakri and Moslem references 288
When Abō Bakr is cornered 296
Fāṭimah's public speeches 297
Omm Salamah objects to Abō Bakr 300
Do the prophets leave inheritance?! 301
An interesting Bakri explanation! 306

Fadak Between Usurping And Returning 307

SAYYEDAT NESĀ' AL-ᶜĀLAMĒN'S MARTYRDOM 309

Fāṭimah's wish to be buried secretly at night 309

Fāṭimah prepares for death 311

ᶜAli and Fāṭimah just before her death 313

Fāṭimah in her last minutes 315

Abō Bakr and ᶜOmar want to attend Fāṭimah's burial ceremonies 317

Fāṭimah's burial ceremonies 318

ᶜAli on Fāṭimah's grave 320

Abō Bakr and ᶜOmar attempt to exhume Fāṭimah's body!! 321

ᶜĀ'eshah and Fāṭimah's death 324

GLOSSARY 325

MOSLEM REFERENCES 333

BAKRI REFERENCES 336

ARABIC TRANSLITERATION

In the Arabic language, there are a number of letters that do not have a corresponding equivalent in the English language. The English reader can easily pronounce some of them, whereas he would find others difficult to pronounce, if he has not already been exposed to the sounds of the Arabic alphabet. This is an effort to describe sounds of these letters, and or explain how their sounds are generated, hoping that the reader may have some idea about these particular letters.

To distinguish these letters, either a combination of two letters are used or, in the case of the majority of them, a normal Latin letter is used in association with a dot below it or a line or diacritic above it. Furthermore, there is another letter in the Arabic alphabet which we have indicated using the symbol (ᶜ).

The easier letters are:

(dh)
As in the word "there".

(gh)
The nearest sound for this is that of the French R.

(th)
As in the word "three".

(Ā or ā)
The diacritic or the small horizontal line above the letter, like (Ā or ā), represents a 'long' A; an alternative to writing aa. The

nearest example for the 'long' A, or (Ā or ā), in English words is: "far" as opposed to "fat". In the case of "far", the 'A' is elongated in the pronunciation, whereas in the case of "fat", the 'A' is short.

(Ē or ē) and (Ō or ō)

The diacritic or the small horizontal line above the letters (Ē or ē) and (Ō or ō) represents a 'long' E and a 'long' O; an alternative to writing ee and oo. Example of these letters in English words are: "need" and "noon".

And the more difficult letters are:

(ᶜ)

This symbol is used to characterize an Arabic letter that represents the sound of 'strong' A. Creating the sound of (ᶜ) is similar to that of the normal 'A', with the difference that the former is generated further up in the beginning of the throat, where more muscles are contracted to block more of the throat. And just as in the case of the normal 'A', the sound is actually generated at the time of the release of the contraction of the muscles involved.

(Ḍ or ḍ)

The sound of this letter is somewhere near the sound of (Ẓ). (Ḍ or ḍ) is generated by slightly pressing the tip of the tongue against the tip of the front upper teeth, whilst caving in the middle part of the tongue.

(Ḥ or ḥ)

The sound of this letter resembles the sound of 'strong' H. The sound for (Ḥ or ḥ) is generated from the proximity of the throat that the normal H is, but from an area slightly further up the throat, with the back end of the tongue closing in against the roof of the throat immediately before the uvula whilst forcing the air though in the outward direction.

(Kh)

The sound for this is perhaps somewhere between that of 'H' and 'K', as far as the location of mouth where it is generated is concerned. It is generated by pressing the back end of the tongue against the uvula whilst forcing the air though in the outward direction causing the uvula to vibrate between the tongue and the hard pallet.

Some examples of the sound of (kh) found in English words or words that the English reader may be familiar with are:

"Loch", the Scottish word for lake, where the 'ch' in loch is pronounced as the designated (kh) in Arabic. And "Mikhail", as in Mikhail Gorbachev, where the 'kh' is, or should be pronounced as it is required in the Arabic language.

(Q)

The sound for this letter is a short and sharp version of the letter (gh) or the French R. Whereas in the process of generating the sound of (gh), the back end of the tongue is pressed slightly against the uvula, allowing some air to flow, in the case of the sound of the Arabic alphabet represented by Q, the same process takes place with the difference that the passage is completely blocked, and the sound is actually generated by the sudden release of the blockage.

(Ṣ or ṣ)

The sound of this letter resembles the sound of 'strong' S. In aid of pronouncing (Ṣ or ṣ), it would be helpful if you consider saying the letter 'S' when the front upper and lower teeth are brought closer together reducing the airflow, thus producing the sound of the letter 'S'. The opposite process is used to generate the sound of (Ṣ or ṣ), i.e. the sound is produced when slightly moving apart the upper and lower teeth whilst slightly curving the center of the front half of the tongue in the downwards direction, thus pronouncing (Ṣ or ṣ).

(Ṭ or ṭ)

The sound of this letter resembles the sound of 'strong' T. Whereas a normal T is generated by involving the front end of the tongue, (Ṭ or ṭ) is generated by pressing the front end of the trunk of the tongue against the front end of the hard palate or the roof of the mouth with the tip of the tongue actually touching the back of the upper front teeth.

(Ẓ or ẓ)

The sound of this letter nowhere near that of a normal Z! The best description of this sound is that it could be the strong version of (dh) as in the word "*th*ere". Whereas (dh) is generated by placing the tip of the tongue between the upper and lower front teeth, whilst slightly pressing against the upper front teeth, the sound for (Ẓ or ẓ) is generated by placing more of the front end of the tongue between the upper and lower front teeth, whilst slightly pressing against the upper front teeth, and curving the center of the tongue downwards.

'Double' letters

In the Arabic language, there are many instances where a letter in a word has double pronunciations with a very slight or no pause between the two. For correct pronunciation of the word, it is important that there is a very slight pause between the sounds of the double letters. Some examples are as follows:

"Allāh", where the 'll' indicate the double pronunciation of the letter 'l'. It may help if the word is considered as "Al-lāh", but the pause due to the hyphen is very light. And "Makkah", where the presence of 'mm' indicate the requirement of double pronunciation of the letter 'm'.

INTRODUCTION

Muslims believe that Allāh created the worlds and the creations to test the creatures to whom He would grant the power of intellect and the ability of choice. Those who succeed will enter Heaven where they shall reside forever in complete and continuous pleasure; and those who fail will fall into Hell where they shall remain in utter and constant pain.

In this gigantic examination hall, man knows the good and the evil both of which are equally visible to him, as Allāh says in the Holy Qor'ān:

﴿*AND POINTED OUT TO HIM THE TWO CONSPICUOUS WAYS*[1].﴾.

And in this corridor to the Hereafter, Allāh created various magnets that pull human beings towards Heaven, and in parallel to this he also created different inducements that push them in the direction of Hell. And these armies of good and evil are very well matched and equal in force.

The evil-commanding self is countered with the self-reproaching self; the bad friend is matched with the good friend; animal desires can be controlled by the intellect... And in this hard battle between the good and the evil pulling powers, the examinee remains in total choice; he can choose Heaven over Hell or the other way round.

Moslems also believe that in the previous worlds Allāh tested these rational beings, and chose a number of them to become His messengers to His creatures in the next worlds, to guide them to

[1] Holy Qor'ān = sōrah (chapter) 90, āyah (verse) 10.

the right path and to help them elevate through the levels of perfection and completion.

After passing their tests, these messengers were given special qualities and powers that were necessary for Allāh's representatives and by which they were distinguished. And this was not subject to race or age, thus ᶜĒsā was born a prophet whose conception and birth were miraculous as Allāh reveals in the Holy Qor'ān[1]. And Moḥammad's birth was surrounded with many

---

1

﴿AND MENTION MARYAM IN THE BOOK WHEN SHE DREW ASIDE FROM HER FAMILY TO AN EASTERN PLACE * SO SHE HANGED A CURTAIN (TO SCREEN HERSELF) FROM THEM; THEN WE SENT TO HER OUR RŌḤ, AND THERE APPEARED TO HER A WELL-MADE MAN * SHE SAID: SURELY I TAKE REFUGE FROM YOU TO THE BENEFICENT GOD, IF YOU ARE ONE GUARDING (AGAINST EVIL) * HE SAID: I AM ONLY A MESSENGER OF YOUR LORD: THAT I WILL GIVE YOU A PURE BOY * SHE SAID: WHEN SHALL I HAVE A BOY AND NO MORTAL HAS YET TOUCHED ME, NOR HAVE I BEEN UNCHASTE? * HE SAID: EVEN SO; YOUR LORD SAYS: IT IS EASY TO ME: AND THAT WE MAY MAKE HIM A SIGN TO MEN AND A MERCY FROM US; AND IT IS A MATTER WHICH HAS BEEN DECREED * SO SHE CONCEIVED HIM; THEN WITHDREW HERSELF WITH HIM TO A REMOTE PLACE * AND THE THROES (OF CHILDBIRTH) COMPELLED HER TO BETAKE HERSELF TO THE TRUNK OF A PALM TREE. SHE SAID: OH, WOULD THAT I HAD DIED BEFORE THES, AND HAD BEEN A THING QUITE FORGOTTEN! * THEN (THE CHILD) CALLED OUT TO HER FROM BENEATH HER: GRIEVE NOT, SURELY YOUR LORD HAS MADE A STREAM TO FLOW BENEATH YOU; * AND SHAKE TOWARDS YOU THE TRUNK OF THE PALMTREE, IT WILL DROP ON YOU FRESH RIPE DATES: * SO EAT AND DRINK AND REFRESH THE EYE. THEN IF YOU SEE ANY MORTAL, SAY: SURELY I HAVE VOWED A FAST TO THE BENEFICENT GOD, SO I SHALL NOT SPEAK TO ANY MAN TODAY * AND SHE CAME TO HER PEOPLE WITH HIM, CARRYING HIM (WITH HER). THEY SAID: O MARYAM! SURELY YOU HAVE DONE A STRANGE THING * O SISTER OF HĀRŌN! YOUR FATHER WAS NOT A BAD MAN, NOR WAS YOUR MOTHER AN UNCHASTE WOMAN * BUT SHE POINTED TO HIM. THEY SAID: HOW SHOULD WE SPEAK TO ONE WHO WAS A CHILD IN THE CRADLE? * HE SAID: SURELY I AM A SERVANT OF ALLĀH; HE HAS GIVEN ME THE BOOK AND MADE ME A PROPHET; * AND HE HAS MADE ME BLESSED WHEREVER I MAY BE, AND HE HAS ENJOINED ON ME PRAYER AND PPOR-RATE SO LONG AS I LIVE; * AND DUTIFUL TO MY MOTHER, AND HE HAS NOT MADE ME INSOLENT, UNBLESSED; * AND PEACE BE ON ME ON THE DAY I WAS

miracles that were witness around the world[1], and his light was seen in the faces of his grandfathers so much that the Idolaters made countless attempts to kill them, and even his twentieth grandfather, ᶜAdnān, was attacked by around eighty worriers who wanted to kill him to prevent the birth of Moḥammad[2].

These people who are called prophets and awṣeyā' have different ranks and positions; each one is senior to some and junior to others. Every prophet is senior to his waṣi[3] or awṣeyā'; and Nōh, Ebrāhēm, Mōsā, ᶜEsā and Moḥammad are the most senior prophets, the latter being senior to the former.

Moḥammad is the most complete of Allāh's creations, and he is senior to all of the prophets before him; and his Twelve Awṣeyā' are the most complete of Allāh's creations after him, and as such they are more senior to all of the prophets and the awṣeyā' before Moḥammad.

However, Fāṭimah the daughter of Moḥammad is senior to eleven of her father's awṣeyā', thus she is the third most complete of Allāh's creations after Moḥammad and his first waṣi, ᶜAli; and she is senior to all the prophets and their awṣeyā' before Moḥammad.

Allāh and Rasōlollāh[4] said that her satisfaction and anger is that of Allāh; her content and discontent is that of Allāh; her love and hate is that of Allāh. Loving her is a redemption of sins; hating her would render all one's good deeds void. She is the Chief of the Women of the World; she is the Chief of the Women of the Heaven.

Among other things, Allāh granted her the highest levels of ᶜEṣmah[5], ᶜElm al-Ghayb[1], al-Walāyah al-Takwēneyyah[2]... She was one of the reasons for the creation of the worlds as Allāh reveals:

BORN, AND ON THE DAY I DIE, AND ON THE DAY I AM RAISED TO LIFE.. (Holy Qor'ān = sōrah 19, āyāt 16-33)

[1] Rasolollah, the Messenger of Allāh / by the author = page 29.

[2] Montahā al-Āmāl / al-Qommi (Arabic translation) = vol. 1, page 43.

[3] A successor of a prophet, chosen by Allāh and appointed by that prophet. A waṣi is not, himself, a prophet. Also khalēfah or caliph. Plural awṣeyā'.

[4] Messenger of Allāh; a title exclusively given to Prophet Moḥammad by Allāh.

[5] The state of immunity from committing sins, making mistakes, or any act of forgetfulness, etc. whilst the choice to commit sin remains open to the individual. Prophets and their awṣeyā' have this attribute and are called maᶜṣōm.

> *((O Moḥammad! if it were not for you, I would not have created the universe; and if not for ᶜAli, I would not have created you; and if not for Fāṭimah, I would not have created either of you[3].)).*

> *((Verily, I have not created any erected sky nor any flattened land nor any illuminating moon nor any shining sun nor any circling planet nor any flowing sea nor any sailing ship but for the love of these five [Moḥammad, ᶜAli, Fāṭimah, Ḥasan and Ḥosayn][4].)).*

But because this world is a gigantic examination hall in which the examinees have to choose a path on their own without being forced into any direction, Allāh subjected both the good and the bad, and the right and the wrong to the law of "sabab and mosabbab", cause and effect; as Imām[5] Ṣādiq*(AS)*[6] says:

---

[1] Knowledge-of-the-Unseen. An all-encompassing knowledge granted by Allāh to a person without the usual methods of learning; a knowledge that covers everything and everyone, and is not limited by time or space, neither is it crippled by what plagues the knowledge gained through education, such as inaccuracy, forgetfulness, etc. ᶜElm al-Ghayb includes the Unseen-World just as it includes the Seen-World; and it has various levels. Prophets and their awṣeyā' have ᶜElm al-Ghayb.

[2] Authority over the laws of nature. A power and ability granted by Allāh to a person. al-Walāyah al-Takwēneyyah has different levels of strength in accordance with its bearer's position to Allāh, and the degree of his obedience to Him. Some levels are limited to the earth and earthly things, whereas other levels exceed our planet.

[3] Min Feqh al-Zahrā' / The Martyr Āyatollāh al-ᶜOẓmā Sayyed Moḥammad Shērāzi = vol. 1, page 19.

[4] See page 129 of this book.

[5] Leader, good or bad, religious or otherwise. This title has been used for any person with a religious leading role, such as a public prayer leader or leader of a religious group or movement. But in this book it is only used as a title for one of the twelve God-appointed successors of the Prophet Moḥammad. Plural a'emmah.

[6] *ᶜAlayhes Salām,* peace be upon him.

((Allāh has declined to run the affairs of creation except through [their] causes[1].)).

And He subjected His Message and His Messengers to this rule; so at times they were loved and they were revered and they were followed, and at other times they were hated and they were hurt and they were killed; and similarly, the propagation of their messages depended on the amount of support they had from the people. Allāh says:

﴿ALL DO WE AID—THESE AS WELL AS THOSE—OUT OF THE BOUNTY OF YOUR LORD; AND THE BOUNTY OF YOUR LORD IS NOT CONFINED[2].﴾.

And Fāṭimah was not an exception to this rule, she was hated and she was hurt and she was killed when she supported the Rightful Khelāfah[3] against its usurpers; and the propagation of her message—Islam depended and will forever depend on the amount of support from her followers.

And these messengers repeatedly pointed to this fact and called their followers to make known their Way to the people, so that those worthy of Heaven may be guided to it, as the scholars narrate from many of the ma^cṣōmēn[4] who said:

((Make known our Way, may Allāh have Mercy on those who make known our Way[5].)).

---

[1] Beḥār al-Anwār / al-Majlesi = vol. 2, page 90.

[2] Holy Qor'ān = sōrah (chapter) 17, ayah (verse) 20.

[3] Successorship of Rasōlollāh. Also caliphate.

[4] Plural of ma^cṣōm: a person who does not commit sins, does not make mistakes, does not forget, etc. although he/she has the choice to commit sins. Prophets and their awṣeyā' are ma^cṣōm. The Fourteen Ma^cṣōmēn are the Prophet Moḥammad, his daughter Fāṭimah, and his twelve God-appointed successors.

[5] For some instances of these narrations see: Beḥār al-Anwār / al-Majlesi = vol. 2, pages 30 and 151; vol. 52, page 126; vol. 71, page 187; vol. 74, page 223; vol. 81, page 219.

And because of this repeated call, I decided to compile this wok and carry out some of my duty to help the younger generation of Moslems living in the West to know something about the life and mission of their Prophet's only daughter; and in the second place to give the Western people a brief account of the life and mission of this eighteen year old lady who literally shook the world; and in the third place to provide the fair-minded Bakris[1] with some of the information recorded in their references about Sayyedat Nesā' al-ᶜĀlamēn[2]. And I hope that Allāh will honor me and grant me the strength to finish this journey, and what greater honor?!

In many subjects of this book I have relied on highly respected and widely used Bakri references, not because I have any special regard or appreciation for them as a whole or for their authors, but for the fact that one's confession about himself is more effective and more penetrating than someone else's testimony.

GRIEVANCE

After the assassination of Rasōlollāh*(SAA)*[3] when the Bakri party forcefully usurped his khelāfah, it fabricated numerous commendations for its leader Abō Bakr*(LA)*[4], and worked very hard to hide the countless praises of the late prophet about his God-appointed successor, Amēr al-Mo'menēn[5]. These tireless efforts to create and strengthen this false legitimacy and to hide and enshroud that holy appointment continued for centuries.

---

[1] Plural of Bakri: a follower of Abō Bakr. Opposite Moslem, Shēᶜah, follower of Rasōlollāh. Some people unknowingly call the followers of Abō Bakr "Sonni". Sonni means a follower of the tradition of Rasōlollāh; and since the followers of Abō Bakr follow him and not Rasōlollāh, it is wrong to call them Sonnis.

[2] Chief of the Women of the World; a title given exclusively to Fāṭimah, the Daughter of Rasōlollāh, by Allāh.

[3] *Ṣallallāh ᶜAlayh wa Ālih,* Allāh's Blessings be upon him and his descendants.

[4] *Laᶜnatollāh ᶜAlayh,* may Allāh distance him from His Blessings and Mercy.

[5] Commander of the Faithful; a title given exclusively to Imām ᶜAli by Allāh.

Since the first day Abō Bakr sat in that usurped position until today, the Bakris have always oppressed the Moslems for refusing to give in to their regime and for rejecting their many alterations and distortions of the Islamic history.

They call the Moslems many names, including: "al-Rāfiḍah", the Rejecters, and even Communists and Infidels and Polytheists and Idolaters. They persistently tell their children wild fairy-tales, making them grow up hating the Moslems; they have even made a scary image for the Moslems not entirely human—a creepy being with a tail! This sounds unbelievable in the fifteenth Hejri[1] century, the era of the space travel and cloning, but it is exactly what the Bakri Grand Mofti of Syria, Shaykh Kaftārō, firmly asserted in 1983 in a public gathering in Damascus-Syria, and despite the outrage he never retracted his statement!!

All of this is expected from the Bakris, after all in some parts of the world such as Iran, the Bakris burned any Moslem they could find with fire for the sole reason of being a Moslem, and for decades to come they called the victims' children and grandchildren "Pedar-Sōkhteh", Burnt-Father, or the Son of the Burnt [father][2]. And this 'heroic', 'courageous', 'Islamic' and 'humane' treatment of Moslems has been well documented in Bakri references. For instance they write in the biography of Aḥmad ibn Esmāᶜēl Abō al-Khayr, a prominent Bakri scholar who resided in Qazween-Iran:

> *((...And the Shaykh (Abō al-Khayr) said: I will not stay in Qazween after this. And he left the city, and the people left with him, and the king also went with him.*

---

[1] The Moslem lunar calendar. It has 12 months and 355 days in a year; it starts from the year of Rasōlollāh's migration to Madinah. AH: after the Hejrah (Rasōlollāh's migration), BH: before the Hejrah.

[2] Pāidāri tā Pāye Dār / Mondhir = page 85. Many books have been written about the suffering of Moslems at the hands of the Bakris throughout the Islamic history. These books record names and give detailed accounts of barbaric executions and horrific tortures which targeted Moslem men and women of all ages and social standings, especially the scholars.

He then said: I will not return until you engrave the names of Abō Bakr and ᶜOmar on an iron and brand the foreheads of Shēᶜah[1] leaders.
So they accepted his condition, and they did as he had requested!![2])).

However what is not expected and what is most hurtful is that some people who call themselves Moslems stab other Moslems in the back and oppress them for the excuse or in the name of Moslem Unity.

Their hidden agenda to destroy Islam, or at least their ignorance and lack of knowledge about Islam and its beliefs and teachings, brings them to change and distort its principles and practices.

Instead of achieving a political and economical and social unity between all those who recite the Shahādatayn and stand facing the Kaᶜbah, they want to completely destroy the structure of Moslem belief so that it becomes indistinguishable from the Bakri system of belief.

However, some groups within this powerful minority have proceeded so far away from Islam, abandoned numerous principles, introduced various beliefs, rejected innumerable historic facts and invented many falsifications, that they can hardly call themselves Moslems.

But regardless of the different levels of deviation within this minority, one can attribute this movement, in the recent times, mainly to two schools of thought: One in Iran which, on top of everything else, promotes the idea of Waḥdat al-Mawjōd[3]; and the other in Iraq which, on top of everything else, preaches that hurting Fāṭimah is not forbidden by Islam, contrary even to what the Bakris say!![4]

---

[1] Moslem: a follower of Rasōlollāh and Amēr al-Mo'menēn. Opposite Bakri: a follower of Abō Bakr. Shēᶜah is used as singular and as plural.

[2] Āthār al-Belād wa Akhbār al-ᶜEbād / al-Qazwēni = page 402.

[3] The belief that everything is one thing and that thing is God, thus man is God, and the feces of a pig is also God; and so the eye that sees these as two different things is defective!!

[4] In recent times, this particular school of thought in Iraq has had three influential promoters—a "grand teacher", a "teacher" and a "student".

Between them, they introduced many grave deviations, one worse than the other, which evolved to something hardly called Islam.
In "al-Mabāni fi Sharh al-ᶜOrwah al-Wothqā = al-Nekāḥ, page 364" the "grand teacher" says that hurting Sayyedat Nesā' al-ᶜĀlamēn is not prohibited by Islam, where he states: ((...And the mere fact that it hurts Fāṭimah does not make it forbidden!!)).
This is despite the fact that countless Bakri scholars narrate many aḥādēth from Rasōlollāh about Fāṭimah such as:

> *((And she (Fāṭimah) is a part of me, and she is my heart, and my soul that is between my sides. So whoever annoys her, he has surely annoyed me, and whoever annoys me, he has surely annoyed Allāh.)).*
> *((Fāṭimah is a part of me, tires me what tires her.)).*
> *((Fāṭimah is a part of me, saddens me what saddens her.)).*
> *((Fāṭimah is a part of me, makes me suspicious what makes her suspicious.)).*
> *((Fāṭimah is a part of me, angers me what angers her.)).*
> *((Fāṭimah is a part of me, so whoever makes her angry, he has surely made me angry.)).*
> *((Verily, Fāṭimah is a part of me, enrages me what enrages her and annoys me what annoys her.)).* (To read more of these aḥādēth with their Bakri references, see the section 'Sayyedat Nesā' al-ᶜĀlamēn in the Holy Ḥadēth' of this book).

And in "Feqh al-Shēᶜah = vol. 3, page 126" the "grand teacher" states: ((And therefore we say that the first two usurpers of the khelāfah of Amēr al-Mo'menēn were Moslems, because they did not show hostility towards Ahl al-Bayt, but rather challenged them in coming to power, whilst recognizing their status and rank!!)).
This is despite the fact that Abō Bakr and ᶜOmar took part in several futile attempts on Rasōlollāh's life. And despite the fact that many of the Maᶜṣōmēn have said that Abō Bakr and ᶜOmar planned and ordered the assassination of Rasōlollāh; and despite the fact that even the Bakris record some of the evidence which point to Abō Bakr and ᶜOmar. (For more details see: Rasōlollāh, the Messenger of Allāh / by the author = page 181).
And this is despite the fact that all Moslem scholars and a very large number of Bakri scholars agree that Abō Bakr ordered his men to raid the home of ᶜAli and Fāṭimah; and that ᶜOmar, along with three hundred Bakri ruffians, attacked their home, surrounded it with firewood and set fire to it with its Ahl al-Bayt occupants: Amēr al-Mo'menēn, Sayyedat Nesā' al-ᶜĀlamēn, Imām Ḥasan and Imām Ḥosayn still inside, crushed the six-month-pregnant Fāṭimah between the burning door and the wall, penetrated her chest with the nail, lashed her with the whip, hit her with the sword,

slapped her face, kicked her in the stomach, killed her six-month fetus Moḥassin, put a rope around ᶜAli's neck and pulled him in the streets, unsheathed the swords to execute him in the mosque… And Moslem and Bakri scholars agree that Abō Bakr actually ordered Khālid ibn al-Walēd to assassinate ᶜAli. And Moslem and Bakri scholars also agree that the first two usurpers of the khelāfah repeatedly and systematically denied the status and the ranks of Ahl al-Bayt; rejected their testimonies and accused them of lying.

So how can a person who just speaks against Ahl al-Bayt be called a Nāṣibi (a person who shows hostility towards Ahl al-Bayt), yet Abō Bakr and ᶜOmar who were the killers of Ahl al-Bayt and the founders of the hostility against them not be Nāṣibis but be Moslems instead?!!

And in "Baḥth Ḥawl al-Walāyah" the "teacher" states: ((ᶜOmar's slapping Fāṭimah on the face was a matter of his jurisprudential opinion!!?)).

Besides the fact that no Bakri scholar brings this excuse for ᶜOmar's actions, since when did ᶜOmar become a mojtahid (jurist—a scholar who is able to extract Islamic laws from its sources)?! According to Bakri references, ᶜOmar did not even have enough knowledge of the Holy Qor'ān which is one of the sources of Islamic law; so how can the "teacher" call ᶜOmar a mojtahid?! But supposing that ᶜOmar was a qualified mojtahid, what part of Islam did allow him to hit Sayyedat Nesā' al-ᶜĀlamēm?!! The person who was chosen by Allāh and appointed by Him as the Chief of the Women of the World; a person about whom Rasōlollāh said:

> *((Fāṭimah is the mother of her father.)).*
> *((I won't agree until she agrees.)).*
> *((Your father be your sacrifice.)).*
> *((I am at war with whoever fights you, and I am in peace with whoever is in peace with you.)).* (To read more of these aḥādēth with their Bakri references, see the section 'Sayyedat Nesā' al-ᶜĀlamēn in the Holy Ḥadēth' of this book).

And if we agree with what the "teacher" writes in the above book, then we must believe that ᶜOmar will actually be rewarded by Allāh for hitting Sayyedat Nesā' al-ᶜĀlamēn!! Since Allāh rewards a mojtahid twice, if his jurisprudential opinion is right, and He rewards him once, if his jurisprudential opinion is wrong; as the Bakris say. Now maybe he was rewarded twice!!?

And in "Mabāḥith al-Oṣōl = part 1, section 2" the "teacher" states: ((And the Sonni rule which was headed by the first three Wise Kholafā' and which was based on Islam and justice, ᶜAli took his sword to defend it when he fought as a regular soldier in the battles of al-Raddah under the leadership of the First Khalēfah Abō Bakr!!?).

Although Bakri scholars have always tried desperately to create some kind of legitimacy for Abō Bakr as the first khalēfah of Rasōlollāh, but none of them has ever claimed what the "teacher" writes in the mentioned book!!
This gives total legitimacy to Abō Bakr, something that Ahl al-Bayt were suppressed for two hundred and fifty years for insistently refusing to do.
Now, if the Bakri rule was based on Islam and justice, then why did Amēr al-Mo'menēn and Sayyedat Nesā' al-ᶜĀlamēn oppose it so strongly?! And if the Bakri rule was based on Islam and justice, then it must have been right in suppressing Amēr al-Mo'menēn and Sayyedat Nesā' al-ᶜĀlamēn, who must have become traitors to Islam and justice when they rose up against Abō Bakr and his rule and therefore deserved to be punished!!?
And what part of the Bakri rule was based on Islam?! The Bakri party claimed that the successor of Rasōlollāh must be chosen by the Moslems, and they claimed that Abō Bakr was chosen by the Moslems, who really was not. And later on his deathbed, Abō Bakr appointed ᶜOmar as his successor; so what happened to the right of the Moslems to choose their leader?! And later on his deathbed, ᶜOmar formed an all-time joke of a council of six for choosing his successor, with the swords unsheathed to kill them if they strayed from his specific instructions!! Besides, does the "teacher" not claim that he believes, like other Moslems, that Allāh chose the thirteen leaders of Islam—the Prophet and his twelve successors?! So did the Bakri rule follow the leadership of Allāh's chosen leaders of Islam to be based on Islam?! How can the "teacher" say that the Bakri rule was based on Islam when it fought Islam and its God-appointed leaders?! And if the Bakri rule was based on Islam, then the "teacher" must be an infidel, since he claims that he does not follow it.
And what part of the Bakri rule was based on justice?! Killing Moḥassin?! Killing Sayyedat Nesā' al-ᶜĀlamēn?! Usurping her positions?! Usurping Rasōlollāh's inheritance?! Assassinating opposition leaders?! Raping their women?!
Besides, if one really believes that ᶜAli unsheathed his sword to defend the Bakri rule, then he must forget all about Ahl al-Bayt and grab onto the blood-stained robes of their killers—the Bakri rulers such as Abō Bakr and ᶜOmar.
And the "student" who is the creation and the invention of the fist two, has broken all records in the number of deviations he has introduced in numerous Islamic fields. In the field of Islamic history, he denies the fact that the Bakri leaders raided the home of ᶜAli and Fāṭimah and killed Moḥassin and Fāṭimah!! In the field of Islamic theology, he disputes the prophethood of some of the prophets and he rejects many of the powers and abilities and attributes of the Fourteen Maᶜṣōmēn!! In the field of Islamic

This powerful minority fiercely attacks everything and everyone that transmits information damaging to the Bakri party, even if it has been recorded in Bakri references; and it condemns and denounces everything and everyone that speaks highly in favor of the Rightful Khelāfah.

And in this regard, a number of individuals and some groups all of whom call themselves Moslems, and who are adherents of either school, showed a lot of aggression when I published my first book: 'Rasōlollāh, the Messenger of Allāh'.

They had two main objections to the book:

First: that I called the followers of Abō Bakr: 'Bakris' (followers of Abō Bakr), instead of how they call themselves: Sonnis (followers of the tradition of Rasōlollāh) or Moslems (believers in the Islamic religion). This is when everyone agrees and admits that the Bakris follow Abō Bakr; and this is when neither the Holy Qor'ān nor Rasōlollāh or any of his Rightful Kholafā' ever called the followers of Abō Bakr "Sonnis" or "Moslems". In fact the Holy Qor'ān and Rasōlollāh and his Rightful Kholafā' clearly state that the followers of Abō Bakr are non-Moslem[1].

---

law, he has declared as permissible many prohibitions and has marked as prohibited many permissibles!! In the numerous fields of the Holy Qor'ān and the Holy Ḥadēth, he has also left his dirty finger prints; he even says that there is a mistake in the Holy Qor'ān!!

The list of his deviations and distortions and aberrations is virtually endless; it is such that many of the marājiᶜ have issued decrees and statements against him and his beliefs, announcing that they are not part of Islam; and several scholars have written books against him and his beliefs. To read more about the opinions and the beliefs of this man, see: 'Ma'sāt al-Zahrā' and 'Khalfiyyat Ketāb Ma'sāt al-Zahrā'.

[1] For instance, while returning from the Farewell Pilgrimage, Allāh revealed the following āyah to Rasōlollāh:

> ﴿*O Apostle! deliver what has been revealed to you from your Lord; and if you do it not, then you have not delivered His message, and Allāh will protect you from the people; surely Allāh will not guild the infidels.*﴾ (Holy Qor'ān = sōrah 5, āyah 67)

And after Rasōlollāh appointed Amēr al-Mo'menēn, by the order of Allāh, as his first khalēfah, Allāh revealed the following āyah:

Second: that after mentioning the names of the Bakri party leaders, I wrote "May Allāh distance them from His Mercy", instead of writing: "May Allāh Be Pleased with them", as the Bakris say and write. This is when the Holy Qor'ān and Rasōlollāh and his Rightful Kholafā' repeated on innumerable occasions about these people what I wrote about them.

This aggression became so intense that some of these so called Moslem priests in the UK threatened me with injury and even death; and some of them publicly marked the book as: 'A Book of Aberration'. And a so called Moslem group in a Western country threatened the distributors of 'Rasōlollāh, the Messenger of Allāh' to stop distributing copies, and the group put sand in the engine oil of one of the distributors' cars and put sugar in the petrol tank of another one of their cars!!

This happened, when I only repeated some of what the ma^{c}ṣōmēn had said, the very people whom this minority reveres as its leaders. And this happened despite the fact that some researchers and scholars have compiled a number of multi-volume works recording what the Holy Qor'ān and the Fourteen Ma^{c}ṣōmēn*(AmS)*[1] had said against Bakri leaders.

But the tongues utter one thing and the hearts hold another. Is anyone listening and is anyone seeing?!

﴾THIS DAY HAVE I PERFECTED FOR YOU YOUR RELIGION AND COMPLETED MY FAVOR ON YOU AND CHOSEN FOR YOU ISLAM AS A RELIGION.﴿. (Holy Qor'ān = sōrah 5, āyah 3)

These two āyāt clearly show that the Islam without the khelāfah of Amēr al-Mo'menēn is not the complete Islam, just as the Islam without the Prophethood of Rasōlollāh is not the complete Islam; and they show that accepting these teachings without accepting the appointment of Amēr al-Mo'menēn as Rasōlollāh's first khalēfah is not the same as accepting Islam, just as accepting these teachings without accepting the appointment of Rasōlollāh as the last prophet is not the same as accepting Islam. Therefore a person who does not believe in the khelāfah of Amēr al-Mo'menēn cannot be called a Moslem, just as the person who does not believe in the Prophethood of Rasōlollāh cannot be called a Moslem.

Furthermore, in the last part of the first āyah, Allāh actually calls those who do not accept this revelation Infidels.

[1] *^{c}Alayhemos Salām,* peace be upon them.

SAYYEDAT NESĀ' AL-ᶜĀLAMĒN BEFORE MARRIAGE

Fāṭimah's creation

Five years after Rasōlollāh[1] started his mission in Makkah, Jabra'ēl the angel revelation descended upon him in Abtah, a Makkah suburb, while he was among some of his followers, saying:

> *((O Moḥammad! The ᶜAli (one of Allāh's names), the Highest, sends you greetings, and orders you to isolate yourself from Khadējah for forty days.)).*

Obeying Allāh's command, he did not return home to his wife Khadējah that night, and spent the next forty days in his uncle Abō Ṭālib's[2] home; fasting every day, and worshiping every night.

On completion of the forty-day period, Jabra'ēl once again descended upon Rasōlollāh[(SAA)3] saying:

> *((O Moḥammad! The ᶜAli, the Highest sends you greetings, and orders you to prepare yourself for his gift.*
> *Soon after, other angels descended carrying some Heavenly produce on a plate, and put it before him.*

---

[1] Messenger of Allāh; a title exclusively given to Prophet Moḥammad by Allāh.

[2] Father of Amēr al-Mo'menēn.

[3] *Ṣallallāh ᶜAlayh wa Ālih,* Allāh's Blessings be upon him and his descendants.

Jabra'ēl said: O Moḥammad! Your Lord orders you to break your today's fast with these fruits.)).

Amēr al-Mo'menēn^(AS)[1] narrates:

((Whenever Rasōlollāh wanted to break his fast, he ordered me to open the door and let in anyone who wanted to break his fast. But on that night he ordered me to sit at the door, and not permit anyone to enter, saying:
O son of Abō Ṭālib! This food is forbidden to anyone but me[2].)).

After eating, when Rasōlollāh stood to pray as usual, Jabra'ēl told him:

((Ṣalāt is forbidden to you at this time, until you go to Khadējah. The Almighty Allāh has indeed taken upon Himself to create for you in this night an excellent progeny. Thus he went to Khadējah's home.)).

According to many aḥādēth[3], Rasōlollāh had one hundred and twenty ma^cārij[4/5], and at least one of them was near the end of this forty-day period; when he ate some Heavenly produce, before approaching Khadējah.

Heavenly child

A series of questions arises when a person reaches this part of Rasōlollāh's life; why forty days of isolation from his wife Khadējah, during which he had to fast the days and worship the

---

1 *^cAlayhes Salām,* peace be upon him.
2 Montahā al-Āmāl (Arabic translation) / Qommi – vol. 1, page 256.
3 Plural of ḥadēth: a narration from one of the Fourteen Ma^cṣōmēn.
4 Ma^cārij plural of me^crāj = Rasōlollāh's voyage through the skies.
5 For more detailed information, see: Rasōlollāh, the Messenger of Allāh / by the author = page 60.

nights?! And why eat Heavenly food, after which he was prohibited from worshiping and ordered to meet with Khadējah?!...

Forty days of fasting and worshiping in isolation from Khadējah was a further preparation for something very important. Numerous Bakri aḥādēth clearly state that the semen that produced Fāṭimah was extracted from Heavenly food, eaten by Rasōlollāh in Heaven and on earth, shortly before he approached his wife Khadējah[1].

What strengthens these narrations further is the fact that her staunchest enemies such as her murderer, ᶜOmar*(LA)*[2], and ᶜĀ'eshah*(LAa)*[3] narrated many of them.

One such ḥadēth[4] narrated from ᶜĀ'eshah is as follows:

> *((I frequently saw Rasōlollāh kiss Fāṭimah; so one day I said: O Rasōlollāh! I see you do something I had not seen you do before.*
> *So he told me: O Ḥomayrā'![5] Indeed, on the night during which I was taken to the sky, I entered Heaven and I stood by its most beautiful tree, with the whitest leaves, and the most delicious fruit. So I took from its fruit and ate...*
> *And when I descended to the earth, I approached Khadējah; and she became pregnant with Fāṭimah from that produce.*

---

[1] Besides the large number of Moslem narrations on the subject, many Bakri aḥādēth can also be found in their prominent references such as:
al-Dorr al-Manthōr / al-Soyōṭi. Dorar al-Semṭayn / al-Zarandi. Lesān al-Mēzān / al-ᶜAsqalāni. Maqtal al-Ḥosayn / al-Khārazmi. Mēzān al-Eᶜtedāl / al-Dhahabi. Tārēkh Baghdād / al-Baghdādi. Talkhēṣ al-Mostadrak / al-Dhahabi. Dhakhā'er al-ᶜOqbā / al-Ṭabari. Yanābēᶜ al-Mawaddah / al-Qandōzi.

[2] *Laᶜnatollāh ᶜAlayh,* may Allāh distance him from His Blessings and Mercy.

[3] *Laᶜnatollāh ᶜAlayha,* may Allāh distance her from His Blessings and Mercy.

[4] A narration from one of the Fourteen Maᶜṣōmēn. Plural aḥādēth.

[5] A name by which the Prophet sometimes called ᶜĀ'eshah.

So whenever I yearn for the scent of Heaven, I smell the scent of Fāṭimah. O Ḥomayrā'! Verily, Fāṭimah is not like the human women[1].)).

cĀ'eshah also narrates:

((Whenever Rasōlollāh returned from his journeys, he went to Fāṭimah, kissed her throat and said: From her I smell the scent of Heaven[2].)).

The pregnancy

As Fāṭimah was a product of Heaven, according to Bakri narrations, her pregnancy was also extraordinary. It was accompanied by many karāmāt[3], one of which was that she talked to her mother whilst in her womb.

Besides the Moslem accounts of this great karāmah[4] that repeatedly happened during the pregnancy, Bakri references also provide many convincing statements, such as:

((After Khadējah became pregnant with Fāṭimah, Rasōlollāh came and heard her talking. He asked her: Whom are you talking to?
Khadējah: The fetus in my womb talks to me and amuses me[5].
Rasōlollāh: O Khadējah! This is Jabra'ēl telling me that it is a female, and that she is a pure and

---

[1] Farā'ed al-Semṭayn / al-Ḥamō'i = vol. 2, page 61. Lesān al-Mēzān / al-cAsqalāni = vol. 1, page 134; vol. 5, page 160. Majmac al-Zawā'ed / al-Haythami = vol. 9, page 202. al-Majrōḥēn / al-Bosti = vol. 2, pages 29 and 30. Mēzān al-Ectedāl / al-Dhahabi = vol. 1, page 212; vol. 4, page 220. al-Mocjam al-Kabēr / al-Ṭabarāni = vol. 22, page 400. Tārēkh Baghdād / al-Baghdādi = vol. 5, page 87.

[2] Yanābēc al-Mawaddah / al-Qandōzi.

[3] Plural of karāmah.

[4] A supernatural action, etc. performed by or for a Godly person, but not as part of a challenge and not to prove that he or she is a Godly person. Plural karāmāt.

[5] Dhakhā'er al-cOqbā / al-Ṭabari.

blessed child; and that the Almighty Allāh will indeed create my lineage through her, and will choose from my lineage a number of a'emmah appointing them as His kholafā' on His earth after the completion of His revelation[1].)).

Bakri scholars also narrate from Khadējah who said:

((When I became pregnant with Fāṭimah, it was an easy pregnancy; and she talked to me from my womb[2].)).

Bakri scholars also narrate:

((When Idolaters asked Rasōlollāh to cut the moon in half for them, during Khadējah's pregnancy with Fāṭimah, Khadējah said:
What a failure for the person who accuses Moḥammad of lying, when he is the greatest Messenger from my Lord.
Suddenly Fāṭimah said from her womb: O Mother! do not worry and do not be afraid; Allāh is indeed with my father[3].)).

Her birth

The birth of Fāṭimah also accompanied many supernatural events, just as the births of her father, husband and the a'emmah from her lineage accompanied similar karāmāt and moᶜjezāt[4]/[5].

At that time, in the fifth year of Rasōlollāh's mission, Idolaters had already taken a strong and often violent stance against

---

[1] Tajhēz al-Jaysh / al-Dehlawi.
[2] Nozhat al-Majālis = vol. 2, page 227.
[3] al-Rawḍ al-Fā'eq / al-Meṣri = page 214.
[4] Moᶜjezāt plural of moᶜjezah: a supernatural action, etc. performed by or for a Godly person to show others the right path.
[5] For more information, see: Rasōlollāh, the Messenger of Allāh / by the author = page 29.

Moslems. This harsh stance equally affected Khadējah despite her being the richest Arab woman when she married Rasōlollāh.

In fact the Idolaters' hatred of Khadējah was more intense than of many other Moslems, as her social and economic position obliged her to marry one of the most prominent Idolater leaders, many of whom had asked for her hand in marriage, and join with them in their confrontational stance against the Moslems. But instead, she had turned them down and married Rasōlollāh; and on top of that, she had spent and continued to spend her wealth in the cause of propagating Islam and strengthening the Moslems. Therefore her former friends and peers had broken all ties with her, and ignored her kind attempts to show them the right path.

As the time of giving birth to Fāṭimah approached, she sent for them once again to come to her, hoping that they will see a moᶜjezah[1] at the time of birth that will convince them of the truth. But as before they returned her messengers with ugly words.

Moments before giving birth, four Godly women descended from Heaven along with many angels, to take part in delivering that Heavenly creature.

Moslem scholars are not alone in reporting this extraordinary event; many Bakri scholars report similar narrations, such as:

> *((Moments before giving birth to Fāṭimah, four women entered Khadējah's room with such a beauty and light that words cannot describe.*
> *One of them told her: I am your mother Ḥawwā'[2]; another said: I am ᶜĀ'eshah bint Mozāḥim; another said: I am Kolthoom, sister of Moses; and the forth said: I am Maryam[3] bint ᶜEmrān, mother of Jesus. We have come here to deliver Fāṭimah.*
> *After she was born she fell on the ground to perform sojōd[4], raising and extending her forefinger to show one[1].)).*

---

[1] A supernatural action, etc. performed by or for a Godly person to show others the right path. Plural moᶜjezāt.

[2] Also Eve.

[3] Also Mary.

[4] A particular position in ṣalāt in which the forehead, the palms, the knees and the toes of both feet are placed on the ground. Sojōd is also performed

Human Houri

Since Fāṭimah was created from the produce of Heaven, even by her enemies' testimony, she is therefore a Human Houri. Thus no other person can be compared to her as she is not just human, and others are not partly houries.

Bakri scholars in their ḥadēth references narrate from Rasōlollāh who often said:

((Fāṭimah is a human houri[2].)).

Naming the newly born

The newly born child who was created from Heavenly fruit, who repeatedly talked to her mother whilst in her womb, who was delivered by saints who descended from Heaven, had to be named by her Creator, Allāh.

Bakri scholars narrate from Rasōlollāh who said:

((Allāh indeed named her Fāṭimah, because He forbade her and those who love her to the fire of Hell[3].)).

Bakri scholars also narrate from Rasōlollāh who said:

((The Almighty Allāh most assuredly forbade Fāṭimah, her children, and those who love them to

---

on its own—not as part of a ṣalāt—for a number of reasons, some of which are mandatory whereas others are recommended.

[1] Mokhtaṣar Dhakhā'er al-ᶜOqbā / al-Ṭabari = page 72.

[2] Tārēkh Baghdād / al-Baghdādi = vol. 12, page 331. al-Rawḍ al-Fā'eq / al-Meṣri = page 214. al-Fawā'ed al-Majmōᶜah / al-Shawkāni = page 392. Mokhtaṣar Dhakhā'er al-ᶜOqbā= page 47.

[3] Mokhtaṣar Dhakhā'er al-ᶜOqbā / al-Ṭabari = page 47. Tārēkh Baghdād / al-Baghdādi = vol. 12, page 331. al-Fawā'ed al-Majmōᶜah / al-Shawkāni = page 392.

the fire of Hell. And for that reason she was called Fāṭimah[1].)).

Date of birth

According to Moslem scholars, Fāṭimah was born on the 20th of Jomādā al-Thāneyah, 5 years after the start of Rasōlollāh's mission; therefore she was eighteen years old when she was killed by cOmar 11 years after the Hejrah.

However some Bakri scholars insist that she was born five years before the start of Rasōlollāh's mission, adding ten years to her age, which puts her death at the age of 28.

Obviously this is just another attempt to hide her greatness. Otherwise, for example, in what way can they explain how an eighteen year old woman, who had not been educated by human teachers, could give those public speeches at the very peak of eloquence that remains unmatched and unchallenged throughout the centuries, without admitting the fact that she was directly taught by Allāh; enabling her to combine Islamic theology, law, Qor'ānic sciences, politics, literature... in one stunning speech, in such a way sending shockwaves through the foundations of the Bakri rule, causing it to violently tremble forever.

And how can they elucidate her death at that age without mentioning that their leaders Abō Bakr and cOmar were forced to resolve to violence when they ran out of reason in front of an eighteen-year-old woman; marching three hundred vicious ruffians to her home in an attempt to silence her, setting her house on fire, crushing her between the door and the wall, penetrating her chest with a hot nail, breaking her ribs, lashing her, causing the miscarriage of her son Mohassin(AS)[2]... and ultimately killing her.

This Bakri attempt to increase her age causes a number of contradictions, one of which is when Abō Bakr and cOmar consecutively asked Rasōlollāh for Fāṭimah's hand in marriage, he

---

[1] Kanz al-cOmmāl / al-Hendi = vol. 12, page 109. Mokhtaṣar Dhakhā'er al-cOqbā / al-Ṭabari = page 47. Mokhtaṣar al-Maḥāsin al-Mojtamicah = page 182.

[2] *cAlayhes Salām,* peace be upon him.

refused their requests by saying she is very young[1]; and everyone agrees that these requests were made shortly before Amēr al-Mo'menēn's request for her hand in marriage which was eight years before her martyrdom.

So how could Rasōlollāh say that a twenty year old woman is very young for marriage, especially at a time when boys and girls in Arabia married at a much younger age due to their early and fast physical and mental growth?! And especially when he encouraged parents to help their sons and daughter to marry at a young age?!

Khadējah dies

At the young age of five, Fāṭimah was to wear the mourning dress when her mother, the loyal Qorashi[2] woman, answered the call of her Lord and parted this world, on 10 Ramaḍān in the tenth year of Rasōlollāh's mission, after years of suffering much hardship at the hands of the despicable Idolater tyrants.

And the short period between her death and the death of Abō Ṭālib, Rasōlollāh's uncle, was the reason for calling that year "the year of grief."

It has been narrated that before her death, Khadējah made a number of requests from Rasōlollāh, amongst which was:

> *((And the third request O Rasōlollāh! I will make it to my daughter Fāṭimah, and she will tell you.*
> *When he left her room, she called Fāṭimah, telling her: O my darling, and the delight of my eye! Tell your father that my mother says: I am afraid of the grave, and I want you to shroud me in the robe that you always wear when receiving revelation.*
> *So Fāṭimah went to Rasōlollāh conveying her mother's message.*
> *He then sent her his robe with Fāṭimah, which made her extremely happy.*

---

[1] According to some Bakri narrations Rasōlollāh refused their requests by saying: She is very young; but according to other Bakri narrations he refused their requests by turning his back to them without saying anything.

[2] A member of the Qoraysh, the largest Arab tribe in the world.

After she died, Rasōlollāh carried out the religious preparations before her burial himself, and when he wanted to shroud her with that special robe, Jabra'ēl the angel of revelation descended telling him:
Allāh sends you His greetings and says: O Moḥammad! We will provide Khadējah's shroud, as she gave in our cause what she owned[1].)).

Thus, Rasōlollāh first shrouded her with his robe, and on top of that he covered her with the Heavenly shroud.

Fāṭimah and the Idolaters

Although she was a young child, but history records heartrending accounts of when Faṭimah took brave stances against the Idolaters in the defense of her father.

She would clean him when they threw rubbish on him; she would treat his wounds when they injured him; she would defend him when they accused him; she would answer them when they insulted him.

At around one years of age, she was sent with her father and his followers and their families to the desert outside Makkah, where they remained under Idolater siege for three years, in an attempt to force them to renounce their god and religion and worship useless idols.

Idolaters reported that during the three-year siege, they often heard children crying at night from the other side of the mountain, from sickness and hunger.

At around eight years of age, Fāṭimah and the rest of Rasōlollāh's family migrated to Madinah, guided by Amēr al-Mo'menēn, three days after Rasōlollāh had left Makkah, to escape Idolater suppression.

In Madinah, despite her young age, she had a very active role in educating women who had been mistreated and ignored by the Arabs, teaching them literacy and Islam.

---

[1] Fāṭimah al-Zahrā' min Qabl al-Mēlād elā Ba^c^d al-Estesh-hād / al-Hāshimi = page 22.

In the second year after the Hejrah[1], she was among the few women who left Madinah for the Oḥod Mountain, where Moslems had defended their city against an overwhelming Idolater attack and suffered great losses. There she once again treated her father's familiar wounds.

[1] Rasōlollāh's migration from Makkah to Madinah in the thirteenth year of his mission. Moslems start their lunar calendar from the year of the Hejrah.

SAYYEDAT NESĀ' AL-ᶜĀLAMĒN'S MARRIAGE

Abō Bakr and ᶜOmar ask for her hand in marriage

After Rasōlollāh had settled in Madinah, a number of prominent Moslems from Mohājirēn[1] and Anṣār[2] came to him to request his daughter's hand in marriage. In most cases he respectfully refused their requests either by saying:

((This matter lies with her Creator; if He wanted her to marry, the she will marry.)).

Or by saying:

((I await in my decision Allāh's command.))

However, in a few cases history records that Rasōlollāh responded to the question of marriage from certain people, in a way completely different from his usual social etiquette, a behavior rarely witnessed from him, in which he disrespectfully refused a request by intentionally and dramatically turning his back to the person.

---

[1] Plural of Mohājir: the Moslems who migrated from Makkah to Madinah to escape Idolater suppression, before the liberation of Makkah.

[2] Plural of Anṣāri: a citizen of Madinah who converted to Islam before the liberation of Makkah.

Bakri scholars name two of the highest ranking members of the Bakri party, ᶜOmar and ᶜAbdorraḥmān ibn Awf along with Abō Bakr, himself, to be the bearers of that everlasting shame.

Bakri historians narrate:

> *((Abō Bakr came to the Prophet, sat in front of him and said: O Rasōlollāh! You surely know my faithfulness and precedence in Islam...*
> *Rasōlollāh: So what do you want?*
> *Abō Bakr: Fāṭimah's hand in marriage.*
> *Rasōlollāh then turned his back on him. And Abō Bakr returned to ᶜOmar saying: You perished and caused me to perish*[1]
> *Omar: And how is that?*
> *Abō Bakr: I asked his daughter's hand in marriage, but he turned his back on me.*
> *Omar: Stay here while I go to him to ask him as you did.*
> *Thus ᶜOmar came to the Prophet, sat in front of him and said: O Rasōlollāh! You surely know my faithfulness, and precedence in Islam...*
> *Rasōlollāh: So what do you want?*
> *Omar: Fāṭimah's hand in marriage.*
> *Rasōlollāh then turned his back on him; and ᶜOmar left*[2]*.)).*

It has also been recorded that Abō Bakr and ᶜOmar made a second attempt to win Fāṭimah's marriage, as Bakri historians narrate:

> *((Both Abō Bakr and ᶜOmar told their daughters to ask Rasōlollāh for Fāṭimah's hand in marriage, on their behalf; and each of them went to Rasōlollāh asking for his daughter's marriage to her father. But Rasōlollāh refused.*

---

[1] This statement shows that it was ᶜOmar's suggestion that Abō Bakr asks for Fāṭimah's hand in marriage.

[2] Kanz al-ᶜOmmāl / al-Hendi = vol. 2, page 99.

And both of them wished they had not mentioned to the Prophet the question of Fāṭimah's marriage[1].)).

Amēr al-Mo'menēn asks for her hand in marriage

Besides the Moslem accounts of the miraculous marriage of Amēr al-Mo'menēn[(AS)2] and Sayyedat Nesā' al-ᶜĀlamēn[(AaS)3], Bakri historians also record it along with its accompanying supernatural events.

Omm Salamah narrates that when Amēr al-Mo'menēn[4] came to Rasōlollāh, who was in her home, to ask for Fāṭimah's hand in marriage, the following happened:

> *((He knocked on the door.*
> *I asked: Who is at the door?*
> *And before he could answer, Rasōlollāh told me: Stand up O Omm Salamah! and open the door, and ask him to enter. For he is surely a man who loves Allāh and His Messenger and they love him.*
> *So I said: My father and mother be your sacrifice, who is this person about whom you say such things without having seen him?!*
> *Rasōlollāh: O Omm Salamah! He is my brother and cousin and the most beloved person to me.*
> *So I harried to the door, stumbled in my Merṭ[5] on the way and almost fell to the ground, and when I opened the door I saw ᶜAli. By Allāh! He did not enter*

---

[1] Majmaᶜ al-Zawā'ed / al-Haythami.

[2] *ᶜAlayhes Salām,* peace be upon him.

[3] *ᶜAlayhas Salām,* peace be upon her.

[4] Commander of the Faithful; a title given exclusively to Imām ᶜAli by Allāh.

[5] A piece of cloth that covers the body from head to toe. This kind of ḥejāb was often worn by Arab women.

the house until he was sure I had returned to my Khedr[1]*.*

Then he came to Rasōlollāh saying: Peace and Allāh's Mercy and Blessing be upon you O Rasōlollāh!

Rasōlollāh: And peace be upon you O ᶜAli!

So ᶜAli sat in front of him and looked down at the ground, as if he wanted to ask something but was shy to put it in words.

Knowing what was on his mind, Rasōlollāh told him: O ᶜAli! I truly know that you have come here with a request, so ask of me your request and make clear what is in your mind[2]*.*

But ᶜAli stayed silent.

Rasōlollāh: Maybe you have come here to ask for Fāṭimah's hand in marriage?

Ali: Yes[3]*.*

I saw Rasōlollāh's face glowing with happiness and joy. He then told ᶜAli: O ᶜAli! Do you want me to give you a good news?

Ali: Yes, my father and mother be your sacrifice O Rasōlollāh...

Rasōlollāh: Rejoice O ᶜAli! For surely Allāh the Almighty has made you and Fāṭimah man and wife in the sky before I make you man and wife on the earth.)).

Marriage in the sky

Besides the Moslem accounts, Bakri scholars also narrate a large number of aḥādēth that Rasōlollāh was ordered by Allāh to make ᶜAli and Fāṭimah man and wife, before ᶜAli asked for her hand in marriage.

---

[1] A section of a room, etc. separated by a curtain, behind which women sit if there are any stranger men present.

[2] Fāṭimah al-Zahrā' min Qabl al-Mēlād elā Baᶜd al-Estesh-hād / al-Hāshimi = page 27.

[3] Mokhtaṣar Dhakhā'er al-ᶜOqbā / al-Ṭabari = page 48. Osd al-Ghābah / Ibn al-Athēr = vol. 7, pages 221 and 222.

Bakri scholars also narrate a large number of aḥādēth that says the marriage was performed in the sky before it was performed on the earth, and explains, in some detail, the manner in which the marriage was performed in the sky in the presence of countless angels with numerous ceremonies[1].

Fāṭimah takes ᶜAli as her husband

A question may come to mind, that if Allāh had ordered His Messenger to make ᶜAli and Fāṭimah man and wife, and that if the marriage was actually performed in the sky before being performed on the earth, then what was the point of ᶜAli asking Rasōlollāh for Fāṭimah's hand?

The answer is clear; asking someone for his daughter's hand in marriage is ceremonial and part of a tradition accepted by Islam. And the messengers of Allāh and their awṣeyā' always followed and abided by such traditional rules, to make known to their followers, through their actions, which rules are accepted in their religion and which and rejected.

It has been narrated that after Imām ᶜAli asked for Fāṭimah's hand in marriage, Rasōlollāh said:

> *((O ᶜAli! Others asked me for her hand in marriage before, and I mentioned them to her, but saw disagreement and discontent in her face. So wait here until I ask her about your proposal.*
> *Thus Rasōlollāh left ᶜAli waiting for the result, and went to his daughter Fāṭimah, saying: O Fāṭimah! ᶜAli ibn Abi Ṭālib is a person whom you have known his relation, merit and the quality of his faith; and surely I have asked my Lord to make you the wife of His best creature and their most beloved to Him; and*

[1] The following are some of the more prominent Bakri references that record these aḥādēth: Ḥelyat al-Awleyā' / Abō Noᶜaym. Lesān al-Mēzān / al-ᶜAsqalāni. Maqtal al-Ḥosayn / al-Khārazmi. Nozhat al-Majālis / al-Ṣafōri. Tahdhēb al-Tahdheb / al-ᶜAsqalāni. Taḥdhēr al-Khawāṣ / al-Soyōṭi. Yanābēᶜ al-Mawaddah / al-Qandōzi.

indeed cAli has mentioned the question of marriage with you, so what do you say?
She stayed silent and did not turn away her face, and he did not see in her face any sign of disapproval. So he said: Allāh is the greatest; her silence is her agreement[1].)).

The marriage gift

Another pre-Islamic tradition that was accepted by Islam and included in the marriage, as an mandatory part, was the marriage gift. An amount of money, or piece of jewelry, or any other valuable given as a gift to the bride by her would be husband at the time of their marriage.

But knowing that in an effort to score a higher social status most people would raise the value of the marriage gift beyond their capabilities, and thus often encounter unpleasant consequences, or if they happened to content themselves to an affordable level they would risk social contempt, Rasōlollāh set an affordable standard for the marriage gift and insistently requested the Moslems not to ask for nor provide a higher value, in another attempt to quash social distinctions and bring the poor closer to the rich.

And when the time for his daughter's marriage came, he followed the same standard and did not ask for a marriage gift more compatible with Fāṭimah's God-given title: Sayyedat Nesā' al-cĀlamēn, or with his own social standing and powerful position; making himself, yet again, an Idolater target.

It has been narrated that some members of Qoraysh looked down on Rasōlollāh and made clear their stance by saying:

((You have indeed taken cAli as your son-in-law with a vile marriage gift[2].)).

Rasōlollāh, then, divided his daughter's small marriage gift into three. One portion for buying the necessary tools of life such as pottery, one portion for buying perfume and scents, and he gave the

[1] Fāṭimah al-Zahrā' min al-Mahd elā al-Laḥd / al-Qazwēni = page 171.
[2] Man Lā Yaḥḍoroh al-Faqēh / al-Ṣadōq = vol. 3, page 401.

third portion back to Amēr al-Mo'menēn[(AS)1] to help him with his wedding banquet.

When the humble dowry was purchased and brought to Rasōlollāh, he turned them up and down and said:

> *((O Allāh! Bless a people most of whose containers are earthenware[2].)).*

The wedding

When a house was prepared for the newly married couple, the wedding was set to take place. And like the marriage, many supernatural events occurred during the wedding, some of which were also reported and recorded by the couple's enemies.

Bakri testimonies in their highly respected references include:

> *((Jabra'ēl descended and told the Prophet: O Moḥammad! Allāh sends you greetings, and has ordered me to greet Fāṭimah and give her a gift from Heavenly clothes for her wedding[3].)).*

Prominent Bakri scholars also record the following:

> *((During the wedding, when Fāṭimah was ceremoniously escorted to ᶜAli's house, the Prophet was walking in front of her, Jabra'ēl was walking on her right, Mēkā'ēl[4] was walking on her left and seventy thousand angels were walking behind them, praising and glorifying Allāh until dawn break[5].)).*

---

[1] *ᶜAlayhes Salām,* peace be upon him.

[2] Fāṭimah min al-Mahd elā al-Laḥd / al-Qazwēni = page 181.

[3] Nozhat al-Majālis / al-Ṣafōri = vol. 2, page 226.

[4] Also: Michael.

[5] Akhbār al-Dowal wa Āthār al-Owal / al-Qermāni. Dorar al-Semṭayn / al-Zarandi. al-Fawā'ed al-Majmōᶜah / al-Shawkāni. Lesān al-Mēzān / al-ᶜAsqalāni. al-Majrōḥēn / Ibn Ḥabbān. Mēzān al-Eᶜtedāl / al-Dhahabi. Mokhtaṣar Dhakhā'er al-ᶜOqbā / al-Ṭabari. Tārēkh Baghdād / al-Baghdādi. Yanābēᶜ al-Mawaddah / al-Qandōzi.

The wedding banquet

The wedding banquet also accompanied supernatural events, one of which is that thousands of people from Madinah, and even the farmers in the city suburbs gathered for the banquet, after an open invitation, and ate until they were full, and took out more food with them; but the small amount of food that according to Bakri historians was prepared from one sheep and a few kilos of corn flour[1] for making bread, did not finish, and it did not even reduce in quantity[2].

It has been narrated from Amēr al-Mo'menēn who said:

> *((...Then Rasōlollāh told me: Invite whoever you like for the banquet.*
> *So I went to the mosque and saw it crowded with the Ṣaḥābah[3], and because I did not like to invite a particular group and ignore a particular group, I stepped on a high platform and raised my voice: Attend Fāṭimah's wedding banquet.*
> *Suddenly I saw groups and groups of people coming for the banquet and I felt modest because of the large numbers of attendants and the small quantity of food.*
> *Rasōlollāh who sensed what I was thinking, told me: O ᶜAli! I will surely pray to Allāh for His Blessing.*
> *Later all the people ate, drank, prayed for us and left, and their number was well over four thousand, but the food remained the same and did not reduce[4].)).*

---

[1] Mokhtaṣar Dhakhā'er al-ᶜOqbā / al-Ṭabari = page 57. Osd al-Ghābah / Ibn Athēr = vol. 7, page 222. al-Sonan al-Kobrā / al-Nasā'i = vol. 6, page 72. Tārēkh Demashq / Ibn ᶜAsākir = vol. 17, page 336.

[2] Fāṭimah min al-Mahd elā al-Laḥd / al-Qazwēni = page 192.

[3] Plural of ṣaḥābi: a companion of the Prophet Moḥammad.

[4] Beḥār al-Anwār / al-Majlesi = vol. 43, page 95.

SAYYEDAT NESĀ' AL-ᶜĀLAMĒN'S CHILDREN

Moslem and Bakri historians agree that Sayyedat Nesā' al-ᶜĀlamēn*(AaS)*[1] and her husband Amēr al-Mo'menēn*(AS)*[2] had three sons and two daughters.

Moslem historians and many Bakri historians also agree that their first child was a boy named Ḥasan, their second child was also a boy named Ḥosayn, their third child was a girl named Zaynab, their fourth child was also a girl named Omm Kolthoom and their fifth and last child was a boy named Moḥassin.

Birth of Imām Ḥasan

Sayyedat Nesā' al-ᶜĀlamēn gave birth to her first child on 15 Ramaḍān in the third year of Hejrah[3].

Bakri scholars narrate:

((Then Rasōlollāh asked ᶜAli: What have you named my son?
Ali: I would not precede you in naming him.
Rasōlollāh: And I would not precede my Lord.
Suddenly Jabra'ēl descended, saying: O Moḥammad! Your Lord sends you greetings and tells you: ᶜAli's

[1] *ᶜAlayhas Salām*, peace be upon her.

[2] *ᶜAlayhes Salām*, peace be upon him.

[3] Rasolollāh's migration from Makkah to Madinah in the thirteenth year of his mission. Moslems start their lunar calendar from the year of the Hejrah.

position to you is similar to that of Hārōn[1] to Mōsā[2], with the difference that there is no prophet after you. Therefore name your son by the name of Hārōn's son.
Rasōlollāh: And what was the name of Hārōn's son O Jabra'ēl?
Jabra'ēl: Shobbar.
Rasōlollāh: My tongue is Arabic.
Jabra'ēl: So call him Ḥasan[3]/[4].)).

Bakri scholars narrate from a high-ranking member of the Azd tribe, who said:

((I heard Rasōlollāh say about his grandson Ḥasan: Whoever loves me should love him; let those who are present tell those who are absent.
And if it were not for Rasōlollāh's insistence, I would not have told you this[5].)).

Birth of Imām Ḥosayn

Sayyedat Nesā' al-ᶜĀlamēn gave birth to her second child on 3 Shaᶜbān in the fourth year of Hejrah.

Bakri historians narrate that Allāh revealed to his messenger to name the newly born child by the name of Hārōn's second son, which in Hebrew was Shobayr[6].

Moslem and Bakri historians narrate that the period of Fāṭimah's pregnancy with Imām Ḥosayn[(AS)1] was only six months[2]; Prophets Yaḥyā[3] and ᶜĒsā[4] were also born in their sixth month.

---

[1] Also Aaron.
[2] Also Moses.
[3] Shobbar is a Hebrew name and its Arabic translation is Ḥasan.
[4] Mokhtaṣar Dhakhā'er al-ᶜOqbā / al-Ṭabari = page 201.
[5] Mokhtaṣar Dhakhā'er al-ᶜOqbā / al-Ṭabari = page 207. Mokhtaṣar Tārēkh Demashq / Ibn ᶜAsākir = vol. 7, page 11. Mosnad / Aḥmad = vol. 5, page 366. al-Mostadrak / al-Ḥākim = vol. 3, page 173. Seyar Aᶜlām al-Nobalā' / al-Dhahabi = vol. 3, page 253. Tahdhēb al-Kamāl / al-Mazzi = vol. 6, page 228.
[6] Mokhtaṣar Dhakhā'er al-ᶜOqbā / al-Ṭabari = page 201.

It has been narrated that every day Rasōlollāh came to Ḥosayn and put either his tongue or his index finger in Ḥosayn's mouth, and the baby boy suckled it until his flesh grew and his bones strengthened. And he did not suckle milk from his mother or from any other woman[5].

Bakri scholars narrate from Asmā' bint ᶜOmays who said:

((Then Rasōlollāh put Ḥosayn on his lap and started to weep.
I said: My father and mother be your sacrifice; what makes you cry?
Rasōlollāh: My son, O Asmā'! He will surely be killed at the hands of a group of oppressors[6].)).

Bakri scholars narrate from Rasololläh who said:

((Whoever loves Ḥasan and Ḥosayn loves me, and whoever hates them hates me[7].)).

Bakri scholars also narrate from Rasōlollāh who said:

((Ḥosayn is of me and I am of Ḥosayn; Allāh loves those who love Ḥosayn[8].)).

Birth of Sayyedah Zaynab

Sayyedat Nesā' al-ᶜĀlamēn gave birth to her third child on 5 Jomādā al-Ōlā in the fifth year of Hejrah.

---

[1] *ᶜAlayhes Salām,* peace be upon him.

[2] Mokhtaṣar Dhakhā'er al-ᶜOqba / al-Ṭabari = page 199.

[3] Also John.

[4] Also Jesus.

[5] Fāṭimah al-Zahrā' min al-Mahd Elā al-Laḥd / al-Qazwēni = page 225.

[6] Mokhtaṣar Dhakhā'er al-ᶜOqbā / al-Ṭabari = page 199.

[7] Mokhtaṣar Tārēkh Demashq / Ibn ᶜAsākir = vol. 7, page 10. Mokhtaṣar Dhakhā'er al-ᶜOqbā / al-Ṭabari = page 208. Sharaf al-Nobowwah / Abō Saᶜd.

[8] Mokhtaṣar Dhakhā'er al-ᶜOqbā / al-Ṭabari = page 226. Mosnad / Aḥmad = ḥadēth 3777.

It has been narrated:

((When Fāṭimah gave birth to her first daughter, she told her husband ᶜAli: Name this newly born girl.
Amēr al-Mo'menēn: I would not precede Rasōlollāh. But Rasōlollāh was on a trip.
When he returned, Amēr al-Mo'menēn asked him to name his daughter, but he said: I would not precede my Lord.
Then Jabra'ēl descended conveying Allāh's greeting, and said: The name of this newly born girl is Zaynab. Allāh has indeed chosen this name for her[1].)).

Moḥassin, the Martyred Fetus

Although all Moslem and many Bakri historians agree that Moḥassin(AS)[2] was ᶜAli and Fāṭimah's fifth and last child, there are a number of Bakri historians who falsely claim that Moḥassin was born after Ḥosayn and before Zaynab, making him the third child.

This distortion of history was initiated by a few Bakri historians, who had sold their pens to the usurpers of the khelāfah[3], in an attempt to cover-up what had been ordered and executed by their leaders shortly after Rasōlollāh's martyrdom, and to erase the most evil and villainous dark spot from their history books; one which for ever altered the course of Moslem and world history: when the First Usurper, Abō Bakr(LA)[4], gave the order to attack Fāṭimah's home, and his second-in-command, ᶜOmar(LA)[5], along with around three hundred ruffians executed the order; setting fire to the house, and crushing Fāṭimah between the door and the wall while beating her, as a result of which she miscarried the fetus that was named Moḥassin by the Prophet.

---

[1] al-Ḥosayn wa Baṭalat Karbala / al-Moghneyah from a Bakri source.

[2] *ᶜAlayhes Salām,* peace be upon him.

[3] Successorship of Rasōlollāh. Also caliphate.

[4] *Laᶜnatollāh ᶜAlayh,* may Allāh distance him from His Blessings and Mercy.

[5] *Laᶜnatollāh ᶜAlayh,* may Allāh distance him from His Blessings and Mercy.

Fortunately many Bakri historians do not follow suit in this perversion, and choose to disagree with their peers in their falsification of Moḥassin's time of birth.

However some of these historians still refuse to tell the whole truth; so they content themselves only in reporting that Moḥassin was the fifth and last child who died in a miscarriage, but still fail to mention what caused the miscarriage.

SAYYEDAT NESĀ' AL-ᶜĀLAMĒN'S MORALS

Good morals and bad morals are what separate good people from bad people, and admired characters and evil characters are what distinguish gracious human beings from wicked ones.

And as praised qualities are the revelations of God and dispraised qualities are the revelations of Shayṭān[1], we can thereby identify Godly icons and satanic idols. Thus whoever is decorated with many virtuous standards is a Godly person, and whoever is stained with many villainous standards is a satanic person.

Here we stand while history, written by enemies alongside friends, points to Fāṭimah as the most complete Godly woman in the world. A female messenger of Islam who, despite her eighteen years of age, overtook all human beings, except two, to become the third maᶜṣōm[2], and be awarded by Allāh with the title: Sayyedat Nesā' al-ᶜĀlamēn, Chief of the Women of the world.

As the third delegate of God to His creations, she retained the highest levels of Godly morals and kept herself away from satanic morals, teaching others with her actions before her words.

The following are examples of her holy characters:

---

[1] Also Satan.

[2] A person who does not commit sins, does not make mistakes, does not forget, etc. although he/she has the choice to commit sins. Prophets and their awṣeyā' are maᶜṣōm. Plural: maᶜṣōmēn. The Fourteen Maᶜṣōmēn are the Prophet Moḥammad, his daughter Fāṭimah, and his twelve God-appointed successors.

Altruism

The quality of considering the well-being and happiness of others before one's own, is the foundation of the Islamic society. However this is only a lower level of the Islamic altruism.

Therefore we see that the messengers of Islam maintain its highest levels; not only giving the precedence to others, but also giving their very essential needs to others; something hardly called altruism.

And Fāṭimah observed the highest degree of this praised character throughout her life; as the following Bakri narration testifies:

> *((One day Ḥasan and Ḥosayn became ill, so their grandfather Moḥammad along with Abō Bakr, ᶜOmar and a number of the Ṣaḥābah[1] went to visit them.*
> *They told ᶜAli: O Father of Ḥasan! You could make a Nadhr[2] for the cure of your sons.*
> *Ali said: If my sons recover from their illness, I will fast three days as thanksgiving to Allāh. Then Fāṭimah said the same thing and Feḍḍah said: If my masters regain their health, I will fast for Allāh three days.*
> *So Allāh clothed the two boys with good health, at a time when the descendants of Moḥammad did not have any food or money.*
> *Thus ᶜAli went to Shamᶜoon, a Jew from Khaybar, and borrowed a few kilos of barley. When he returned, Fāṭimah took one third of the barley, grinded it and baked five loafs of bread, one loaf for each person.*
> *At night, when ᶜAli returned home after praying with the Prophet, they sat to break their fast with barley bread. Suddenly there was a knock on the door, and*

---

[1] Plural of ṣaḥābi: a companion of Rasōlollāh.

[2] A conditional religious vow, that if a certain condition is met, etc. the person who has made the Nadhr will do what he has vowed to do. There are several forms of Nadhr.

someone said: Peace be upon you O Descendants of Moḥammad. I am a very poor Moslem; feed me, may Allāh feed you from Heavenly food. So they gave him all their bread and thus they went with just water that evening having fasted all day. On the second day they continued fasting.

Later in the day, Fāṭimah took a second portion of the borrowed barley, grinded it and baked another five loafs of bread.

At night, when ᶜAli returned home after praying with the Prophet, they sat down to break their second day's fast. Suddenly there was a knock on the door, and someone said: Peace be upon you O Descendants of Moḥammad! I am an orphan from Mohājirēn; my father was killed on the day of Aqabah. Feed me, may Allāh feed you from Heavenly food. So they gave him all their bread and tasted nothing but water. And on the third day the continued fasting.

Later in the day, Fāṭimah took the last portion of the borrowed barely, grinded it and baked another five loafs of bread.

On the third night, when ᶜAli return after praying with the Prophet, they sat down to break their fast. Suddenly there was a knock on the door and someone said: Peace be upon you O Descendants of Moḥammad! I am a captive (slave); feed me, may Allāh feed you from Heavenly food. So they gave him all their bread and tasted nothing except water.

On the fourth day, when they had fulfilled their Nadhr and finished their three days of fasting, ᶜAli came to Rasōlollāh taking Ḥasan's hand in his right hand and Ḥosayn's hand in his left hand, while they were shivering from hunger like young birds.

When the Prophet saw them, he said: O Father of Ḥasan! how sorry I feel to see you in this condition. Let us go to my daughter. So they went home to see her in her meḥrāb[1], while her stomach was stuck to her back from hunger, and her eyes had caved in her head. When Rasōlollāh saw her he said: O Allāh! The descendants of Moḥammad are dying from hunger. Suddenly Jabra'ēl descended and revealed to Rasōlollāh the seventy sixth Sōrah[2] of the holy Qor'ān:

*"THERE SURELY CAME OVER MAN A PERIOD OF TIME WHEN HE WAS A THING NOT WORTH MENTIONING * SURELY WE HAVE CREATED MAN FROM A SMALL LIFE-GERM UNITING (ITSELF): WE MEAN TO TRY HIM, SO WE HAVE MADE HIM HEARING, SEEING * SURELY WE HAVE SHOWN HIM THE WAY: WHETHER HE MAY BE THANKFUL OR THANKLESS * SURELY WE HAVE PREPARED FOR THE UNBELIEVERS CHAINS AND SHACKLES AND A BURNING FIRE * SURELY THE RIGHTEOUS SHALL DRINK OF A CUP, THE ADMIXTURE OF WHICH IS CAMPHOR * A FOUNTAIN FROM WHICH THE SERVANTS OF ALLĀH SHALL DRINK; THEY MAKE IT TO FLOW A (GOODLY) FLOWING FORTH * THEY FULFILL VOWS AND FEAR A DAY THE EVIL OF WHICH SHALL BE SPREADING FAR AND WIDE * AND THEY GIVE FOOD, OUT OF LOVE FOR HIM, TO THE POOR AND THE ORPHAN AND THE CAPTIVE: * WE ONLY FEED YOU FOR ALLĀH'S SAKE; WE DESIRE FROM YOU NEITHER REWARD NOR THANKS: * SURELY WE FEAR FROM OUR LORD A STERN, DISTRESSFUL DAY * THEREFORE ALLĀH WILL GUARD THEM FROM THE EVIL OF THAT DAY, AND CAUSE THEM TO MEET WITH EASE AND HAPPINESS; * AND REWARD THEM, BECAUSE THEY WERE PATIENT, WITH GARDEN AND SILK, * RECLINING THEREIN ON RAISED COUCHES, THEY SHALL FIND THEREIN NEITHER (THE SEVERE HEAT OF) THE SUN NOR INTENSE COLD * AND CLOSE DOWN UPON THEM (SHALL BE) ITS SHADOWS, AND ITS FRUITS SHALL BE MADE NEAR (TO THEM), BEING EASY TO REACH. * AND THERE SHALL BE MADE TO GO ROUND ABOUT THEM VESSELS OF SILVER AND GOBLETS WHICH ARE OF GLASS, * (TRANSPARENT AS) GLASS, MADE OF*

[1] Place of worship, where a Moslem worships Allāh. Meḥrāb also means a place, especially in a mosque, where the public prayer leader performs the ṣalāt.

[2] A chapter from the Holy Qor'ān. Plural sowar.

*SILVER; THEY HAVE MEASURED THEM ACCORDING TO A MEASURE. * AND THEY SHALL BE MADE TO DRINK THEREIN A CUP THE ADMIXTURE OF WHICH SHALL BE GINGER, * (OF) A FOUNTAIN THEREIN WHICH IS NAMED SALSABEEL. * AND ROUND ABOUT THEM SHALL GO YOUTHS NEVER ALTERING IN AGE; WHEN YOU SEE THEM YOU WILL THINK THEM TO BE SCATTERED PEARLS. * AND WHEN YOU SEE THERE, YOU SHALL SEE BLESSINGS AND A GREAT KINGDOM. * UPON THEM SHALL BE GARMENTS OF FINE GREEN SILK AND THICK SILK INTERWOVEN WITH GOLD, AND THEY SHALL BE ADORNED WITH BRACELETS OF SILVER, AND THEIR LORD SHALL MAKE THEM DRINK A PURE DRINK. * SURELY THIS IS A REWARD FOR YOU, AND YOUR STRIVING SHALL BE RECOMPENSED. * SURELY WE OURSELVES HAVE REVEALED THE QOR'ĀN TO YOU, REVEALING (IT) IN PORTIONS. * THEREFORE WAIT PATIENTLY FOR THE COMMAND OF YOUR LORD, AND OBEY NOT FROM AMONG THEM A SINNER OR AN UNGRATEFUL ONE. * AND GLORIFY THE NAME OF YOUR LORD MORNING AND EVENING. * AND DURING PART OF THE NIGHT ADORE HIM, AND GIVE GLORY TO HIM (A) LONG (PART OF THE) NIGHT. * SURELY THESE LOVE THE TRANSITORY AND NEGLECT A GRIEVOUS DAY BEFORE THEM. * WE CREATED THEM AND MADE FIRM THEIR MAKE, AND WHEN WE PLEASE WE WILL BRING IN THEIR PLACE THE LIKES OF THEM BY A CHANGE. * SURELY THIS IS A REMINDER, SO WHOEVER PLEASES TAKES TO HIS LORD A WAY. * AND YOU DO NOT PLEASE EXCEPT THAT ALLĀH PLEASE; SURELY ALLĀH IS KNOWING, WISE; * HE MAKES WHOM HE PLEASES TO ENTER INTO HIS MERCY; AND (AS FOR) THE UNJUST, HE HAS PREPARED FOR THEM A PAINFUL CHASTISEMENT. *"[1])).*

---

[1] Fāṭimah al-Zahrā' fi al-Qor'ān / Āyatollāh al-ᶜOẓmā Sayyed Ṣādiq Sherāzi = page 313; from the prominent Bakri reference: Rōḥ al-Maᶜāni / al-Ālōsi = vol. 29, page 157. Āyatollāh al-ᶜOẓmā Sherāzi also mentions other important Bakri references which have confirmed this subject, they include: Gharā'eb al-Qor'ān / al-Naysābōri. al-Jāmiᶜ le-Aḥkām al-Qor'ān / al-Qorṭobi. Lobāb al-Ta'wēl fi Maᶜāni al-Tanzēl / al-Khāzin. Maᶜālim al-Tanzēl / al-Baghawi. al-Tashēl le-ᶜOlōm al-Tanzēl / al-Kalbi. Yanābēᶜ al-Mawaddah / al-Qandōzi.

Contentment

Contentment and altruism always go hand in hand. Without contentment there is no altruism, and with altruism there is always contentment.

Therefore Fāṭimah, who had the highest level of altruism, was also distinguished by the highest level of contentment. She did not use her position or that of her father to gather wealth, welfare or any of the luxuries of life. Furthermore she did not keep anything that her position brought her.

The following are just three examples of her contentment:

It was the custom in those days to give valuable gifts to a newly wed couple; and the quantity and quality of these gifts increased in accordance to the social standing of the couple. And since ᶜAli and Fāṭimah were the closest people to Rasōlollāh[2], and were, themselves, highly important, the people of Madinah and city leaders showered them with precious gifts.

But altruism, excessive generosity, and contentment played their roles; and after receiving the costly gifts, the newly wed couple

---

[1] Besides these references, there are over thirty well-known Bakri references for this narration recorded in the al-Ghadēr encyclopedia, some of which are:

Bahjat al-Nofōs / al-Ḥāfiẓ al-Azdi = vol. 4, page 225. al-Dorr al-Manthōr / al-Soyōṭi = vol. 6, page 299. al-ᶜEqd al-Farēd / Ibn ᶜAbderabbeh = vol. 3, page 42. Farā'ed al-Semṭayn / al-Ḥamō'i. Fatḥ al-Qadēr / al-Shawkāni = page 338. al-Fawā'ed / al-Ḥāfiẓ al-Azdi. al-Eṣābah / al-ᶜAsqalāni = vol. 4, page 387. al-Kash-shaf / al-Zamakhshari = vol. 2, page 511. al-Kashf wa al-Bayān / al-Thaᶜlabi. Kefāyat al-Ṭālib / al-Kanji = page 210. al-Manāqib / al-Kharazmi, page 180. Manāqib Fāṭimah / al-Naysābōri. Maṭālib al-Sa'ōl / Abō Sālim al-Shāfeᶜi = page 31. al-Reyāḍ al-Naḍirah / al-Ṭabari = vol. 2, page 207. Rōḥ al-Bayān / al-Borōsawi = vol. 10, page 268. Sharh Nahj al-Balāghah / Ibn Abi al-Ḥadēd = vol. 3, page 257. Tadhkerat Khawāṣ al-Ommah / Ibn al-Jawzi. Tafsēr / al-Ḥāfiẓ al-Eṣbahāni. Mafāteḥ al-Ghayb / al-Rāzi = vol. 8, page 276. Tafsēr al-Khazin / al-Baghdādi = vol. 4, page 358. Tafsēr / al-Bayḍāwi = vol. 2, page 571. Zayn al-Fata fi Tafsēr Sōrat Hal Atā / al-Ḥāfiẓ al ᶜĀsimi. (al-Ghadēr / al-Amēni = vol. 3, page 107.)

[2] Messenger of Allāh; a title exclusively given to Prophet Moḥammad by Allāh.

gave most of it to the poor, and used the remaining gifts to buy male and female slaves and free them. Meanwhile they remained content with a very poor life, as Bakri scholars narrate from Amēr al-Mo'menēn who said:

> *((We had a blanket, if we used it in length it did not cover our sides, and if we used it in width it did not cover our heads and our feet[1].)).*

And in the seventh year after the Hejrah, a group of Arabia's Jews, and according to some researchers a Jewish convert to Islam, gave the famous land of Fadak to the Prophet, who in turn and by the order of Allāh passed it to Fāṭimah[2].

The annual profit of Fadak is recorded to have been around seventy thousand gold Dēnārs. But when it came under Fāṭimah's ownership, she spent all of its large profits on poor people and in charity projects, and she and her husband did not use any of its profits to sleep with a full stomach at night or change their very poor and humble life style.

It has been narrated:

> *((One of his (Rasōlollāh) companions went to her (Fāṭimah) home when she was grinding barley and reciting: "And what is with Allāh is better and more lasting[3]". So she put on an old worn-out cloak that had been patched in twelve places with palm leaves.*
> *When she came out, Salmān looked at her cloak and cried, saying: What a sadness; the Roman and Persian emperors are covered with sarcenet and silk, and Mohammad's daughter is covered with an old worn-out woolen cloak patched in twelve places.*
> *Later when Fāṭimah met with the Prophet, she told him: O Rasōlollāh! Salmān was surprised to see this dress. I swear by Him Who gave you the mission, in the past five years ᶜAli and I have only had one*

---

[1] Dhakhā'er al-ᶜOqbā / al-Ṭabari = page 49.
[2] You will read about Fadak in more detail later in this book.
[3] Holy Qor'ān = sōrah 42, āyah 36.

animal skin on which our camel feeds during the day and we sleep during the night; and our pillow is of animal skin stuffed with leaves[1].)).

Courage

Any kind of person who has any kind of mission in life has to have a certain degree of courage. This is because a mission is often accompanied by some sort of confrontation; and lack of courage usually means failure. And the more serious the nature of the mission is, the stronger and more impenetrable the courage should be.

And since the mission of those who deliver the word of God is the most heavy and more confronted, they should be equipped with unprecedented courage.

We read in history books how the prophets and their successors were persecuted and suppressed and how a large number of them were tortured and killed. So if they had lacked the much-needed courage, they would not have been able to spread the message whilst suffering the pain.

And the Prophet of Islam was no exception, and his successors were not treated differently. In fact they were, altogether, subjected to harsher treatment than any of the prophets and their successors.

Rasōlollāh himself said:

((No prophet was harassed as much as I was[2].)).

He also said:

((We (Rasōlollāh and his successors) are either poisoned to death or killed by a sword[3].)).

This aggression was not directed, exclusively, from those who openly fought Islam, but mostly from those who carried its flag

[1] Beḥār al-Anwār / al-Majlesi = vol. 8, page 303.
[2] Beḥār al-Anwār / al-Majlesi = vol. 39, page 56.
[3] Beḥār al-Anwār / al-Majlesi = vol. 44, page 139.

in order to destroy it. The attempts on Rasōlollāh's life were mainly carried out by those who shammed Islam, and the persecution of his kholafā' were solely undertaken by them.

And Fāṭimah, as the third leader of Islam, had her share of persecution from both enemies. And when we read about her life we clearly see that there was no comparison between what she suffered from the overt front with what she suffered from the covert front. Thus her courageous stances against the covert enemies surpassed and outshined the ones against the overt enemies.

She showed great courage when she went all-out to unveil the true identities and beliefs of Abō Bakr and his party members, ignoring the imminent most serious repercussions that this exposure would yield.

It takes more than courage to openly and publicly tell a person like Abō Bakr what she told him, and speak about Abō Bakr and his party the way she did; as you will read later in this book.

Equality

One of the most obvious moral qualities that Godly people are characterized by is equality. This is because Godly people always try to teach out to others with their actions before their words. And since equality comes in the forefront of God's teachings, it reflects in their actions early on in their lives.

Therefore equality has become a criterion with which to test Moslem leaders and distinguish between the true and the fake people of God.

And as in the other fields, Fāṭimah was decorated with the highest degrees of equality. After several years of marriage during which she cared for her children, and carried out all the work at home such as: grinding barley, baking bread, carrying water, cleaning the house, etc. she brought a housemaid to help her. Although Feḍḍah, as a housemaid, lived in Fāṭimah's home and was expected to do all the housework, but to the amazement of others Fāṭimah told her that the work should be evenly divided between them. One day Feḍḍah should do the work and Fāṭimah have a rest, and the next day Fāṭimah should do the work and Feḍḍah have a rest!!

After her martyrdom, Amēr al-Mo'menēn spoke to one of his followers telling him something about Fāṭimah's housework:

> *((She carried water with a Qerbah*[1] *so often that it put a mark on her chest; and she grinded with the mill until her hands indurated and became callous; and she swept the home until her clothes became dusty; and she made fire under the pot until...*[2]*)).*

Excessive generosity

Any person can be generous, especially if he is in touch with his humanity, and more so if he believes in the Hereafter. Therefore if this humane character is historically attributed to a person living in past centuries, it does not necessarily mean that its bearer is someone special who should be taken as a role model.

However, if this generosity oversteps its expected boundaries and finds no limits and thus becomes excessive, then its bearer is certainly special. And as much as this excessive generosity is accompanied with more splendid characters and fewer ugly characters, its holder stands out more clearly.

When we read about Fāṭimah, we see that she had the highest grades of excessive generosity, something hard to grasp; and only possible to rationalize as teaching her followers with her actions before her words.

There are more instances than I can possibly count, but the two following narrations will give you some idea of her limitless excessive generosity:

> *((The Prophet had prepared a new dress for Fāṭimah for her wedding night, as she only had a patched dress.*
> *And before the wedding, suddenly a beggar came to the door saying: I ask from the House of Prophethood a worn-out dress. So she wanted to give him her old*

---

[1] A leathern container for liquids usually water, carried with its handle on the shoulder.

[2] Beḥār al-Anwār / al-Majlesi = vol. 85, page 329.

patched dress, but she remembered the holy āyah[1]*: "BY NO MEANS SHALL YOU ATTAIN TO RIGHTEOUSNESS UNTIL YOU SPEND (BENEVOLENTLY) OUT OF WHAT YOU LOVE*[2]*" ; thus she gave out her wedding dress instead, and decided to wear her old patched dress in her wedding*[3]*.)).*

It has also been narrated:

((One day after Rasōlollāh performed the noon ṣalāt[4] *with us, he sat and Moslems surrounded him. Suddenly an ageing Arab wearing an old torn dress, hardly able to control himself from old age and weakness, came to him.*
Rasōlollāh asked him about his condition and his needs.
The old Arab: O Prophet of Allāh! I am hungry, so feed me; and I am naked, so cover me with clothes; and I am poor, so donate some money to me.
Rasōlollāh: I do not have anything at the moment, but he who points to goodness is such as him who accomplishes it. Go to the home of the person who loves Allāh and His Messenger, and is loved by them; who gives precedence to Allāh's wishes over himself; go to Fāṭimah's room.
When the Arab arrived at Fāṭimah's door, he called out with all his voice: Peace be upon you O Ahl Bayt al-Nobowwah![5] *and the point of come-and-go for the*

---

[1] A verse from the Holy Qor'ān. Plural āyāt.
[2] Holy Qor'ān = sōrah 3, āyah 92.
[3] Nozhat al-Majālis / al-Ṣafōri = vol. 2, page 226.
[4] Prayer, certain connected movements during which parts of the Holy Qor'ān, as well as several adhkār (plural of dhekr) and adᶜeyah (plural of doᶜā') are recited. There are many different forms of ṣalāt for different reasons and with different effects; some of which are wājib (mandatory), whereas others are mostaḥab (recommended). Some of these ṣalawāt (plural of ṣalāt) should only be performed in specific times and/or places, whereas other ṣalawāt are not bound to any time or place restrictions.
[5] Ahl al-Bayt, the Fourteen Maᶜṣōmēn.

angels, and the place of descent for Jabra'ēl carrying the Qor'ān from the Creator of the creatures.

Fāṭimah: And Peace be upon you too. Who are you?

The old Arab: I am an ageing Arab. I came to your father... and I am O daughter of Moḥammad! naked and hungry, so help me, may Allāh bless you.

This happened when it was three days since Rasōlollāh, ᶜAli and Fāṭimah had last eaten food.

So Fāṭimah picked up the animal skin on which Ḥasan and Ḥosayn slept and gave it to the Arab, saying: Take this; may Allāh give you what is better for you.

The old Arab: O daughter of Moḥammad! I complained to you from hunger and you gave me an animal skin?! What do I do with it for my hunger?!

When Fāṭimah heard him, she took the only piece of jewelry she had, a necklace given to her by her cousin daughter of Ḥamzah, and gave it to the Arab, saying: Take this and sell it; may Allāh exchange it for you with what is better.

So the Arab took the necklace and went back to the mosque where Rasōlollāh and his Ṣaḥābah were sitting, telling him: O Rasōlollāh! Fāṭimah gave me this necklace and told me: Sell it; may Allāh fulfill your needs.

Hearing him, Rasōlollāh cried and said: And how is it possible that Allāh does not fulfill your needs when Fāṭimah, the daughter of Moḥammad, the Foremost of the Daughters of Ādam has given you her necklace?!

Suddenly ᶜAmmār ibn Yāsir stood up and said: O Rasōlollah! Do you permit me to buy this necklace?

Rasōlollāh: Buy it ᶜAmmār...

ᶜAmmār: How much will you sell it O Arab?

The old Arab: I will sell it for a full stomach with bread and meat, a Yemeni garment to cover my body in which I can pray for my God, and one gold Dēnār to take me to my family.

ᶜAmmār: You will have twenty gold Dēnārs, and two hundred silver Derhams, and my camel to take you to your family.
The old Arab: How generous you are!
Then ᶜAmmār gave him what he had promised, and the Arab returned to Rasōlollāh where he asked him: Did you eat and dress?
The old Arab: Yes and I became rich, my parents be your sacrifice.
Rasōlollāh: So reward Fāṭimah for what she did for you.
The old Arab: O Allāh! You are a God we did not create, and we do not have a God to worship except you. You are our provider in every circumstance. O Allāh! Give Fāṭimah what no eye has seen and no ear has heard...
Later, ᶜAmmār took the necklace, smeared it with musk, wrapped it with a Yemeni garment and gave it to his slave called Sahm, telling him: Take this and give it to Rasōlollāh, and from now on you will belong to him.
The slave took the necklace and went to the Prophet, telling him what ᶜAmmār had said.
Rasōlollāh: Go to Fāṭimah's home and give her this; and you will belong to her.
So the slave went to Fāṭimah and told her what Rasōlollāh had said. Fāṭimah took the necklace and freed the slave.
Sahm laughed, and so Fāṭimah asked her: What makes you laugh?
Sahm: The importance of this necklace made me laugh. It fed a hungry, clothed a naked, made a poor rich, freed a slave and returned to its owner[1].)).

Honor for knowledge

---

[1] Beḥār al-Anwār / al-Majlesi = vol. 43, page 56.

Honor for knowledge is what keeps a person knowledgeable. Understanding the importance of what a person has learnt and is learning is most necessary for maintaining it. And knowing what a person carries inside his head will continue to drive him to acquire more of it. Without this, the scholar stops learning and often becomes as good as an illiterate.

However this honor dramatically increases when the gained information relates to God and Godly things, in contrast with what relates to world and worldly things; because the latter kind does not have much value beyond the limits of this life and this world, whereas the former yields even more outside the boundaries of this world.

Therefore we see Fāṭimah had an unprecedented honor for knowledge so much that she says in the following narration: "To me it (some of her father's teachings) equals Ḥasan and Ḥosayn".

> *((After Rasōlollāh's death a man came to Fāṭimah, saying: O Daughter of Rasōlollāh! Did Rasōlollāh leave anything with you that I can see?*
> *Fāṭimah said to her student: O Feḍḍah! Bring me that piece of silken cloth.*
> *So she looked for it but could not find it.*
> *Fāṭimah: Woe on to you! Find it. To me it equals Ḥasan and Ḥosayn!!*
> *When she found the cloth, it was written on it: Prophet Moḥammad said: He is not a believer whose neighbor is not safe from his calamity; and whoever believes in Allāh and the Hereafter should not annoy his neighbor; and whoever believes in Allāh and the Hereafter should say good things or remain silent.*
> *Indeed Allāh loves him who is charitable, forbearing and abstinent; and hates him who swears, uses obscene language and is a persistent demander.*
> *Indeed shyness is of faith and faith is in Heaven; and indeed indecency is of obscenity and obscenity is in Hell[1].))*

---

[1] Mostadrak al-Wasā'el / al-Nōri = vol. 12, page 81.

Love for teaching

Without having love for teaching no one can teach, because teaching is surrounded with difficulties. And the lesser knowledge a student has, the harder it is to teach him; and the more ignorant the society is, the more unbarring its education becomes.

So it is easy to imagine how hard it must have been for Rasōlollāh*(SAA)*[1] and the other maᶜṣōmēn[2] to teach the ignorant illiterate Arabs of their time, fourteen centuries ago, and transform them, in a relatively short period, to a new knowledgeable people.

And as the first woman teacher in Islam, whose students did not only consist of women, Fāṭimah had enormous love for teaching. So much that, to her, the impossible job of educating those people was a very pleasant and a satisfying undertaking.

The following narration sheds some light on Fāṭimah's love for teaching:

> *((One day a woman came to Fāṭimah and said: I have an old weak mother who has made a mistake in her ṣalāt, and has sent me to you to ask about it.*
> *So Fāṭimah answered the mother's question.*
> *And the woman asked a second question and a third question and a fourth question, until she asked her tenth question. Then wanting to ask yet more questions, she said to Fāṭimah: I do not want to annoy you more O Daughter of Rasōlollāh!*
> *Fāṭimah: Come and ask whatever questions you wish to ask. Would it be difficult for a person who is hired for one hundred thousand gold Dēnārs to take a heavy load to the roof?!*

---

[1] *Ṣallallāh ᶜAlayh wa Ālih,* Allāh's Blessings be upon him and his descendants.

[2] Plural of maᶜṣōm: a person who does not commit sins, does not make mistakes, does not forget, etc. although he/she has the choice to commit sins. Prophets and their awṣeyā' are maᶜṣōm. The Fourteen Maᶜṣōmēn are the Prophet Moḥammad, his daughter Fāṭimah, and his twelve God-appointed successors.

The woman: No.

Fāṭimah: I was hired for more than what fills between the earth and the Arsh with pearls for every question I answer. So it is more appropriate for me not to feel the heavy load of these questions.

I heard my father say: When the scholars of our followers are resurrected, robes of honor are put on them to the extent of their knowledge, and their seriousness in guiding their people, such that any one of them would be given one million robes of light[1].

Then an angel announces: O you crowd of guardians of the orphans of Moḥammad's descendants! The revivers of the orphans after they were separated from their fathers who were their A'emmah[2]. *These are your students and the orphans whom you guarded and revived and clothed with the robes of knowledge in the previous world.*

The scholars are then given robes of light to the extent of what they had taught their orphans. They are given as many as one hundred thousand robes for a particular student.

---

[1] In this world we are unable to understand the affairs of the Hereafter in measurement to the affairs of this world. This is because our brains are designed to grasp limited things in a limited world, thus we cannot use it to absorb a limitless world. For instance we do not exactly know what is a robe of honor in the Hereafter, or what is a robe of light, or what does it mean for a scholar to be given one million robes of light… We can either believe in them if we believe in God and His attributes, or reject them if we choose not to believe in God and His attributes.

Therefore a person who does not even believe in God and His attributes should not really bother to try to understand these minor issues, and must before everything examine the evidence for the existence of God and study them. And when he finds himself a creature of a limitless God, then and only then, can he start believing in robes of light, etc. without understanding them.

If you do not believe in God, then you can only believe in the few things that you see, but if you do believe in God, then believing in the limitless things that you do not see becomes possible and easier.

[2] Plural of imām. The twelve successors of Prophet Moḥammad.

And then the students themselves are given robes to the extent of what they had taught their own students.

Later Allāh says: Repeat the process and give them more... So every teacher is given robes to the extent of what he had taught his students, and his students are then given robes to the extent of what they had taught their students, and so on.

Then Fāṭimah said: O Servant of Allāh! A thread of those robes is a million times more valuable than what the sun shines upon[1].)).

Patience

A person who has a constructive mission in life, faces two kinds of hardship which vary in accordance with the nature and the circumstances of the mission:

One source of hardship is a friendly source, from people who want to participate, cooperate, be receptive, be useful, etc. but do not quite know what to do and how best to do it.

And fourteen centuries ago the teachers of Islam constantly and continuously faced such difficulties. This was because the Arabs and non-Arabs in those times were in a period of transformation, and were not yet familiar with all the etiquettes of learning and the formalities of education.

And the other source of hardship, which was the most serious and the harshest, was naturally the enemy.

And during her life, Fāṭimah suffered unlimited aggression especially from the disguised enemies of Islam, those who shammed tawheed[2] to propagate Idolatry.

However, armed defense against this enemy, who immediately ceased power after the martyrdom of Rasōlollāh and swiftly usurped his khelāfah, was not possible as it would have ended in the deaths of the real carriers of Islam, who were followed by only a very small minority, and would have resulted in the complete destruction of all that the Prophet had constructed.

---

[1] Beḥār al-Anwār / al-Majlesi = vol. 2, page 3.

[2] Belief in the one indivisible God.

So the only feasible option for the Ahl al-Bayt[1], to insure the survival of Islam, was teaching in relative secret and occasional public speeches that differed in temperature.

And in parallel to this, they had to exercise great patience and endure what was thrown at them as a result of their public and secret stances against the usurpers.

One of the instances when Rasōlollāh ordered Fāṭimah to exercise patience after his death, was while he was on his deathbed; he told her:

> *((...Leave everything to Allāh and be patient, just as your fathers, who were prophets, were patient...[2])).*

Bakri scholars also narrate in their respected references that a few days before her death, Fāṭimah addressed Abō Bakr's party in the Prophet's Mosque in Madinah, and said in her famous public speech:

> *((...And we remain patient with you of things similar to the cutting of the saw, and the stabbing of the stomach with a spear[3].)).*

And as part of their patience, the Fourteen Maᶜṣōmēn*(AmS)*[4] did not complain of their suffering to their families or followers. So much that the husband did not speak of his pain to the wife, neither did the wife show her injuries to her husband...

And sometimes, when their wounds and hurt were obvious, they tried their utmost to keep their family away so that they do not see the heartrending scenes.

Therefore, when ᶜOmar*(LA)*[5] viciously slapped Fāṭimah in the street, she covered her face at home, so that her husband and her

---

[1] The Fourteen Maᶜṣōmēn, who are Rasōlollāh, Sayyedat Nesā' al-ᶜĀlamēn, and the twelve God-appointed successors of Rasōlollāh.

[2] Beḥār al-Anwār / al-Majlesi – vol. 40, page 66.

[3] Sharh Nahj al-Balāghah / Ibn Abi al-Ḥadēd = vol. 16, page 251.

[4] *ᶜAlayhemos Salām,* peace be upon them.

[5] *Laᶜnatollāh ᶜAlayh,* may Allāh distance him from His Blessings and Mercy.

young children do not see its marks, and she did not tell them about it.

And after the final assault on her home, when ᶜOmar and around three hundred Bakri ruffians attacked her house, set fire to it, crushed her between the door and the wall, broke her ribs, lashed her body, hit her with sword, caused the miscarriage of her son Moḥassin… she hid her wounds as much as she possibly could from her husband and children, and did not mention her pains to them.

Therefore, hours before she died, she cleaned her wounds, and washed her bloodstained clothes, so that after she dies her husband does not see much of her suffering. But after her death, when they were washing her body, Amēr al-Mo’menēn, Asmā’ bint ᶜOmays[1], and Feḍḍah saw and felt the injuries and bruises she had so long tried to hide from them; and they wept in silence, suppressing the sound of their crying to avoid alerting the people who did her injustice[2].

Simplicity

Although other people who were in similar social, political and financial positions as Fāṭimah enjoyed the finest of life’s luxuries, and untiringly submerged themselves in formalities and never ending ceremonies, Fāṭimah did the exact opposite.

She avoided all these unnecessary burdens and did not introduce any of them to her life. Because unlike the others, she wanted to be readily accessible to all kinds of people, rich and poor, influential and ordinary…

By living as the poorest Moslem woman in the poorest Moslem family, leading a most simple life, she prevented people from thinking that a large gap separated her and her family from them; and taught others in similar social standing to erase any distinction between them and the ordinary man in the street.

---

[1] Asmā’ bint Omays was Abō Bakr’s wife, and at the same time she was one of Fāṭimah’s finest students. She once alerted Amēr al-Mo’menēn about her husband’s plot to assassinate him the next day in the Prophet’s Mosque. And she was also one of the few people who were allowed to participate in Fāṭimah’s secret burial ceremonies in the middle of the night.

[2] You will read more on this subject later in this book.

So when a poor person visited her, he or she would feel better off financially; and when a person of a low class came to her, he or she would feel as if visiting a person of the same or even a lower class.

Zohd[1]

The Fourteen Maᶜṣōmēn have given a number of meanings and descriptions for zohd from different angles. In one of his descriptions for zohd, Amēr al-Mo'menēn says:

((Zohd in this world means: Shortening the hope[2].)).

And when someone asks him: What is zohd in this world? He answers:

((It is avoiding its prohibitions[3].)).

And Imām Ṣādiq[(AS)4] describes zohd by its opposite, when he says:

((The opposite of zohd is desire[5].)).

And in an attempt to correct a misconception of zohd that some people may have, he says:

((Zohd in this world does not mean avoiding money, and it does not mean prohibiting what God has allowed[6].)).

But perhaps the best all-inclusive description of zohd from the Fourteen Maᶜṣōmēn[(AmS)1] is:

---

[1] Non-attachment to material things.
[2] al-Kāfi / al-Kolayni = vol. 5, page 71.
[3] Wasā'el al-Shēᶜah / al-Ḥorr al-ᶜĀmili = vol. 16, page 15.
[4] *ᶜAlayhes Salām,* peace be upon him.
[5] al-Kāfi / al-Kolayni = vol. 1, page 20.
[6] Wasā'el al-Shēᶜah / al-Ḥorr al-ᶜĀmili = vol. 17, page 35.

> *((Zohd means: That this world does not own you, but you own this world.)).*

And we see that in the short eighteen years of her life, Fāṭimah was an embodiment of zohd, who owned the world and was not enslaved by it.

She lived the life of the poorest of the poor, although the vast yielding Fadak was among her positions; she lived the simplest possible life, although she was the daughter of the ruler of nine countries in today's geography; and she requested her husband to burry her in secret and hide her grave[2], although she could have had the best burial ceremony, and attract countless pilgrims to her grave, like her father, husband and sons.

---

[1] *ᶜAlayhemos Salām,* peace be upon them.

[2] You will read more on this subject later in this book.

SAYYEDAT NESĀ' AL-[c]ĀLAMĒN'S MISSION

We could never fully understand the whole mission of any of the Fourteen Ma[c]ṣōmēn, and can only believe in what has been passed down to us from Allāh, and from them, about themselves and their missions.

This is because on the one hand our brain and intellectual capability is limited, and on the other hand their mission is even bigger than our imagination.

Their mission overlap human beings and covers all the creatures of Allāh, irrespective of time and place and regardless of whether or not they have a soul; and their authority extends over everything and overspreads whole planets.

And it does not stop at the highest levels of al-Walāyah al-Takwēneyyah[1], but goes further to encompass creation itself; after

---

[1] Authority over the laws of nature. A power and ability granted by Allāh to a person. al-Walāyah al-Takwēneyyah has different levels of strength in accordance with its bearer's position to Allāh, and the degree of his obedience to Him. Some levels are limited to the earth and earthly things, whereas other levels exceed our planet.

Having authority over nature has not been limited to the followers of Prophet Moḥammad. The followers of previous prophets were also able to acquire this enormous power. For example at the time of Prophet Dāwōd (also David) his followers were shown the way to achieve this goal, when Allāh told Dāwōd:

> *((Deliver to your people: that there is no servant among them, whom I command my obedience and he obeys me, except that it becomes necessary for Me to obey him.)).* (Kalimatollāh / The Martyr Āyatollāh Ḥasan Shērāzi = page 141)

God empowered them and deputized them to create His creatures, just as He ordered some of his angels to give and take lives.

And about this fact, the second Bakri leader ᶜOmar, said to Prophet Moḥammad's third khalēfah[1] Imām Ḥosayn*(AS)*[2]:

> *((...Verily, you caused to grow what is on our heads (hair) after Allāh[3].)).*

And he repeated this recognition on another occasion when he said to Imām Ḥosayn:

> *((...And has anyone caused to grow the hair on the head after Allāh, except you[4].)).*

Allāh also says:

> *((O My servant! obey Me, you will become like Me. I say to things: Be, and they are; and you will say to things: Be, and they are.)).*

And in the Holy Qor'ān, when Allāh reveals the story of Prophet Solaymān (also Solomon) to Prophet Moḥammad, He says:

> *﴿HE (SOLAYMĀN) SAID: O CHIEFS! WHICH OF YOU CAN BRING TO ME HER THRONE BEFORE THEY COME TO ME IN SUBMISSION? * ONE AUDACIOUS AMONG THE JINN SAID: I WILL BRING IT TO YOU BEFORE YOU RISE UP FROM YOU PLACE; AND MOST SURELY I AM STRONG [AND] TRUSTY FOR IT * ONE WHO HAD SOME KNOWLEDGE OF THE BOOK SAID: I WILL BRING IT TO YOU IN THE TWINKLING OF AN EYE. THEN WHEN HE SAW IT SETTLED BESIDE HIM, HE SAID: THIS IS OF THE GRACE OF MY LORD THAT HE MAY TRY ME WHETHER I AM GRATEFUL OR UNGRATEFUL; AND WHOEVER IS GRATEFUL, HE IS GRATEFUL ONLY FOR HIS OWN SOUL, AND WHOEVER IS UNGRATEFUL, THEN SURELY MY LORD IS SELF-SUFFICIENT, HONORED.﴿.* (sōrah 27, āyāt 38-40)

What that person did in the presence of Solaymān was surely by the power of al-Walāyah al-Takwēneyyah.

[1] A God-appointed successor of Rasōlollāh. Also caliph. Bakris wrongfully use this title for the leaders of the Bakri party who usurped the Rightful Khelāfah from the a'emmah. Plural Kholafā'.

[2] *ᶜAlayhes Salām,* peace be upon him.

[3] Tārēkh Baghdād / al-Baghdādi = Vol. 7, page 141.

[4] Kanz al-ᶜOmmāl / al-Hendi = vol. 7, page 105. al-Ṣawāᶜiq al-Moḥreqah / Ibn Ḥajar = page 107.

But their mission does not end there either, as God has tied our being to their being. Thus if a ḥojjah[1] of Allāh is no longer amongst us, we will seizes to exist.

As Prophet Moḥammad's eighth khalēfah Imām Reḍa[(AS)2] said:

> *((If the earth became vacant of a ḥojjah for a blink of an eye, it would certainly swallow its inhabitants[3].)).*

Bakri[4] scholars also narrate in their references from Rasōlollāh who said:

> *((...And if my descendants seize to exist, so will the earth's inhabitants seize to exist[5].)).*

And after this world, the Fourteen Maṣōmēn remain in charge in the Hereafter, as Bakri scholars agree and narrate:

> *((Abō Bakr and ᶜAli ibn Abi Ṭālib met one day, and Abō Bakr smiled in his face. ᶜAli asked him: Why did you smile?*
> *Abō Bakr: I heard Rasōlollāh say: No one can cross over the Ṣerāṭ[6] without a pass from ᶜAli[7].)).*

---

[1] Ḥojjah (plural: ḥojaj) means a representative of Allāh on earth, who is the link between Him and His creatures. Only the prophets and their awṣeyā' are ḥojaj.

[2] *ᶜAlayhes Salām,* peace be upon him.

[3] Beḥār al Anwār / al-Majlesi – vol. 23, page 29.

[4] A Bakri is a follower of Abō Bakr. Opposite Moslem, Shēᶜah, follower of Rasōlollāh. Some people unknowingly call the followers of Abō Bakr "sonnis". Sonni means a follower of the tradition of Rasōlollāh; and since the followers of Abō Bakr follow him and not Rasōlollāh, it is wrong to call them sonnis.

[5] Mokhtaṣar Dhakhā'er al-ᶜOqbā / al-Ṭabari = page 30.

[6] Ṣerāṭ is the bridge from the place of resurrection to Heaven, passing over Hell. It is thinner than a hair and sharper than a sword; and as such, only those worthy of Heaven are able to cross it, and those worthy of Hell will lose their balance and fall into their deserving abode.

[7] Mokhtaṣar Dhakhā'er al-ᶜOqbā / al-Ṭabari = page 115.

And because Allāh granted the Fourteen Maᶜṣōmēn the highest levels of al-Walāyah al-Takwēneyyah, and made them his instruments for creation, and chose them to be the sustainers of the world, etc. He instructed all of His prophets to believe in them and submit to their will, before they could become prophets.

It has been narrated from Rasōlollāh who said:

> *{{The prophethood of no prophet became complete in Aẓellah, until my authority and the authority of my descendants were presented to them, and my descendants were shown to them, and they recognized their obedience and submitted to their authority[1].)).*

And after the world of Aẓellah the Fourteen Maᶜṣōmēn remained ever so important to the prophets, so much that in times of danger and oppression, they prayed to Allāh and put the Fourteen Maᶜṣōmēn as the intermediary between them and Allāh for relief and victory.

Prophet Nōḥ[2], for example, asked God in their name for safety and relief, and wrote the names of Rasōlollāh, Amēr al-Mo'menēn, Sayyedat Nesā' al-ᶜĀlamēn, Imām Ḥasan and Imām Ḥosayn[(AmS)3] on a board which he put on his ship for blessing.

And Fāṭimah was one of these Fourteen Maᶜṣōmēn, whose authority over God's creations encompassed everything and everyone including the prophets and their awṣeyā', except her father and her husband.

And throughout their lives, prophet Moḥammad's kholafā' repeatedly recognized her authority over them in front of their followers, so that they may know her better and understand her position to God as much as they can.

For instance Rasōlollāh's eleventh khalēfah Imām ᶜAskari[(AS)4] says:

---

[1] Beḥār al-Anwār / al-Majlesi = vol. 26, page 281.

[2] Also Noah.

[3] *ᶜAlayhemos Salām,* peace be upon them.

[4] *ᶜAlayhes Salām,* peace be upon him.

((We are Allāh's Ḥojaj[1] over people, and Fāṭimah is Allāh's Ḥojjah over us[2].)).

This is Fāṭimah, who is a Ḥojjah over eleven of her father's successors, who are, themselves, Ḥojaj over all the creation.

We may not know exactly what she is and who she is with our limited intellectual capability, which so far has not comprehended all there is to comprehend about the human body which is only a part of its larger being, but we know something about her mission, to an extent that relates to us.

Here are some highlights of a part of Fāṭimah's mission that relates to the propagation of Islam:

HER DOᶜĀ'[3]

Islam as the last divine religion is the most complete religion, and it is universal and for all times.

Islam, as its predecessors, works to elevate its followers' souls as much as they allow it to elevate, through listening to Allāh and speaking to Him. Listening to Allāh, when reciting the Holy Qor'ān; and speaking to Him, when reciting the Holy Doᶜā'.

Fortunately a large number of adᶜeyah[4] have been passed down to us from the Fourteen Maᶜṣōmēn, for every day of the week; for every month of the year; for every aspect of life; for every kind of

---

[1] Plural of ḥojjah: a representative of Allāh on earth. Prophets and their awṣeyā' are ḥojaj.

[2] Mostadrakāt ᶜAwālim al-ᶜOlōm / al-Abṭaḥi = vol. 11, page 7

[3] Praying to Allāh, asking Him for something for oneself and/or for others… Doᶜā' can be positive or negative, and has many forms and many uses and effects. Some adᶜeyah (plural of doᶜā') should only be recited in specific times and/or places, whereas other adᶜeyah are not bound to any time or place restrictions. There is a huge number of set formal adᶜeyah narrated from the Fourteen Maᶜṣōmēn, the recitation of which is highly recommended, but it is also possible for any Moslem to compose his own doᶜā', in any language format, provided that he has a considerable knowledge of Islam.

[4] Plural of doᶜā'.

need; for every type of fear; for all forms of thanking Allāh for His gifts; for all sorts of estekhārah[1], etc.

These adᶜeyah teach us Islamic law, theology, sociology, politics, economics, morals, etiquettes, etc. They include prophecies and scientific facts centuries before they happen and are discovered.

These adᶜeyah are the peaks of eloquence of the Arabic language, and the main sources of knowledge. Something that separates the true representatives of Allāh from the pretenders. Something that the maᶜṣōmēn have plentiful, and their foes lack totally.

In her adᶜeyah, Fāṭimah turns herself into the smallest of things in front of the largest of things. She looks at Allāh as if He is looking at her, and she talks to Allāh as if He is talking to her. She speaks of herself as the worst sinner on the face of earth, who has no chance of forgiveness; and yet she shows so much confidence in forgiveness, as if she is sinless.

In her adᶜeyah, she portrays Allāh as the most powerful king from Whose justice nothing escapes, and Who holds His subjects accountable for every tiny mistake; and at the same time, she portrays Him as the most affectionate mother towards her only child who always turns a blind eye to her child's mischief.

In her adᶜeyah, she places the person between Allāh's wrath and His Mercy in such proximity that he feels he will be engulfed in God's wrath in one minute, and becomes certain of God's Mercy in the next minute.

In her adᶜeyah, she makes a person see, hear and feel the comforts of Heaven; and simultaneously see, hear and feel the tortures of Hell.

Many scholars have collected the narrated adᶜeyah from the maᶜṣōmēn in various specialized books; and other scholars have put great efforts into write explanations and interpretations to these adᶜeyah in their multi-volume encyclopedias.

Fāṭimah's adᶜeyah could be divided into three categories:

---

[1] Asking Allāh, after reciting a doᶜā', etc. whether something should or should not be done. Estekhārah is taken only when the person has remained undecided after thinking, and consulting the relevant persons. There are numerous methods for estekhārah.

A- SECRET AD^cEYAH:

The ad^ceyah that were between her and her God which she recited in secrecy, and did not allow others to learn for various reasons.

B- PRIVATE AD^cEYAH:

The ad^ceyah that she recited for specific purposes, without the intention to teach them to others; although saying them out loud in front of others so that they may use them as a source of knowledge. They include:

1-[1] *((O My Lord! and my Master! this is Moḥammad, Your Prophet; and this is ^cAli, Your Prophet's cousin; and these are Ḥasan and Ḥosayn, Your Prophet's grandsons.*
O My Lord! Descend upon us food from the sky, just as You descended it to the children of Israel. They ate from it and disbelieved it. O Allāh! Descend it upon us; in it we are surely believers[2].)).

2-[3] *((O Ever-Living! O Self-Subsisting! By Thy Mercy I ask for relief, so relieve me. O Allāh! Move me away from Hell and enter me into Heaven; and join me with my father*

---

[1] It has been narrated (in Beḥār al-Anwār / al-Majlesi = vol. 43, page 74 as well as other references) that one day Rasōlollāh went to Fāṭimah's home to see if there was any food to eat, but learned that like him, his daughter, son-in-law and their two sons Ḥasan and Ḥosayn had not eaten for three days. Later Fāṭimah performed a ṣalāt and recited this do^cā'. She had not completed her do^cā' when suddenly they saw Heavenly food before them.

[2] ^cAwālim al-^cOlōm / al-Baḥrāni = vol. 11, page 323.

[3] It has been narrated that after the series of attacks on Fāṭimah by the usurpers of the khelāfah, and shortly before her death, she recited a large number of long and short ad^ceyah, some of which are mentioned here.

Moḥammad, may Allāh's Blessing be upon him and his descendents[1].
O my Lord! I have indeed become tired of life, and have been annoyed by the people, so take me to my father[2].
To You my Lord, not to Hell. O Allāh! With Your Messenger. O Allāh! In Your Heaven and in Your vicinity and in Your house, the house of peace[3]*.)).*

3- *((O Allāh! I ask You in Moḥammad the Moṣṭafa's name, and his yearning for me; and in my husband ᶜAli the Mortaḍā's name, and his grief for me; and in Ḥasan the Mojtabā's name, and his crying for me; and in Ḥosayn the Martyr's name, and his sorrow for me; and in my daughters' names, and their heartbreak for me; that You have Mercy upon the sinners of the followers of Moḥammad, and forgive them, and take them to Heaven. You are indeed the Most Noble, and the Most Merciful*[4]*.)).*

C- PUBLIC ADᶜEYAH:

The adᶜeyah that she taught others so that they may recite them. These adᶜeyah fall into several categories including:

- asking Allāh for forgiveness and pardon;
- freedom from prison;
- fulfillment of needs;
- glorifying Allāh;
- physical healing, such as: recovery from a fever;

[1] Beḥār al-Anwār / al-Majlesi = vol. 81, page 233.
[2] al-Ṣaḥēfah al-Fāṭimeyyah / al-Abṭaḥi = page 70.
[3] al-Ṣaḥēfah al-Fāṭimeyyah / al-Abṭaḥi = page 71.
[4] Bahjat Qalb al-Moṣṭafa / al-Raḥmāni = page 301. al-Ṣaḥēfah al-Fāṭimeyyah / al-Abṭaḥi = page 77.

- praising Allāh;
- protection from an unjust ruler, etc;
- settlement of a debt;
- specific ad^c^eyah for morning and night;
- specific ad^c^eyah for every day of the week;
- specific ad^c^eyah to be recited after the mandatory and the recommended ṣalawāt (plural of ṣalāt).
- warding off anxiety and worry.

Some of these ad^c^eyah are:

1-[1] *((O Allāh! Protect us with Your eye which does not go to sleep; and Your support which will never be weaken; and with Your great names. And descend Your Blessing upon Moḥammad and his descendents. And protect for us that which would be lost if someone other than You protects it; and conceal for us that which would be known if someone other than you conceals it; and make all of this conformable for us. You are indeed a Listener to the Do^c^ā', and a Fast Responder[2].)).*

2-[3] *((Praise be to Allāh, He Whose Praise cannot be culminated by those who commend. And praise be to Allāh, He Whose gifts cannot be counted by those whose expertise is to count. And praise be to Allāh, He who cannot be recompensed by the continuous worship of the devout worshipers.*
And there is no God except Allāh, the First and the Last. And there is no God except Allāh, the Evident and the Hidden. And there

---

[1] This is a special do^c^ā' to be recited on Wednesday.

[2] al-Do^c^ā' wa al-Zeyārah / The Martyr, Āyatollāh al-^c^Oẓmā Sayyed Moḥammad Shērāzi = page 40.

[3] The following are parts of a special do^c^ā' to be recited after the maghreb prayer.

is no God except Allāh, the Giver of Life and the Taker of Life.
And Allāh is Greater, the Almighty. And Allāh is Greater, the Eternal.
And praise be to Allāh, He whose knowledge cannot be comprehend by the knowledgeable; and whose forbearance cannot be weakened by the ignorant; and whose praise cannot be culminated by those whose expertise is to praise; and whose attributes cannot be described by those whose expertise is to describe; and whose qualities cannot be adequately explained by His creatures.
And praise be to Allāh, He who has the reign and the kingdom; and the grandeur and the mightiness; and the pride and the exaltedness; and the magnificence and the gravity; and the beauty and the prestige; and the power and the strength; and the force and the grace; and the victory and the merit; and the might and the justice; and the truth and the noble character; and the eminence and the highness; and the glory and the virtue; and the wisdom and the sufficiency; and the profusion and the expansion and the contraction; and the forbearance and the knowledge; and the conclusive proof; and the encompassing benefaction; and the graceful and beautiful commendation; and the noble spiritual gifts. The king of this world and the Hereafter and the Heaven and the Hell and all of what they include. Blessed be Him, Allāh, and be He raised far above.
Praise be to Allāh, He Who knows the secrets of the invisibles; and is aware of the sins that the hearts commit; so there is no way of escape and getaway from Him.
And praise be to Allāh, He Who is the Proud in His rule; and is the Venerated in His Place; and is the Haughty in his Reign; and the

Powerful in his Assault; and is the High over his Arsh; and is the Informed of His people; and attains whatever He wishes.

And praise be to Allāh, He by Whose command the massive skies were upheld; and the flat lands became firm; and the unshakable deep-rooted mountains stood erect; and the pollinating air flew; and the clouds moved in the sky; and the seas stood at their limits; and the hearts became apprehensive of His fear; and the lords were subdued by His Lordship.

Blessed You are, O Who counts the rain drops; and the leaves of the trees; and the Giver of life to the corps of the dead for the resurrection.

Glory be to You, O You Who possesses the Exaltedness and Honor; what would You do to the stranger, the destitute if he came to You appealing for aid and asking for help?

What would You do to the one who remains at Your Court; and exposes himself to Your Approval; and comes to You, until he kneels between Your Hands, complaining to You of the things that are not hidden from You?

So do not let O my Lord! the outcome of my invocation to be deprivation, and nor my share of what I wish from you to be disappointment.

O He Who has not and will not vanish; and has been and will continue to be watching every soul as to what it attains.

O He Who has made the days of this world to pass, and its months to change, and its years to go round. And You are the Everlasting. The times do not afflict You, and nor do the worlds.

O He to Whom every day is new; and by Him every means of living for the weak and the strong and the tough are prepared. You have divided the means of living for the creatures, and have equaled between the small ant and the bird.

I ask of You O Allāh! By these praises to forgive me, and pardon me, and cloth my body with health, and grant me soundness in my religion.

Thus I ask of You and I am confident of Your Response; and I call upon You and I know that You can hear my call; so listen to my call, and do not sever my hope, and do not refuse my laudatory, and do not block my call. I am in need of Your Satisfaction and of Your Forgiveness. I ask of You and I am not disheartened of Your Mercy, and call upon You while I am not being cautious of Your Discontentment.

O Lord! Fulfill my requests, and have favor on me with Your Forgiveness; and take my life as a Moslem and join me with the good. O Lord! Do not forbid me Your Kindness, O Beneficent! And do not make me depend on myself in abandonment, O Compassionate!

O Lord! Be Merciful to me when I leave my beloveds and die, and when I stay alone in my grave, and when I am a stranger in the desert on the Day of Resurrection, and when I stand in poverty between Your Hands in Your Court of justice.

O Lord! I seek refuge to You from the Fire, so give me refuge. O Lord! I seek Your Protection from the Fire, so protect me. I run to You from the Fire, so take me away.

O Lord! Being anguished, I seek Your Mercy, so have Mercy on me; O Lord! I seek Your Forgiveness for when I was ignorant, so forgive me.

Indeed doᶜā' for my need has taken me to You, so do not disappoint me, O Bountiful! He

Who has the Gifts, and the Benevolence and the Overlooking.

O My Master! O Beneficent! O Merciful! Grant my request amongst those who pray humbly to You; and have Mercy on my tears amongst those who cry to You; and on the day I leave this world, make my meeting with You as my Comfort; and conceal amongst the dead O He in Whom there are great wishes, my shameful acts; and have Compassion for me when I am being moved to my grave alone. You are my hope, and You are the one Whom I ask my needs from, and the one Who knows what I am going to ask Him; so fulfill my needs, O Fulfiller of needs!

So, to You is the complaint, and You are the Helper and the Giver of hope. I run to You fleeing from the sins, so accept me; and I seek refuge from Your Justice to Your Forgiveness, so aid me; and I seek shelter to Your Forgiveness from Your Assault so keep me away from it; and I seek Your Mercy from Your Punishment, so rescue me; and I seek to get close to You by Islam, so get me close.

And from the greater fear, so keep me safe; and in the shadow of Your Arsh, so shade me; and two shares of Your Mercy, so present to me; and safely from this world, so deliver me; and from the darkness to the light, so send me; and on the Day of Resurrection, so brighten my face; and with a light questioning, so question me; and with what I have concealed, so do not expose me; and for Your Affliction, so give me patience.

And just as You diverted the evil and the adultery from Yōsof[1]*, so divert it from me; and what I do not have the capacity for, so do not load on my shoulder; and to the House of*

[1] Also Joseph.

Peace, so guide me; and by the Qor'ān, so benefit me; and by the firm belief, so make me firm; and from the accursed Shayṭān[1]*, so keep me safe; and by Your Strength and Power and Might, so shield me; and by Your Forbearance and Knowledge and broad Mercy, so rescue me from Hell; and in Your Heaven of Ferdaws, so house me; and looking at Your Face, so bestow upon me; and with Your Prophet Moḥammad, so join me; and from the Shayāṭēn*[2] *and their followers and from all those who possess evil, so keep me away...*[3]*)).*

3-[4] *((Glory be to Him for Whose Greatness everything became humble. Glory be to Him for Whose High Standing everything became low. Glory be to Him to Whose Control and Rule everything yielded. Glory be to Him Who is obeyed by everything.*

Praise be to Allāh Who does not forget whoever remembers Him. Praise be to Allāh Who does not disappoint whoever prays to Him. Praise be to Allāh Who is Sufficient for those who rely on Him.

Praise be to Allāh Who is the Thickener of the sky; and the Builder of the earth; and Who limits the seas; and Who piles up the mountains; and Who creates the animals; and Who creates the trees; and who opens the earth's springs; and Who arranges things; and Who moves the clouds; and Who causes the wind and the water and the fire to flow from the earth up to sky; and Who descends the heat and the cold.

---

[1] Also Satan.

[2] Shayāṭēn plural of Shayṭān (also Satan).

[3] ᶜAwālim al-ᶜOlōm / al-Baḥrāni = vol. 11, page 315.

[4] The following are parts of a special doᶜā' to be recited after the ᶜEshā' prayer.

The one with Whose Gift the good deeds are completed; and by thanking Him they are increased; and by His Order the skies started to exist; and by His Greatness the unshakable mountains stood; and the wild animals glorified Him in the deserts and the birds in the nests.

O Allāh! I ask You by Your stored name, the pleasant, the pure, the one by which the skies and the earth started to exist; and the darkness was lit for it; and the angels glorified for it; and the hearts feared it; and the necks became humble for it; and the one by which You brought the dead back to life; to forgive every sin that I committed in the darkness of the night and in the light of the day, intentionally or inadvertently, in secrecy or in public; and to give me a conviction, and a guidance, and a light, and a knowledge, and an understanding so that I may implement your book, and allow what it allows, and prohibit what it prohibits; and to perform what You have made mandatory for me, and to practice Your prophet's tradition.

O Allāh! Join me with the virtuous of those who have passed away, and make me one of the virtuous of those who remain alive; and finish my deeds at its best; for You are the Most Forgiving and the Most Merciful.

O Allāh! If my life were to finish, and my days were to sever, and I were to meet you, so I ask You, O Kind! to put me in a place in Heaven where others will envy me.

O Allāh! I entrust my religion and my soul and all the gifts You have given me to You; and so put me in Your shade, and in Your protection, and in Your might, and in Your prevention.

Your neighbor is mighty, and Your tribute is grand, and Your names are sanctified, and there is no God but You. You are Sufficient for me in joy and in sorrow, and in hard times and in prosperity; and You are the best [one who can be] in charge[1].)).

HER POLITICS

Islam as the last universal religion, attaches great importance to politics and engages in all political affairs. This means that Islam is political as much as it is economical, educational, social, ritual, moral, legal, etc.

However, there are some people who claim Islam is non-political, and therefore call for a separation between Islam and politics.

To reject their assertion, one has to look at the history of Islam and see how Prophet Moḥammad and his Rightful Kholafā' played major political roles as the messengers of Islam.

Prophet Moḥammad was the founder of the Islamic rule in Madinah, which in a period of ten years spread to nine countries in today's geography. After his martyrdom, his successorship was usurped by Abō Bakr's party and remained usurped for centuries[2].

However during this time, Amēr al-Mo'menēn the first khalēfah, was able to attain his usurped position, and headed the Islamic rule for about five years until he was assassinated.

He was succeeded by Imām Ḥasan[(AS)3], the second khalēfah, who headed the Islamic rule for several months until his position was usurped by Moᶜāwiyah[(LA)4], the fourth Bakri usurper, the first Amawi ruler and son of the Idolater leader Abō Sofyān. Later Moᶜāwiyah poisoned Imām Ḥasan to death.

Thus Rasōlollāh[5], Amēr al-Mo'menēn and Imām Ḥasan personally headed the Islamic rule for a total of around sixteen years.

---

[1] ᶜAwālim al-ᶜOlōm / al-Baḥrāni = vol. 11, page 318.

[2] For more detailed information, see: Rasōlollāh, the Messenger of Allāh / by the author.

[3] *ᶜAlayhes Salām,* peace be upon him.

[4] *Laᶜnatollāh ᶜAlayh,* may Allāh distance him from His Blessings and Mercy.

[5] Messenger of Allāh; a title exclusively given to Prophet Moḥammad by Allāh.

And the other a'emmah up to the eleventh Imām, were consecutively suppressed and were assassinated, because they had major political functions and continuously opposed the usurpers of their times.

So politics is an integral part and a major component of Islam. Without politics, Islam will not be complete.

And Fāṭimah as a representative of Allāh had huge political roles, the results of which are everlasting. Her political mission was more noticeable after her father's martyrdom when she became the focus of attention in the struggle between the Rightful Khalēfah and the usurpers.

In a period, the shortest of which is said to be thirty days and the longest of which is said to be nine months, she unveiled the Bakri party, showing its true identity.

Despite her very young age, she managed to draw a line between the true Islam taught by the rightful successors of Prophet Moḥammad, and the false Islam used by the usurpers of the khelāfah to rule their growing empire and destroy the true Islam.

Her politics proved to be so intolerable and dangerous for the Bakri party that it decided to crush her immediately, directly and without much cover.

ᶜOmar*(LA)*[1], the Second Usurper, personally headed several attacks on her home in full view of the public that had enormous love and great respect for her as the daughter of the late Prophet.

Below are highlights of her politics:

COMPLETE ENDORSEMENT FOR AMĒR AL-MO'MENĒN

Importance of a pledge of allegiance

From the start, the pre-Islamic Arabs had much respect for a pledge of allegiance. A pledge of allegiance was made in public to a leader of some sort. If an Arab gave his pledge of allegiance to a fellow Arab, he would remain loyal to him.

[1] *Laᶜnatollāh ᶜAlayh,* may Allāh distance him from His Blessings and Mercy.

When Rasōlollāh[(SAA)1] migrated to Madinah and established the Islamic rule, influential leaders and other people gave him their pledge of allegiance. And his governors also received such pledges from their people, especially from those who had leading roles in their society, such as tribe leaders.

And before his death, Rasōlollāh himself sought pledge of allegiance for Amēr al-Mo'menēn[2] as his Khalēfah, from the Moslems on numerous occasions. The most dramatic being on 18 Dhol-Ḥejjah in the tenth year of Hejrah, seventy days before his martyrdom, known as the day of "Ghadēr Khom", when he gathered one hundred and twenty thousand Moslems in the desert while returning from the Farewell Pilgrimage. There, after a lengthy public speech, Rasōlollāh asked them to give their pledge of allegiance to Imām ᶜAli[(AS)3] and call him by his God-given title: "Amēr al-Mo'menēn". It took three days for all the people to give their individual pledges[4].

When the Bakri party assassinated the Prophet and made its swift move to usurp the khelāfah, it struggled to gain the much needed pledges of allegiance. But how could it render void the pledges already given to Amēr al-Mo'menēn[(AS)5] that were insistently sought by Rasōlollāh?

With its titanic influence, secret deals and promises of friendship and enmity, which meant wealth or death, it brought many influential Arab leaders to its corner. By securing the allegiance of a few men, the Bakri party won the loyalty and the swords of countless people[6]. The tribal ruling system of that day meant the automatic endorsement of tribe members of whomsoever their leader supported.

---

[1] *Ṣallallāh ᶜAlayh wa Ālih,* Allāh's Blessings be upon him and his descendants.

[2] Commander of the Faithful; a title given exclusively to Imām ᶜAli by Allāh.

[3] *ᶜAlayhes Salām,* peace be upon him.

[4] For more detailed information see: Rasōlollāh, the Messenger of Allāh / by the author = page 171.

[5] *ᶜAlayhes Salām,* peace be upon him.

[6] For more detailed information, see: Rasōlollāh, the Messenger of Allāh / by the author = page 222.

As more tribes came under its wings, the Bakri party multiplied its pressure on the defaulters.

The opposition was led by Amēr al-Mo'menēn who maintained his claim for the khelāfah, and proved to be the biggest barrier between the Bakri party and legitimacy. But violence and assassination continued to reduce the resistance in numbers.

Here, Sayyedat Nesā' al-ᶜĀlamēn[1] became the focus of attention. Would the Prophet's daughter give her pledge of allegiance to Abō Bakr*(LA)*[2] or to Amēr al-Mo'menēn?

Importance of Fāṭimah's endorsement

In the events that followed Rasōlollāh's martyrdom, people kept their eyes set on Fāṭimah, and their ears open to any words she said, in an effort to learn who she supported as the khalēfah.

Fāṭimah was Rasōlollāh's daughter and was very dear to him. He showed his love for her to the point that it made others like ᶜĀ'eshah*(LAa)*[3] repeatedly burst in jealousy[4]. She was the most beloved woman to the Prophet and ᶜAli was the most beloved man.

Bakri scholars narrate:

> *((Some people came to Rasōlollāh and asked him: O Rasōlollāh! Who is the most beloved person to you? Rasōlollāh: Fāṭimah[5].)).*

---

[1] Chief of the Women of the World; a title given exclusively to Fāṭimah, the Daughter of Rasōlollāh, by Allāh.

[2] *Laᶜnatollāh ᶜAlayh,* may Allāh distance him from His Blessings and Mercy.

[3] *Laᶜnatollāh ᶜAlayha,* may Allāh distance her from His Blessings and Mercy.

[4] For more details see the following Bakri references:
al-Fawā'ed al-Majmōᶜah / al-Shawkāni = page 389. Mezān al-Eᶜtedāl / al-Dhahabi = vol. 1, pages 81 and 541. Mokhtaṣar Dhakhā'er al-ᶜOqbā / al-Ṭabari = page 60.

[5] Mokhtaṣar Dhakhā'er al-ᶜOqbā / al-Ṭabari = page 59. Mosnad / Aḥmad = vol. 5, page 240.

((One day ᶜAli asked the Prophet: O Rasōlollāh! Which of your family is most beloved to you? Rasōlollāh: Fāṭimah[1].)).

ᶜĀ'eshah also admitted to this fact when she said:

((They asked me: Who was more beloved to Rasōlollāh?
And I answered: Fāṭimah.
I was asked again: And of men?
I answered: Her husband[2].)).

ᶜAbdollāh son of the Second Usurper ᶜOmar narrates:

((Rasōlollāh kissed Fāṭimah on the head and said: Your father be your sacrifice[3].)).

ᶜĀ'eshah daughter of the First Usurper Abō Bakr narrates:

((Whenever Fāṭimah went to Rasōlollāh, he welcomed her, kissed her hands and offered her to sit in his place[4].)).

The importance of this action can only be understood when we learn that kissing the hand was a very rare thing in the Arab culture, and showed the greatest respect for a person.

But the reason for the importance of Fāṭimah's endorsement was not merely the fact that she was close to Rasōlollāh, it was rather because of her close position to Allāh, and the nature of her Godly-being. And it was because Rasōlollāh had said that her approval and

---

[1] Mokhtaṣar Tārēkh Demashq / Ibn ᶜAsākir / vol. 4, page 219. Mokhtaṣar Dhakhā'er al-ᶜOqbā / al-Ṭabari = page 60.

[2] al-Estēᶜāb / Ibn ᶜAbdelbarr = vol. 4, page 1894. Jāmiᶜ al-Oṣōl / Ibn al-Athēr = vol. 9, page 125. al-Manāqib = ḥadēth No. 3873. Mokhtaṣar Tārēkh Demashq / Ibn ᶜAsākir = vol. 17, page 336. Mokhtaṣar Dhakhā'er al-ᶜOqbā / al-Ṭabari = page 59. Osd al-Ghābah / Ibn al-Athēr = vol. 7, page 223.

[3] Fāṭimah al-Zahrā' Min al-Mahd Ela al-Lahd / al-Qazwēni = page 269.

[4] Fāṭimah al-Zahrā' Min al-Mahd Ela al-Lahd / al-Qazwēni = page 268.

disapproval is his approval and disapproval and Allāh's approval and disapproval.

Bakri scholars narrate:

((Rasōlollāh said: O Fāṭimah! Indeed the Almighty Allāh becomes angry for your anger; and approves for your approval[1].)).

Fāṭimah's pledge of allegiance

After the martyrdom of her father, Fāṭimah immediately showed support for Amēr al-Mo'menēn, as the Bakri leaders were coming out of hiding to gather in Bani Sāʿedah's gethering place to appoint Abō Bakr as the Khalēfah.

Bakri scholars narrate that she said:

((Have you forgotten Rasōlollāh's speech on the day of Ghadeer Khom: For whomsoever I am master, ʿAli is his master?! And that he said to ʿAli: You are to me what Hārōn[2] was to Mōsā[3]?![4].)).

It has also been narrated that she said:

((It is as though you have not learned what Rasōlollāh said on the day of Ghadeer Khom. By Allāh, indeed he appointed him on that day to sever your hopes for it. But you severed the routs between you and your Prophet!!

---

[1] Mēzān al-Eʿtedāl / al-Dhahabi = vol. 2, page 492. Moʿjam / Ibn al-Mothanna. Mokhtaṣar Dhakhā'er al-ʿOqbā / al-Ṭabari = page 62. Osd al-Ghābah / Ibn al-Athēr = vol. 7, page 224. Sharaf al-Nobowwah / Abō Saʿd.
[2] Also: Aaron.
[3] Also: Moses.
[4] Asnā al Maṭālib fi Manāqib ʿAli ibn Abi Ṭālib / Ibn al-Jazari. al-Badr al-Ṭāliʿ / al-Shawkāni = vol. 2, page 297. al-Ḍaw' al-Lāmiʿ / al-Sakhāwi = vol. 9, page 256.

And Allāh is the Judge between us and you in this world and the Hereafter[1].)).

It has also been narrated:

((When people were giving their oath of allegiance to Abō Bakr, Fāṭimah the daughter of Moḥammad came out of her home and stood at the door, saying: I have never seen a day like this! People attended the worst meeting and left their Prophet unburied, and usurped our right[2].)).

Maḥmōd ibn Lobayd (Abō ᶜOmar) narrates:

((I said to Fāṭimah: O my Lady, I want to ask you a question that stammers in my chest.
Fāṭimah: Ask.
Abō ᶜOmar: Did Rasōlollāh appoint ᶜAli as the Khalēfah before his death?
Fāṭimah: What a surprise! Have you forgotten the day of Ghadeer Khom?!
Abō ᶜOmar: No my Lady; but I want to know what Rasōlollāh told you.
Fāṭimah: I hold the Almighty Allāh as my witness that I heard him say: ᶜAli is the best person whom I leave with you. And he is the Imām and the Khalēfah after me. And my two grandsons and nine of Ḥosayn's lineage are A'emmah[3].
If you follow them, you will find them learned leaders; and if you disobey them, there will be great conflict among you[4] until the Day of Judgment.

---

[1] Beḥār al-Anwār / al-Majlesi = vol. 28, page 205. ᶜAwālim al-ᶜOlōm / al-Baḥrāni = vol. 11, page 877.

[2] Beḥār al-Anwār / al-Majlesi = vol. 28, page 233. ᶜAwālim al-ᶜOlōm / al-Baḥrāni = vol. 11, page 883.

[3] Plural of imām.

[4] Among those who disobey the a'emmah; as every group tries to seize power.

Abō ᶜOmar: O my Lady! so why did he (Ali) not get back his right?
Fāṭimah: O Abā ᶜOmar! Rasōlollāh said: The example of ᶜAli is that of the Kaᶜbah; people go to it and it does not go to people. Then she said:
But they gave precedence to whom Allāh had held back; and held back whom Allāh had given precedence to...
They appointed [a khalēfah] with their desire and acted according to their decisions. Woe unto them; have not they heard the Almighty Allāh say: "And your Lord creates and chooses whom He pleases; to choose is not theirs[1]". They did hear, but as Allāh says: "For surely it is not the eyes that are blind, but blind are the hearts which are in the chests[2]".
How far! They spread their wishes in this world, and weaved their fates. "For them is destruction, and He has made their deeds ineffective[3]".
I seek protection from you, O Lord! from injustice...[4])).

Fāṭimah's support for ᶜAli as the Khalēfah did not start after the assassination of Rasōlollāh, but during his life.

It has been narrated that she said:

((The two fathers of this nation are Moḥammad and ᶜAli.
They straighten its bends, and deliver it from the continuous punishment (Hell) if it obeyed them; and they bring it the continuous bliss (Heaven) if it followed them[5].)).

---

[1] Holy Qor'ān = sōrah 28, āyah 68.
[2] Holy Qor'ān = sōrah 22, āyah 46.
[3] Holy Qor'ān = sōrah 47, āyah 8.
[4] ᶜAwālim al-ᶜOlōm / al-Baḥrāni – vol. 11, page 875. Beḥar al-Anwār / al-Majlesi = vol. 36, page 352. Ghāyat al-Marām / al-Sayyed al-Baḥrāni.
[5] ᶜAwālim al-ᶜOlōm / al-Baḥrāni = vol. 11, page 867.

Complete Rejection Of Abō Bakr's Party

As the Bakri party lacked truth and originality, and as it was usurping the khelāfah and trying to push back Amēr al-Mo'menēn who possessed all the truth and originality, it could not tolerate much opposition.

Confrontation even from an unknown Bedouin was serious, as it undermined the legitimacy of the False Khalēfah.

At this time, Sayyedat Nesā' al-ᶜĀlamēn*(AaS)*[1] posed a grave threat to Abō Bakr's throne as she went all out to expose this assumed pious and sincere Moslem.

Her rejection of Abō Bakr and his party varied from simple criticisms—which coming from Fāṭimah meant quite more—to calling for an uprising to strip him from his undeserved position.

Below are highlights of her rejecting stance against the Bakri party:

Open confrontation with the Bakri party

As a maᶜṣōm and a carrier of God's message, Fāṭimah was frank and outright in her mission. She did not show fear from her powerful enemies and did not allow her personal interests compromise her duties.

And when it came to the question of the khelāfah, she did not give the Bakri party any corners; and like Amēr al-Mo'menēn, she did not offer nor did she accept any compromises.

Open confrontation was a method by which she showed people where she stood and where they should stand.

Prominent Bakri and Moslem scholars narrate:

> *((When Fāṭimah's condition worsened[2], a group of women from Mohājirēn and Anṣār came to visit her;*

[1] *ᶜAlayhā's Salām,* peace be upon her.

[2] This was caused by the numerous injuries she had sustained from the Second Usurper ᶜOmar and other Bakri ruffians, when they raided her

they asked: How are you feeling, O Daughter of Rasōlollāh?
She praised Allāh and saluted her father; then she said: By Allāh, I am disgusted with your world; and I am angry with your men, I spat them after I bit them, and loathed them after I tasted them. How shameful is a notch in a sharp sword; and playfulness after seriousness; and hitting a hard stone; and a crack in a spear; and foolish thoughts; and devious wishes!! "Certainly evil is that which their souls have sent before for them, that Allāh became displeased with them and in chastisement shall they abide[1]".
Undoubtedly, by Allāh, I have put its noose around their necks, and loaded them its heavy burden, and sent them its shame. So, cut be their noses, and severed be their legs, and far be the group of wrongdoers.
Woe unto them, where to did they move it (khelāfah) from pillars of the messengerhood and foundations of the prophethood and guidance, and Jabra'ēl's place of descent, and the intelligent knowledgeable in the fields of the world and religion?! "Now surely, that is the clear loss[2]".
What did they resent from the father of Ḥasan?! They resented, by Allāh, the sharpness of his sword, and his little concern for his death, and the strength of his movement, and the force of his strike, and his turning into a tiger in the way of Allāh, the Powerful and Exalted.
By Allāh, if they had not touched the rein that Rasōlollāh had dropped, he surely would have taken it and would have advanced them an easy advance. He would not cause the khashāshah[3] to injure, and

---

home. She later died from her injuries. You will read more on the subject later in this book.

[1] Holy Qor'ān = sōrah 5, āyah 80.

[2] Holy Qor'ān = sōrah 39, āyah 15.

[3] A piece of wood that is put in a camel's mouth and attached to the reins, or a piece of rope that is pierced through a camel's nose.

would not tire his ride, and would not irritate the riders. And would have led them to a wide clear spring that overflows its banks, and would have let them fill all their stomachs with water. And he would have been sincere with them in private and in public. They would have been lost in much wealth, while he did not decorate himself with any of it, and would not enjoy of this living except a little water that does not fully satisfy his thirst, and a little food that only stops the sting of his hunger.

And they would have distinguished the zāhid[1] *from the desirous, and the truthful from the liar. And much blessing would have come to them from the sky and the earth. "And if the people of the towns had believed and guarded (against evil) We would certainly have opened up for them blessings from the Heaven and the earth, but they rejected, so We overtook them for what they had earned*[2]*".*

Oh come and listen; and as you live, time will show you surprises. And if you ever become surprised, this will surprise you the most.

I wish I knew! On what reasoning did they rely?! And to what handle did they cling?! And what progeny did they overtake and suppress?!

Verily, what a bad master, and what a bad companion; and bad is what they exchanged for themselves. They replaced, by Allāh, the heads with the tails, and the crucial with the unimportant. So dirt be on the noses of those who "think they are well versed in skill of the work of hands[3]*"; "Now surely they themselves are the mischief makers, but they do not perceive*[4]*".*

Woe unto them; "IS HE THEN WHO GUIDES TO THE TRUTH MORE WORTHY TO BE FOLLOWED, OR HE WHO HIMSELF DOES

---

[1] A person who practices zohd: non-attachment to material things.
[2] Holy Qor'ān = sōrah 7, āyah 96.
[3] Holy Qor'ān = sōrah 18, āyah 104.
[4] Holy Qor'ān = sōrah 2, āyah 12.

NOT GO ARIGHT UNLESS HE IS GUIDED? WHAT THEN IS THE MATTER WITH YOU; HOW DO YOU JUDGE?[1]".

Indeed, by the religion of your Lord, it has become pregnant; so wait and see what it shall bear. Then milk until the cup overflows with fresh blood, and killer poison. There, shall the wrongdoers lose; and those who come shall learn the results of what those who passed had founded.

Then see if you can clear your conscience; and let your hearts rest assured that conflict shall come, and be certain of a sharp sword, and the suppression of a tyrant aggressor, and an all-inclusive agitation, and despotism from unjust rulers...

What a pity, and how far from the solution you shall be when you have been made blind. "Shall we constrain you to accept it while you are averse from it?![2]".

Then the women returned to their husbands, and told them what she had said. So a group of Mohājirēn and Anṣār leaders came to her to apologize.

They said: O Chief of the Women! If Abō al-Ḥasan (Amēr al-Mo'meneen) had told us about this before we concluded the pledge [to Abō Bakr] and tied the knot, we would not have deviated from him to anyone else.

Fāṭimah: Leave! There is no apology after your action, and no making up after your failure[3].)).

Total condemnation

---

[1] Holy Qor'ān = sōrah 10, āyah 35

[2] Holy Qor'ān = sōrah 11, āyah 28.

[3] Bakri references: A^clām al-Nesā' / Kaḥḥālah = vol. 3, page 1219. Balāghāt al-Nesā' / Ibn Ṭayfōr = page 19. Sharh Nahj al-Balāghah / Ibn Abi al-Ḥadēd = vol. 16, page 233.

Moslem references: Beḥār al-Anwār / al-Majlesi = vol. 43, page 158. Eḥqāq al-Ḥaqq / al-Tostari = vol. 10, page 306. al-Eḥtejāj / al-Ṭabarsi = vol. 1, page 384. Kashf al-Ghommah / al-Erbelli = vol. 1, page 492. Nafaḥāt al-Lāhōt fi La^cn al-Jebt wa al-Ṭāghōt / al-Karaki = page 124.

At the same time when Sayyedat Nesā‘ al-ᶜĀlamēn supported the True Khalēfah, she denounced the False Khalēfah; and as she continued to advocate the Rightful Khelāfah, she condemned its usurpers.

Below are some excerpts from her famous public speech in the mosque, after the usurpation of the khelāfah, during which publicly and strongly condemned the usurpers:

> *((...And when Allāh chose for His Prophet the house of the prophets, and the adobe of His most sincere friends, the spite of hypocrisy appeared on you, and the garment of faith became worn out, and the silent aberrant spoke out, and the indolent of the inferiors emerged, and the wrongdoers' most favored camel roared, so he wiggled his tail in your courtyards.*
> *And Shayṭān raised his head from his hiding place calling upon you, and he found you answering to his call and looking into his deceit. Then he aroused you and found you quick to respond; and caused you to become angry, so he found you angry for his anger.*
> *Thus you marked a camel which you did not own, and came to a drinking place other than your own.*
> *This! and the memory is near?! And the wound is wide open?! And the injury has not healed?! And the Messenger has not been buried?!*
> *...And the Book of Allāh is among you. Its affairs are clear, and its rules are shining, and its signs are dazzling, and its prohibitions have been made clear, and its commands are plain; and you have surely left it behind you. Is it because you do not want it? Or is it because you judge according to something else? "Evil is (this) change for the unjust[1]", "And whoever desires a religion other than Islam, it shall not be accepted from him, and in the Hereafter he shall be one of the losers[2]"[3].)).*

---

[1] Holy Qor'ān = sōrah 18, āyah 50.

[2] Holy Qor'ān = sōrah 3, āyah 85.

[3] A considerable number of Bakri references have recorded parts of Fāṭimah's speech through different chains of narrators, they include: Aᶜlām

She also said:

((O You crowd of Moslems who rush towards the uttering of falsehood, and agree to disgraceful and deviating actions, "DO YOU NOT THEN REFLECT ON THE QOR'ĀN?! NAY! ON THE HEARTS THERE ARE LOCKS[1]". "NAY! RATHER WHAT YOU HAVE DONE HAS BECOME LIKE RUST UPON YOUR HEARTS[2]". So it has seized your hearing and your sight; and truly how vile is what you have pointed to; and how wicked is what you have taken for an exchange.
You shall, by Allāh, find bearing it a heavy burden, and its consequence a harsh punishment, when the cover is removed for you and appears to you what is behind it of wrath, and comes into your sight from your Creator what you had never expected, "AND THOSE WHO TREATED (IT) AS A LIE WERE LOST[3]".)).

She also said:

((...Verily I have said all that I have said with full knowledge of the betrayal that has mixed with you, and the treachery that has covered your hearts; but it is the effusion of distress, and cooling the rage, and the explosion of the chest, and the presentation of proof.
So here it is, load it on the injured back of a she-camel with thin hooves, with permanent disability, marked by the wrath of the Omnipotent, with eternal

---

al-Nesā' / Kaḥḥālah = vol. 4, page 116. Balāghāt al-Nesā' / Ibn Ṭayfōr = page 12. al-Fā'eq / al-Zamakhshari = vol. 3, page 331; vol. 4, page 116. Lesān al-ᶜArab / Ibn Manẓōr = vol. 12, page 331. Manāl al-Ṭālib / Ibn al-Athēr = page 501. al Nehāyah / Ibn al-Athēr = vol. 4, page 273. Sharh Nahj al-Balāghah / Ibn Abi al-Ḥadēd = vol. 6, page 46; vol. 16, page 210.

[1] Holy Qor'ān = sōrah 47, āyah 24.

[2] Adaptation from the Holy Qor'ān = sōrah 83, āyah 14.

[3] Holy Qor'ān = sōrah 40, āyah 78.

*shame, which is lead to "THE FIRE KINDLED BY ALLĀH * WHICH PENETRATES THE HEARTS[1] ".*
Surely it is in the presence of Allāh what you do, "AND THEY WHO ACT UNJUSTLY SHALL KNOW TO WHAT FINAL PLACE OF TURNING THEY SHALL TURN BACK[2] ".)).

Severe protests

As part of the larger package of rejecting Abō Bakr and his party, Sayyedat Nesā' al-ᶜĀlamēn often criticized them publicly.

And in accordance with the seriousness their deviations and their unIslamic policies and actions, the severity of her protests increased.

The following are some instances of her protests in her famous public speech in the mosque:

((...Then you did not wait for its stampede to calm and until it obeys its reins, so you added fuel to its fire, and instigated its burning coal; and you complied with the call of the deceitful Shayṭān, extinguishing the lights of the clear religion, and suppressing the traditions of the Prophet.
You show sincerity while concealing your own agenda, and you proceed towards his family and children in a secretive manner.
And we remain patient with you of things similar to cutting with a saw, and stabbing the stomach with a spear.)).

She also said:

((O Moslems! Will my inheritance be usurped?! O Son of Abi Qoḥāfah! (Abō Bakr), is it in the Book of Allāh that you inherit your father but I do not inherit my father?! You have surely come up with an unprecedented lie.)).

---

[1] Holy Qor'ān = sōrah 104, Āyāt 6-7.
[2] Holy Qor'ān = sōrah 26, āyah 227.

She also said:

((So here is the she-camel, take it, with its nose rope and its saddle in place; it will see you on the day of your resurrection. Then, what an excellent Judge is Allāh, and what an excellent prosecutor is Moḥammad. And the appointment is the resurrection day; and on the Hour shall the wrongdoers lose; and it shall not benefit you when you regret. "FOR EVERY PROPHECY IS A TERM, AND YOU WILL COME TO KNOW [IT][1]". "WHO IT IS TO WHOM THERE SHALL COME A PUNISHMENT WHICH WILL DISGRACE HIM AND TO WHOM WILL BE DUE A LASTING PUNISHMENT[2].)).

LABELING THE BAKRI PARTY AS NON-MOSLEM

If we believe that Sayyedat Nesā' al-ᶜĀlamēn was a produce of Heaven, as Bakri scholars narrate; and if we believe that she was one of the people about whom the āyah *"ALLĀH ONLY DESIRES TO KEEP AWAY THE UNCLEANNESS FROM YOU, O PEOPLE OF THE HOUSE! AND TO PURIFY YOU A [THOROUGH] PURIFYING"* was revealed, as Bakri scholars narrate; and if we believe that she was one of the people about whom the āyah "SAY: I DO NOT ASK OF YOU ANY REWARD FOR IT BUT LOVE FOR MY NEAR RELATIVES" was revealed, as Bakri scholars narrate; and if we believe that whomsoever was in peace with her was as such as he was in peace with the Prophet, and whomsoever was at war with her was as such as he was in war with the Prophet, as Bakri scholars narrate; and if we believe that Allāh's satisfaction and anger are tied to her satisfaction and anger, as Bakri scholars narrate... we can only come to the conclusion that the Bakri party deviated from Islam when it entered into a war with Sayyedat Nesā' al-ᶜĀlamēn and subsequently killed her.

---

[1] Holy Qor'ān = sōrah 6, āyah 67.
[2] Holy Qor'ān = sōrah 39, āyah 40.

This is not a conclusion that only the Moslems reach after fourteen centuries of the events, but it is a fact that Fāṭimah herself repeatedly announced and publicized.

Below are instances of her labeling the Bakri party as Non-Moslem:

In her famous public speech in the mosque she said:

((Is it then the judgment of (the times of) ignorance that you desire?! And who is better than Allāh to judge for a people who are sure?[1])).

She also said:

((Do you intentionally abandon the Book of Allāh and cast it behind your back?!)).

She also said:

((...So to what direction did you go after announcement? And why did you conceal after declaring? And turn on your heels after daring? And become polytheists after believing?
Misery be upon "A PEOPLE WHO BROKE THEIR OATHS AFTER THEIR PROMISE, AND AIMED AT THE EXPULSION OF THE APOSTLE, AND THEY ATTACKED YOU FIRST, DO YOU FEAR THEM? BUT ALLĀH IS MOST DESERVING THAT YOU SHOULD FEAR HIM, IF YOU ARE BELIEVERS[2]".
Indeed I can surely see that you are inclined to easy living; and that you have kept away who is more worthy of the caliphate; and have secluded yourselves with comfort; and have taken refuge from wideness to narrowness. So you spitted out what you had kept, and vomited what had smoothed down your throats. "IF YOU DISBELIEVE, YOU AND THOSE ON EARTH ALL TOGETHER, MOST SURELY ALLĀH IS SELF-SUFFICIENT, PRAISED[3]".)).

---

[1] Holy Qor'ān = sōrah 5, āyah 50.
[2] Adaptation from the Holy Qor'ān = sōrah 9, āyah 13.
[3] Holy Qor'ān = sōrah 14, āyah 8.

She also said:

((Do you then unite in treachery, justifying it with fabrication?! And this after his death is similar to what was directed at him during his life[1].)).

Calling for uprising

After Abō Bakr[(LA)2] and his party succeeded in usurping the khelāfah from Amēr al-Mo'menēn, through bringing the tribe chiefs to their court by making promises of wealth and power and also threats of death and persecution, Sayyedat Nesā' al-ᶜĀlamēn embarked on the hard and dangerous mission of reminding the sold hearts of the many promises and numerous oaths they had made in favor of the Rightful Khalēfah.

And as part of that package she accompanied her husband and her two sons on visits to the homes of the heads of Mohājirēn[3] and Anṣār[4], for a number of days and nights, asking for their support.

Fāṭimah ignores her injuries

From what history tells us we know that the attacks on Amēr al-Mo'menēn[(AS)5] and Sayyedat Nesā' al-ᶜĀlamēn[(AaS)1] were carried

---

[1] A considerable number of Bakri references have recorded parts of Fāṭimah's speech through different chains of narrators, they include: Aᶜlām al-Nesā' / Kaḥḥālah = vol. 4, page 116. Balāghāt al-Nesā' / Ibn Ṭayfōr = page 12. al-Fā'eq / al-Zamakhshari = vol. 3, page 331; vol. 4, page 116. Lesān al-ᶜArab / Ibn Manẓōr = vol. 12, page 331. Manāl al-Ṭālib / Ibn al-Athēr = page 501. al-Nehāyah / Ibn al-Ather = vol. 4, page 273. Sharh Nahj al-Balāghah / Ibn Abi al-Ḥadēd = vol. 6, page 46; vol. 16, page 210.

[2] *Laᶜnatollāh ᶜAlayh,* may Allāh distance him from His Blessings and Mercy.

[3] Plural of Mohājir: the Moslems who migrated from Makkah to Madinah to escape Idolater suppression, before the liberation of Makkah.

[4] Plural of Anṣari: a citizen of Madinah who converted to Islam before the liberation of Makkah.

[5] *ᶜAlayhes Salām,* peace be upon him.

out in the first half of her life after the Prophet's death, and that the numerous meetings with the heads of Mohājirēn and Anṣār took place in the second half.

Therefore during that time she was suffering from the many injuries she had sustained at the hands of the Bakri party, nevertheless she performed her duty and accomplished her task. Making the sin of those who did not answer her call even greater.

This is supported by the fact that ᶜAli took her to those homes on a female donkey. As the normal transport for short trips in those days was the horse, and people rarely used a donkey for traveling in or outside the city. And it was news if a famous person chose to ride a donkey. For example Rasōlollāh was known for riding a donkey in the city as part of his humility, and used to say:

> *((There are five things I will not give up until death: Eating with slaves on the ground, riding a donkey without a saddle, milking a she-goat with my hand, wearing wool*[2] *and greeting children*[3]*.)).*

It is also supported by the fact that the female donkey is shorter than the male, and therefore it is easier to mount and

---

[1] *ᶜAlayhas Salām,* peace be upon her.

[2] Wearing wool has had three stages in the Islamic era:

1- In the first centuries of Islam, when woolen wear was rough and it hurt and scratched the skin, causing discomfort for the person. During that stage wearing wool was recommended by Islam as a means of training the self in zohd (non-attachment to material things) and humility.
2- Later a group of people, who had deviated from the Islam taught by the Prophet and his kholafā', started to wear woolen clothing, making it a sign for their identity and affiliation. That group came to be known as the Ṣōfēs (also Sufis), in relation to the Arabic word ṣōf which means: wool.
   During that stage, Islam discouraged wearing wool, unless it was not assumed to be a sign for taṣawwof (also Sufism).
3- Currently, when woolen wear is a comfortable clothing, and as such it is no longer used as a means for training the self, and is no longer a sign for taṣawwof.

[3] Beḥār al-Anwār / al-Majlesi = vol. 5, page 215. Rasōlollāh, the Messenger of Allāh / by the author = page 81.

dismount. And by the fact that she was riding when Amēr al-Mo'menēn was walking, a serious disrespect, unless she was unable to walk!!

Completion of proof

Just as Rasōlollāh had persevered in his mission and endured much pain in his insistence to convince the Idolaters, Jews, Christians, etc to believe in the one indivisible God, and stop associating people and things with Him, Amēr al-Mo'menēn and Sayyedat Nesā' al-ᶜĀlamēn also suffered a great deal in their pertinacious attempts to keep the nation on the right track on which Rasōlollāh had first placed it.

Therefore after his martyrdom, when the nation took another rout and began to go astray, Sayyedat Nesā' al-ᶜĀlamēn rose up to guide it back to the right path.

Although she had been badly injured in several attacks by the Bakri party, she ignored all the pain and joined the Khalēfah and their sons Imām Ḥasan and Imām Ḥosayn to meet with the leaders of Mohājirēn and Anṣār, who were able to stand up and stop the Bakri party.

The high position of Imām ᶜAli put aside, Fāṭimah and her two sons had the highest ranks and respect after the martyrdom of Prophet Moḥammad. People –including Bakris- remember to this day what Allāh and the Prophet had said about them, and know that they were with the truth and that the truth was with them.

Therefore, Imām ᶜAli, Fāṭimah and their two sons$^{(AmS)}$[1] took advantage of their position and set out on another mission to complete the proof for the people of that day, leaving no space for any excuse produced by the Bakris today, justifying the actions and affiliations of the Companions of the Prophet for choosing Abō Bakr over Amēr al-Mo'menēn. And to clearly show that the so-called Companions of the Prophet deliberately left the truth to followed the falsehood, and even admitted it.

---

[1] *ᶜAlayhemos Salām,* peace be upon them.

Why did she not ask for uprising publicly

The question may occur to the mind that considering their high standing, if Amēr al-Mo'menēn, *Fāṭimah* and their two sons had publicly asked for support, the Bakri party would have lost all of its following, and Amēr al-Mo'menēn would have become the khalēfah. So why did they instead go to the homes of the influential leaders?

Perhaps the reasons were the following:

1- Tribal rule. In those days people were members of tribes, and as tribe members they had to follow their chiefs and do whatever they ordered, whether or not they agreed to it. As tribe members they did not own anything, including their lives; the chief owned everything and everyone.
Therefore people would not have supported Amēr al-Mo'menēn if their chiefs did not support him.
We read in history books that people cried when they witnessed the attacks on Fāṭimah's home, but they did not interfere. We also read that the people who attended Fāṭimah's famous public speech in the mosque cried so much that she had to wait for them to calm down before she could continue, but again they did not interfere.

2- Risk of internal clashes. Although the tension and fighting amongst the Arab tribes had come to an end when they accepted Islam, and the hostility between them had extinguished, but everyone still remembered their dead, and everyone still had traces from the days of ignorance.
So if Fāṭimah had publicly called for uprising and had openly encouraged the people to topple the regime, tribal instincts may have been aroused and as tribes took sides, door to door fighting may have been resurrected. And if that were to happen, Islam would have been crushed by the two neighboring powers of Persia and Rome who were extremely vigilant of its amazing progress.

3- A public call for uprising would have given the Bakri party the best excuse to totally suppress the opposition and execute its leaders.

4- Amēr al-Mo'menēn and *Sayyedat Nesā' al-ᶜĀlamēn* knew perfectly well that without promises of wealth and power and threats of persecution and death, they could not outdo the Bakri party in gathering important allies; and as they denounced such methods as unIslamic, they were certain of their inability to topple the regime.
However, they wanted to register their resounding objections to the usurpers and their strong claim to the khelāfah, so that no one may be left in the comfortable position to justify his support for Abō Bakr. And the best way for registering this in the history books was through repeated visits to the leaders of Mohājirēn and Anṣār, overwhelming them in argument and giving them a second chance to undo the damage they had caused.

Therefore instead of openly asking the public for support, she approached their leaders and influential people, who were able to turn the tide without much noise and risk.

Who did she ask?

There is a slight difference in the historic accounts narrating this crucial chapter of history. According to some narrations Sayyedat Nesā' al-ᶜĀlamēn asked the leaders of both the Mohājirēn and the Anṣār to rise up against the Bakri party; where as other narrations only mention the Anṣār leaders.

A part from the different authenticity levels of these aḥādēth, some scholars favor the latter group, arguing that the Mohājirēn, with the exception of a very small minority, were either leaders or strong supporters of the Bakri party and seriously despised Amēr al-Mo'menēn; so there was no point in asking them to rise up against their allies and take their sworn enemy as their beloved leader instead; whereas the Anṣār did not have such a bond with the Bakri party.

However other scholars argue that the point of asking for uprising was not the uprising itself, as Amēr al-Mo'menēn and Sayyedat Nesā' al-ᶜĀlamēn knew well that it was not going to happen, but it was rather another attempt to complete the proof and to eliminate any grounds for any excuse; thus contacting the Mohājirēn leaders would also have been necessary.

Fāṭimah calls for uprising

The famous Bakri scholar Ibn Qotaybah narrates in his well-known book "al-Imāmah wa al-Seyāsah" the following:

((Ali carried Fāṭimah the Daughter of Rasōlollāh on a riding animal, at night, to the gathering places of the Anṣār, asking them for support.
They would say: O Daughter of Rasōlollāh! we have pledged our allegiance to this man (Abō Bakr), and if your husband had come to us before Abō Bakr we would not have chosen anyone over him.
And ᶜAli would say: Was I to leave Rasōlollāh in his house without burying him, and go out to seek his rule from the people?!
And Fāṭimah would say: The father of Ḥasan did what he should have done; and they (the Bakris] surely did what Allāh shall take them to account and question them.)).

And it has been narrated:

((Ali took Fāṭimah on the back of a female donkey to the houses of Mohājirēn and Anṣār for forty days, along with Ḥasan and Ḥosayn.
She would say: O Mohājirēn and Anṣār! support Allāh and the daughter of your Prophet. You had indeed pledged to Rasōlollāh, on the day you gave him your allegiance, to protect him and his family from what you protect yourselves and your families. So fulfill your pledge to Rasōlollāh.

But no one supported her[1].)).

Feeble excuses

As supporting Fāṭimah and ᶜAli, at that crucial time, meant washing one's hands off a comfortable life and seriously risking death, the leaders of Mohājirēn and Anṣār responded to her request with feeble excuses and unacceptable justifications for taking Abō Bakr as their Khalēfah.

One such excuse is as follows:

((She went to Maᶜādh ibn Jabal[2] and said: O Maᶜādh ibn Jabal! I come to you asking for your support. And you have indeed given your pledge to Rasōlollāh to support him and his family, and protect him from what you protect yourself and your family. And Abō Bakr has usurped my Fadak and ordered my trustee out of it.
Maᶜādh: Will there be others with me?
Fāṭimah: No, no one has agreed to support me.
Maᶜādh: So where can I reach in your support?!
So Fāṭimah left his house saying: By Allāh, I will never talk to you until I see Rasōlollāh.
Then Maᶜādh's son entered and asked his father: What brought Moḥammad's daughter to you?
Maᶜādh: She came to ask my support over Abō Bakr. He has indeed taken Fadak from her.
Maᶜādh's son: And what did you tell her?
Maᶜādh: I told her: What can be gained with my support alone?!
Maᶜādh's son. So you refused to support her?!
Maᶜādh: Yes.
Maᶜādh's son: And what did she tell you?
Maᶜādh: She told me: By Allāh, I will never talk to you until I see Rasōlollāh.

---

[1] Fāṭimah min al-Mahd elā al-Laḥd / al-Qazwēni = page 578.
[2] One of the Anṣār leaders.

Maᶜādh's son: By Allāh, I will also never talk to you until I see Rasōlollāh[1].)).

Moᶜāwiyah admits

As in many other areas, Bakri scholars are pushed into a corner here. On the one hand they say that Amēr al-Mo'menēn was the forth khalēfah, who outwitted the others in knowledge, morals, etc. And many of them go further to say that he was the leading Moslem after Rasōlollāh who was not peered even by Abō Bakr and ᶜOmar.

And on the other hand, they respect the Bakri party and its leaders so much that they take their criticism as the biggest sin that cannot be cleansed accept by the fire of Hell. Moreover, they favor the Bakri party leaders*(LAm)*[2] to Rasōlollāh himself. So if Rasōlollāh said one thing and a party leader said the exact opposite, they would obey the latter and avoid the former as an unforgivable sin.

So how can the Bakris explain the words and actions of Amēr al-Mo'menēn and Sayyedat Nesā' al-ᶜĀlamēn inciting the people against the Bakri party, if both sides are on the right path?! Thus some of their historians choose not to mention anything about it, trying to avoid another question mark that they will remain unable to answer as long as they choose to follow Abō Bakr.

However Moᶜāwiyah, the second Amawi ruler, who fought with Amēr al-Mo'menēn and brought about his assassination, writes to him in one of his insulting letters:

((And I still remember you carrying your wife on a donkey at night, and your hands in your sons' hands Ḥasan and Ḥosayn, when Abō Bakr was given allegiance; so you did not forget any of the people of the Badr and those who accepted Islam early on and called them to yourself, and went to them along with your wife and your sons[3].)).

---

[1] Fāṭimah al-Zahrā' min al-Mahd elā al-Laḥd / al-Qazwēni = page 579.

[2] *Laᶜnatollāh ᶜAlayhem,* may Allāh distance them from His Blessings and Mercy.

[3] Sharh Nahj al-Balāghah / Ibn Abi al-Ḥadēd = vol. 2, page 47.

Continuous Mourning

Another highlight in Fāṭimah's mission was her continuous mourning after the martyrdom of her father. A very unique kind of mourning: heartrending; shocking; intensifying; gaining momentum; public; provocative; and most importantly full of meaning.

Mourning on Rasōlollāh

Waraqah ibn ᶜAbdollāh narrates that he asked Feḍḍah, one of Fāṭimah's students, about what she had seen from Fāṭimah after her father's martyrdom, who said:

> *((When Rasōlollāh died, every child and adult mourned him, and there was a lot of crying; and this catastrophe was so heavy for his relatives, and his companions, and the faithful, and the friends, and the strangers; and you did not see anyone not crying. But there was no one more saddened and grieving and lamenting than my mistress Fāṭimah. And her sadness regenerated and increased, and her crying intensified as time passed.*
>
> *She sat in her home for seven days, crying and lamenting. Everyday that came her crying was more than the day before. When the eighth night came, she showed what she had kept of sadness, so she went out and lamented, as if she was speaking from Rasolollāh's mouth.*
>
> *So the women and children gathered around her and there was a big roar of crying, and people came from everywhere. Then the lights were put out so that the features of the women could not be seen. The women thought that Rasōlollāh had risen from his grave. The people were surprised and they were confused and tired...*
>
> *She then went stumbling in her clothes, unable to see anything from her tears until she came close to her father's grave. When she looked at his room and her*

eye caught the Ma'dhanah[1]*, her steps became shorter, and her lamenting and crying continued until she lost consciousness. The women splashed water on her face, chest and forehead until she regained, then she stood saying:*
"My strength has been taken, my endurance has betrayed me; and my enemy has rejoiced at my misfortune; and sadness is killing me. O Father! I am left distracted and alone, confused and lonely; my voice has faded; and my back has broken; and my life has become embittered; and my world has become turbid...
O Father! The ways changed after you, and the doors closed to me. So I abhor the world after you, and I will continue to cry over you as long as I shall breath; and my longing for you will not run out, and my sadness over you will not decrease...[2]*)).*

Why so much mourning?

There are numerous narrations about Fāṭimah's mourning on her father, so many that some historians have devoted entire sections of their books to the subject. Her mourning was so much full of content that one cannot limit it to a particular theme. As well as the emotional grief that a daughter shows for her father's death, and a follower shows for his/her leader's death, Fāṭimah's mourning contained theology, law, poetry, politics...

A very emotional person may mourn the loss of the closest person to them for sometime, they may feel deeply depressed and they may intensely cry; but if they know, for a fact, that their loved one has left a world full of hardship and difficulty and entered into a world full of pleasure and comfort, they would not remain so unhappy.

And since Fāṭimah knew, better than anyone, the closeness of her father to Allāh, and had seen the kind of hardship he was

---

[1] A place for the performer of adhān (call to the daily wājib ṣalawāt), usually a manārah (also minaret).
[2] Beḥār al-Anwār / al-Majlesi = vol. 43, page 175.

suffering either from his overt or covert enemies or by his own choosing as the Islamic ruler[1], perhaps she should not have grieved the way she did.

But when a person studies this chapter of her life, he comes to the conclusion that her constant mourning was not merely because of her father's death, but rather to show that something significant was seriously wrong. Was it because she wanted to put a bold question mark on his death?! and a tall exclamation mark on the movement that seized power after his death?!

It is evident from her lamentations and brief statements that all was not well at all, and that a well planned, devastating conspiracy had been unfolding.

"What" and "Who"?

But what was wrong, and who were the wrongdoers?

In her lamentations she gave short damaging statements about those who seized power after Rasōlollāh's death, as well as brief descriptions of their betrayal.

Moslem and Bakri scholars narrate many of her statements and poems in her father's mourning, some of which are:

> *((O Father! after you we became weak; O Father! the people are keeping away from us[1].)).*

---

[1] Besides the normal moral standards that Islam encourages all Moslems to meet, such as altruism, contentment, generosity, simplicity, etc. it instructs the Islamic ruler to keep its highest levels, and moreover to live in a poorer state than the poorest person under his rule, so that every Moslem and non-Moslem living in Moslem territories be better off than the ruler.
Islam also encourages Moslems, and makes it mandatory for those in a leading role (i.e. a public prayer leader "imam", a judge, etc.) to practice patience and forbearance with people; and it instructs the ruler even more strictly to show respect for disrespect, and forgiveness for disobedience, and gentleness for boldness, etc. all of which makes life very hard for those who have to meet these requirements.
And when we read about the life of Rasōlollāh, we understand that he was in great difficulty living among those people and keeping the highest levels of what was required from him. Thus life in this world for Rasōlollāh and his kholafā' was very unpleasant.

((And Islam cried for you as it became a stranger between people, like other strangers.
If you see the menbar[2] on which you used to rise, darkness has risen on it after light.
O My Lord! make my death very near, as life has indeed become embittered[3].)).

((Say! to the one hidden under levels of the earth: If you can hear my scream and my call,
calamities have poured on me that if were to pour on the days, they will have become nights.
Indeed I had protection in the shade of Moḥammad; I was not afraid of injustice, and he was my protector.
But today I am humble for the lowly, and cautious of injustice; and I ward off my oppressor with my robe.
So if a turtledove weeps in her night from sadness on a branch, I weep in my day.
I shall make sadness my friend after you, and I shall make the tear for you my scarf[4].)).

((Indeed, there were news and many difficulties after you; if you had witnessed them, there would not be much talk.
We surely missed you, as the earth misses her downpour; and your people became disordered, so witness them and do not be absent...
Some people showed us the animosities they had hidden in their chests when you left and the earth shielded you.
Some people frowned on us and disparaged us when you became absent, and all the earth is usurped[1].)).

---

[1] Beḥār al-Anwār / al-Majlesi = vol. 43, page 176.

[2] A raised platform for a Moslem speaker in a mosque, Ḥosayneyyah, etc. where he/she would either stand or sit to give a speech.

[3] Beḥār al-Anwār / al-Majlesi = vol. 43, page 177.

[4] Fāṭimah al-Zahrā' Min Qabl al-Mēlād elā Baᶜd al-Estesh-hād / al-Hāshimi = page 219. al-Fotōḥāt al-Rabbāneyyah / Ibn al-ᶜAllān = vol. 3, page 160.

Now I leave it to the reader to decide "What" and "Who".

The Bakri party bans Fāṭimah from mourning

It comes as a big shock to those who do not know the reality of the Bakri party to read that after Rasōlollāh's martyrdom, the party banned his daughter Fāṭimah to mourn him and prohibited her to cry.

This forbiddance comes, exactly, in line with the Bakri motives behind the assassination of Prophet Moḥammad, and usurping his khelāfah, and suppressing his family. If the Bakri party had not denied Fāṭimah her right to cry, she would have grievously harmed its agenda. And as the party was struggling to gain legitimacy and support, it could not tolerate the slightest disturbance and disregard the smallest danger.

Therefore it decided to stop her, and sent a number of people to her husband Amēr al-Mo'menēn.

Scholars narrate:

> *((City leaders gathered and went to Amēr al-Mo'menēn ᶜAli, and said: O Father of Ḥasan! Fāṭimah cries night and day, so none of us enjoys sleep at night, and none of us can work during the day; so we are here to tell you to ask her: either to cry during the night or the day...*
>
> *Thus Amēr al-Mo'menēn went to Fāṭimah while she was crying profusely, and when she saw him she calmed down for some moments.*
>
> *So he told her: O Daughter of Rasōlollāh! The city leaders have asked me to ask you "either to cry during the night or the day".*
>
> *Fāṭimah: O Father of Ḥasan! How short is my stay among them!! And how early is my absence from them!! So by Allāh, I will not be silent either during the night or the day until I join my father Rasōlollāh.*

---

[1] Fāṭimah al-Zahrā' Min Qabl al-Mēlād elā Baᶜd al-Estesh-hād / al-Hāshimi = page 289.

Ali: Do O Daughter of Rasōlollāh! what you want.)).

What seems to be interesting is that the Bakri party did not contact Amēr al-Mo'menēn directly in this matter, in an attempt to keep well away from the controversy of denying the daughter of the late prophet, her most basic right to mourn his death, but rather chose a group of its supporters to accomplish the task.

Were all of these people neighbors of Fāṭimah who heard her crying?! Were they so close to her home that her crying affected their sleep?! If they were her neighbors, did they all work from home, as they complained that her crying also affected their business?!

But Fāṭimah's persistence and perseverance and the Bakri party's suppressive policy, betrayed its stance in this matter.

Reasons behind the ban

Why should the Bakri party ban Fāṭimah from crying?! She was a young woman who had lost her beloved father, and as any other affectionate daughter she was expected to mourn her father's death; especially when all the people of Madinah cried for him.

And even if her mourning was out of the ordinary and more than what was usual, why should a ruler, who at that time ruled nine countries in today's world map, go as far as prohibiting it and insist upon enforcing its prohibition at all costs?!

Perhaps some of the reasons are:

A- Her personality and high position as the Daughter of Rasōlollāh[1] and the wife of Amēr al-Mo'menēn and the mother of Imām Ḥasan and Imām Ḥosayn; and as Sayyedat Nesā' al-ᶜĀlamēn, Chief of the Women of the World, a title given to her by Allāh. She was a produce of Heaven. Allāh had revealed over two hundred and fifty āyāt in the Holy Qor'ān about her[2]. Rasōlollāh*(SAA)*[1] had given countless aḥādēth about her...

---

[1] Messenger of Allāh; a title exclusively given to Prophet Moḥammad by Allāh.

[2] In his book Fāṭimah al-Zahrā' fi al-Qor'ān, Āyatollāh al-ᶜOẓmā Sayyed Ṣādiq Shērāzi has gathered around two hundred and fifty āyāt that were

B- Fāṭimah, like her father, was distinguished for practicing the highest levels of patience and forbearance; so if she insisted on something, people knew that it was for an important reason.

C- Her crying was such that it raised questions and stirred the conscience and aroused sentiments and gathered supporters.

D- Fāṭimah was seen as the second person in the strongest opposition against the Bakri party. She had strongly defended Amēr al-Mo'menēn in his claim for the khelāfah, and had equally attacked the Bakri party for usurping it. So whatever she did, supported one camp as it rejected the other. Whatever she gained, Imām ᶜAli gained, and whatever she lost, Imām ᶜAli lost. Whatever she lost Abō Bakr gained, and whatever she gained Abō Bakr lost.

E- The time of her crying was also very important, as it was after her father's assassination, and the usurpation of the khelāfah, and the attack on her home, and the assault on her, and the miscarriage of her son, and the seizure of her positions…

F- The place of her crying—her home—was also very important, as it was in the Prophet's Mosque in Madinah, which had become the center of the Bakri rule.

G- Bakri Party's hidden enmity and hostility against her.

H- Bakri party's devious views about mourning the dead.

ᶜOmar's view about mourning the dead

Here is ᶜOmar*(LA)*[2], the "Second Khalēfah" to the Bakris; whom they title as "al-Fārōq", he who always distinguishes between

---

revealed about Sayyedat Nesā' al-ᶜĀlamēn in the Holy Qor'ān from Bakri references.

[1] *Ṣallallāh ᶜAlayh wa Ālih,* Allāh's Blessings be upon him and his descendants.

[2] *Laᶜnatollāh ᶜAlayh,* may Allāh distance him from His Blessings and Mercy.

the truth and the falsehood[1]; whom they claim to be the most just Moslem after the Prophet[2].

And here is his perverted view about mourning the dead, and his torturous methods of suppressing it, as Bakri scholars narrate:

> *((When Zaynab the daughter of Rasōlollāh died, Rasōlollāh said: Bury her near our charitable deceased cOthmān ibn Maḍcōn.*
> *The women cried, and cOmar started to lash them with his whip. Rasōlollāh took his hand and said: Slowly, O cOmar! Let them cry[3].)).*

Bakri scholars also narrate:

> *((The women cried when Roqayyah (daughter of Rasōlollāh) died, so cOmar began to stop them[4].*
> *cOmar lashed them with his whip, and Rasōlollāh took his hand saying: Leave them, O cOmar![5].)).*

Bakri scholars also narrate:

---

[1] This title was exclusively awarded by Rasōlollāh to Amēr al-Mo'menēn, but was later used by cOmar as his own. (Rasōlollāh, the Messenger of Allāh / by the author = page 6)

[2] Among the many fabricated aḥādēth that the Bakris relate to the Prophet about their leaders, is that they claim the Prophet said: ((cOmar is the most just person in this nation)). Even though the Bakris, themselves, confess that cOmar knew nothing about justice and the Islamic judicial laws, and that he even ordered the execution of a number of people whom according to the Islamic law were not guilty!!

[3] al-Estēcāb / Ibn cAbdelbarr = vol. 2, page 482. Majmac al-Zawā'ed / al-Haythami vol. 3, page 17. Mosnad / Abi Dāwōd = page 351. Mosnad / Aḥmad = vol. 1, page 237. al-Mostadrak / al-Ḥākim = vol. 3, page 191. Talkhēṣ al-Mostadrak / al-Dhahabi .

[4] al-Sonan al-Kobrā / al-Bayhaqi = vol. 4, page 70.

[5] al-Eṣābah / al-cAsqalāni = vol. 4. Tārēkh al-Madinah / Ibn Shobbah = vol. 1, page 103.

((A member of Rasōlollāh's family died, so the women gathered crying over him; and ᶜOmar stood up prohibiting them and dispersing them.
Rasōlollāh said: Leave them, O ᶜOmar! The eye is surely tearful, and the heart is stricken by grief, and the time is near[1].)).

Bakri scholars also narrate:

((When Abō Bakr died, ᶜĀ'eshah held a mourning ceremony for him. And when the news reached ᶜOmar, he came and prohibited them from mourning Abō Bakr. But they refused to stop.
So he ordered Hoshām ibn al-Walēd: Bring the daughter of Abō Qoḥāfah (Abō Bakr's sister) before me. Then he began to lash her with his whip until the women dispersed[2].)).

Bakri scholars also narrate:

((ᶜOmar heard the sound of crying from a house, so he entered while holding the whip in his hand, and began lashing them severely until he reached the Nā'eḥah[3].
He lashed her until her covering fell. Then he said to his servant: Lash the Nā'eḥah. Woe unto you! Lash her. She is a Nā'ehah; she does not deserve any respect[4].)).

Bakri scholars also narrate:

---

[1] ᶜOmdat al-Qāri' / al-ᶜAyni = vol. 4, page 87.

[2] al-Eṣābah / al-ᶜAsqalāni = vol. 3, page 696. Kanz al-ᶜOmmāl / al-Hendi = vol. 8, page 119. al-Ṭabaqāt al-Kobra / Ibn Saᶜd = vol. 3, page 208.

[3] Nā'eḥah: a woman hired by the family of a deceased to mourn his/her death in a gathering, by reading poems, etc. while his/her family and friends cried.

[4] Sharh Nahj al-Balāghah / Ibn Abi al-Ḥadēd = vol. 12, page 68.

((When Khālid ibn al-Walēd died, a group of women gathered in his aunt's home mourning his death.
Then ᶜOmar came and started to lash them with his whip until the covering of one of the women fell. Some of his men said: O Commander of the Faithful! Her covering!
Omar: Leave her, she does not deserve any respect[1].)).

Bakri scholars also narrate:

((...And ᶜOmar lashed with his whip all the Bani Makhzoom women who had attended the ceremony, mourning the death of Khālid ibn Walēd.
ᶜOmar raided the home of Omm Maymōnah, Khālid's aunt, and personally lashed the Nā'eḥah, and dispersed the women[2].)).

The above are just a few examples of ᶜOmar's favored method to suppress what he thought was wrong. Recorded and preached by his supporters and followers.

Now, one has to ask whether lashing a grief stricken woman is the most appropriate way to stop her from crying over her loved one?!

And whether crying over a deceased is indeed an unIslamic act?!

And whether preceding Rasōlollāh in approval or disapproval is Islamic?!

And whether insisting upon what Rasōlollāh has repeatedly forbidden by his words and his actions is Islamic?!

And whether ᶜOmar was more impressed by Islamic or Jewish teachings, such as the belief that crying over the dead is forbidden?!

---

[1] Kanz al-ᶜOmmāl / al-Hendi = vol. 8, page 118.
[2] Naẓariyyāt al-Khalēfatayn / al-Ṭā'i = vol. 1, pages 30 and 31, from: Kanz al-ᶜOmmāl / al-Hendi.

And whether a person with a sound mind would lash members of his prophet's family, in his presence, on several occasions, and insist upon it?!...

Fāṭimah's persistence

After the Bakri party banned Fāṭimah from crying in her home in the Prophet's Mosque, she and a number of women regularly went to the Baqē[c] cemetery in every morning, and cried under a tree.

Although the place where they had chosen in the cemetery was far from Abō Bakr's court, but he and his associates remained unhappy about it and wary of its consequences.

People who were not aware of this ban, started to ask why the daughter of their late Prophet goes to the cemetery every day, to cry under a tree?!

Fāṭimah's perseverance

Thus the Bakri party decided to continue its suppression of Fāṭimah, and take away her shade from the burning sun of Arabia by cutting down the tree; hoping that she will be forced to stop going to the cemetery.

But Fāṭimah was the Daughter of Rasōlollāh and the wife of Amēr al-Mo'menēn, and her patience and perseverance in spreading God's message and in standing up to His enemies were similar to those of her father and husband. Therefore she continued with her daily routine, and ignored the scorching heat.

Every morning she would go to the same place, and sit where there once was a shade, and cry and cry besides the fallen tree.

The House of Grief

Later Amēr al-Mo'menēn built a room for her in that place, so that she could continue her mourning away from the sun.

On the one hand, the room concealed her from the people who could no longer see her sitting without a shade in that hot weather, but on the other, it raised new questions as to why should she leave her home and come to room in the cemetery to cry?!

Things became worse for the Bakri party, as people named that room the House of Grief.

The Bakri party demolishes the House of Grief

And as expected, the usurpers demolished the House of Grief.

But since Allāh does not let His light be extinguished, Moslems soon built a mosque where once stood the symbol of resistance.

And even the Bakris wrote about it in their books, and recommended their followers to visit the “Mosque of Fāṭimah” in the Baqēᶜ cemetery, also known as the House of Grief. Thus it became a shrine, not only for her followers, but also for the followers of her enemies.

HER POLITICAL LEGACY

During her short life, as mentioned above, Fāṭimah was an intolerable obstacle in the way of the usurpation of the khelāfah, and a serious opposing force facing the Bakri party. However, after her death, she proved to be more of a barrier and posed greater opposition!!

Bakri rulers have always had their scholars sweep Fāṭimah’s opposition under the rug, and convinced them not to mention it in their lectures and their compilations. And the little of it that managed to leak into their works has been professionally stained in order to defuse them.

Some Bakri scholars have developed methods with which they attempt to control the damage, and decrease the effects of what has been mentioned in their books about the opposition of Fāṭimah to the Bakri party, and the suppression of the former by the latter. These methods include:

Impugning Bakri narrators who have narrated such narrations, and slandering them as fabricators; labeling Bakri scholars as reporters of lies and rumors; disowning Bakri scholars and denouncing them as non-Bakris; marking a whole source book, often of several volumes, as unauthentic and denying that it was written by its Bakri author; etc.

However, disowning and marking as unauthentic are not always possible when the targeted reports are mentioned in Bakri master references; that is where falsifying and fabricating comes to use. They create false narrations to counter the unwanted genuine reports; and invent lies to combat the truth.

But there still remain a number of facts in their respected references that no amount of denial can delete and no quantity of fiction can weaken. These backbreaker historic accounts include reports about Fāṭimah's opposition to the Bakri party, particularly those referring to the events after her death.

Secret burial ceremonies

After the assassination of Rasōlollāh, leaders of the Bakri party did not attend his burial ceremonies, and worse still, they used force to delay his burial to give them enough time for usurping his khelāfah.

And when they killed his daughter Fāṭimah, they felt a strong need to fully participate in her burial ceremonies, to stop criticisms, and also make people forget what had caused her death.

However, Sayyedat Nesā' al-ᶜĀlamēn*(AaS)*[1] knew that the usurpers would want to use this opportunity in their favor, to show the world how much they cared about the Prophet and his family. Therefore she decided to keep them from participating in her burial ceremonies, and preferred to be buried, secretly, in the middle of the night, and have her grave concealed.

A sign that to her last breath she opposed the Bakri party and despised its leaders, so much that she preferred to be buried secretly in order to keep her enemies away, when she could have had the best burial ceremony where Moslems and non-Moslems thronged to pay their respects.

And a reminder for the next generations of Moslems, that she, with her high religious, social and political standing, sacrificed

---

[1] *ᶜAlayhas Salām,* peace be upon her.

everything, even a known grave, to support her Imām[1] and to guarantee the continuation of her religion; so that the Moslems may not refrain from doing what they can in order to protect and spread their faith.

And a reminder for the Bakris, that no matter how highly and saintly they think of Abō Bakr and ᶜOmar, but Fāṭimah, the only daughter of Rasōlollāh, opposed them and hated them so much that she stipulated in her will to be buried secretly at night, and have her grave concealed, in order to stop them from participating and attending.

Endless opposition to the Bakri party

The importance of Fāṭimah's preference to have a secret burial and concealed gravesite, and the reason behind her choice, is better understood when we compare her secret burial and concealed graveside to that of her husband Amēr al-Mo'menēn thirty nine years later.

Imām ᶜAli*(AS)*[2] was assassinated in the Koofah Mosque, in Koofah-Iraq, capital of the Islamic rule at that time, while leading the morning ṣalāt[3] on 19 Ramaḍān, 40 AH[4].

His main enemy, the Bakri party, led by the Second Amawi ruler Moᶜāwiyah, was gaining ground by bringing influential leaders

---

[1] Leader, good or bad, religious or otherwise. This title has been used for any person with a religious leading role, such as a public prayer leader or leader of a religious group or movement. But in this book it is only used as a title for one of the twelve God-appointed successors of the Prophet Moḥammad. Plural a'emmah.

[2] ᶜAlayhes Salām, peace be upon him.

[3] Prayer, certain connected movements during which parts of the Holy Qor'ān, as well as several adhkār (plural of dhekr) and adᶜeyah (plural of doᶜā') are recited. There are many different forms of ṣalāt for different reasons and with different effects; some of which are wājib, whereas others are mostaḥab. Some of these ṣalawāt (plural of ṣalāt) should only be performed in specific times and/or places, whereas other ṣalawāt are not bound to any time or place restrictions.

[4] The Moslem lunar calendar. It has 12 months and 355 days in a year; it starts from the year of Rasōlollāh's migration to Madinah. AH: after the Hejrah (Rasōlollāh's migration), BH: before the Hejrah.

to his court through promises and threats. And the enmity of the Amawis towards Imām ᶜAli and the descendants of Rasōlollāh had no limits.

Their hatred was such that they would have exhumed his body from the grave to burn it, just as they had placed the body of Moḥammad ibn Abi Bakr, his loyal supporter and student, inside a donkey skin and set it on fire. This kind of cruelty and viciousness was no surprise from Moᶜāwiyah; after all, it was his parents Abō Sofyān and Hend who before shamming Islam, mutilated the body of Ḥamzah, Prophet Moḥammad's uncle and his long-time protector, and it was his mother Hend^(LAa)[1] who cut out Ḥamzah's liver to eat it, and made a necklace of Ḥamzah's body parts…

Therefore Amēr al-Mo'menēn^(AS)[2] stated in his will to his son Imām Ḥasan^(AS)[3] what his wife had asked him thirty nine years earlier, to have secret burial ceremonies, and a concealed gravesite.

Thus after his martyrdom, he was washed, shrouded in his kafan, and the few people who were allowed to attend performed the *Prayer of the Deceased*; then he was secretly curried to an unknown location outside the city where he was buried.

As expected, Moᶜāwiyah continued the hatred after the Imām's death, and gave strict orders to every priest to publicly curse Amēr al-Mo'menēn in their public prayers and speeches, as he had done during the Imām's life.

This Amawi show of hatred continued for the duration of their one thousand month rule, until they were overthrown by the ᶜAbbāsiyyēn[4], who became the new leaders of the Bakri party.

The ᶜAbbāsi animosity towards the descendants of Rasōlollāh was quite different. Although they assassinated Rasōlollāh's Rightful Kholafā' one after the other, and viciously killed their families, but they did it in a more subtle way; and at times they even showed great affection, publicly, towards the descendants of Prophet Moḥammad.

---

[1] *Laᶜnatollāh ᶜAlayha,* may Allāh distance her from His Blessings and Mercy.

[2] *ᶜAlayhes Salām,* peace be upon him.

[3] *ᶜAlayhes Salām,* peace be upon him.

[4] Also Abbasids.

Therefore, decades after the martyrdom of Amēr al-Mo'menēn, finally the imām of the time revealed the location of his concealed grave, and allowed Moslems to embark on its pilgrimage.

Hiding his gravesite was because of the threat of exhuming his body and burning it; and revealing its location was because that danger no longer existed. So today countless Moslems flock to visit his shrine, twenty-four hours a day, and seven days a week.

But the heartrending question remains, where is Fāṭimah's gravesite?

The location of her husband's gravesite was handed down to later generations and was revealed when the reason for its secrecy no longer existed; and the location of her gravesite has been handed down through generations, but why has not it been revealed?!

Is it because of the threat of exhuming her body by her enemies?! Or is it because of another reason?!

It is true that after her martyrdom, her murderers who were angry for not being allowed to participate in her burial ceremonies announced their intention to exhume her body to perform the *Prayer of the Deceased*, but after those first few days the danger lifted.

So what is the reason?!

She wanted her gravesite to be kept hidden because she did not want the line that she had drawn between the real Islam, represented by Amēr al-Mo'menēn, and the fake Islam, represented by Abō Bakr*(LA)*[1], to fade away; and she wanted it to remain as divisive, inclusive and exclusive as possible at all times.

She was killed because she drew the line, and she kept her gravesite hidden to preserve the line and keep it distinctive.

HER TEACHINGS

When Rasōlollāh migrated to Madinah in the thirteenth year of his mission, and established the Islamic rule, he embarked on the objective to educate the people.

Education in Madinah comprised religious teachings, and literacy lessons, and they were both provided to all males and females. In fact all Moslems regardless of sex, origin, race, prior

---

[1] *Laᶜnatollāh ᶜAlayh,* may Allāh distance him from His Blessings and Mercy.

faith, background, social standing, etc. were instructed by the Prophet to seek both kinds of knowledge. Thus a number of classes in a variety of levels were opened in Madinah as a first step in this undertaking.

Regarding education and seeking knowledge Rasōlollāh said:

((Seeking knowledge is an obligation for every male and female Moslem.)).

He also said:

((Seek knowledge from the cradle to the grave.)).

He also said:

((Seek knowledge, even in China.)).

And Fāṭimah at the young age of eight started to educate women in Madinah.

After a few years when Moslems formed the majority of the literate people in the Arabian peninsula, education became more focused on religion.

Once again, Fāṭimah was the leading woman teacher not only for women, but also for men.

Her teachings were of two sorts: She would repeat and narrate what her father had either told her privately, or what he had said publicly. Or she would teach from her own.

And as in those days Islam was very young and people generally knew little about its message, both sorts of Fāṭimah's teachings included various Islamic themes. She taught health and cleanliness as she taught theology and philosophy; she taught Islamic law and jurisprudence as she taught comparative religion and Islamic beliefs; she taught morals and social etiquettes as she taught politics and economics; etc.

As an Islamic teacher she was well known; she taught Arabs alongside non-Arabs; slaves alongside masters; rich alongside poor.

And although Rasōlollāh and Amēr al-Mo'menēn were both present and easily accessible, people also came to her with their questions.

1- Narrating from Rasōlollāh

Fāṭimah often narrated from her father in various Islamic fields. Below are a few examples:

Regarding health and cleanliness she narrated:

> *((Should not blame but himself [when he becomes ill], he who sleeps while having fat [from the meat he had eaten] on his hand[1].)).*

Regarding good and bad morals she narrated:

> *((Beware of closefistedness, for surely it is a handicap not found in a noble. Beware of closefistedness, for surely it is a tree in Hell, with branches in this world; so anyone who clings to one of its branches, it shall take him to Hell.*
> *And practice generosity, for surely it is a tree in Heaven, with branches in this world; so anyone who clings to one of its branches, it shall guide him to Heaven[2].)).*

Regarding freeing slaves she narrated:

> *((Whoever frees a faithful slave, there would be for him for every part of the slave's body a ransom from the fire[3].)).*

There is also a very interesting ḥadēth[4] called the Ḥadēth of the Blanket, one of her most famous narrations. It is about an event

---

[1] Bahjat Qalb al-Moṣṭafa / al-Raḥmāni = page 302.
[2] Bahjat Qalb al-Moṣṭafa / al-Raḥmāni = page 266.
[3] Beḥār al-Anwār / al-Majlesi = vol. 104, page 194.
[4] A narration from one of the Fourteen Maᶜṣōmēn. Plural aḥādēth.

that happened in Madinah, concerning the first five ma^cṣōmēn[1]: Rasōlollāh, Amēr al-Mo'menēn, Sayyedat Nesā' al-^cĀlamēn, Imām Ḥasan and Imām Ḥosayn. Following that event, Fāṭimah, her father, husband and two sons became known as the "People of the Blanket".

That event shows the importance of the "People of the Blanket" in the creation of the world, and their closeness to Allāh.

This ḥadēth is unique, in the sense that it has a do^cā'[2] like effect; it has psychological and physical healing power, and it functions in the fulfillment of needs etc.

What also makes this ḥadēth stand out even more is the fact that despite its important contents, it is laid out in a theatrical shape.

Despite its strong and heavy content, many Bakri scholars also narrate it in their references alongside Moslems.

Fāṭimah narrates:

((One day my father Rasōlollāh came to my home and said: Peace be upon you, O Fāṭimah!
So I said: Upon you be peace.
He said: I feel weakness in my body.
So I said: May Allāh protect you from weakness.
Then he said: O Fāṭimah! bring me the Yemeni blanket and cover me with it. So I brought him the Yemeni blanket and covered him. And I began to look at him, his face was shining as a full moon at night.
A moment later my son Ḥasan came and said: Peace be upon you, O mother!
So I said: And upon you be peace, O delight of my eye and fruit of my heart!

---

[1] Plural of ma^cṣōm: a person who does not commit sins, does not make mistakes, does not forget, etc. Prophets and their successors are ma^cṣōm.

[2] Praying to Allāh, asking Him for something for oneself and/or for others... Do^ca' can be positive or negative, and has many forms and many uses and effects. Some ad^ceyah (plural of do^cā') should only be recited in specific times and/or places, whereas other ad^ceyah are not bound to any time or place restrictions. There is a huge number of set formal ad^ceyah narrated from the Fourteen Ma^cṣōmēn, the recitation of which is highly recommended, but it is also possible for any Moslem to compose his own do^cā', in any language format, provided that he has a considerable knowledge of Islam.

Then he said: O mother! I smell a pleasant scent here; is it the scent of my grandfather Rasōlollāh?
So I said: Yes, your grandfather is under the blanket. So Ḥasan went towards the blanket and said: Peace be upon you, O grandfather! O Rasōlollāh! Do you permit me to come with you under the blanket?
So he said: And upon you be peace, O my son! and O owner of my pool! I permit you. So he went under the blanket with him.
A moment later my son Ḥosayn came and said: Peace be upon you, O mother!
So I said: And upon you be peace, O my son! and O delight of my eye and fruit of my heart!
Then he said: O mother! I smell a pleasant scent here; is it the sent of my grandfather Rasōlollāh?
So I said: Yes, your grandfather and brother are under the blanket. So Ḥosayn went near the blanket and said: Peace be upon you, O grandfather! Peace be upon you, O whom Allāh has chosen! Do you permit me to be with you two under the blanket?
So he said: And upon you be peace, O my son! and O interceder of my nation! I permit you. So he went under the blanket with them.
Then came Abō al-Ḥasan ᶜAli ibn Abi Ṭālib and said: Peace be upon you, O Daughter of Rasōlollāh!
So I said: And upon you be peace, O Abā al-Ḥasan! and O Amēr al-Mo'menēn!
Then he said: O Fāṭimah! I smell a pleasant scent here; is it the scent of my brother and my cousin Rasōlollāh?
So I said: Yes, that is he with your sons under the blanket. So ᶜAli went towards the blanket and said: Peace be upon you, O Rasōlollāh! Do you permit me to be with you under the blanket?
Rasōlollāh said: And upon you be peace, O my brother! and O my Waṣi![1] and O my Khalēfah! and O

[1] A successor of a prophet, chosen by Allāh and appointed by that prophet. A waṣi is not, himself, a prophet. Also khalēfah or caliph. Plural awṣeyā'.

holder of my flag! I permit you. So ᶜAli went under the blanket.

Then I went near the blanket and said: Peace be upon you, O father! O Rasōlollāh! Do you permit me to be with you under the blanket?

He said: And upon you be peace, O my daughter! and O part of my body! I permit you. So I went under the blanket.

When we were all under the blanket, my father Rasōlollāh held the edges of the blanket and pointed with his right hand to the sky and said: O Allāh! These are indeed my Ahl al-Bayt, and my confidants, and my defenders; their meat is my meat and their blood is my blood; hurts me what hurts them and saddens me what saddens them; I am at war with whomsoever is at war with them and I am at peace with whomsoever is at peace with them; and I am an enemy for whomsoever is their enemy and I love whomsoever loves them; they are from me and I am from them. So descend Your Blessing and Your Benevolence and Your Mercy and Your Forgiveness and Your Pleasure upon me and upon them; and keep away the uncleanness from them, and purify them a (thorough) purifying.

So Allāh the Great and the Almighty said: O My angels! And O residents of my skies! Verily, I have not created any erected sky and nor any flattened land and nor any illuminating moon and nor any shining sun and nor any circling planet and nor any flowing sea and nor any sailing ship but for the love of these five who are under the blanket.

The trustworthy angel Jabra'ēl said: O Lord! and who are under the blanket?

So the Great and Almighty said: They are Ahl Bayt al-Nobowwah[1] and the source of messengerhood. They are Fāṭimah and her father and her husband and her sons.

---

[1] Here, Ahl Bayt al-Nobowwah refers to the first five of the Fourteen Maᶜṣōmēn.

Then Jabra'ēl said: O Lord! Do you permit me to descend to the earth to be the sixth of them?
So Allāh said: Yes, I permit you.
Thus the trustworthy angel Jabra'ēl descended and said: Peace be upon you, O Rasōlollāh! The Most High, the All-Highest sends you greetings and says to you: By My Greatness and by My Exaltedness; verily, I have not created any erected sky and nor any flattened land and nor any illuminating moon and nor any shining sun and nor any circling planet and nor any flowing sea and nor any sailing ship but for your sake and love. And He has permitted me to enter (under the blanket) with you; so do you permit me, O Rasōlollāh?
So Rasōlollāh said: And upon you be peace, O trusted bearer of the revelation of Allāh! I permit you.
Thus Jabra'ēl came under the blanket with us. Then my father said: Verily, Allāh has revealed to you: "ALLĀH ONLY DESIRES TO KEEP AWAY THE UNCLEANNESS FROM YOU, O PEOPLE OF THE HOUSE! AND TO PURIFY YOU A (THOROUGH) PURIFYING"[1].
Then ᶜAli said to my father: O Rasōlollāh! tell me what significance our gathering under the blanket has before Allāh.
So the Prophet said: By Him Who appointed me a prophet, and chose me a messenger for the salvation; whenever this event is mentioned anywhere on earth in an assembly in which there are a group of our followers and friends, Allāh shall descend upon them His Benevolence, and angels shall surround them asking Allāh for the redemption of their sins until the assembly disperses.
Then ᶜAli said: Thus by Allāh we have won and our followers have won by the Lord of the Kaᶜbah.
Rasōlollāh said: O ᶜAli! By Him Who appointed me a prophet, and chose me a messenger for the salvation, whenever this event is mentioned anywhere on earth in an assembly in which there are a group of our

[1] Holy Qor'ān = sōrah 33, āyah 33.

followers and friends, there shall remain no person with anxieties except that Allāh shall relieve him, and there shall remain no grieving person except that Allāh shall remove his grief, and there shall remain none in need except that Allāh shall fulfill his need. Then ᶜAli said: Thus, by Allāh we are winners and blessed, and our followers are winners and blessed, in this world and in the Hereafter, by the Lord of the Kaᶜbah[1].)).

2- Teaching from her own

Fāṭimah, like her father, was a learned person who had not seen a teacher, and an educated person who had not seen an educator. Thus, at a young age, she was able to teach people the things she had not learned from others.

To this day, scholars of both Moslem and Bakri faiths have written countless books interpreting and explaining her sayings and speeches. And Moslem jurisprudents have treated her teachings as a source for Islamic law, as that of her father, and as such they have extracted and derived Islamic laws from them.

Min feqh al-Zahrā' is an encyclopedia of several volumes, four of which has been published to date. In this work, the Martyr Āyatollāh al-ᶜOẓmā Sayyed Moḥammad Shērāzi compiles a large number of Islamic laws which he has extracted from the sayings of Sayyedat Nesā' al-ᶜĀlamēn*(AaS)*[2].

Her teachings cover many fields, below are a few examples:

Regarding social contacts she said:

((The best of you is the softer of you in social contacts, and the most noble to his wife[3].)).

Regarding the philosophy of Islamic laws… she said:

---

[1] al-Doᶜā' wa al-Zeyārah / The Martyr, Āyatollāh al-ᶜOẓmā Sayyed Moḥammad Shērāzi = page 805.

[2] *ᶜAlayhas Salām,* peace be upon her.

[3] Nahj al-Ḥayāt / al-Dashti = page 88.

((...Allāh made faith your purification from polytheism; and ṣalāt, your purity from haughtiness; and Zakāt[1]*, the chastening for the self and the growth in the livelihood; and ṣawm*[2]*, the strengthening of the sincerity; and hajj*[3]*, the erection of the religion; and justice, the harmony for the hearts; and our obedience, the order for the nation; and our leadership, the safety from separation; and jehād*[4]*, the glory for Islam; and patience, the support for deserving the reward; and directing to good deeds, the benefit for the people; and being dutiful to the parents, the protection from wrath; and having close bonds with the family, the lengthening of the life and the growth in numbers; and Qeṣāṣ*[5]*, the prevention from bloodshed; and fulfilling a vow, the exposure to forgiveness...*[6]*)).*

Regarding serving Allāh she said:

((The pleasure of serving Allāh distracted me from asking Him. I have no need other than looking at His gracious face[7]*.)).*

---

[1] An Islamic tax of different rates levied on a number of items beyond a certain limit.

[2] Moslem fasting—refraining from eating, drinking, smoking, inhaling steam and thick vapor, sexual intercourse, etc. from fajr to maghreb. Fajr is one to two hours before sunrise, depending on the time of the year and geographical location. And maghreb is ten to twenty minutes after sunset.

[3] Pilgrimage to Makkah.

[4] Linguistically jehād means struggle, religious or otherwise. But as an Islamic term jehād is only used for religious struggle. Religious struggle in Islam is unlimited, in the sense that it can be in the field of worship, education, economics, politics, society, self training, etc. Therefore the meaning of jehād is determined by the context in which it is used. Here, martial jehād is meant.

[5] Retaliation within the Islamic law.

[6] Fāṭimah min al-Mahd elā al-Laḥd / al-Qazwēni = page 386.

[7] Nahj al-Ḥayāt / al-Dashti = page 136.

Regarding ṣawm she said:

((What can a Ṣā'em[1] do with his ṣawm, if he does not guard his tongue and ear and eye and his external body parts [from sin]?![2])).

Regarding the position of mothers and the need to respect them she said:

((Hold on to her foot, for indeed Heaven is under her feet[3].)).

Regarding the Fourteen Maᶜṣōmēn(AmS)[4] she said:

((And praise be to Him by Whose Greatness and Light those who are in the skies and the earth seek the means to reach Him. And we are His means among His creatures; and we are His dignitaries and the place of His sanctity; and we are His representatives in His absence[5]; and we are the inheritors of His prophets[6].)).

Regarding the effect of worship she said:

((Whomsoever sends his sincere worship to Allāh, Allāh shall send Him much benefit[7].)).

Regarding the usurped khelāfah[8] she said:

---

[1] A person who is fasting.
[2] Nahj al-Ḥayāt / al-Dashti = page 127.
[3] Nahj al-Ḥayāt / al-Dashti = page 199.
[4] *ᶜAlayhemos Salām,* peace be upon them.
[5] Allāh is present at all times and in all places through His knowledge and power. But contact between Him and His creatures is through the prophets and their awṣeyā'... who are the only links. Thus they are the representatives of Allāh in his absence among His creatures.
[6] Bahjat Qalb al-Moṣṭafa / al-Raḥmāni = page 265.
[7] Beḥār al-Anwār / al-Majlesi = vol. 71, page 183.
[8] Successorship of Rasōlollāh. Also caliphate.

((By Allāh! If they had left it with its people, and followed the ᶜEtrah[1] of His Prophet, no two people would have differed among themselves in religion; and it would have been handed down until our Qā'em[2] the ninth descendent of Ḥosayn rises. But they brought forward whom Allāh had moved back, and moved back whom Allāh had brought forward.
When they buried the Messenger and put him in the grave, they chose with their desire, and acted upon their decisions. Woe onto them. Had not they heard Allāh say: "AND YOUR LORD CREATES WHATSOEVER HE WILLS, AND CHOOSES; TO CHOOSE IS NOT THEIRS"[3]. Yes they did hear, but as Allāh says: "FOR SURELY IT IS NOT THE EYES THAT ARE BLIND, BUT BLIND ARE THE HEARTS WHICH ARE IN THE CHESTS"[4].
How far; they broadened their hopes in this world, and forgot the moment of their deaths. Woe onto them...[5])).

ACTIONS BEFORE WORDS

As the effect of an action can be much more than that of a word in the field of persuasion and encouragement, Fāṭimah's actions preceded her words.

Before she taught the importance of patience and forbearance in the Islamic faith, she became the embodiment of patience and forbearance. Before she spoke about the importance of doᶜā' and ṣalāt in nearing the creature to the Creator, she filled much of her time with the various adᶜeyah and the numerous ṣalawāt. Before she explained the essential role of zohd and altruism in the

---

[1] Sayyedat Nesā' al-ᶜĀlamēn and the twelve God-appointed successors of Rasōlollāh.
[2] One of the titles of Prophet Moḥammad's twelfth khalēfah, Imām Mahdi.
[3] Holy Qor'ān = sōrah 28, āyah 68.
[4] Holy Qor'ān = sōrah 22, āyah 46.
[5] Beḥār al-Anwār / al-Majlesi = vol. 36, page 353.

correct formation of the self, she practiced the highest levels of zohd and excessive altruism.

The following are three examples of Fāṭimah's teachings with her actions before her words:

((A hungry person stood in the Prophet's Mosque and said: O you crowd of Moslems! I have indeed become strained with enduring hunger; so host me.
Rasōlollāh stood and said: Who will host this man tonight?
So ᶜAli stood and said: I will, O Rasōlollāh!
Shortly after, he went home and asked Fāṭimah: Do we have any food? I have brought a hungry guest.
So Fāṭimah said: We only have food for the little girl, but we will offer it to our guest[1].
Then ᶜAli held the light, pretending to fix it, but put it out instead, and said to Fāṭimah: Stall in lighting it until the guest finishes eating, then bring it.
And Amēr al-Mo'menēn was moving his mouth [making noises as if he was chewing food], making the guest believe he was eating with him, until the guest finished eating and was satisfied. Fāṭimah then brought the light and put it there.
The food was as much as before, as if no one had eaten. So Amēr al-Mo'menēn said to his guest: Why did you not eat the food?
So he said: I ate the food, O father of Ḥasan! and became satisfied; but the Almighty Allāh blessed it.
Then Amēr al-Mo'menēn and Sayyedat Nesā' al-ᶜĀlamēn and their children ate, and gave some of it to their neighbors[2].
The next morning he prayed with the Prophet, and when the Prophet finished his ṣalāt he looked at Amēr al-Mo'menēn and cried heavily and said: O Amēr al-Mo'menēn! The Lord was amazed with your actions

---

[1] Fāṭimah al-Zahrā' fi al-Qor'ān / Āyatollāh al-ᶜOẓmā Sayyed Ṣādiq Sherāzi = page 290, from Shawāhid al-Tanzēl / al-Ḥasakāni. Nahj al-Ḥayāt / al-Dashti = page 130, from La'āli al-Akhbār / al-Soyōṭi.
[2] Mostadrak al-Wasā'el / al-Nōri = vol. 7, page 216.

last night, and he recited: "AND THEY GIVE PREFERENCE OVER THEMSELVES EVEN THOUGH THEY MAY BE IN NEED. AND WHOSOEVER IS SAVED FROM HIS OWN COVETOUSNESS, THESE IT IS THAT ARE THE SUCCESSFUL ONES"[1]/[2].)).

Bakri scholars also narrate from Salmān who described seeing Fāṭimah one day:

((Fāṭimah was sitting with a hand mill in front of her, grinding barely, and there was blood on the handle [from the blisters on her hand caused by grinding]; while Ḥosayn was, in a corner, writhing with hunger. So I said: O Daughter of Rasōlollāh! see to your palms, and this is Feḍḍah[3], [she will grind the barely for you].
But she said: Rasōlollāh told me to share the housework with her; and yesterday was her day of work[4].)).

It has also been narrated from Imām Ḥasan who said:

((I saw my mother Fāṭimah standing in her meḥrāb[5] the night of Friday, performing rokōᶜ[6] and sojōd[7] until

---

[1] Holy Qor'ān = sōrah 59, āyah 9.
[2] Mostadrak al-Wasā'el / al-Nōri = vol. 7, page 215.
[3] Feḍḍah was her housemaid, and one of her best students.
[4] Nahj al-Ḥayāt / al-Dashti = page 181, from: Dhakhā'er al-ᶜOqbā / al-Ṭabari; al-Kāmil / al-Jorjāni; Majmaᶜ al-Zawā'ed / al-Haythami; Mosnad / Aḥmad; Tārēkh Demashq / Ibn ᶜAsākir; Yanābēᶜ al-Mawaddah / al-Qandōzi; etc.
[5] Place of worship, where a Moslem worships Allāh. Meḥrāb also means a place, especially in a mosque, where the public prayer leader performs the ṣalāt.
[6] A particular position in ṣalāt in which a person bows down, placing the palms on the knees, whilst keeping the legs and the back in a straight position.
[7] A particular position in ṣalāt in which the forehead, the palms, the knees and the toes of both feet are placed on the ground. Sojōd is also performed on its own—not as part of a ṣalāt—for a number of reasons, some of which are mandatory whereas others are recommended.

the fajr[1]; and I heard her praying for the faithful men and women, mentioning their names, and praying for them extensively. But she would not pray for her self and ask for anything.
So I said: O mother! Why do you not pray for yourself as you pray for others?!
She said: O my son! First the neighbors, then the home[2].)).

THE BOOK OF FĀṬIMAH

Besides the seen world, parts of which we understand, there is an unseen world, which we do not know anything about; and which is infinite compared to the former.

Comprehending the seen world is conditioned to studying the relevant sciences, etc. and the results of such comprehension are limited by the limitations of the seen world; but gaining insight into the unseen world is by training the self, and its results are limitless by the infinity of the unseen world.

It has been narrated from Rasōlollāh who said:

((Were it not for the Shayāṭēn[3] who swarm around the hearts of the children of Ādam, they could indeed look at the treasures of the skies and the earth[4]/[5].)).

And in the Holy Qor'ān, Allāh mentions the story of one of Prophet Solaymān's[6] aids who had acquired some *knowledge-of-the-unseen* and was able to carry out an extraordinary, supernatural task. Allāh refers to him saying:

---

[1] One to two hours before sunrise, depending on the time of year and geographical location.
[2] Beḥār al-Anwār / al-Majlesi = vol. 43, page 81.
[3] Plural of Shayṭān; also: Satan.
[4] Jāmi^c al-Sa^{c}ādāt / al-Narāqi – vol. 1, page 43.
[5] Meaning that if a person resists the Shayāṭēn and trains his self, he would be able to see the creatures that can not be seen by the normal person, such as the angels, as part of his knowledge-of-the-unseen.
[6] Also: Solomon.

﴾ONE WHO HAD SOME KNOWLEDGE OF THE BOOK SAID: I WILL BRING IT TO YOU IN THE TWINKLING OF AN EYE[1]/[2].﴿.

---

[1] Holy Qor'ān = sōrah 27, āyah 40.

[2] A brief account of the story of Prophet Solaymān and the Queen of Saba' (also Sheba) Belqēs, has been narrated in the Holy Qor'ān as follows:

> *﴾AND HE TARRIED NOT LONG, THEN SAID: I COMPREHEND THAT WHICH YOU DO NOT COMPREHEND AND I HAVE BROUGHT TO YOU A SURE INFORMATION FROM SHEBA.*
>
> *SURELY I FOUND A WOMAN RULING OVER THEM, AND SHE HAS BEEN GIVEN ABUNDANCE AND SHE HAS A MIGHTY THRONE.*
>
> *I FOUND HER AND HER PEOPLE ADORING THE SUN INSTEAD OF ALLĀH, AND THE SHAYṬĀN [ALSO: SATAN] HAS MADE THEIR DEEDS FAIR-SEEMING TO THEM AND THUS TURNED THEM FROM THE WAY, SO THEY DO NOT GO ARIGHT.*
>
> *THAT THEY DO NOT MAKE OBEISANCE TO ALLĀH, WHO BRINGS FORTH WHAT IS HIDDEN IN THE HEAVENS AND THE EARTH AND KNOWS WHAT YOU HIDE AND WHAT YOU MAKE MANIFEST.*
>
> *ALLĀH, THERE IS NO GOD BUT HE: HE IS THE LORD OF MIGHTY POWER.*
>
> *HE SAID: WE WILL SEE WHETHER YOU HAVE TOLD THE TRUTH OR WHETHER YOU ARE OF THE LIARS.*
>
> *TAKE THIS MY LETTER AND HAND IT OVER TO THEM, THEN TURN AWAY FROM THEM AND SEE WHAT (ANSWER) THEY RETURN.*
>
> *SHE SAID: O CHIEFS! SURELY AN HONORABLE LETTER HAS BEEN DELIVERED TO ME.*
>
> *SURELY IT IS FROM SOLAYMĀN AND SURELY IT IS IN THE NAME OF ALLĀH, THE BENEFICENT, THE MERCIFUL.*
>
> *SAYING: EXALT NOT YOURSELVES AGAINST ME AND COME TO ME IN SUBMISSION.*
>
> *SHE SAID: O CHEIFS! GIVE ME ADVICE RESPECTING MY AFFAIR: I NEVER DECIDE AN AFFAIR UNTIL YOU ARE IN MY PRESENCE.*
>
> *THEY SAID: WE ARE POSSESSORS OF STRENGTH AND POSSESSORS OF MIGHTY PROWESS, AND THE COMMAND IS YOURS, THEREFORE SEE WHAT YOU WILL COMMAND.*
>
> *SHE SAID: SURELY THE KINGS, WHEN THEY ENTER A TOWN, RUIN IT AND MAKE THE NOBLEST OF ITS PEOPLE TO BE LOW, AND THUS THEY (ALWAYS) DO.*
>
> *AND SURELY I AM GOING TO SEND A PRESENT TO THEM, AND SHALL WAIT TO SEE WHAT (ANSWER) DO THE MESSENGERS BRING BACK.*
>
> *SO WHEN HE CAME TO SOLAYMĀN, HE SAID: WHAT! WILL YOU HELP ME WITH WEALTH?! BUT WHAT ALLĀH HAS GIVEN ME IS BETTER THAN WHAT HE HAS GIVEN YOU.*

However, training the self, in this sense, is for people who want to elevate themselves and be closer to God but are not ma^cṣōm; as the ma^cṣōmēn are already close to Allāh and have knowledge-of-the-unseen.

And Fāṭimah, as the third highest ma^cṣōm, had knowledge-of-the-unseen. And one of her names was Mohaddathah the woman to whom angels speak.

NAY, YOU ARE EXALTANT BECAUSE OF YOUR PRESENT.
GO BACK TO THEM, SO WE WILL MOST CERTAINLY COME TO THEM WITH HOSTS WHICH THEY SHALL HAVE NO POWER TO OPPOSE, AND WE WILL MOST CERTAINLY EXPELL THEM THEREFROM IN ABASEMENT, AND THEY SHALL BE IN A STATE OF IGNOMINY.
HE SAID: O CHEIFS! WHICH OF YOU CAN BRING TO ME HER THROWN BEFORE THEY COME TO ME IN SUBMISSION?
ONE AUDACIOUS AMONG THE JINN SAID: I WILL BRING IT TO YOU BEFORE YOU RISE UP FROM YOUR PLACE; AND MOST SURELY I AM STRONG (AND) TRUSTY FOR IT.
ONE WHO HAD SOME KNOWLEDGE OF THE BOOK SAID: I WILL BRING IT TO YOU IN THE TWINKLING OF AN EYE. THEN WHEN HE SAW IT SETTLED BESIDE HIM, HE SAID: THIS IS OF THE GRACE OF MY LORD THAT HE MAY TRY ME WHETHER I AM GRATEFUL OR UNGRATEFUL; AND WHOEVER IS GRATEFUL, HE IS GRATEFUL ONLY FOR HIS OWN SOUL, AND WHOEVER IS UNGRATEFUL, THEN SURELY MY LORD IS SELF-SUFFICIENT, HONORED.
HE SAID: ALTER HER THRONE FOR HER; WE WILL SEE WHETHER SHE FOLLOWS THE RIGHT WAY OR IS OF THOSE WHO DO NOT GO ARIGHT.
SO WHEN SHE CAME, IT WAS SAID: IS YOUR THRONE LIKE THIS? SHE SAID: IT IS AS IT WERE THE SAME; AND WE WERE GIVEN THE KNOWLEDGE BEFORE IT AND WE WERE SUBMISSIVE.
AND WHAT SHE WORSHIPPED BECIDES ALLĀH PREVENTED HER, SURELY SHE WAS OF AN UNBELIEVING PEOPLE.
IT WAS SAID TO HER: ENTER THE PALACE; BUT WHEN SHE SAW IT SHE DEEMED IT TO BE A GREAT EXPANSE OF WATER, AND BARED HER LEGS.
HE SAID: SURELY IT IS A PALACE MADE SMOOTH WITH GLASS. SHE SAID: MY LORD! SURELY I HAVE BEEN UNJUST TO MYSELF, AND I SUBMIT WITH SOLAYMĀN TO ALLĀH, THE LORD OF THE WORLDS.﴾.
(Holy Qor'ān = sōrah 27, āyāt 22-44)

After the martyrdom of Rasōlollāh, according to a large number of aḥādēth, Allāh revealed to Fāṭimah what came to be known as the "Book of Fāṭimah".

In terms of size, the Book of Fāṭimah is described to be three times the size of the Holy Qor'ān; and in terms of content, it is described to include knowledge about what has happened in the world from the beginning of the creation, and what will happen until the last day before the Hereafter; it includes the names of all the prophets and their awṣeyā', and all those who believed and disbelieved in them; it includes the names of all those who ruled and those who will rule; it includes Jewish, Christian and Islamic laws as they were revealed; it includes a complete description of all the creatures; etc.

And like the Qor'ān, the content of the Book of Fāṭimah is not much in terms of volume, but it includes everything about everything; and like the Qor'ān only the people to whom it was reveled can understand and use it[1].

---

[1] The Holy Qor'ān has what can be translated as an 'outer layer' and seventy 'inner layers'. Those who study the sciences of the Arabic language and the many Qor'ānic sciences can only understand the 'outer layer', and remain unable to comprehend even the first 'inner layer'. And even in understanding the 'outer layer', Qor'ānic scholars who have produced well over two thousand encyclopedias in its explanation some of which consists of around sixty volumes, are paralyzed without the help and insight of the Fourteen Maᶜṣōmēn. As Imām Ṣādiq says:

> *((Verily, understands the Qor'ān only he to whom it was revealed.)).* (Wasā'el al-Shēᶜah / al-ᶜĀmili = vol. 27, page 185)

But in some cases, the Fourteen Maᶜṣōmēn revealed some knowledge of the 'inner layers' of the Holy Qor'ān. For instance, Ibn ᶜAbbās, who is one of the top Qor'ānic scholars and most trusted narrators of aḥādēth to the Bakris, narrates:

> *((One night, Amēr al-Mo'menēn, from the beginning of the darkness until the beginning of the light [the next day], taught me some of the meanings of the first letter of Besmellāh [the first word of the first āyah of the first sōrah of the Holy Qor'ān], and said: If I wanted, I can overload forty camels with the interpretation of Besmellāh [In the name of Allāh].)).* (Beḥār al-Anwār / al-Majlesi = vol. 40, page 186)

And the Imām is not exaggerating about his ability, as the 'inner layers' of the Holy Qor'ān are codes where even a single dot in a single letter gives a

After her martyrdom, her husband Amēr al-Mo'menēn held the book, and he passed it to his son Imām Ḥasan before his martyrdom, and it was handed down by one imām to the other until the awaited savior Imām Mahdi(AS)[1].

These ma^cṣōmēn[2] used the Book of Fāṭimah as a means of knowing the unseen world, and they often referred to it.

HER STUDENTS

Fāṭimah(AaS)[3] had many students who narrated a large number of aḥādēth from her. And as she believed in and preached and practiced equality, her narrators included Arab and non-Arab, rich and poor, influential and ordinary, master and slave, white and black, man and woman, etc. And as she allowed her knowledge to flow to all willing seekers, both enemy and friend profited to the extent of their capability.

Thus we see the names of ᶜĀ'eshah, the enemy, alongside Omm Salamah, the friend; Asmā' bint ᶜOmays, the woman, alongside Ibn Mas'ood, the man; Belāl al-Habashi, the black, alongside Abō Sa'eed al-Khodri, the white; Salmā, the ordinary, alongside Ibn ᶜAbbās, the influential; Zaynab bint Abi[4] Rāfiᶜ, the poor, alongside Abō Ayyoob al-Anṣāri, the rich; Salmān, the non-Arab, alongside Jābir ibn ᶜAbdollāh al-Anṣāri, the Arab.

Below are a few highlights about some of her students:

---

lot of meanings, and its position to other dots before and after it in that word produces yet more meanings. Even to this day, we have remnants of the Science of the Dot, in some libraries in the Middle East.

1 *ᶜAlayhes Salām*, peace be upon him.

2 Plural of maᶜṣōm: a person who does not commit sins, does not make mistakes, does not forget, etc. although he/she has the choice to commit sins. Prophets and their awṣeyā' are maᶜṣōm. The Fourteen Maᶜṣōmēn are the Prophet Moḥammad, his daughter Fāṭimah, and his twelve God-appointed successors.

3 *ᶜAlayhas Salām*, peace be upon her.

4 Abā, Abō and Abi have the same meaning, but their usage differs based on the Arabic grammar.

1- Asmā' bint ᶜOmays

Asmā' was one of the first people who accepted Islam. She and her husband Jaᶜfar ibn Abi Ṭālib, who was put in charge of a group of around eighty Moslems, migrated to Ethiopia from Makkah after the Idolaters tightened their grip on Moslems and subjected them to all sorts of torture, and in some cases death under torture[1]. After a number of years in exile, they returned to Madinah just after the Battle of Khaybar.

After about a year, in the eighth year of Hejrah[2], Asmā's husband Jaᶜfar was put in charge of an army, three thousand strong, to Mo'tah in today's Jordan, after an ally of the Roman Empire killed Rasōlollāh's courier Hārith ibn Omayr. But Jaᶜfar was not to return, after the Romans sent a reinforcement of more than one hundred thousand soldiers; and he met his fate among a number of his loyal men.

After Jaᶜfar's martyrdom, Asmā' married Abō Bakr; and gave birth to Abō Bakr's son Moḥammad. A few years later, when Abō Bakr was assassinated by ᶜOmar, Asmā' married Amēr al-Mo'menēn. Moḥammad ibn Abi Bakr was three years old at that time.

During the time when Asmā' was with Rasōlollāh, after she accepted Islam in Makkah until her migration to Ethiopia, and after her return to Madinah until the martyrdom of Rasōlollāh, she learned a lot from him, allowing her to narrate a large number of aḥādēth.

After his martyrdom, Asmā' followed and supported Imām ᶜAli*(AS)*[3], even though she was married to Abō Bakr, the person who had forcefully usurped the khelāfah from him.

She continued studying under Fāṭimah, showing support for the oppressed camp over the oppressors. And when her husband usurped Fadak[4] from Fāṭimah, she testified that Rasōlollāh had given it to her. And when her testimony was shamelessly rejected by Abō

[1] For more detailed information, see: Rasōlollāh, the Messenger of Allāh / by the author = page 46.

[2] Rasōlollāh's migration from Makkah to Madinah in the thirteenth year of his mission. Moslems start their lunar calendar from the year of the Hejrah.

[3] *ᶜAlayhes Salām,* peace be upon him.

[4] You will read more about Fadak later in this book.

Bakr and ᶜOmar as biased, Fāṭimah stepped forward and made them admit that Asmā' was not a liar.

Bakri scholars narrate alongside Moslems:

> *((...Then she (Fāṭimah) said to Abō Bakr and ᶜOmar: Have you two not heard my father say: Asmā' bint ᶜOmays and Omm Ayman are among the residents of Heaven?!*
> *So Abō Bakr and ᶜOmar said: Yes*[1]/[2]*.)).*

She was so close to Fāṭimah that Fāṭimah asked her to participate in her secret burial ceremonies.

And after her death, Asmā' showed great courage and loyalty standing up to ᶜĀ'eshah(LAa)[3], who was one of the main players in the usurpation of the khelāfah.

As Abō Bakr's wife, she once sent word to Amēr al-Mo'menēn that her husband had ordered his assassination, and that he should take care and be ready for it.

2- Feḍḍah

Feḍḍah is reported to have been the daughter of an Indian king. The Prophet brought her to Fāṭimah to be her student and housemaid.

After Rasōlollāh's martyrdom she stood up to the Bakri party, firmly supported Amēr al-Mo'menēn and shared some of Fāṭimah's pain and grief.

Feḍḍah studied under both ᶜAli and Fāṭimah, and narrated from both of them. From what has been reported in history books we

---

[1] Mostadrakāt ᶜAwālim al-ᶜOlōm / al Abṭaḥi – vol. 11, page 889.

[2] When a maᶜṣōm, using his/her ᶜElm al-Ghayb or Knowledge-of-the-Unseen, declares that someone will go to Heaven, it means that they are special. Very few people have been declared by the maᶜṣōmēn to be among the residents of Heaven. Thus when Rasōlollāh says that these two women will go to Heaven it means that they do not lie, especially in such an important issue.

[3] *Laᶜnatollāh ᶜAlayha,* may Allāh distance her from His Blessings and Mercy.

learn that she was very special. Her capability to receive knowledge was amazing, and that is why her teachers took her to where few of their students had been taken, and showed her what few people had been shown, and enabled her to do what few people had been enabled to do.

Below are some examples:

((Rasōlollāh brought his daughter Fāṭimah a housemaid called Feḍḍah al-Nawbeyyah, to help her with the housework; and he taught her a doᶜā' to recite.
One day, Fāṭimah asked her: Do you want to make the dough or do you want to bake?
Feḍḍah: I will make the dough and gather wood. So she went out, gathered the wood and wrapped it, but could not carry it. Then she recited the doᶜā' the Prophet had taught her, which was: "O One! Like Whom there is no one. You cause everyone to die, and exterminate everyone. And You are one on Your throne. Slumber does not overtake Him nor sleep". Suddenly a Bedouin appeared and carried the bundle to Fāṭimah's home[1]/[2].)).

It has also been narrated:

((When Feḍḍah came to Fāṭimah's home, she could not see anything but the sword, and the armor, and the hand mill.
She was the daughter of the Indian king and had a supply of elixir, so she took a piece of copper, softened it, shaped it as a piece of silver, put the elixir on it and turned it into gold.

---

[1] Mostadrakāt ᶜAwālim al-ᶜOlōm / al-Abṭaḥi = vol. 11, page 1043.

[2] There are some special adᶜeyah that have specific effects when recited by the people to whom they had been taught; however, the subjects of these adᶜeyah may not seem consistent with their effects. In this case, for instance, the doᶜā' is about God's qualities and powers, not about asking for help, etc. but its effect is more like that of a request for assistance.

When Amēr al-Mo'menēn returned, Feḍḍah put the gold before him. Seeing it, he said: Bravo, O Feḍḍah! But if you had melted the body, the color would have become better and the price more expensive.
So Feḍḍah said: O Master! Do you know this science?
Imām ᶜAli: Yes, and this child knows it too, pointing to Imām Ḥosayn [who was a child of around three years old]. Then Ḥosayn came and told Feḍḍah exactly what Amēr al-Mo'menēn had said.
Then Amēr al-Mo'menēn said: We know greater than this; he pointed with his hand, suddenly large pieces of gold and treasures of the earth appeared flowing. He said: Put your gold with its sisters; so she did and it flowed away[1].)).

It has also been narrated:

((Fāṭimah had taught Feḍḍah some strange sciences... One day, using what she had learned, Feḍḍah made some gold, sold it and bought everything Fāṭimah and ᶜAli needed in their home. When Fāṭimah saw all those things, she asked Feḍḍah how she had bought them. And Feḍḍah told her what she had done.
So Fāṭimah said: Give this all to the poor, and do not repeat it again. We have not acquired this science and other sciences[2] to ascend through the levels of this world, but to practice contentment and zohd so that our ranks increase in the Hereafter[3].)).

Through training, Feḍḍah had become able to speak only with Qor'ānic āyāt. As Abō al-Qāsim al-Qoshayri narrates:

---

[1] Mostadrakāt ᶜAwālim al-ᶜOlōm / al-Abṭaḥi = vol. 11, page 1044. Beḥār al-Anwār / al-Majlesi = vol. 41, page 273.

[2] A person who has ᶜElm al-Ghayb or Knowledge-of-the-Unseen necessarily knows everything about the seen world, including all sciences.

[3] Eᶜlamō Anni Fāṭimah / al-Mohājir = vol. 3, page 542.

((I was left behind the caravan in the desert where I found a woman. I asked her: Who are you?
She said: "AND SAY SALĀM (PEACE), FOR THEY SHALL SOON COME TO KNOW[1]". So I greeted her. And asked: What are you doing here?
She said: "AND WHOM ALLĀH GUIDES, THERE IS NONE THAT CAN LEAD HIM ASTRAY[2]".
So I asked: Where are you coming from?
She said: "THESE SHALL BE CALLED TO FROM A FAR-OFF PLACE[3]".
So I asked: Where are you going?
She said: "AND PILGRIMAGE TO THE HOUSE IS INCUMBENT UPON PEOPLE[4]".
So I asked: When were you left behind?
She said: "AND CERTAINLY WE CREATED THE HEAVENS AND THE EARTH AND WHAT IS BETWEEN THEM IN SIX DAYS[5]".
So I asked: Would you like some food?
She said: "AND WE DID NOT MAKE THEM BODIES NOT EATING THE FOOD[6]".
So I gave her food and told her: Walk faster.
She said: "ALLĀH DOES NOT IMPOSE UPON ANY SOUL A DUTY BUT TO THE EXTENT OF ITS ABILITY[7]".
So I asked: Do you want to ride with me?
She said: "IF THERE HAD BEEN IN THEM ANY GODS EXCEPT ALLĀH, THEY WOULD BOTH HAVE CERTAINLY BEEN IN A STATE OF DISORDER[8]".
So I dismounted and helped her mount.
She said: "GLORY BE TO HIM WHO MADE THIS SUBSERVIENT TO US[9]".

---

[1] Holy Qor'ān = sōrah 43, āyah 89.
[2] Holy Qor'ān = sōrah 39, āyah 37.
[3] Holy Qor'ān = sōrah 41, āyah 44.
[4] Holy Qor'ān = sōrah 3, āyah 97.
[5] Holy Qor'ān = sōrah 50, āyah 38.
[6] Holy Qor'ān = sōrah 21, āyah 8.
[7] Holy Qor'ān = sōrah 2, āyah 286.
[8] Holy Qor'ān = sōrah 21, āyah 22.
[9] Holy Qor'ān = sōrah 43, āyah 13.

When we reached the caravan, I asked her: Do you have someone here?
She said: "O DĀWŌD! SURELY WE HAVE MADE YOU A RULER IN THE LAND[1]"; "AND MOḤAMMAD IS NO MORE THAN AN APOSTLE[2]"; "O YAḤYĀ! TAKE HOLD OF THE BOOK"; "O MŌSĀ! SURELY I AM ALLĀH YOUR LORD[3]".
So I called these names, and four youths came towards her.
I asked her: Who are these people to you?
She said: "WEALTH AND CHILDREN ARE AN ADORNMENT OF THE LIFE OF THIS WORLD[4]".
When they reached her, she said: "O MY FATHER! EMPLOY HIM, SURELY THE BEST OF THOSE THAT YOU CAN EMPLOY IS THE STRONG MAN, THE FAITHFUL ONE[5]". So they rewarded me. Then she said: "AND ALLĀH MULTIPLIES FOR WHOM HE PLEASES[6]". And they increased my reward.
So I asked them who she was, and they said: This is our mother Feḍḍah, who used to be Fāṭimah's housemaid. She has not spoken for twenty years, except with Qor'ān[7].)).

After Fāṭimah's martyrdom, Feḍḍah remained a strong supporter of Amēr al-Mo'menēn against the Bakri party, courageously exposing its leaders. In one instance, after a debate with ᶜOmar, she made the Second Usurper admit the truth and say:

((A single hair from the family of Abō Ṭālib[8] is more learned than ᶜOday[1]/[2].)).

---

[1] Holy Qor'ān = sōrah 38, ayah 26.
[2] Holy Qor'ān = sōrah 3, āyah 144.
[3] Holy Qor'ān = sōrah 20, āyāt 10 and 11.
[4] Holy Qor'ān = sōrah 18, āyah 46.
[5] Holy Qor'ān = sōrah 28, āyah 26.
[6] Holy Qor'ān = sōrah 2, āyah 261.
[7] Mostadrakāt ᶜAwalim al-ᶜOlōm / al-Abṭaḥi = vol. 11, page 1045. Beḥār al-Anwār / al-Majlesi = vol. 43, page 86.
[8] Abō Ṭālib was the father of Amēr al-Mo'menēn.

3- Jābir ibn ᶜAbdollāh al-Anṣāri

Jābir was one of Rasōlollāh’s Ṣaḥābah[3] who, according to some historic reports, was among the Moslem soldiers at the Battle of Badr[4].

After Rasōlollāh’s martyrdom, Jābir continued to support Amēr al-Mo’menēn courageously. His opposition to the Bakri party was well known. In the streets and public gatherings of Madinah, he often recited Rasōlollāh’s famous ḥadēth[5]:

> *((Ali is the best person; and whomsoever denies it, he is surely an infidel[6].)).*

He was also among the Moslem army at the Battle of Ṣeffēn against Moᶜāwiyah, the Second Amawi ruler and leader of the Bakri party.

He was the first person to visit the gravesite of Imām Ḥosayn[(AS)7] after his tragic martyrdom in 61 AH, at the hands of the Bakri party leader, the Third Amawi ruler Yazēd.

Jābir had gone through many levels of learning, and because of his surrender to the truth, his teachers revealed more and more of

---

[1] ᶜOday is the Arab tribe in which ᶜOmar was freed as a slave. At that time, slaves who were freed in a tribe became members of that tribe. For more information about ᶜOmar and Abō Bakr’s origins see: Rasōlollāh, the Messenger of Allāh / by the author = page 181.

[2] al-Kawthar / al-Mōsawi = vol. 7, page 433.

[3] Plural of ṣaḥābi: a companion of the Prophet Moḥammad.

[4] For more detailed information about the Battle of Badr see: Rasōlollāh, the Messenger of Allāh / by the author = page 126.

[5] A narration from one of the Fourteen Maᶜṣōmēn. Plural aḥādēth.

[6] al-Bedāyah wa al-Nehāyah / Ibn Kothayr = vol. 7, page 359. al-Fawā’ed al-Majmōᶜah / al-Shawkāni = page 372. Kanz al-ᶜOmmāl / al-Hendi = vol. 12, page 221. Mēzān al-Eᶜtedāl / al-Dhahabi = vol. 1, page 531; vol. 2, page271. Montakhab Kanz al-ᶜOmmāl = vol. 5, page 35. Tārēkh Demashq / Ibn ᶜAsākir = vol. 42, page 372. Yanābēᶜ al-Mawaddah / al-Qandōzi = vol. 2, page 78.

[7] *ᶜAlayhes Salām,* peace be upon him.

the unseen world to him. One of his most famous narrations from Fāṭimah is the following:

> *((Imām Ṣādiq narrates: My father [Imām Bāqir] said to Jābir ibn ʿAbdollāh al-Anṣāri: I need to ask you something in private, what time is suitable for you?*
> *Jābir answered him: Any time you like. So my father asked him: O Jābir! Tell me about the tablet you saw in the hands of my mother Fāṭimah, Daughter of Rasōlollāh, and what she told you, and what was written on that tablet.*
> *Jābir said: I take Allāh as my witness, I went to your mother Fāṭimah during the life of Rasōlollāh to congratulate her on the birth of Ḥosayn, and saw in her hand a green tablet which I thought was of emerald; and I saw on it a writing in white similar to sunlight. So I told her: My parents be your sacrifice O Daughter of Rasōlollāh! What is this tablet?*
> *She said: Allāh, the Great and Almighty, gave this to His Messenger. In it, there is my father's name, and my husband's name, and my two sons' names, and the names of the awṣeyā'*[1] *in my lineage. So my father gave it to me.*
> *Then your mother Fāṭimah gave it to me, so I read and copied it.*
> *Then my father said to him: O Jābir! Can you show it to me?*
> *Jābir said: Yes. So they both walked to Jābir's home, where he gave my father a scroll. But my father said: O Jābir! Look in your scroll while I read it to you [from myself].*
> *So Jābir looked in his scroll and my father read; and he did not make any mistakes.*
> *Jābir said: I take Allāh as my witness, I surely saw on the tablet exactly as you said.*
> *It was written:*

---

[1] Plural of waṣi: a successor of a prophet, chosen by Allāh and appointed by that prophet. A waṣi is not, himself, a prophet. Also khalēfah or caliph.

In the name of Allāh, the Most Compassionate, the Most Merciful. This is a written message from Allāh, the Great, the Wise, to Moḥammad, His Light, and His Ambassador, and His Mediator, and His Guide. It is conveyed by Rōḥ al-Amēn[1], from the Lord of the nations.

Glorify O Moḥammad! My names; and be thankful for My material gifts, and do not deny My immaterial gifts[2].

Indeed I am Allāh, there is no God but Me. Breaker of the despots; and Destroyer of the haughty; and Humiliater of the tyrants; and Rewarder and Punisher of the Day of Reward and Punishment.

Indeed I am Allāh, there is no God but Me. So whomsoever wishes other than My Favor, or fears from other than My Punishment, I shall subject him to a punishment to which I do not subject any person. So it is Me you should worship, and on Me you should depend.

I have surely not sent a prophet whose days completed and whose time finished except that I chose a waṣi for him. And I have surely favored you over the prophets, and favored your Waṣi over the awṣeyā'. And I have given you your two sons Ḥasan and Ḥosayn[3] as a present (to become imām) after him.

Thus I made Ḥasan the source of my knowledge after his father's time expired.

And made Ḥosayn the keeper of my revelation, and gifted him with martyrdom, and finished it for him with glory. So he is the best of those who were martyred, and the highest martyr to Me. I put My Word and Conclusive Proof with him. By his lineage I reward and punish.

The first of them (Ḥosayn's lineage) is ᶜAli, master of the worshipers, and the jewel of my servants.

---

[1] An angel.

[2] Any creation that is not felt by one of the five senses, such as: intellect.

[3] Imām Ḥasan and Imām Ḥosayn are called Sons of the Prophet.

And his son looks very much like his grandfather Maḥmōd[1]*. Moḥammad, the splitter of My knowledge, and the source of My wisdom.*

The doubtful will soon go astray in Jaᶜfar. Whomsoever refuses Jaᶜfar, refuses me. I will most definitely make precious Jaᶜfar's stature, and I will most definitely make him happy in his followers and supporters and friends.

And after him, I chose Mōsā, in a difficult test, and blind severe darkness. Because the line of My instruction shall not be cut, and My proof shall not be hidden, and My friends shall not ever go astray. Beware! Whomsoever denies any one of them, he has surely denied My bliss; and whoever changes an āyah from My Book, he has surely fabricated against Me.

And woe unto the fabricating deniers when the time of My servant and friend and My chosen one Mōsā finishes. Beware! Whomsoever accuses the Eighth of lying is indeed accusing all of my friends of lying. ᶜAli is My friend and My supporter, and is he on whom I shall put the burdens of the prophethood, and test him with carrying it. He will be killed by a deceitful haughty; he will be buried in the city that was built by the righteous servant Thol-Qarnayn[2] *alongside my worst creature*[3]*.*

It is a foregone promise; I shall make him extremely happy with Moḥammad, his son and his khalēfah after him. For he is the inheritor of My knowledge, and the source of My wisdom, and the keeper of My secret, and My proof over My creatures; I make Heaven his home, and make him the intercessor for seventy thousand of his lineage, all of whom should indeed go to Hell.

---

[1] One of Rasōlollāh's names.

[2] One of the prophets.

[3] This is a reference to Hārōn, the ᶜAbbāsi (also: Abbasid) ruler and leader of the Bakri party. He was the most evil person of his era.

And I shall finish him with glory with his son ᶜAli, My defender and supporter, and the witness among My creatures, and My trustee over My revelation.
I shall create from him the one who calls to My way, and the holder of my knowledge Ḥasan.
Then I shall complete it with his son, mercy for the creatures of this world. He shall have the perfection of Mōsā[1], and the magnificence of ᶜĒsā[2], and the patience of Ayyōb[3]. My defenders will be humiliated in his era; and their heads will be exchanged as gifts just as the heads of the Turks and the Daylam[4] are exchanged as gifts. They will be killed and burnt; and they will be frightened, terrorized, apprehensive; the earth will be painted with their blood, and grief and resonance will spread in their families. They are truly My friends; by them I push away every blind dark test; and by them I lift the earthquake; and remove from them their burdens and the shekels, "THOSE ARE THEY ON WHOM ARE BLESSINGS AND MERCY FROM THEIR LORD, AND THESE ARE THE FOLLOWERS OF THE RIGHT COURSE"[5]/[6].)).

At an old age, Jābir died in Madinah. He was the last to die of those who had witnessed the oath of allegiance to Rasōlollāh at Aqabah, before the Prophet migrated to Madinah. His lineage has survived to this day, and is well known.

4- Omm Ayman

Barakah bint Thaᶜlabah, known as Omm Ayman, was of an Ethiopian origin. She was the housemaid of Āminah, the mother of Rasōlollāh. After Āminah's death, she stayed with him.

---

[1] Also Moses.
[2] Also Jesus.
[3] Also Jacobs.
[4] The people who lived in today's northern Iran.
[5] Holy Qor'ān = sōrah 2, āyah 157.
[6] Mostadrakāt ᶜAwālim al-ᶜOlōm / al-Abṭaḥi = vol. 11, page 848, from a number of other sources.

She married ᶜObayd ibn Zayd who was killed in the Battle of Khaybar by the Jews in the 7th year after the Hejrah. Later she married Zayd ibn Hārithah who was also killed in the Battle of Mo'tah by the Persians in the 8th year after the Hejrah.

It has been reported that she also participated in some of the battles. In the Battle of Oḥod, in 2 AH[1], she gave water to the soldiers and looked after the injured. She was also present in the Battles of Khaybar and Ḥonayn, in 7 and 8 AH.

Omm Ayman is one of the many women narrators. She has narrated a considerable number of aḥādēth from Rasōlollāh.

As her knowledge increased and her taqwā[2] strengthened, the Prophet promised her paradise. He repeated his testimony, in public, several times[3]; Prophet Moḥammad has given few individuals such an assurance.

After the assassination of Rasōlollāh, Omm Ayman continued to support Amēr al-Mo'menēn against the Bakri party. When Abō Bakr*(LA)*[4] usurped Fadak from Fāṭimah*(AaS)*[5], Omm Ayman was one of the witnesses who stepped forward and testified that Fadak was her property. And although Abō Bakr and ᶜOmar both admitted that she and Abō Bakr's wife, Asmā' bint ᶜOmays, were promised Heaven by Rasōlollāh, they refused their testimony and shamelessly said:

((Two women from Heaven testify to a lie[6].)).

Omm Ayman was very close to Fāṭimah, and before she died from her injuries she called Omm Ayman to come and see her and

---

[1] The Moslem lunar calendar. It has 12 months and 355 days in a year; it starts from the year of Rasōlollāh's migration to Madinah. AH: after the Hejrah (Rasōlollāh's migration), BH: before the Hejrah.

[2] Obeying Allāh in all His commands, thus doing what he makes wājib (mandatory), and refraining from what he makes ḥarām (prohibited).

[3] al-Eṣābah / al-ᶜAsqalāni = vol. 4, page 432.

[4] *Laᶜnatollāh ᶜAlayh,* may Allāh distance him from His Blessings and Mercy.

[5] *ᶜAlayhas Salām,* peace be upon her.

[6] Mostadrakāt ᶜAwālim al-ᶜOlōm / al-Abṭaḥi = vol. 11, page 1047.

witness her will. She was also present among the few who were allowed to attend her secret burial ceremonies.

After her martyrdom, Omm Ayman decided to make her opposition to the Usurpers of the Khelāfah, who were determined to destroy Islam from within, more obvious. Therefore in a public move, she announced her decision to depart from Madinah to be far from the usurpers.

Her departure from Madinah accompanied a karāmah[1], which shows her importance and close position to Allāh. It has been narrated:

> *((When Fāṭimah died, Omm Ayman swore not to stay in Madinah, as she could not bear to look at the places where Fāṭimah had used to be; so she left for Makkah.*
> *On the way she became badly thirsty, so she extended her arms towards the sky and said: O Lord! I am Fāṭimah's housemaid, do you kill me by thirst?!*
> *Suddenly a bucket came down to her from the sky, and she drank from it. After that she did not need food or water for seven years.*
> *So she would go out [to the desert] in a very hot day, and she would not become thirsty[2].)).*

5- Omm Salamah

Hend bint Abi Omayyah, known as Omm Salamah, was married to ᶜAbdollāh ibn ᶜAbdol-asad. They were among those who accepted Islam in Makkah, and therefore suffered greatly from the Idolaters.

The Makhzoom Arab tribe, to which they both belonged, separated between Omm Salamah and her husband and took away their son Salamah to force them to renounce their new religion and

---

[1] A supernatural action, etc. performed by or for a Godly person, but not as part of a challenge and not to prove that he or she is a Godly person. Plural karāmāt.

[2] Beḥār al-Anwār / al-Majlesi = vol. 43, page 28.

reaffirm their belief in their old faith. For a period of around a year she was imprisoned by her tribe and denied the right to see her son or husband. But finally one of her cousins intervened and mediated with the chiefs, securing the return of her son to her and her release. When freed, Omm Salamah took her child and headed towards Madinah, where her husband ᶜAbdollāh was living at the time.

ᶜAbdollāh participated in the Battle of Oḥod, in 3 AH, and was wounded in his upper arm. He died several months later of his wound. And in 4 AH Rasōlollāh married Omm Salamah.

She was not just a wife, but also a student who ceased every chance to acquire more knowledge. Seeing her thirst for learning, the Prophet taught her to her upmost capacity, including many things of the *world-of-the-unseen*. The following narration is just an instance:

> *((One day Rasōlollāh was in Omm Salamah's home, and he told her: Do not let anyone come to see me at this time.*
> *Later Ḥosayn came, he was a child, and Omm Salamah could not stop him from going to the Prophet. So she followed Ḥosayn and saw him on his chest, while the Rasōlollāh was crying and examining something in his hand.*
> *Then the Prophet said: O Omm Salamah! This is Jabra'ēl telling me that Ḥosayn will be killed and this is the soil on which he will be killed; so keep it with you, and when it turns into blood, then surely my beloved has been killed*[1].

---

[1] Imām Ḥosayn has a number of miracles that remain to this day. One of them is that the soil on which he was killed turns into blood on the anniversary of his martyrdom, 10 Moḥarram of every year, known as the day of ᶜĀshōrā'. The soil on which he was killed and its vicinity turns into fresh blood, and that of the surrounding area turns into red mud, and that of further away places turns into red soil. And then gradually transforms into its natural shape and color.

My paternal grandfather Āyatollāh al-ᶜOẓmā Sayyed Mahdi Shērāzi, who died on 28 Shaᶜbān 1380 AH, had a small quantity of Torbat al-Ḥosayn which turned into blood on every day of ᶜĀshōrā'; and he stipulated in his will that a portion of it be placed with him inside his grave.

Omm Salamah said: O Rasōlollāh! Ask Allāh to ward off this thing from him.
Rasōlollāh: I have done so; and Allāh the Great, the Almighty revealed to me that he shall have a level that no one of His creatures will have; and that he shall have followers who will intercede and their intercession shall be accepted; and that Mahdi (the Savior) is of his lineage.
So blessed is him who is a friend of Ḥosayn. And his followers are, by Allāh, the winners in the Hereafter[1].)).

After Rasōlollāh's martyrdom, Omm Salamah continued to support Amēr al-Mo'menēn and stood up against the Bakri party and its leaders.

When ᶜĀ'eshah led the Bakri party and marched an army against Imām ᶜAli(AS)[2], Omm Salamah took courageous stances against her, showing her and her supporters that ᶜĀ'eshah was embarking on a mission contrary to Islam.

Omm Salamah has narrated many aḥādēth from Rasōlollāh, Amēr al-Mo'menēn and Sayyedat Nesā' al-ᶜĀlamēn.

6- Salmā

Salmā was a female slave who belonged to Safiyyah, Rasōlollāh's aunt. Safiyyah gave Salmā to Rasōlollāh, and he freed her. She later married Abō Rāfiᶜ, who was himself a freed slave who used to belong to ᶜAbbās, Rasōlollāh's uncle.

It is reported that Salmā nursed Khadējah after she had given birth to Fāṭimah; she was Māriyah's midwife when she gave birth to Rasōlollāh's son Ebrāhēm; and she also did midwifery for Fāṭimah when she gave birth.

Salmā and her husband were both present in the Moslem army at the Battle of Khaybar.

The area of a radius of twenty-four kilometers around the grave of Imām Ḥosayn is regarded as Torbat al-Ḥosayn or the Soil of Ḥosayn.

[1] Beḥār al-Anwār / al-Majlesi = vol. 44, page 225.

[2] *ᶜAlayhes Salām,* peace be upon him.

After the Bakri party usurped the Khelāfah, Salmā and her family stayed with Amēr al-Mo'menēn. She was very close to Fāṭimah, and after the attacks on her home by the Bakri party, she helped in nursing her.

And as you will read later in this book, she helped Fāṭimah get ready for her death, and stayed with her as she died. After her martyrdom, she helped Imām ᶜAli prepare her for burial.

During Amēr al-Mo'menēn's rule, Abō Rāfiᶜ was in charge of the treasury, and his two sons, ᶜObaydollāh and ᶜAli worked as Imām's secretaries.

7- Salmān

According to the aḥādēth, Salmān was one of the three best Ṣaḥābah[1]. He was an Iranian who migrated to Arabia after he heard about the Prophet and his mission. On arrival, some Arabs captured him and sold him as a slave. It is reported that as a slave he served ten different masters; and as soon as Rasōlollāh heard about him and his thirst for Islam, he bought him from his Jewish master and freed him[2].

The following narration shows the importance of Salmān and his closeness to Allāh, and also the kind of prejudice he was subjected to by those who shammed Islam:

> *((Aṣbagh ibn Nabātah narrates from Amēr al-Mo'menēn who said: One day I went to Rasōlollāh, and Salmān was sitting in front of him. Then a Bedouin[3] came, pushed Salmān aside, and sat in his place.*

---

[1] Companions of the Prophet Moḥammad. Singular ṣaḥābi.

[2] Montahā al-Āmāl / al-Qommi (Arabic translation) = vol. 1, page 226.

[3] From the various indications in this ḥadēth, one comes to the conclusion that this Bedouin was actually ᶜOmar himself, but because he became powerful after the usurpation of the khelāfah, his name, as that of his comrades, is usually changed in the aḥādēth that are damaging to him. This is fully supported and laid out in detail by the great scholar al-Qommi in his famous work: "Toḥfat al-Aḥbāb fi Nawādir Āthār al-Aṣḥāb = page 196".

Seeing that, Rasōlollāh became angry, blood filled the vein between his eyes, and his eyes turned red, and he said: O Bedouin! Do you push aside a man whom Allāh likes in the sky and His Messenger likes on the earth?! O Bedouin! Do you push aside a man whom Jabra'ēl instructs me from My Lord, every time he descends, to convey His greetings to him?! O Bedouin! Indeed Salmān is of me; whomsoever is harsh on him, he has surely been harsh on me; and whomsoever annoys him, he has surely annoyed me; and whomsoever isolates him, he has surely made me isolated; and whomsoever shows favor to him, he has surely shown favor to me. O Bedouin! Do not ever be crude with Salmān, for surely Allāh has instructed me to teach him the sciences of Manāyā and Balāyā[1], Ansāb[2] and Faṣl al-kheṭāb[3].

Then the Bedouin said: O Rasōlollāh! I did not think that Salmān would be as you said. Was not he a Magi before converting to Islam?!

So the Prophet said: O Bedouin! I am telling you from my Lord, and you argue with me?! Indeed Salmān

---

Similarly, the "Two Bedouins" is a code often used in such aḥādēth to refer to Abō Bakr and ᶜOmar.

Besides, there was another incident when ᶜOmar belittled Salmān because of his nationality in front of the Prophet, which made the Prophet show a similar reaction. (For more detailed information, see: Rasōlollāh, the Messenger of Allāh / by the author = page 75).

[1] The science or knowledge of Manāyā and Balāyā is a part of ᶜElm al-Ghayb or Knowledge-of-the-Unseen. The individual who has been granted this knowledge, knows exactly when and how each person dies, and when and what afflictions, etc. they will suffer.

[2] The science or knowledge of Ansāb is also a part of ᶜElm al-Ghayb. The individual who has been granted this knowledge knows the correct ancestry of each person, and their real fathers, rather than what has been recorded or believed to be true.

[3] The science or knowledge of Faṣl al-Kheṭāb is also a part of ᶜElm al-Ghayb. The individual who has been granted this knowledge and ability can present an indisputable argument or proof in any subject and put the argument to rest beyond any doubt.

was not a Magi, but he pretended polytheism, keeping his faith secret.
O Bedouin! Have not you heard Allāh, the Great and the Almighty say: "BUT NO! BY YOUR LORD! THEY DO NOT BELIEVE UNTIL THEY MAKE YOU A JUDGE OF THAT WHICH HAS BECOME A MATTER OF DISAGREEMENT AMONG THEM, AND THEN DO NOT FIND ANY STRAITNESS IN THEIR HEARTS AS TO WHAT YOU HAVE DECIDED AND SUBMIT WITH ENTIRE SUBMISSION[1]"?! Have not you heard Allāh, the Great and the Almighty say: "AND WHATEVER THE APOSTLE GIVES YOU, ACCEPT IT, AND FROM WHATEVER HE FORBIDS YOU, KEEP BACK[2]"?! O Bedouin! Accept what I tell you and be of the grateful ones; and do not refuse, so you will be of those who are punished[3].)).

Salmān's amazing drive for learning and his total submission put him at the top of his teachers' lists. They taught him more than the others, and showed him greater things. As ᶜĀ'eshah narrates:

((Every night Salmān had a meeting with Rasōlollāh, when he would talk to him alone for most of the night[4].)).

After Rasōlollāh's martyrdom, Salmān continued to support Amēr al-Mo'menēn against the usurpers, ignoring his disadvantage of being a non-Arab in the Bakri system. He repeatedly objected to the party in public, and suffered greatly.

In one instance, when the Bakris dragged Amēr al-Mo'menēn to the mosque to force him give his pledge of allegiance to Abō Bakr, Salmān was the second person who courageously stood up in protest. He also risked execution, and was severely beaten

---

[1] Holy Qor'ān = sōrah 4, āyah 65.
[2] Holy Qor'ān = sōrah 59, āyah 7.
[3] al-Ekhteṣāṣ / al-Mofēd = page 221.
[4] Beḥār al-Anwār / al-Majlesi = vol. 22, page 391.

when he followed his True Khalēfah[1] in refusing to pledge his allegiance to the False Khalēfah.

Both during the Prophet's life and after his martyrdom, Salmān learned a great deal from Sayyedat Nesā' al-ᶜĀlamēn[2]. Fāṭimah took him to where she had not taken her other students.

The following narration is an example:

> *((Salmān narrates: Ten days after Rasōlollāh's death, I went out of my home and on the way I saw ᶜAli ibn Abi Ṭālib, Rasōlollāh's Cousin. He said to me: O Salmān! You abandoned us after Rasōlollāh!*
> *So I said: O my beloved Abō al-Ḥasan, your kind is not abandoned. But my grief over Rasōlollāh grew longer, and that is what kept me from visiting.*
> *He said: Go to Fāṭimah's home. She likes to give you a gift she was sent from Heaven.*
> *So I said: Fāṭimah was presented with something from Heaven after Rasōlollāh's death?!*
> *He said: Yes; yesterday.*
> *So I ran to Fāṭimah's home, and found her sitting wearing an ᶜAbā'ah[3]. It was so small that if she covered her head with it, her legs would show; and if she covered her legs with it, her head would show [if she were standing]. When she saw me entering, she covered her head with something. Then said: O Salmān! You abandoned me after my father's death!*
> *I said: My beloved, I have not abandoned you.*
> *She said: So sit and pay attention to what I tell you. Yesterday I was sitting here, and the door was locked [from the inside]. I was thinking about the termination of the revelation, and the departure of the angels from our home. Suddenly the door opened without someone unlocking it, and three ladies*

[1] A God-appointed successor of Rasōlollāh. Also caliph. Bakris wrongfully use this title for the leaders of the Bakri party who usurped the Rightful Khelāfah from the a'emmah. Plural Kholafā'.

[2] Chief of the Women of the World; a title given exclusively to Fāṭimah, the Daughter of Rasōlollāh, by Allāh.

[3] A kind of Arabic cloak worn by women.

entered. No one has seen the likes of their beauty and elegance, and the blooming of their faces, and the purity of their scents. When I saw them, I stood up and asked: Are you from Makkah or Madinah?
They said: O daughter of Moḥammad! We are neither from Makkah nor Madinah; we are not from the earth; we are from Heaven. The Lord of Glory has sent us. We have been yearning to see you.
So I asked the one I thought was the oldest of the three: What is your name? She said: My name is Maqdoodah. I asked: And why were you named Maqdoodah? She said: I was created for Meqdād ibn al-Aswad al-Kendi, companion of Rasōlollāh.
And I asked the second woman: What is your name? She said: Dharrah. I asked: And why were you named Dharrah? She said: I was created for Abō Dharr al-Ghefāri, companion of Rasōlollāh.
And I asked the third: What is your name? She said: Salmā. I asked: And why were you named Salmā? She said: I was created for Salmān al-Fārsi, companion of your father Rasōlollāh.
Then Fāṭimah said: The women gave me a gift from Heaven, and I have kept some of it for you. So she brought a tray of dates, whiter than snow, and with a scent better than musk, and gave me five, saying: Break your fast tonight with these, and bring me their stones tomorrow.
So I took the dates and left, and on my way every one asked me: O Salmān! Do you have musk with you? And I said: Yes.
At night, I broke my fast with the dates, but did not find any stones in them. The next day I went to Rasōlollāh's daughter and said: I broke my fast with your gift, but did not find any stones in them.
She said: O Salmān! They would not have any stones. They are from a palm that Allāh has planted in Heaven because of a doʿā' that my father Moḥammad had taught me, which I recite every morning and night.
I said: Teach it to me O my Lady!

So she said: If you wish fever does not afflict you as long as you live in this world, keep reciting this doᶜā': "In the name of Allāh, the Most Compassionate, the Most Merciful. In the name of Allāh, the Light. In the name of Allāh, the Light of the Light. In the name of Allāh, the Light over Light. In the name of Allāh, He Who manages everything. In the name of Allāh He Who created the Light from the Light. Praise be to Allāh He Who created the light from the Light; and descended the light unto the mountain, in a written message, on a spread skin, in a limited quantity, to a delighted prophet. Praise be to Allāh He Who is mentioned in glory, and famous in pride, and thanked in happiness and sadness. And Allāh's peace be upon our master Moḥammad and his maᶜṣōm descendants".
So I learned the doᶜā' and, by Allāh, I taught it to over one thousand people from Makkah and Madinah who were afflicted with different kinds of the fever disease, and every one of them recovered from his illness by Allāh's permission[1].)).

Finally at a very old age, he died in the Iranian capital of that day, Madā'en, now in Iraq, in 36 AH. His shrine, in an area named after him, Salmān Pāk, attracts many pilgrims every day. And his lineage has survived to this day.

[1] Beḥār al-Anwār / al-Majlesi = vol. 95, page 36.

SAYYEDAT NESĀ' AL-ᶜĀLAMĒN IN THE HOLY QOR'ĀN

Important people, good and evil, and important events are usually mentioned in the Holy Qor'ān. So Rasōlollāh has been mentioned just as Abō Bakr has, and ᶜĀ'eshah has been referred to just as Sayyedat Nesā' al-ᶜĀlamēn has.

But when we come to this lady, the sheer number of āyāt revealed about her, and the subjects, are dazzling. These references certainly show her position to Allāh as His third most important and most complete creature.

In his book Fāṭimah al-Zahrā' fi al-Qor'ān, Āyatollāh al-ᶜOẓmā Sayyed Ṣādiq Shērāzi has gathered two hundred and seventy āyāt in sixty-eight sowar[1], all of which were revealed about her according to Bakri references!!

1- The Āyah of Taṭ-hẹr (purification)

In the second half of the thirty-third āyah of the thirty-third sōrah of the Holy Qor'ān, Allah says:

> *﴾Allāh only desires to keep away the uncleanness from you, O Ahl al-Bayt (People of the House)! And to purify you a (thorough) purifying[2].﴿*

[1] Plural of sōrah = A chapter of the Holy Qor'ān.
[2] Holy Qor'ān = sōrah 33, āyah 33.

A number of very important facts can be drawn from this āyah, including: That Fāṭimah was a maᶜṣōmah[1]. And that she was the only female member of Ahl al-Bayt[(AmS)2], and thus senior to all Moslem women, including the Prophet's wives.

And although Bakri[3] scholars have in large numbers accepted these two facts, but they have obstinately insisted on playing down their importance to minimize serious contradictions within their system of beliefs.

In the first instance, they say Fāṭimah was a maᶜṣōmah[4] who did not commit any sin. However, after her father's martyrdom she testified, on many occasions, in favor of Amēr al-Mo'menēn as the Khalēfah, and against Abō Bakr as the Usurper of the Khelāfah; and publicly and loudly protested against and condemned the unIslamic actions of the Bakri party. Her objections were so intense, that Abō Bakr found no alternative other than killing her.

So if she was a maᶜṣōmah, according to Allāh, who did not lie, then why were her testimonies so shamelessly rejected?!

And in the second instance, the overwhelming majority of Bakri scholars agree that Fāṭimah was the only female member of Ahl al-Bayt[5] who have a special place in Islam, and admit that even ᶜĀ'eshah was not a member.

So, does not this mean Fāṭimah was senior to ᶜĀ'eshah?! If being a member of Ahl al-Bayt does not bring seniority, then what

---

[1] The feminine form of maᶜṣōm: a person who does not commit sins, does not make mistakes, does not forget, etc.

[2] *ᶜAlayhemos Salām,* peace be upon them.

[3] A Bakri is a follower of Abō Bakr. Opposite Moslem, Shēᶜah, follower of Rasōlollāh. Some people unknowingly call the followers of Abō Bakr "Sonnis". Sonni means a follower of the tradition of Rasōlollāh; and since the followers of Abō Bakr follow him and not Rasōlollāh, it is wrong to call them Sonnis.

[4] al-Fakhr al-Rāzi, perhaps the most senior Bakri scholar who has worked on the Holy Qor'ān in the last millennium, writes in his widely used reference "Mafātēḥ al-Ghayb = vol. 2, page 700": ((This āyah means that these five people: Moḥammad, ᶜAli, Fāṭimah, Ḥasan and Ḥosayn are clean from big and small sins.)). (Naẓariyyāt al-Khalēfatayn / al-Ṭā'i = vol. 1, page 153)

[5] The Fourteen Maᶜṣōmēn, who are Rasōlollāh, Sayyedat Nesā' al-ᶜĀlamēn, and the twelve God-appointed successors of Rasōlollāh.

does?! And if it does bring seniority, then why was ᶜĀ'eshah's testimony favored over Fāṭimah's?!

However, a small number of Bakri scholars stubbornly insist that the wives of the Prophet are also included in Ahl al-Bayt. But this false claim is easily refuted by the following facts:

1- The overwhelming majority of Bakri aḥādēth only name Rasōlollāh, Amēr al-Mo'menēn, Sayyedat Nesā' al-ᶜĀlamēn, Imām Ḥasan and Imām Ḥosayn as members of Ahl al-Bayt, and do not mention the Prophet's wives[1]. For instance, Bakri scholars narrate from ᶜĀ'eshah, who said:

> *((While Rasōlollāh was covered with a blanket, Ḥasan came, and he took him under the blanket; then Ḥosayn came, and went under the blanket; then Fāṭimah came, and he took her under the blanket; then ᶜAli came, and he took him under the blanket; then he recited: "ALLĀH ONLY DESIRES TO KEEP AWAY THE UNCLEANNESS FROM YOU, O AHL AL-BAYT (PEOPLE OF THE HOUSE)! AND TO PURIFY YOU A (THOROUGH) PURIFYING[2]"[3].)).*

---

[1] To read some of these aḥādēth, see the following Bakri references: al-Dorr al-Manthōr / al-Soyōṭi = vol. 5, page 198. al-Eṣābah / al-ᶜAsqalāni = vol. 4, page 568. al-Etqān / al-Soyōṭi = vol. 2, page 200. Faḍā'el al-Ṣaḥābah / Ibn Ḥanbal = vol. 2, pages 672, 684 and 786. al-Kash-shāf / al-Zamakhshari = vol. 1, page 193. al-Khaṣā'eṣ al-Kobrā / al-Soyōṭi = vol. 2, page 264. Majmaᶜ al-Zawā'ed / al-Haythami = vol. 7, page 91; vol. 9, pages 119 and 167. al-Moᶜjam al-Awsaṭ / al-Ṭabarāni = vol. 3, page 166; vol. 4, page 134. al-Moᶜjam al-Kabēr / al-Ṭabarāni = vol. 12, page 98; vol. 23, page 337. al-Mostadrak / al-Naysābōri = vol. 3, pages 143 and 159. Ṣaḥēḥ / Moslem = vol. 4 , page 1883. Seyar Aᶜlām al-Nobalā' / al-Dhahabi = vol. 3, page 315. al-Sonan al-Kobrā / al-Bayhaqi = vol. 2, page 149. Jāmiᶜ al-Bayān fi Tafsēr al-Qor'ān / al-Ṭabari = vol. 22, pages 6, 7 and 8.

[2] Holy Qor'ān = sōrah 33, āyah 33.

[3] Moṣannaf / Ibn Abi Shaybah = vol. 6, page 370. Mosnad / Esḥāq ibn Rāhawayh = vol. 3, page 678. al-Mostadrak / al-Naysābōri = vol. 3, page 159. Ṣaḥēḥ / Moslem = vol. 4, page 1883. al-Sonan al-Kobrā / al-Bayhaqi = vol. 2, page 149. Tafsēr al-Qor'ān al-ᶜAẓēm / Ibn Kothayr = vol. 3, page 486. Jāmiᶜ al-Bayān fi Tafsēr al-Qor'ān / al-Ṭabari = vol. 22, page 6.

2- A large number of Bakri aḥādēth clearly limits members of Ahl al-Bayt to those five, excluding others[1]. For instance, Bakri references record:

> *((When the āyah "ALLĀH ONLY DESIRES TO KEEP AWAY THE UNCLEANNESS FROM YOU, O AHL AL-BAYT (PEOPLE OF THE HOUSE)! AND TO PURIFY YOU A (THOROUGH) PURIFYING[2]" was revealed, Rasōlollāh called ᶜAli, Fāṭimah, Ḥasan and Ḥosayn; then he covered them with a Khaybari blanket, and said: O Allāh! These are my Ahl al-Bayt. O Allāh! Keep away the uncleanness from them, and purify them a (thorough) purifying[3].)).*

3- Neither ᶜĀ'eshah nor the other wives of Rasōlollāh did ever claim membership to Ahl al-Bayt, even though some of them

---

[1] To read some of these aḥādēth, see the following Bakri references:
al-Eṣābah / al-ᶜAsqalāni = vol. 8, page 56. al-Esteᶜāb / Ibn ᶜAbdelbarr = vol. 3, page 1100. Faḍā'el al-Ṣaḥābah / Ibn Ḥanbal = vol. 2, page577. Fatḥ al-Bāri / al-ᶜAsqalāni = vol. 7, page 138. Majmaᶜ al-Zawā'ed / al-Haythami = vol. 9, page 167. Mawārid al-Ẓam'ān = vol. 1, page 555. al-Moᶜjam al-Awsaṭ / al-Ṭabarāni = vol. 2, page 371; vol. 7, page 319. al-Moᶜjam al-Kabēr / al-Ṭabarāni = vol. 23, page 334. al-Moᶜjam al-Ṣaghēr / al-Ṭabarāni = vol. 1, page 120. Moᶜjam al-Shoyōkh / al-Ṣaydāwi = vol. 1, page 133. Mosnad / al-Bazzār = vol. 6, page 210. Mosnad / Aḥmad = vol. 4, page 107. Moṣannaf / Ibn Abi Shaybah = vol. 6, page 370. al-Mostadrak / al-Naysābōri = vol. 2, page 251; vol. 3, pages 158 and 159. Seyar Aᶜlām al-Nobalā' / al-Dhahabi = vol. 3, page 254. al-Sonan al-Kobrā / al-Bayhaqi = vol. 2, page 150; vol. 5, pages 107 and 113. al-Sonnah / Ibn Abi ᶜĀsim = vol. 2, page 603. Tafsēr al-Qor'ān al-ᶜAẓēm / Ibn Kothayr = vol. 3, pages 484 and 485. Jāmiᶜ al-Bayān fi Tafsēr al-Qor'ān / al-Ṭabari = vol. 22, page 6. Tahdhēb al-Tahdhēb = vol. 2, page 258.
It has also been narrated:

> *((...And when Rasōlollāh saw the Blessing (revelation) descending, he said: Call for me! Call for me!*
> *Safiyyah asked: Whom O Rasōlollāh?*
> *Rasōlollāh said: My Ahl al-Bayt: ᶜAli, Fāṭimah, Ḥasan and Ḥosayn)).* (al-Mostadrak / al-Naysābōri = vol. 3, page 159)

[2] Holy Qor'ān = sōrah 33, āyah 33.
[3] Jāmiᶜ al-Bayān fi Tafsēr al-Qor'ān / al-Ṭabari = vol. 22, page 7.

were struggling to gain medals and seniority over Fāṭimah and other members of Ahl al-Bayt. On the contrary, they acknowledged Fāṭimah's membership and admitted their exclusion[1]. For instance,

---

[1] All the aḥādēth that name the five members of Ahl al-Bayt and state the exclusion of Rasōlollāh's wives from Ahl al-Bayt, were narrated by either ᶜĀ'eshah or by Omm Salamah. The sentences that exclude the Prophet's wives from Ahl al-Bayt differ in words, but provide the same meaning. The following are some examples:

> *((...I went near them and said: Am I a member of your Ahl al-Bayt? Rasōlollāh said: Step back.)).* (Tafsēr al-Qor'ān al-ᶜAẓēm / Ibn Kothayr = vol. 3, page 486)
>
> *((...And me? But, By Allāh! he [Rasōlollāh] did not agree and said: You are to a good ending [you will die a good person].)).* (Tafsēr al-Qor'ān al-ᶜAẓēm / Ibn Kothayr = vol. 3, page 485. Jāmiᶜ al-Bayān fi Tafsēr al-Qor'ān / al-Ṭabari = vol. 22, page 8)
>
> *((Am I a member of Ahl al-Bayt? Rasōlollāh said: You are my family, and these are my Ahl al-Bayt.)).* (al-Mostadrak / al-Naysābōri = vol. 2, page 451)
>
> *((...Count me with them. Rasōlollāh said: You are a member of my family.)).* (Tafsēr al-Qor'ān al-ᶜAẓēm / Ibn Kothayr = vol. 3, page 486. Jāmiᶜ al-Bayān fi Tafsēr al-Qor'ān / al-Ṭabari = vol. 22, page 8)
>
> *((Am I a member of Ahl al-Bayt? Rasōlollāh said: You are a member of my family.)).* (al-Moᶜjam al-Kabēr / al-Ṭabarāni = vol. 3, page 53. Mo'tasar al-Mokhtaṣar / Abō al-Maḥāsin al-Ḥanafi = vol. 2, page 266. Ṣaḥēḥ / Ibn Ḥabbān = vol. 15, page 432)
>
> *((Am I a member of Ahl al-Bayt? Rasōlollāh said: You are in your position, and you are good.)).* (al-Moᶜjam al-Kabēr / al-Ṭabarāni = vol. 9, page 25. Sonan / al-Termedhi = vol. 5, pages 351 and 663. al-Jāmiᶜ le Aḥkām al-Qor'ān / al-Qorṭobi = vol. 14, page 183. Jamiᶜ al-Bayān fi Tafsēr al-Qor'ān / al-Ṭabari = vol. 22, page 8)
>
> *((Am I a member of Ahl al-Bayt? Rasōlollāh said: You are with your neighbors to a good ending.)).* (Mosnad / Aḥmad = vol. 6, page 292)
>
> *((Am I a member of Ahl al-Bayt? Rasōlollāh said: You are to a good ending.)).* al-Moᶜjam al-Kabēr / al-Ṭabarāni = vol. 3, page 52; vol. 23, pages 249, 333 and 396. Mosnad / Abi Ya'li = vol. 12, page 451. Mosnad / Aḥmad = vol. 6, page 304. Seyar Aᶜlām al-Nobalā' / al-Dhahabi = vol. 3, page 283; vol. 10, page 347. Sonan / al-Termedhi = vol. 5, page 699. Tārēkh Baghdād / al-Baghdādi= vol. 9, page 126; vol. 10, page 278. Tahdhēb al-Kamāl / al-Mazzi =

Bakri scholars narrate from cĀ'eshah*(LAa)*[1], Fāṭimah's enemy, who said in a long ḥadēth:

> *((...Indeed, I saw Rasōlollāh one day call cAli, Fāṭimah, Ḥasan and Ḥosayn; then he covered them with a cloth and said: O Allāh! These are my Ahl al-Bayt, so keep away the uncleanness from them and purify them a (thorough) purifying.*
> *So I went near them and said: O Rasōlollāh! Am I a member of your Ahl al-Bayt?*
> *And he said: Step back*[2]*.)).*

Bakri references also narrate from Omm Salamah, Fāṭimah's friend, who said:

> *((One day Rasōlollāh came to my home, and said: Do not let anyone come in. Later Fāṭimah came, and I could not keep her away from her father; then Ḥasan came, and I could not keep him away from his grandfather and mother; then Ḥosayn came, and I could not keep him away from his grandfather and mother; then cAli came, and I could not keep him away.*
> *So they gathered, and Rasōlollāh covered them with the blanket that was on him and said: These are my Ahl al-Bayt, so keep away the uncleanness from them, and purify them a (thorough) purifying. Then,*

---

vol. 6, page 229. Tafsēr al-Qor'ān al-cAẓēm / Ibn Kothayr = vol. 3, page 485. Jāmic al-Bayān fi Tafsēr al-Qor'ān / al-Ṭabari = vol. 22, page 7)

((Am I a member of Ahl al-Bayt? Rasōlollāh said: You are to a good ending, you are a wife of the Prophet.)). (al-Mocjam al-Kabēr / al-Ṭabarāni = vol. 3, page 54; vol. 23, page 281. Mo'tasar al-Mokhtaṣar / Abō al-Maḥāsin al-Ḥanafi = vol. 2, page 267. Tafsēr al-Qor'ān al-cAẓēm / Ibn Kothayr = vol. 3, page 485. Jāmic al-Bayān fi Tafsēr al-Qor'ān / al-Ṭabari = vol. 22, page 7)

[1] *Lacnatollāh cAlayha,* may Allāh distance her from His Blessings and Mercy.

[2] Tafsēr al-Qor'ān al-cAẓēm / Ibn Kothayr = vol. 3, page 486.

when they were all under the blanket, this āyah descended.
So I said: O Rasōlollāh! And me? But, by Allāh! he did not agree, and said: You are to a good ending [you will die a good person][1].)).

4- There is not a single ḥadēth in which the Prophet or the other members of Ahl al-Bayt mention the inclusion of the Prophet's wives in Ahl al-Bayt. On the contrary, they only name themselves, as the only members. For instance, Bakri references narrate from Rasōlollāh, who said:

((This āyah was revealed about five people: About me, ᶜAli, Ḥasan, Ḥosayn and Fāṭimah. "ALLĀH ONLY DESIRES TO KEEP AWAY THE UNCLEANNESS FROM YOU, O AHL AL-BAYT (PEOPLE OF THE HOUSE)! AND TO PURIFY YOU A (THOROUGH) PURIFYING[2]"[3].)).

5- The revelation of this āyah was followed by many theatrical acts by Rasōlollāh over a long period of time, practically showing who were members of Ahl al-Bayt and who were not.

He would gather them under a cloth, recite the Āyah of Taṭhēr and call them Ahl al-Bayt. He would regularly go to the house of ᶜAli and Fāṭimah, recite the Āyah and call them Ahl al-Bayt. He did these things intentionally and frequently and regularly to show its importance.

And in the hundreds of times when he performed these shows, he never missed one person of the five, and never included one person other than the five; even though he could have included at least ᶜĀ'eshah—whom the Bakris regard as the most noble woman in Islam and the closest to the Prophet—or Umm Salamah, both of whom asked to be included.

---

[1] Tafsēr al-Qor'ān al-ᶜAẓēm / Ibn Kothayr = vol. 3, page 485. Jāmiᶜ al-Bayān fi Tafsēr al-Qor'ān / al-Ṭabari = vol. 22, page 8.
[2] Holy Qor'ān = sōrah 33, āyah 33.
[3] Majmaᶜ al-Zawā'ed / al-Haythami = vol. 9, page 167. Tafsēr al-Qor'ān al-ᶜAẓēm / Ibn Kothayr = vol. 3, page 486. Jāmiᶜ al-Bayān fi Tafsēr al-Qor'ān / al-Ṭabari = vol. 22, page 6.

And these theatrical acts were witnessed by countless people who narrated them in large numbers, surviving the tight Bakri censorship. Therefore, today, Bakri references contain a significant number of these narrations; for instance they narrate from Ibn ᶜAbbās, ᶜOmar's first secretary, who said:

> *((During nine months, I witnessed Rasōlollāh go everyday at the time of every ṣalāt—five times a day—to the door of ᶜAli ibn Abi Ṭālib, saying: Assalāmo ᶜAlaykom wa Raḥmatollāh wa Barakātoh (peace and Allāh's Mercy and Blessing be upon you) O Ahl al-Bayt! "ALLĀH ONLY DESIRES TO KEEP AWAY THE UNCLEANNESS FROM YOU, O AHL AL-BAYT (PEOPLE OF THE HOUSE)! AND TO PURIFY YOU A (THOROUGH) PURIFYING[1]". ṣalāt! May Allāh be Merciful to you[2].)).*

---

[1] Holy Qor'ān = sōrah 33, āyah 33.

[2] al-Dorr al-Manthōr / al-Soyōṭi = vol. 5, page 199. Others have also narrated similar aḥādēth, varying in the period of time during which they were with the Prophet. Some of them narrate that they witnessed him going to Fāṭimah's door and reciting the Āyah of Taṭ-hēr, everyday for seventeen months. To read some of these aḥādēth see the following Bakri references: al-Esteᶜāb / Ibn ᶜAbdelbarr = vol. 4, page 1542. Faḍā'el al-Ṣaḥābah / Ibn Ḥanbal = vol. 2, page 761. Kanz al-ᶜOmmāl / al-Hendi = vol. 7, page 103. al-Konā / al-Bokhāri = vol. 1, page 25. Majmaᶜ al-Zawā'ed / al-Haythami = vol. 9, pages 121, 168 and 169. Mēzān al-Eᶜtedāl / al-Dhahabi = vol. 4, page 47. al-Moᶜjam al-Kabēr / al-Ṭabarāni = vol. 3, page 56; vol. 22, pages 200 and 402. Mo'tasar al-Mokhtaṣar / Abō al-Maḥāsin al-Ḥanafi = vol. 2, page 267. Moṣannaf / Ibn Abi Shaybah = vol. 6, page 388. Moshkel al-Āthār / al-Ṭaḥāwi = vol. 1, page 338. Mosnad / al-Ḥomaydi = vol. 1, pages 173 and 367. Mosnad / Abi Yaᶜlā = vol. 7, page 59. Mosnad / Aḥmad = vol. 3, page 285. Mosnad / al-Ṭayālisi = vol. 1, page 274. al-Mostadrak / al-Naysābōri = vol. 3, page 172. Osd al-Ghābah / Ibn al-Athēr = vol. 5, page 521. Seyar Aᶜlām al-Nobalā' / al-Dhahabi = vol. 2, page 134. Sonan / al-Termedhi = vol. 5, page 352. Ṭabaqāt al-Moḥaddethēn be-Eṣbahān = vol. 4, page 148. Tafsēr al-Qor'ān al-ᶜAẓēm / Ibn Kothayr = vol. 3, page 484. Jāmiᶜ al-Bayān fi Tafsēr al-Qor'ān / al-Ṭabari = vol. 22, page 6. Tahdhēb al-Kamāl / al-Mazzi = vol. 33, page 259; vol. 35, page 251.

Aside from Bakri scholars and their references, when we look at this part of the āyah and look at the context in which it was used, we find a most extraordinary thing. Opposite pronouns.

In the related āyāt before and after this āyah, the pronouns are all feminine plural; and even the first part of this āyah has as many as six feminine plural pronouns. But the second part of this āyah has two, out of place, masculine plural pronouns. Irregular, inconsistent, improper and immethodical use of pronouns, a mistake!! But does Allāh the Almighty make mistakes?! Of course not; anyone who believes Allāh makes mistakes does not believe in Islam. So why this unexampled choice of pronoun?

A small minority of scholars who believe in the distortion of the Holy Qor'ān[1] say this āyah is a clear example of distortion. The

---

[1] In the fourteen hundred year history of Islam, there has been a small but sometimes powerful group of people who propagated the idea of the distortion of the Holy Qor'ān. This belief has not been specific to a particular sect, but scholars of many sects, if not all, have at times firmly asserted it.

Distortion can take several forms: It can be an addition, when something is added to the Holy Qor'ān; it can be a deletion, when something is deleted from the Holy Qor'ān; it can be a displacement, when some part of the Holy Qor'ān is taken from its right place and put in a wrong place; or it can be an alteration, when something is changed in the Holy Qor'ān. And the adherents of this opinion differ amongst themselves about the definition of "distortion".

However, according to numerous scholars who have tackled this issue in recent times, the school of distortion has less pupils now than it used to have centuries before. This maybe related to the absence of knowledgeable and senior scholars of the Bakri faith who would be able to conduct fresh examinations of the subject; and to lack of new exhaustive researches and extensive studies by Moslem scholars.

In any case, prominent Bakri references such as: Ṣaḥēḥ / al-Bokhāri (which the Bakris claim to be the most reliable book after the Holy Qor'ān) narrate from their leaders like ᶜOmar, who loudly advocated the idea of the distortion of the Holy Qor'ān*

And respected Moslem references such as Beḥār al-Anwār (which is one of the two largest hadēth encyclopedias) narrate from Moslem leaders such as Amēr al-Mo'menēn, who pointed to places of distortions in the Holy Qor'ān during the rule of the Usurpers of the Khelāfah**

The Bakri's explanation for the distortions has been that throughout the years people forgot parts of the Qor'ān and little by little distortion inadvertently accord. But Moslems strongly reject the idea of people's inattentiveness to the Holy Qor'ān, especially during those first years of Islam; stating that numerous people had memorized the whole of the Qor'ān, and that the Holy Qor'ān had been gathered and written during the life of Prophet Moḥammad, so it could not have been mistakenly distorted.

Therefore, those Moslems who believe in the distortion of the Holy Qor'ān firmly state that it was carried out by Bakri rulers after the martyrdom of Rasōlollāh; and that most, if not all, of the distortion had to do with ousting the Rightful Kholafā' and stripping them of their God-given honors.

And according to them, it continued beyond the second Hejri century, around one hundred and seventy years after the Third Usurper of the Khelāfah, the first Amawi ruler, ᶜOthmān, distributed many copies of the Holy Qor'ān to chosen cities within his great empire, supposedly for safekeeping.

And because those Moslems who believe in the idea of distortion point their finger at Bakri rulers, the Bakris are lately saying: only the Moslems believe in the idea of the distortion, and use this as a weapon against the Moslems; ignoring the fact that Bakri propagators of this idea have been much more, in number and strength, than the Moslems.

But no matter what they exaggerate and what they forget, Bakris either have to believe in the idea of distortion, or they have to reject the idea that their ṣeḥaḥ (plural of ṣaḥēḥ) including "Ṣaḥēḥ / al-Bokhāri" are immune from falsification. As these ṣeḥaḥ, which are claimed to be entirely authentic, include a significant number of narrations that clearly state distortion did happen, and in many cases even point to the places of distortion.

But as far as the Moslems are concerned, no ḥadēth reference is recognized as entirely authentic, and all aḥādēth are subject to examination by specialists; and those that are marked as ṣaḥēḥ by one specialist are not automatically marked as such by others. Therefore as far as the Moslems are concerned, the mere fact that there are numerous aḥādēth pointing to distortion does not necessarily mean it did take place, as in this field, like every other field, a Moslem scholar has to determine the authenticity of the relevant aḥādēth before reaching the conclusion. And in this case, like any other case, it could go either way.

---

* You can read one such ḥadēth in: Ṣaḥēḥ / al-Bokhāri = vol. 6, page 2504; other ṣeḥaḥ and other Bakri references also record this narration. There are also many other narrations from Bakri leaders such as ᶜOmar, in which they state that entire chapters of the Holy Qor'ān were deleted, etc.

construction of this sentence is completely different to that of its environment; the second part of the āyah, with its masculine references, is obviously stranger to this entire passage. They say this part of the āyah was taken from the seventy-sixth sōrah—where at least half the sōrah refers to Rasōlollāh, Amēr al-Mo'menēn, Sayyedat Nesā' al-ᶜĀlamēn, Imām Ḥasan and Imām Ḥosayn—and placed here, within a number of āyāt that refer to the Prophet's wives, to cause confusion.

But this opinion is rejected by the overwhelming majority of scholars who do not agree with the idea of the distortion of the Holy Qor'ān.

Others say that there is no irregularity what so ever. The masculine pronouns were used to include the Prophet himself, who was addressed by Allāh in the beginning of the section. And in the Arabic grammar, masculine pronoun is used when referring to a male together with several females.

But this opinion is also rejected, as according to all Bakri and Moslem scholars, the masculine pronouns in question also include Amēr al-Mo'menēn, Sayyedat Nesā' al-ᶜĀlamēn, Imām Ḥasan and Imām Ḥosayn, none of whom are referred to either before or after this verse.

This brings us to the third and widely believed opinion: that the second part of the āyah is indeed out of place, but it is not due to distortion. This sentence was especially placed here to make it more eye-catching and draw more attention to its meaning.

** One such narration from Amēr al-Mo'menēn is as follows:

> *((...And another example [another instance of distortion] in the seventy-eighth sōrah: "AND THE UNBELIEVER SHALL SAY: O! I WISH I WERE TORĀBIYYAN!" (Holy Qor'ān = 78:40) So they distorted it and said: "torāban"; and that is because Rasōlollāh often called me Abō Torāb.)).* (Beḥār al-Anwār / al-Majlesi = vol. 93, page 27).

Torāban or torāb means: dust. It sounds very similar to Torābiyyan which means: a Torābi, a follower of Abō Torāb. According to this ḥadēth, on the Day of Judgment, when the unbeliever sees his position and that of the Moslems who follow Imām ᶜAli, he wishes he were also one of his followers.

2- The Āyah of Mobāhalah

One of the many āyāt that refer to Fāṭimah is the sixty-first āyah of the third sōrah in the Holy Qor'ān, known as the "Āyah of Mobāhalah".

In a series of āyāt, Allāh speaks of His prophets and their successors, highlighting a number of very important events in their lives. Concentrating on the family of ᶜĒsā[1], Allāh narrates the story of the birth of the Virgin Maryam[2], showing her closeness to Him and recounting some of what Prophet Zakariyyā[3] had witnessed from Maryam. Then the revelation focuses on ᶜĒsā himself, his miraculous conception and birth, his God-given powers, his struggle to guild the Jews, their blind bigotry, and his rise to the sky; rejecting the belief that he is the Son of God.

At the end of this passage Allāh says to His Prophet Moḥammad:

> ﴿*BUT WHOEVER DISPUTES WITH YOU IN THIS MATTER AFTER WHAT HAS COME TO YOU OF KNOWLEDGE, THEN SAY: COME LET US CALL OUR SONS AND YOUR SONS AND OUR WOMEN AND YOUR WOMEN AND OUR SELVES AND YOUR SELVES, THEN LET US BE EARNEST IN PRAYER, AND PRAY FOR THE CURSE OF ALLĀH ON THE LIARS*[4].﴾.

In the tenth year of Hejrah when Moslem rule expanded to a number of countries beyond the Arabian peninsula, the Christian leaders of Arabia who had not entered a war with Moslems decided to have a decisive debate with Rasōlollāh. Hoping to overcome him and destroy his rule with the power of logic, rather than that of the sword, as other groups had futilely attempted.

Thus Abō Hārithah, ᶜAqib and Sayyed, the highest Arab Christian leaders came to Madinah to meet with the Prophet.

---

[1] Also Jesus.
[2] Also Mary.
[3] Also Zacharias.
[4] Holy Qor'ān = sōrah 3, āyah 61.

During the debate, Abō Hārithah who spoke for the Christians, lost on every point he raised, but nevertheless insisted on his beliefs and refused to concede defeat.

Finally, after Rasōlollāh had exhausted all other intellectual methods, Allāh revealed this āyah, and His Messenger called his challengers to mobāhalah, when they would go out to the desert and each party would pray to their God to descend a calamity on the liar; leaving it to God to show who is truthful and who is not. And Rasōlollāh announced that he will be the victorious party and that his God will bring disaster to the Christians after the Mobāhalah; and the Christians promised to be the only party standing after the Mobāhalah, when the Moslems would wither.

Time and place were agreed upon, and the unusual show of strength was set to bring conclusive proof for one side and ultimate defeat for the other.

As the moment of truth approached, Christians decided to go ahead with the Mobāhalah only if Moḥammad came with a large number of people, which to them was a sign of showmanship; but would refuse to take part in the Mobāhalah if he had come with few people, which to them was a sign prophethood.

The next day, Moḥammad approached the Christians who had gathered in the desert, taking the hands of his grandsons, Ḥasan and Ḥosayn, and having his nephew and son-in-law, ᶜAli, walking in front of him, and his daughter Fāṭimah behind him. When they reached the agreed spot, Moḥammad sat and told his family to say āmēn[1] to his prayers as soon as the Mobāhalah started.

Suddenly, the Christians refused to start the Mobāhalah, when their leader Abō Hārithah told them:

> *((I see faces that if it were to ask God to remove a mountain from its place, He would do it for them. Do not enter into a Mobāhalah with them, or you will be destroyed and no Christian will remain on the face of the earth[2].)).*

---

[1] Also amen.

[2] Rasōlollāh, the Messenger of Allāh / by the author = page 114.

So instead of Mobāhalah, they reached an agreement with the Prophet to come under his rule. Later, both ᶜĀqib and Sayyed announced their conversion to Islam.

In this āyah, Allāh instructs His Prophet to challenge his enemies to Mobāhalah, using it as his last weapon of logic; and orders him to be accompanied by his "sons", "women" and "selves" (the closest people to him).

And since Allāh tells His creatures about Moḥammad, saying:

> ﴿*I SWEAR BY THE STAR WHEN IT GOES DOWN * YOUR COMPANION (MOḤAMMAD) DOES NOT ERR, NOR DOES HE GO ASTRAY * NOR DOES HE SPEAK OUT OF DESIRE * IT IS NAUGHT BUT REVELATION THAT IS REVEALED * THE LORD OF MIGHTY POWER HAS TAUGHT HIM * THE LORD OF STRENGTH; SO HE ATTAINED COMPLETION*[1].﴾

We learn that his choices reflect God's will, and not human desire. Thus when he chooses to take Amēr al-Mo'menēn with him to the Mobāhalah, as his "self", we know that ᶜAli is the closest man to Allāh after Moḥammad; and when he chooses to take Imām Ḥasan and Imām Ḥosayn as his "sons", we know that Ḥasan and Ḥosayn are the closest men to Allāh after Moḥammad and ᶜAli; and when he chooses to take Sayyedat Nesā' al-ᶜĀlamēn as his "women", we know that Fāṭimah is the closest woman to Allāh.

Also, not having anyone else go with him to the Mobāhalah as his "sons", "women" or "selves" has a lot of meaning. He could have chosen Abō Bakr and/or ᶜOmar as his "selves", for example; as he could have chosen ᶜĀ'eshah and/or Ḥafṣah as his "women". But he did not.

To escape from this difficult and embarrassing position, a number of Bakris have tried to cause confusion and in some way suggest that the Prophet did not take these four people with him to the Mobāhalah, or that he also took others. They say that these three pronouns are all plural: "sons", "women" and "selves", which in the Arabic language mean three and more. So how can the Prophet take only Ḥasan and Ḥosayn as his "sons", Fāṭimah as his "women" and

---

[1] Holy Qor'ān = sōrah 53, āyāt 1 to 6.

ᶜAli as his "selves"?! Therefore he must have also taken others with him.

But they are ignoring the fact that the use of plural pronouns for two and even one is not new in the Arabic language. In fact the Qor'ān, itself, is filled with such examples. For instance, Allāh says in the Holy Qor'ān:

> *﴾SURELY WE HAVE REVEALED THE REMINDER AND WE WILL MOST SURELY BE ITS GUARDIAN[1].﴿.*

Whom besides Allāh has revealed the Holy Qor'ān?! And whom besides Him is its guardian?!

Allāh also says:

> *﴾SURELY WE OURSELVES HAVE REVEALED THE QOR'ĀN TO YOU, REVEALING (IT) IN PORTIONS[2].﴿.*

Some Bakris say that "sons" means ones own sons or those of his sons or grandsons. But Ḥasan and Ḥosayn were the sons of Rasōlollāh's daughter; and the children of ones daughter are not counted as ones children!! So the Prophet could not have taken them to the Mobāhalah as his "sons".

They are also ignoring the fact that this idea was of the pre-Islam Arabs, who did not count their daughters as members of their families, and did not look at women as members of the society; thus they would not call the sons of their daughters, their "sons". But Islam fought this belief, as many other Arab beliefs.

And even in the Holy Qor'ān Allāh counted ᶜĒsā among the children of Ebrāhēm, even though he reached Ebrāhēm[3] through his mother Maryam. Allāh says:

> *﴾AND OF HIS DESCENDANTS, DĀWŌD[4] AND SOLAYMĀN[5] AND AYYŌB[1] AND YŌSOF[2] AND MŌSĀ[3] AND HĀRŌN[4]; AND THUS*

---

[1] Holy Qor'ān = sōrah 15, āyah 9.
[2] Holy Qor'an = sōrah 76, āyah 23.
[3] Also Abraham.
[4] Also David.
[5] Also Solomon.

*DO WE REWARD THOSE WHO DO GOOD (TO OTHERS) * AND ZAKARIYYĀ AND YAḤYĀ[5] AND ᶜĒSĀ AND ELYĀS; EVERYONE WAS OF THE GOOD[6].*﴾.

Some Bakris who are even more desperate say that all of the aḥādēth[7] that say Rasōlollāh took Ḥasan, Ḥosayn, Fāṭimah and ᶜAli with him to the Mobāhalah have been narrated by the Shēᶜah[8], and therefore they are not acceptable.

But a mere glance at the chains of narrators of these aḥādēth clearly shows that a large number of them do not have a single Shēᶜah narrator or a single Shēᶜah reference. In fact, such aḥādēth have also been narrated in certain Bakri references whose authors do not mention any ḥadēth narrated by the Shēᶜah.

The overwhelming majority of Bakri scholars confess that Rasōlollāh only chose ᶜAli, Fāṭimah, Ḥasan and Ḥosayn for the Mobāhalah; and that he did not take anyone else with him[9].

Rasōlollāh's choice shows the positions of these four people, and their closeness to Allāh is such that if they were to ask Him to descend calamity on the Christians, He would have obliged.

3- The Āyah of Qorbā

When Rasōlollāh started his mission and called on the Idolaters, Star-worshippers, Moon-worshippers, Jews, Christians, etc. to turn their backs to their fathers' beliefs and follow him in

[1] Also Job.
[2] Also Joseph.
[3] Also Moses.
[4] Also Aaron.
[5] Also John.
[6] Holy Qor'ān = sōrah 6, āyāt 84 and 85.
[7] Plural of ḥadēth: a narration from one of the Fourteen Maᶜṣōmēn.
[8] Moslem, a follower of Rasōlollāh and Amēr al-Mo'menēn. Opposite Bakri: a follower of Abō Bakr. Shēᶜah is used as singular and as plural.
[9] Maᶜrifat ᶜOlōm al-Ḥadēth / al-Naysābōri = vol. 1, page 50. Sonan / Saᶜēd ibn Manṣōr = vol. 3, page 1044. Tafsēr / al-Jalālayn = vol. 1, page 75. al-Jāmiᶜ le Aḥkām al-Qor'ān / al-Qorṭobi = vol. 4, page 104. Jāmiᶜ al-Bayān fi Tafsēr al-Qor'ān / al-Ṭabari = vol. 3, page 299. Toḥfah / al-Āḥōdhi = vol. 8, page 278.

worshipping the one indivisible God instead, not only did he put his high social standing in jeopardy, but his life.

He was subjected to unbearable pressure from every corner, isolated, tortured both physically and psychologically, imprisoned, and survived from several assassination attempts.

The Truthful, the Trustworthy, as the Arabs used to call him, suddenly became: the Sorcerer, the Liar. His wife, Khadējah, the richest and most influential woman in the Arabian Peninsula, was shown less respect than her servants. And those who answered his call had their own share of troubles. Some of them perished under brutal torture.

But the Arabs wanted to have their once-adored Moḥammad back; so alongside suppression, they offered him a way to return. To renounce his God and show devotion to their idols, and thus become the chief of all the tribe leaders, controlling all of their wealth and having all the power.

However as the Prophet insisted more and more on his mission, his enemies insisted more and more on destroying him. Finally, he had to leave Makkah migrating to Madinah, where he had a significant number of followers.

After he reached Madinah and established the Islamic rule, Moslems came and offered him great wealth as a reward for prophethood, pledging to give all their remaining assets should the newly born rule come under financial difficulty.

That is when Allāh ordered His Messenger in the twenty-third āyah of the forty-second sōrah of the Holy Qor'ān to convey to his people:

> ﴿*SAY: I DO NOT ASK OF YOU ANY REWARD FOR IT BUT LOVE*[1] *FOR MY NEAR RELATIVES.*﴾.

As Rasōlollāh's Prophethood was the best thing that has ever happened to humanity, and at the same time the hardest mission for any prophet, no amount of financial reward could recompense him. Therefore Allāh took it upon Himself to pay His Messenger for transmitting His message. But as the people had insisted so long to

---

[1] The Arabic word in the āyah is *al-mawaddah* which means: show of devotion, external manifestation of love as well as internal.

do something for their prophet in return for his tireless efforts in guiding them to the right path, Allāh chose the love for his maᶜṣōm descendents instead, which is the only reward Moslems can give their prophet that is consistent with what their prophet had given them.

And to love Rasōlollāh's maᶜṣōm descendents is to follow them after his death, who would continue his mission and keep his followers on the right path. And the continuation of Rasōlollāh's mission after his death is for the benefit of Moslems, as his mission was. And this is what we read in the other āyat of the Holy Qor'ān:

> ﴾*SAY: I DO NOT ASK YOU AUGHT IN RETURN EXCEPT THAT HE WHO WILL, MAY TAKE THE WAY TO HIS LORD*[1].﴿.

> ﴾*SAY: WHATEVER REWARD I HAVE ASKED OF YOU, THAT IS ONLY FOR YOURSELVES; MY REWARD IS ONLY WITH ALLĀH*[2].﴿.

In which Allāh asks His Messenger to tell his people that he does not ask for a reward for his prophethood, except from those who want to get closer to their God. And that the reward he asks those people is for their own benefit, and not for his benefit; as his reward lies with Allāh.

And finally, in this āyah, Allāh asks His messenger to tell Moslems that the only reward he wants from those who like to get closer to Allāh is to follow his maᶜṣōm descendents.

Thus our obedience to our Prophet's maᶜṣōm descendents is the only suitable reward we can offer him; and as this means the continuation of his mission, it is therefore in our own benefit.

This āyah is one of the most important āyāt that have been revealed about the maᶜṣōm descendants of Rasōlollāh, in which Allāh orders Moslems to follow them. It is equally damaging for their enemies, whom suppressed them and usurped the khelāfah. As it is, beside other things, impossible to love someone (Ahl al-Bayt), and at the same time follow their enemy (the Bakri party); and it is impossible to follow someone (the Bakri party) without loving them;

---

[1] Holy Qor'ān = sōrah 25, āyah 57.
[2] Holy Qor'ān = sōrah 34, āyah 47.

and it is impossible to love someone (Ahl al-Bayt) without hating their enemy (the Bakri party).

Therefore some Bakri scholars have put together ridiculous explanations to escape from this serious contradiction. For instance they say: Rasōlollāh is telling his people that my reward is that you should honor my relation to you, and for the sake of this relation to many of you, you must not annoy me!! Of course this interpretation could not be further from truth, as it is clear that a Moslem who has chosen to turn his back on his fathers' beliefs and follow the Prophet instead, automatically respects him as the "Messenger of Allāh", and this respect is much more than what relation brings; in fact he would sacrifice himself to protect his prophet. So there is no need for Rasōlollāh to ask his followers to love him for the fact that he happens to be related to many of them.

And if the Bakris say that the addressee in this āyah are the Idolaters, then their lie becomes more apparent: Is it logical for the Prophet to ask his enemies to reward him for his prophethood which is the very reason for their animosity?! And how can he expect his enemies who want to kill him, to love him instead, because he happens to be related to many of them?!

Besides, Rasōlollāh himself explained the āyah, and named the people whose love is mandatory for the Moslems; as the Bakris themselves narrate in their many ḥadēth references:

> *((When this āyah descended, someone asked Rasōlollāh: O Rasōlollāh! Who are these people whose love has become mandatory for us?*
> *Rasōlollāh said: ᶜAli, Fāṭimah, and their two sons[1].)).*

---

[1] Faḍā'el al-Ṣaḥabah / Ibn Ḥanbal = vol. 2, page 669. Fayḍ al-Qadēr / al-Monāwi = vol. 1, page 219. Kashf al-Khafā' = vol. 1, page 18. Majmaᶜ al-Zawā'ed / al-Haythami = vol. 7, page 103; vol. 9, page 168. al-Moᶜjam al-Kabēr / al-Ṭabarāni = vol. 3, page 47; vol. 11, page 444. Tafsēr al-Qor'ān al-ᶜAẓēm / Ibn Kothayr = vol. 4, page 113. al-Jāmiᶜ le Aḥkām al-Qor'ān / al-Qorṭobi = vol. 16, page 21. Toḥfah / al-Āḥōdhi – vol. 9, page 91.

ᶜAllāmah Amēni has gathered over forty well-known Bakri references in his highly praised encyclopedia al-Ghadēr all of which say that this āyah was revealed about ᶜAli, Fāṭimah and their two sons Ḥasan and Ḥosayn. (al-Ghadēr / al-Amēni = vol. 2, page 307)

Bakri scholars also narrate from Rasōlollāh who said:

((Indeed, Allāh has made mandatory for you, as my reward, the love for my Ahl al-Bayt; and I will, surely, ask you tomorrow (in the Hereafter) about them[1].)).

4- The Āyah of Ahl al-Dhekr

In the forty-third āyah of the sixteenth sōrah and in the seventh āyah of the twenty-first sōrah of the Holy Qor'ān, Allāh says:

﴿*SO ASK "AHL AL-DHEKR" IF YOU DO NOT KNOW.*﴾.

On two separate occasions Allāh reveals this āyah, ordering people to ask "Ahl al-Dhekr" the things they do not know.

Several *a'emmah* have explained Ahl al-Dhekr as the "People of the Qor'ān", or the people to whom the Holy Qor'ān was revealed; or as "Ahl al-Bayt", who are the very people to whom the Holy Qor'ān was revealed; including themselves and excluding others. For instance Bakri scholars narrate:

((When this āyah descended, ᶜAli said: We are Ahl al-Dhekr[2].)).

Bakri scholars also narrate from Rasōlollāh's fifth khalēfah, Imām Bāqir*(AS)*[3], who said:

((We are Ahl al-Dhekr[1].)).

---

[1] Jawāhir al-ᶜEqdayn / al-Samhōdi = page 245. al-Ṣawāᶜeq al-Moḥreqah / Ibn Ḥajar = pages 171 and 228. Dhakhā'er al-ᶜOqbā / al-Ṭabari = page 25. Wasēlat al-Motaᶜabbedēn / Omar ibn Moḥammad = vol. 5, page 199.

[2] Jāmiᶜ al-Bayān fi Tafsēr al-Qor'ān / al-Ṭabari = vol. 17, page 5. al-Jāmiᶜ le Aḥkām al-Qor'ān / al-Qorṭobi = vol. 11, page 272.

[3] *ᶜAlayhes Salām,* peace be upon him.

They also narrate from Rasōlollāh's sixth khalēfah, Imām Ṣādiq, who said:

> *((Al-Dhekr has two meanings: The Holy Qor'ān, and Moḥammad; and we are Ahl al-Dhekr by both definitions[2].)).*

And the fact that Ahl al-Dhekr has been limited to these people means that they are the only authentic sources of knowledge whom have been appointed by Allāh to teach and lead His creatures. Thus it is logically understood that if anyone contradicts any of these people in any field, the former would be in the wrong.

Now, Rasōlollāh being the only authentic source of knowledge does not cause too much worry for the Bakris, but when Amēr al-Mo'menēn[3], Sayyedat Nesā' al-ᶜĀlamēn, Imām Ḥasan and Imām Ḥosayn[(AmS)4] are also mentioned, temperatures hit the roof and the Bakri world is literally upset.

How can Sayyedat Nesā' al-ᶜĀlamēn be the leader and ᶜĀ'eshah be the follower?! How can Amēr al-Mo'menēn be the leader and Abō Bakr be the follower?! How can Imām Ḥasan be the leader and Moᶜāwiyah be the follower?! How can Imām Ḥosayn be the leader and Yazēd be the follower?! And the fact that after Rasōlollāh's martyrdom, the second of the pairs suppressed the first instead of obeying them, only makes things more troublesome, as it means that the latter intentionally changed the course of Islam by disobeying a direct order by Allāh the Almighty in the Holy Qor'ān to obey the former.

Therefore some Bakri scholars have chosen to take the easy way out, resorting to their preferred method of distortion and falsification. To avoid naming the true members of Ahl al-Dhekr,

---

1 Jāmiᶜ al-Bayān fi Tafsēr al-Qor'ān / al-Ṭabari = vol. 14, page 109. Rōḥ al-Maᶜāni / al-Ālōsi = vol. 14, page 147. Tafsēr al-Qor'ān al-ᶜAẓēm / Ibn Kothayr = vol. 2, page 571.

2 Yanābēᶜ al-Mawaddah / al-Qandōzi = vol. 1, page 119.

3 Commander of the Faithful; a title given exclusively to Imām ᶜAli by Allāh.

4 *ᶜAlayhemos Salām,* peace be upon them.

they say that Ahl al-Dhekr are the Jewish and Christian scholars!!! And that Allāh has ordered Moslems to ask them what they do not know!!!

It has been narrated that when the Bakri ruler, Ma'mōn, forcefully brought Rasōlollāh's eighth khalēfah, Imām Reḍa(AS)[1], to Marw his second capital in today's Turkmenistan, he gathered a number of top Bakri scholars from Iraq and Khorāsān[2] in a public gethering, to challenge the Imām in a debate and prove that the Bakris are superior in knowledge. In that long discussion the Imām said:

> *((...We are Ahl al-Dhekr about whom Allāh the Great, the Almighty, says: "SO ASK "AHL AL-DHEKR" IF YOU DO NOT KNOW[3]"; so ask us if you do not know.*
> *The [Bakri] scholars said: On the contrary, Allāh meant the Jews and Christians!!*
> *So Abō al-Ḥasan [Imām Reḍa] said: Allāh is far above; and is that possible?! Then they would call us to their religion, and say that it is better than the religion of Islam.*
> *Then Ma'mōn said: Do you have an explanation other than what they said O Abā al-Ḥasan[4]?*
> *So Abō al-Ḥasan said: Yes, al-Dhekr is Rasōlollāh and we are his Ahl; and this is quite clear in the Book of Allāh, the Great, the Almighty where he says in the sōrah of Divorce: "THEREFORE BE CAREFUL OF (YOUR DUTY TO) ALLĀH, O MEN OF INTELLECT WHO BELIEVE! ALLĀH HAS INDEED REVEALED TO YOU A (DHEKR) REMINDER * AN APOSTLE WHO RECITES TO YOU THE CLEAR*

---

[1] *ᶜAlayhes Salām,* peace be upon him.

[2] The largest province in Iran, situated in the northeast of the country. Khorāsān was much larger in that day, extending to today's northern Afghanistan and Turkmenistan.

[3] Holy Qor'ān = sōrah 16, āyah 43; sōrah 21, āyah 7.

[4] Abā, Abō and Abi have the same meaning, but their usage differs according to the Arabic grammar.

COMMUNICATIONS OF ALLĀH[1]". Therefore al-Dhekr is Rasōlollāh and we are his Ahl[2].)).

The insistence of Ahl al-Bayt[(AmS)3] that they are Ahl al-Dhekr and that no one else is included, comes in parallel with the fact that none of their foes has ever claimed to be among Ahl al-Dhekr. Neither Abō Bakr and ᶜOmar and people of such caliber, nor Jewish and Christian scholars.

A large number of Bakri scholars confess that Ahl al-Dhekr are the "People of the Holy Qor'ān"[4]; and some Bakri scholars say that they are the close relatives of Rasōlollāh[5]. In either case no prejudiced Bakri scholar can exclude Amēr al-Mo'menēn, Sayyedat Nesā' al-ᶜĀlamēn, Imām Ḥasan and Imām Ḥosayn from Ahl al-Dhekr. And according to the second opinion it would be impossible to include their foes such as Abō Bakr and ᶜOmar. And based on the first conviction, it would still be preposterous to regard the Bakri party leaders[(LAm)6] as members of Ahl al-Dhekr.

How can Allāh order us to ask Abō Bakr what we do not know, when he often screams after being proved wrong:

((*I have a Shayṭān who comes upon me. Discharge me! as I am not your best...*[7])).

---

[1] The Holy Qor'ān = sōrah 65, āyāt 10 and 11.
[2] ᶜOyōn Akhbār al-Reḍā / al-Ṣadōq = vol. 1, page 492.
[3] *ᶜAlayhemos Salām,* peace be upon them
[4] Jamiᶜ al-Bayān fi Tafsēr al-Qor'ān / al-Ṭabari = vol. 14, page 109; vol. 17, page 5. al-Jāmiᶜ le Aḥkām al-Qor'ān / al-Qorṭobi = vol. 10, page 108; vol. 11, page 272. Moᶜtasar al-Mokhtaṣar / Abō al-Maḥāsin al-Ḥanafi = vol. 2, page 183.
[5] al-Jāmiᶜ le Aḥkām al-Qor'an / al-Qorṭobi = vol. 11, page 268.
[6] *Laᶜnatollāh ᶜAlayhem,* may Allāh distance them from His Blessings and Mercy.
[7] Abō Bakr, as the First Usurper of the Khelāfah, claimed to be both the political and the religious leader for the whole of the fast-growing Moslem nation; and as an ignorant Arab who had heard of Islam only its name, he made gigantic blunders throughout his unjust rule.
These gross shortcomings were terribly damaging to his status and highly destructive to his legitimacy as the Prophet's successor; and as these exposing occasions repeated, the language of his theatrical confessions

How can Allāh order us to ask ᶜOmar what we do not know, when he does not know the Qor'ān[1]?!

---

varied accordingly. Therefore in difficult times, he acted as if he had been forced to accept that position, and admitted that he was not suitable for that role, and shouted himself hoarse asking the people to depose him!!
And Moslems are not the only ones who record these events, as many Bakri scholars have also narrated them in some detail. The following are some examples of such Bakri references:
al-Bedāyah wa al-Nehāyah / Ibn Kothayr = vol. 5, page 247. Eᶜjāz al-Qor'ān / al-Bāqillāni = page 209. al-ᶜEqd al-Farēd / Ibn ᶜAbderabbeh = vol. 2, page 158. al-Imāmah wa al-Seyāsah / Ibn Qotaybah = vol. 1, page 16. Kanz al-ᶜOmmāl / al-Hendi = vol. 3, pages 126, 135 and 136; vol. 5, page 588. Majmaᶜ al-Zawā'ed / al-Haythami = vol. 5, page 183. al-Mojtaba / Ibn Dorayd = page 27. Mosnad / Aḥmad = vol. 1, page 14. ᶜOyōn al-Akhbār / Ibn Qotaybah = vol. 2, page 234. al-Reyāḍ al-Naḍirah / al-Ṭabari = vol. 1, pages 167 and 177; vol. 2, pages 207 and 219; vol. 3, page 157. Ṣefat al-Ṣafwah / Ibn al-Jawzi = vol. 1, pages 99 and 260. Sērah / Ibn Hoshām = vol. 4, pages 311 and 340. al-Sērah al-Ḥalabiyyah / al-Ḥalabi = vol. 3, page 388. Sharh Nahj al-Balāghah / Ibn Abi al-Ḥadēd = vol. 2, page 56; vol. 6, page 20; vol. 17, page 156. Tārēkh / al-Ṭabari = vol. 2, page 440; vol. 3, pages 203, 210 and 245. Tārēkh / al-Yaᶜqōbi = vol. 2, pages 107 and 127. Tārēkh al-Kholafā' / al-Soyōṭi = pages 47 and 48. al-Ṭabaqāt al-Kobrā / Ibn Saᶜd = vol. 3, pages 139, 151 and 183. Tahdhēb al-Kamāl = vol. 1, page 6. Dhakhā'er al-ᶜOqbā / al-Ṭabari = page 88.

[1] The instances when ᶜOmar confessed to his lack of knowledge about the Qor'ān, or when he was proved wrong in an argument about the Qor'ān, during the life of Rasōlollāh and during Abō Bakr's rule and during his own rule, are more than what I could mention here.
This indigence became so embarrassing for ᶜOmar as someone who claimed to be a Moslem, and so problematic, as someone who assumed both religious and political leadership, that he prohibited Moslems from asking about the Qor'ān, and went so far as lashing the people who asked him about the Qor'ān. To catch a glimpse of ᶜOmar's Qor'ānic disability, besides his other incapacities, see the following Bakri references:
Aḥkām al-Qor'ān / al-Jaṣṣāṣ = vol. 2, pages 87 and 105. Anwār al-Tanzēl / al-Bayḍāwi = vol. 1, pages 545 and 667. Arbaᶜēn / al-Rāzi = pages 466 and 467. Asnā al-Maṭālib / Ibn Darwēsh = pages 166 and 335. al-Dorar al-Montathirah / al-Soyōṭi = pages 152, 243 and 488. al-Dorr al-Manthōr / al-Soyōṭi = vol. 1, pages 21, 54, 288 and 688; vol. 2, pages 133, 249, 251, 344, 466, 753, 754 and 757; vol. 3, pages 45, 226, 269 and 356; vol. 5, page 62;

vol. 6, pages 40, 79, 111, 317, 321, 374, 378 and 682; vol. 7, pages 441, 442, 535 and 614; vol. 8, pages 161, 422, 432, 433, 576 and 587. Eḥyā' cOlōm al-Dēn / al-Ghazāli = vol. 1, pages 28, 30, 241 and 242. Ershād al-Sāri / al-Qasṭalāni = vol. 3, page 195; vol. 8, page 57; vol. 10, page 298. al-Etqān / al-Soyōṭi = vol. 2, page 5; vol. 3, page 7. Fatḥ al-Bāri / al-cAsqalāni = vol. 4, pages 211 and 262; vol. 8, pages 17, 211, 215 and 268; vol. 13, pages 230 and 271. Fatḥ al-Qadēr / al-Shawkāni = vol. 1, pages 407 and 443; vol. 2, pages 379 and 398. al-Foṣōl al-Mohemmah / Ibn al-Ṣabbāgh = page 34. Jāmic Bayān al-Elm / Ibn cAbdelbarr = pages 150, 158, 311 and 799. Jāmic al-Bayān fi Tafsēr al-Qor'ān / al-Ṭabari = vol. 1, page 7; vol. 6, pages 30, 42 and 43; vol. 7, page 119; vol. 11, page 8. al-Jāmic al-Kabēr / al-Soyōṭi = vol. 3, page 35. al-Jāmic le Aḥkām al-Qor'ān / al-Qorṭobi = vol. 1, pages 30, 31, 34, 107 and 132; vol. 5, pages 66 and 99; vol. 6, page 29; vol. 8, pages 151, 152 and 238; vol. 10, pages 73 and 110; vol. 14, pages 84, 126, 178 and 277. Jamc al-Jawāmic / al-Soyōṭi = vol. 8, page 298. Kanz al-cOmmāl / al-Hendi = vol. 1, pages 227 to 229, 257, 278, 279, 285, 287 and 334; vol. 2, pages 331, 470, 568, 569, 596, 597 and 605; vol. 3, pages 35, 96 and 228; vol. 5, page 457; vol. 6, pages 2, 20 and 205; vol. 11, pages 78 and 80; vol. 16, pages 535, 536 and 538. Kashf al-Khafā' / al-cAjlōni = vol. 1, pages 269 and 388, vol. 2, page 118. Kefāyat al-Ṭālib / al-Kanji = pages 105, 218 and 226. Mafātēḥ al-Ghayb / al-Rāzi = vol. 7, page 484; vol. 28, page 15. Majmac al-Zawā'ed / al-Haythami = vol. 4, page 284; vol. 7, page 150. al-Manāqib / al-Khārazmi = page 57. Mokhtaṣar Jāmic al-Elm = page 150. Mokhtaṣar Tārēkh Demashq = vol. 11, page 46. al-Moṣannaf / cAbdorrazzāq = vol. 3, page 207; vol. 7, page 352. Mosnad / Aḥmad = vol. 4, page 30; vol. 5, page 117; vol. 6, page 136. Mosnad cOmar / al-Sadōsi = page 87. al-Mostadrak / al-Naysābōri = vol. 1, pages 438, 457 and 604; vol. 2 pages 177, 193, 245, 303, 332 and 514; vol. 3, pages 305 and 354. al-Mostaṭraf / al-Ebshēhi = vol. 1, pages 55, 56 and 70. al-Nehāyah / Ibn al-Athēr = vol. 1, page 10. Nōr al-Abṣār / al-Shablanji = page 161. cOmdat al-Qāri' / al-cAyni = vol. 4, page 606. Oṣōl al-Tafsēr / Ibn Taymeyyah = page 30. al-Reyāḍ al-Naḍirah / al-Ṭabari = vol. 2, pages 49 and 194; vol. 3, page 142. Rōḥ al-Macāni / al-Ālōsi = vol. 11, page 8. Sērat cOmar / Ibn al-Jawzi = pages 106, 109, 117, 120, 129, 136, 137, 165 and 171. Sharh Nahj al-Balāghah / Ibn Abi al-Ḥadēd = vol. 1, pages 61 and 182; vol. 3, pages 96, 111 and 122; vol. 12, pages 17, 66 and 102. Sonan / al-Bokhāri = vol. 3, page 90. Sonan / al-Dārimi = vol. 1, pages 54 and 55; vol. 2, page 365. Sonan / Sacēd ibn Manṣōr = vol. 1, page 166. al-Sonan al-Kobrā / al-Bayhaqi = vol. 3, page 227; vol. 4, page 313; vol. 6, pages 223, 224 and 463; vol. 7, pages 69, 233 and 442; vol. 8, page 252. Tārēkh Baghdād / al-Baghdādi = vol. 3, page 257; vol. 11, page 468. Tārēkh Demashq / Ibn

How can Allāh order us to ask ᶜOthmān*(LA)*[1] what we do not know, when he is ignorant of the simplest Islamic laws, intent on opposing various Islamic rules, and enjoys torturing, to the point of death, the top Ṣaḥābah who criticize him[2]?!

ᶜAsākir = vol. 6, page 384; vol. 23, page 411. Tārēkh al-Madinah / Ibn Shobbah = vol. 2, page 709. al-Ṭabaqāt al-Kobrā / Ibn Saᶜd = vol. 3, page 327. Tafsēr al-Kash-shāf / al-Zamakhshari = vol. 1, pages 357 and 491; vol. 2, pages 46, 165, 304, 445, 608 and 609; vol. 3, pages 253 and 573. Tafsēr al-Khāzin = vol. 1, pages 339 and 353; vol. 2, pages 51 and 53; vol. 4, page 374. Gharā'eb al-Qor'ān / al-Naysābōri = vol. 2, page 377; vol. 5, page 153; vol. 6, page 120. Tafsēr al-Qor'ān al-ᶜAẓēm / Ibn Kothayr = vol. 1, pages 467, 594 and 595; vol. 2, pages 175 and 383; vol. 4, pages 194, 232, 473 and 533. Talkhēṣ al-Mostadrak / al-Dhahabi = vol. 2, page 191. al-Tamhēd / al-Bāqillāni = page 199. Tadhkerat Khawāṣ al-Ommah / Ibn al-Jawzi = pages 87 and 148. Dhakhā'er al-ᶜOqbā / al-Ṭabari = page 82.

[1] *Laᶜnatollāh ᶜAlayh,* may Allāh distance him from His Blessings and Mercy.

[2] ᶜOthmān's lack of knowledge about basic Islamic laws and rules, and his insistence upon his unIslamic actions and policies, and his harsh treatment and severe punishment of those who dared to criticize him, no matter how highly respected they were, fills the Bakri references. It is such that the Bakris' hopeless arguments, contradictions and sophistry evolves not around the question of whether or not they happened, but around defending these indefensible actions, and debating how far of the right path they have taken ᶜOthmān!!

And because this is a lengthy subject with many different issues, and a huge number of supporting Bakri references, I have content myself with giving only a sample of Bakri references about ᶜOthmān's vicious response to the criticism of a number of great ṣaḥābah who went only as far as questioning and criticizing his actions, among whom Abō Dharr, ᶜAmmār ibn Yāsir and ᶜAbdollāh ibn Masᶜōd catch the eye:

al-Ansāb / al-Samᶜāni = vol. 5, pages 52 and 54. Ansāb al-Ashrāf / al-Balādheri = vol. 5, pages 36, 49, 88 and 480. al-Bedāyah wa al-Nehāyah / Ibn Kothayr = vol. 7, page 163. al-ᶜEqd al-Farēd / Ibn ᶜAbderabbeh = vol. 2, page 272. al-Esteᶜāb / Ibn ᶜAbdelbarr = vol. 1, page 373. Fatḥ al-Bāri / al-ᶜAsqalāni = vol. 3, page 213. al-Imāmah wa al-Seyāsah / Ibn Qotaybah. al-Mostadrak / al-Naysābōri = vol. 3, page 313. al-Nehāyah / Ibn al-Athēr = vol. 2, page 88. al-Sērah al-Ḥalabiyyah / al-Ḥalabi = vol. 2, page 87. Sharh Nahj al-Balāghah / Ibn Abi al-Ḥadēd = vol. 1, pages 236, 239, 240-242; vol. 2, pages 45, 375 and 387; vol. 3, pages 54 and 57; vol. 9, pages 3 and 5. ᶜOmdat al-Qāri' / al-ᶜAyni = vol. 4, page 291. Tārēkh al-Khamēs / al-

5- Sōrah of al-Kawthar

As part of a larger package to suppress Prophet Moḥammad, the Idolaters of Makkah began to call him "Abtar": a man without lineage. Saying that when he dies, he will not have left any children; and without blood-relatives, his memory will fade away.

That is when Allāh revealed the one hundred and eighth sōrah of the Holy Qor'ān:

> ﴿IN THE NAME OF ALLĀH, THE MOST COMPASSIONATE, THE MOST MERCIFUL * SURELY WE HAVE GIVEN YOU AL-KAWTHAR * THEREFORE PRAY TO YOUR LORD AND SACRIFICE CAMEL * SURELY YOUR ENEMY IS THE ONE WHO SHALL BE WITHOUT POSTERITY.﴾.

Scholars of the Holy Qor'ān have given several meanings for the word al-Kawthar, all of which are classified as a great blessing. But perhaps the more suitable meaning for this word is "Sayyedat Nesā' al-ᶜĀlamēn".

The Idolaters taunted the Prophet with being without a child; that is when Allāh said that He has given him al-Kawthar, Fāṭimah, the great blessing, from whom there will be a great quantity and quality of descendents. Many Bakri scholars have also given this meaning for al-Kawthar[1].

And we see that with the assassination of Rasōlollāh, his enemies started to destroy his lineage by killing his grandson, Moḥassin[(AS)2], and his daughter Fāṭimah, only days after his death. Suppression of Rasōlollāh's descendants continued for centuries, during which they were imprisoned, tortured and murdered. Many of

---

Deyārbakri = vol. 2, pages 267 and 268. Tārēkh / al-Yaᶜqōbi = vol. 2, pages 147 and 148. al-Ṭabaqāt al-Kobrā / Ibn Saᶜd = vol. 4, page 168.

[1] Anwār al-Tanzēl / al-Bayḍāwi = page 1156 (handwritten copy). al-ᶜEnāyah / Shahāboddēn = page 403. Hashiyat al-Shaykh-zādeh ᶜalā Tafsēr al-Bayḍāwi = vol. 9, page 341. Mafāteḥ al-Ghayb / al-Rāzi = vol. 30. al-Majālis / Kōseh-zādeh = page 222. al-Qawl al-Fasl / al-Ḥaḍrami = page 457.

[2] *ᶜAlayhes Salām,* peace be upon him.

them had to flee, often in disguise, to the far flanks of the vast Bakri Empire to escape persecution. Those who were identified and caught had to suffer slow and painful deaths. Some of them were buried alive under the foundations of the city of Baghdad-Iraq; some were put in the middle of the walls of the ever-growing castles of Bakri rulers; some were killed under torture.

However, murdering the Prophet's progeny was not enough for the Bakri rulers; so they publicized the pre-Islamic Arab view that the children of one's daughter are not counted as one's children, whereas the children of one's son are counted as one's children; and therefore executed anyone who said that Rasōlollāh had any descendants. This is despite the fact that Islam had refused this pre-Islamic belief, and Rasōlollāh had often called Imām Ḥasan and Imām Ḥosayn, who were the sons of his daughter, as his children.

For instance, al-Sha'bi[1], the famous Bakri scholar, narrates:

> *((I was in Wāsiṭ[2] on the Eid of Aḍḥā[3], so I attended the Ṣalāt of Eid with Ḥajjāj[4], and he gave an eloquent speech. When he left, his messenger came to me, so I went [to Ḥajjāj] and found him sitting as if he wants to leap.*
> *He said: O Sha'bi! This is the day of Aḍḥā, and I surely want to sacrifice a man from Iraq on this day!!*

---

[1] ᶜĀmir al-Shaᶜbi was an influential tābiᶜi (a person who has met any of the ṣaḥābah, plural of ṣaḥābi: a companion of the Prophet). He was a most famous Bakri scholar and poet and was appointed as the judge for the city of Kōfah-Iraq. He narrated many aḥādēth from around one hundred and fifty ṣaḥābah. He died in 104 AH in Kōfah. (al-Konā wa al-Alqāb / al-Qommi = vol. 2, page 327)

[2] Wāsiṭ was a city built by Ḥajjāj, between the two cities of Kōfah and Basrah-Iraq in 83-86 AH.

[3] Eid of Aḍḥā is on the 10th day of the last month of the Hejri year. On this day, Makkah pilgrims must sacrifice one of the specific animals. Other Moslems also make sacrifices on this day.

[4] Ḥajjāj was appointed as the governor for Makkah, Madinah and Iraq by Amawi (also Umayyad) rulers. He was famous for his harsh rule and slaughter of his subjects, especially the Shēᶜah. He demolished the Holy Kaᶜbah.

And I like you to hear what he says, so that you may know that I am right in what I do.
So I said: O Amēr! Would it not be better to follow the tradition of Rasōlollāh and sacrifice what he has ordered to sacrifice and do exactly as he did, and leave what you want to do on this great day to another day?
So he said: O Sha'bi! If you hear what he says, you will support my decision about him, for his relating lies to Allāh and His Messenger, and for introducing doubts in Islam.
I said: Does the Amēr see to excuse me from that?
He said: It is unavoidable. Then he ordered a leather rug to be spread and the executioner to be summoned, and said: Bring the old man, and they brought him.
He was Yaḥyā ibn Yaᶜmor; so I felt extremely sad and said to myself: What is Yaḥyā saying to deserve to die?
So Ḥajjāj said to him: You claim to be the leader of the Iraqi people?
Yaḥyā said: I am a jurisprudent among the jurisprudents of Iraq.
Ḥajjāj: And from what part of your jurisprudence do you allege that Ḥasan and Ḥosayn are the children of Rasōlollāh?!
Yaḥyā: I do not allege that, I rather say it truthfully.
Ḥajjāj: And for what reason do you say that?
Yaḥyā: For the reason from the Book of Allāh, the Great, the Almighty.
So Ḥajjāj looked at me and said: Hear what he says; this is surely what I had not heard from him before. Do you know from the Book of Allah, the Great, the Almighty, that Ḥasan and Ḥosayn are the children of Rasōlollāh?
So I started to think about it, and did not find anything from the Qor'ān to support that. And Ḥajjāj thought for a long time and then said to Yaḥyā: Maybe you mean what Allāh, the Great, the Almighty says: "BUT WHOEVER DISPUTES WITH YOU IN THIS MATTER

AFTER WHAT HAS COME TO YOU OF KNOWLEDGE, THEN SAY: COME LET US CALL OUR SONS AND YOUR SONS AND OUR WOMEN AND YOUR WOMEN AND OUR SELVES AND YOUR SELVES, THEN LET US BE EARNEST IN PRAYER, AND PRAY FOR THE CURSE OF ALLĀH ON THE LIARS[1]". And that Rasōlollāh went to Mobāhalah along with ᶜAli, Fāṭimah, Ḥasan and Ḥosayn?

So as though he gave my heart a great pleasure, and I said to myself: Yaḥyā escaped death.

But Yaḥyā told him: By Allāh! this is a great reason, but it is not the reason I have for what I say. Suddenly the face of Ḥajjāj changed color and he bowed his head for a long time; then he raised his head towards Yaḥyā and said to him: If you bring a reason from the Book of Allāh other than what I recited, I will give you ten thousand darāhim[2]; and if you do not, then can I shed your blood?!

Yaḥyā: Yes.

So I was saddened by what Yaḥyā said, and said to myself: Could not Yaḥyā accept that what Ḥajjāj had said was in fact his reason, and pretend that Ḥajjāj knew it and found it without any help, and thus satisfy him instead of silencing him?! Now whatever reason Yaḥyā brings, Ḥajjāj will refuse, so that Yaḥyā does not say that he knew what Ḥajjāj did not.

So Yaḥyā said to Ḥajjāj: Allāh, the Great, the Almighty, says: "AND OF HIS DESCENDANTS, DĀWŌD AND SOLAYMAN[3]", whom does He mean?

Ḥajjāj: Ebrāhēm.

Yaḥyā: So Dāwōd and Solaymān are his children?

Ḥajjāj: Yes.

Yaḥyā: And who else after Dāwōd and Solaymān does Allāh say are Ebrāhēm's children?

---

[1] Holy Qor'ān = sōrah 3, āyah 61.

[2] Plural of derham, a silver coin. Ten darāhim was equivalent to one dēnār which was a gold coin.

[3] The Holy Qor'ān = sōrah 6, āyah 84.

So Ḥajjāj recited: "AND AYYŌB AND YŌSOF AND MŌSĀ AND HĀRŌN; AND THUS DO WE REWARD THOSE WHO DO GOOD (TO OTHERS)[1]".
Yaḥyā: Who else?
Ḥajjāj: "AND ZAKARIYYĀ AND YAḤYĀ AND ᶜĒSĀ[2]".
Yaḥyā: And how is ᶜĒsā among the children of Ebrāhēm when he does not have a father?!
Ḥajjāj: Through his mother Maryam.
Yaḥyā: So who is nearer? Maryam from Ebrāhēm, or Fāṭimah from Moḥammad?! And ᶜĒsā from Ebrāhēm, or Ḥasan and Ḥosayn from Rasōlollāh?!
It was as if Yaḥyā had put a stone in Ḥajjāj's mouth[3]/[4].)).

---

[1] The Holy Qor'ān = sōrah 6, āyah 84.
[2] The Holy Qor'ān = sōrah 6, āyah 85.
[3] Beḥār al-Anwār / al-Majlesi = vol. 25, page 243.
[4] It has also been narrated from the Bakri scholar ᶜĀmir al-Shaᶜbi who said:

((One night Ḥajjāj summoned me, so I feared for my life and wrote my will and then went to him; and saw a leather rug spread, and the sword unsheathed. So I greeted him and he returned my greeting and said: Do not be scared, I guarantee your safety tonight and tomorrow until the noon. Then he gave me a seat next to him and pointed, and a man who was tied with various shackles and chains was brought and put before him.
So he said: This old man says: Ḥasan and Ḥosayn were the sons of Rasōlollāh. He must bring me a reason from the Qor'ān, or I will surely behead him.
So I said: You must remove these chains from him first. If he brings a reason [from the Qor'ān] then he will be freed, and if not, then the sword cannot cut through all this iron. Thus they removed the shackles and chains, so I saw his face, he was Saᶜēd ibn Jobayr.
Ḥajjāj said to him: Bring me a reason from the Qor'ān for what you claim, or I will behead you.
So Saᶜēd said: Wait, and he stayed silent for a while.
Ḥajjāj then repeated what he had said, and Saᶜēd told him: Wait, and stayed silent for a while.
Ḥajjāj again repeated what he had said. And Saᶜēd recited: I invoke the protection of Allāh from the accursed Shayṭān (also: Satan). IN THE NAME OF ALLĀH, THE MOST COMPASSIONATE, THE MOST MERCIFUL. "AND WE GAVE TO HIM ESḤĀQ AND YAᶜQŌB; EACH DID WE GUIDE, AND NOḤ DID WE GUIDE BEFORE, AND OF HIS

But no matter what the Bakri rulers did and how many they killed, Rasōlollāh's descendants, miraculously, survived and kept growing and growing; and according to some statistics near the end of the fourteenth Hejri century, the number of Rasōlollāh's descendants through Amēr al-Mo'menēn and Sayyedat Nesā' al-ᶜĀlamēn was estimated around thirty five million[1].

DESCENDANTS, DĀWŌD AND SOLAYMĀN AND AYYŌB AND YŌSOF AND MŌSĀ AND HĀRŌN; AND THUS DO WE REWARD THOSE WHO DO GOOD (TO OTHERS)". (Holy Qor'ān = sōrah 6, āyah 84).

Then he said to Ḥajjāj: Recite what is after that. So Ḥajjāj recited: "AND ZAKARIYYĀ AND YAḤYĀ AND ᶜĒSĀ". (Holy Qor'ān = sōrah 6, āyah 85).

So Saᶜēd said: How is ᶜĒsā suitable here?

Ḥajjāj: He was one of his (Ebrāhēm) descendants.

Saᶜēd: If ᶜĒsā, who did not have a father, is counted among the descendants of Ebrāhēm, because he was the son of his daughter, then Ḥasan and Ḥosayn are more appropriate to be called the sons of Rasōlollāh.)). (Beḥār al-Anwār / al-Majlesi = vol. 43, page 229)

[1] Fāṭimah al-Zahrā' min al-Mahd elā al-Laḥd / al-Qazwēni = page 87.

SAYYEDAT NESĀ' AL-ᶜĀLAMĒN IN THE HOLY HADEETH

It has been narrated from Imām Ṣādiq, who said:

((Indeed, she was named Fāṭimah, because the creatures were kept away from knowing her[1].)).

And this is because she was not like any other person, her creation was not the same, her qualities and characters were not similar, her powers were not comparable… And it is clear that a weaker mind cannot understand a stronger mind, and a small drop of water cannot carry within it a large ocean.

Therefore to know her as much as we can, we need to look at the Holy Qor'ān and the Holy Ḥadēth and try to understand what they say about her, and how they present her to our limited minds.

And Fāṭimah's struggle against the Bakri party and her stance against its leaders could not block all of the aḥādēth about her from finding their way into Bakri references. Yes, it is true that Bakri scholars did not record the important aḥādēth, the ones that shed more light on her and her qualities and powers, and that they deliberately cut out important parts of such aḥādeth and distorted and changed other vital sections; but what eventually found its way on Bakri paper is still of great significance and immense value.

So we can say that this unique jewel was so priceless that the malicious hands of vandals could not render her worthless, and that the tireless efforts of knockout artists could not produce exact copies.

---

[1] Beḥār al-Anwār / al-Majlesi = vol. 43, page 65. Tafsēr / For āt al-Kōfi = page 581.

And how could the Bakris do all that, when it was not just Rasōlollāh[1] who praised her, but her most spiteful enemies such as ᶜĀ'eshah?!

1- Fāṭimah's Satisfaction and Anger

Fāṭimah's advancement in the path of the infinite completeness and perfection, and her ascension in the levels of closeness to God, was such that it brought her amongst other things, the ᶜEṣmah—the state of immunity from committing sins, making mistakes, or any act of forgetfulness, etc. whilst the choice to commit sin remains open to the individual... And it brought her amongst other things ᶜElm al-Ghayb—Knowledge-of-the-Unseen. An all-encompassing knowledge granted by Allāh to a person without the usual methods of learning; a knowledge that covers everything and everyone, and is not limited by time or space, neither is it crippled by what plagues the knowledge gained through education, such as inaccuracy, forgetfulness, etc. ᶜElm al-Ghayb includes the Unseen-World just as it includes the Seen-World.

And Rasōlollāh*(SAA)*[2] as God's Messenger, had to inform people of Fāṭimah's great abilities, so that they may use them to the best of their capabilities in their journeys through the various levels of completeness and perfection. Therefore, one of the things he emphasized was Fāṭimah's ability to know, beyond any doubt, what makes God satisfied and what makes Him angry.

And because Allāh had granted her ᶜElm al-Ghayb and the ᶜEṣmah, her satisfaction and anger reflected that of Allāh. Therefore, the Prophet tied Allāh's satisfaction and anger to that of Fāṭimah*(AaS)*[3], so people may know Allāh's satisfaction and anger.

He used every opportunity and used different words and various methods to transmit this to the people in such a way that

[1] Messenger of Allāh; a title exclusively given to Prophet Moḥammad by Allāh.

[2] *Ṣallallāh ᶜAlayh wa Ālih,* Allāh's Blessings be upon him and his descendants.

[3] *ᶜAlayhas Salām,* peace be upon her.

even her Bakri enemies narrated them, despite the fact that they were terribly damaging to their leaders, especially Abō Bakr and ᶜOmar.

For instance, Bakri scholars narrate from Rasōlollāh, who said:

> *((Verily, Allāh, the Great, the Almighty surely becomes angry for Fāṭimah's anger, and becomes satisfied for Fāṭimah's satisfaction[1]/[2].)).*

Bakri scholars also narrate from Rasōlollāh, who said:

> *((So whomsoever my daughter Fāṭimah is satisfied from, I am satisfied from; and whomsoever I am satisfied from, Allāh is satisfied from. And whomsoever she is angry with, I am angry with; and whomsoever I am angry with, Allāh is angry with[3].)).*

---

[1] al-Eṣābah / al-ᶜAsqalāni = vol. 4, page 378. Farā'ed al-Semṭayn / al-Ḥamō'i = vol. 2, page 46. al-Kāmil / Ibn ᶜOday = vol. 2, page 351. Kanz al-ᶜOmmāl / al-Hendi = vol. 6, page 219; vol. 12, page 111; vol. 13, page 674. Kefāyat al-Ṭālib / al-Kanji = page 363. al-Khaṣā'eṣ al-Kobrā / al-Soyōṭi = vol. 2, page 265. Manāqib ᶜAli ibn Abi Ṭālib / Ibn al-Maghāzili = pages 351 and 352. Maqtal al-Ḥosayn / al-Khārazmi = vol. 1, page 15. Maᶜrefat al-Ṣaḥābah / Abō Noᶜaym = vol. 1, page 318. Mēzān al-Eᶜtedāl / al-Dhahabi = vol. 1, page 535. Mosnad Fāṭimah al-Zahrā' / al-Soyōṭi = page 142. Dorar al-Semṭayn / al-Zarandi = page 178. Osd al-Ghābah / Ibn al-Athēr = vol. 5, page 522. Rashfat al-Ṣādi / al-Ḥaḍrami = page 61. Tārēkh Demashq / Ibn ᶜAsākir = vol. 1, page 159. Tahdhēb al-Kamāl / al-Mazzi = vol. 22, page 744. Tahdhēb al-Tahdhēb / al-ᶜAsqalāni = vol. 12, page 441. Tadhkerat Khawāṣ al-Ommah / Ibn al-Jawzi = pages 310 and 320. Dhakhā'er al-ᶜOqbā / al-Ṭabari = page 39. Yanābēᶜ al-Mawaddah / al-Qandozi = pages 173 and 198.

[2] Bakri scholars also narrate from Rasōlollāh, who said:

> *((Verily, Allāh, the Great, the Almighty becomes satisfied for Fāṭimah's satisfaction, and becomes angry for Fāṭimah's anger.)).* (Mēzān al-Eᶜtedāl / al-Dhahabi = vol. 2, page 72. al-Mostadrak / al-Naysābōri = vol. 3, page 153. Osd al-Ghābah / Ibn al-Athēr = vol. 5, page 522)

[3] Farā'ed al-Semṭayn / al-Ḥamō'i = vol. 2, page 67. Maqtal al-Ḥosayn / al-Khārazmi = page 59. Yanābēᶜ al-Mawaddah / al-Qandōzi = page 263.

They also narrate from Rasōlollāh, who said:

((Allāh becomes satisfied for Fāṭimah's satisfaction[1].)).

They also narrate that Rasōlollāh told his daughter Fāṭimah:

((Verily, Allāh becomes angry for your anger, and becomes satisfied for your satisfaction[2]/[3].)).

2- Fāṭimah and Rasōlollāh

As God's Messenger and the link between Him and His creatures, Rasōlollāh's words and deeds reflected God's satisfaction and anger. He did not say anything unless Allāh wanted that thing to be said, and he did not do anything unless Allāh wanted that thing to be done.

And because Rasōlollāh had ᶜElm al-Ghayb, he knew a person's thoughts, intentions, motives, relationship with God,

---

[1] al-Mostadrak / al-Naysābōri = vol. 3, page 153.

[2] al-Āḥād wa al-Mathāni / al-Shaybāni = vol. 5, page 363. Esᶜāf al-Rāghibēn / Ibn al-Ṣabbān = page 171. al-Eṣābah / al-ᶜAsqalāni = vol. 8, page 57. al-Kāmil / Ibn ᶜOday = vol. 2, page 351. Kanz al-ᶜOmmāl / al-Hendi = vol. 7, page 111. Kefāyat al-Ṭālib / al-Kanji = page 219. Majmaᶜ al-Zawā'ed / al-Haythami = vol. 9, page 203. Maqtal al-Ḥosayn / al-Khārazmi = vol. 1, page 52. Mēzān al-Eᶜtedāl / al-Dhahabi = vol. 2, page 289; vol. 4, page 185. al-Moᶜjam al-Kabēr / al-Ṭabarāni = vol. 1, page 108; vol. 22, page 401. al-Mostadrak / al-Naysābōri = vol. 3, page 167. Osd al-Ghābah / Ibn al-Athēr = vol. 5, page 522. al-Ṣawāᶜeq al-Moḥreqah / Ibn Ḥajar = page 105. al-Tadwēn fi Akhbār al-Qazwēn / al-Rāfiᶜi al-Qazwēni = vol. 3, page 11. Tahdhēb al-Tahdhēb / al-ᶜAsqalāni = vol. 12, pages 441 and 443. Tadhkerat Khawāṣ al-Ommah / Ibn al-Jawzi = page 175. Dhakhā'er al-ᶜOqbā / al-Ṭabari = page 39. al-Dhorreyyah al-Ṭāhirah / al-Dōlābi = vol. 1, page 120. Yanābēᶜ al-Mawaddah / al-Qandōzi = page 173.

Bakri scholars also narrate that Rasōlollāh told his daughter Fāṭimah:

((Verily, Allāh becomes angry for your anger.)). (al-Mostadrak / al-Naysābōri = page 351. Dorar al-Semṭayn / al-Zarandi = page 178. al-Ṣawāᶜeq al-Moḥreqah / Ibn Ḥajar = page 175)

ending, etc. And as he was a ma[c]ṣōm, he acted and spoke according to his knowledge, regardless of other people's desires.

And when we look at the history books, we see that Sayyedat Nesā' al-[c]Ālamēn[1] was the closest person to Rasōlollāh among women, just as Amēr al-Mo'menēn was the closest person to him among men, as [c]Ā'eshah*(LAa)*[2], their hateful enemy, testifies:

> *((Jomay' ibn Omayr al-Taymi narrates: I went to [c]Ā'eshah, along with my paternal aunt, and she asked her: Which person was more beloved to Rasōlollāh?*
> *[c]Ā'eshah said: Fāṭimah.*
> *Someone else asked her: And among men?*
> *[c]Ā'eshah said: Her husband. He was surely, in as much as I knew him, a person who fasted very often, and worshipped very often[3].)).*

Bakri scholars also narrate from [c]Ā'eshah, who said:

---

[1] Chief of the Women of the World; a title given exclusively to Fāṭimah, the Daughter of Rasōlollāh, by Allāh.

[2] *La[c]natollāh [c]Alayha,* may Allāh distance her from His Blessings and Mercy.

[3] al-Estē[c]āb / Ibn [c]Abdelbarr = vol. 4, page 1897. al-Mostadrak / al-Naysābōri = vol. 3, page 171. Sonan / al-Termedhi = vol. 5, page 701. Tārēkh Baghdād / al-Baghdādi = vol. 11, page 429.

Bakri scholars also narrate from Jomay' ibn Omayr al-Taymi, who said:

> *((I went to [c]Ā'eshah with my mother, and heard her behind the partition asking [c]Ā'eshah about [c]Ali. So [c]A'eshah said: You ask me about a man! By Allāh, I do not know a man more beloved to Rasōlollāh than [c]Ali; and I do not know a woman on the earth more beloved to him than Fāṭimah))* (al-Sonan al-Kobrā / al-Nasā'i = vol. 5, page 140. A shorter version of this ḥadēth has also been recorded in other Bakri references, such as: al-[c]Eqd al-Farēd / Ibn [c]Abderabbeh = vol. 2, page 194. al-Khaṣā'eṣ / al-Nasā'i = page 109. al-Mostadrak / al-Naysābōri = vol. 3, page 154. al-Reyāḍ al-Naḍirah / al-Ṭabari = vol. 2, page 162. al-Sonan al-Kobrā / al-Nasā'i = vol. 5, page 140. Tārēkh Demashq / Ibn [c]Asākir = vol. 2, page 164. Yanābē[c] al-Mawaddah / al-Qandōzi = page 204)

((I have never seen anyone more similar to Rasōlollāh in speaking than Fāṭimah. Whenever she went to him, he welcomed her and kissed both her hands and sat her in his place; and whenever he went to her, she welcomed him and kissed both his hands[1].)).

The following are some more examples of what Bakri scholars narrate from Rasōlollāh about Sayyedat Nesā' al-ᶜĀlamēn, spoken on different occasions and in different places:

((Your father be your sacrifice[2].)).

((Fāṭimah is the mother of her father[3].)).

((I won't agree until she agrees[4].)).

((Fāṭimah is a part of me, makes me happy what makes her happy[5].)).

((Fāṭimah is a part of me, hurts her what hurts me, and makes me happy what makes her happy[6].)).

((Fāṭimah is a part of me, relieves me what relieves her[7].)).

((Fāṭimah is a part of me, tires me what tires her[8].)).

---

[1] al-ᶜEqd al-Farēd / Ibn ᶜAbderabbeh.

[2] Fatḥ al-Bāri / al-ᶜAsqalāni = vol. 10, page 569. al-Mostadrak / al-Naysābōri = vol. 3, page 156.

[3] Manāqib ᶜAli ibn Abi Ṭālib / Ibn al-Maghāzili = page 340. Maqātil al-Ṭālibeyyēn / al-Eṣbahāni = page 29. al-Moᶜjam al-Kabēr / al-Ṭabarāni = vol. 22, page 397.

[4] Manāqib ᶜAli ibn Abi Ṭālib / Ibn al-Maghāzili = page 342.

[5] al-Mostadrak / al-Naysābōri = vol. 1, page 73. al-Ṣawāᶜeq al-Moḥreqah / al-Haythami = pages 180, 230 and 232. Yanābēᶜ al-Mawaddah / al-Qandōzi = vol. 2, page 468.

[6] al-Manāqib / al-Khārazmi = page 353.

[7] Tāj al-ᶜArōs / al-Zabēdi = vol. 6, page 139.

[8] Tāj al-ᶜArōs / al-Zabēdi = vol. 1, page 485.

((Fāṭimah is a part of me, saddens me what saddens her[1].)).

((Fāṭimah is a part of me, annoys me what annoys her, and tires me what tires her[2].)).

((Fāṭimah is a part of me, makes me suspicious what makes her suspicious, and annoys me what annoys her[3].)).

((Fāṭimah is a part of me, saddens me what saddens her, and delights me what delights her[4].)).

((Fāṭimah is a branch of me, saddens me what saddens her, and delights me what delights her[5].)).

---

[1] al-Ṭabaqāt al-Kobrā / Ibn Saʿd = vol. 8, page 262.
[2] Faḍāʾel al-Ṣaḥābah / Ibn Ḥanbal = vol. 2, page 756. al-Aḥādēth al-Mokhtārah / al-Maqdesi = vol. 9, page 315. al-Mostadrak / al-Naysābūri = vol. 3, page 173.
[3] al-Eṣābah / al-ʿAsqalāni = vol. 4, page 378; vol. 8, page 56. Faḍāʾel al-Ṣaḥābah / al-Nasāʾi = vol. 1, page 78. Ḥelyat al-Awleyāʾ / Abō Noʿaym = vol. 2, page 40. al-Khaṣāʾeṣ / al-Nasāʾi = pages 35, 121 and 122. Maṣābēḥ al-Sonnah / al-Baghawi = vol. 4, page 185. al-Moʿjam al-Kabēr / al-Ṭabarāni = vol. 22, page 404. Mosnad / Abi ʿAwānah = vol. 3, page 70. Mosnad / Aḥmad = vol. 4, page 328. Ṣaḥēḥ / al-Bokhāri = vol. 5, page 2004. Ṣaḥēḥ / Ibn Ḥabbān = vol. 15, page 406. Ṣaḥēḥ / Moslem = vol. 4, page 1902; vol. 5, page 54. Ṣaḥēḥ / Moslem ibn Ḥajjāj = vol. 7, page 140. Ṣaḥēḥ / al-Termedhi = vol. 5, page 698. Sonan / Abi Dāwod = vol. 2, page 226. al-Sonan al-Kobrā / al-Bayhaqi = vol. 7, page 307; vol. 10, page 288. Sonan / Ibn Majah = vol. 1, page 643. Tahdheb al-Kamāl / al-Mazzi = vol. 22, page 599; vol. 35, page 250. Tahdhēb al-Tahdhēb / al ʿAsqalāni = vol. 12, page 468. Tadhkerat Khawāṣ al-Ommah / Ibn al-Jawzi = page 279. Dhakhāʾer al-ʿOqbā / al-Ṭabari = page 38. Yanābēʿ al-Mawaddah / al-Qandōzi = vol. 2, page 59.
[4] Mosnad / Aḥmad = vol. 4, page 323. al Ṣawāʿeq al-Mohreqah / al-Haythami = page 112.
[5] Kanz al-ʿOmmāl / al-Hendi = vol. 13, page 96. al-Mostadrak / al-Naysābōri = vol. 3, page 168. Seyar Aʿlām al-Nobalāʾ / al-Dhahabi = vol. 2, page 132. Tārēkh al-Islam / al-Dhahabi = vol. 2, page 96.

((Fāṭimah is a part of me, annoys me what annoys her[1].)).

((Fāṭimah is a part of me, whoever annoys her, he has surely annoyed me[2].)).

((...And she is a part of me, and she is my heart, and my soul that is between my sides. So whoever annoys her, he has surely annoyed me, and whoever annoys me, he has surely annoyed Allāh[3].)).

((Fāṭimah is the soul that is between my sides; whoever annoys her, he has surely annoyed me, and whoever annoys me, he has surely annoyed Allāh[4].)).

((Verily, Fāṭimah is a part of me, annoys me what annoys her, and makes me angry what makes her angry[5].)).

((Fāṭimah is a part of me, angers me what angers her, and delights me what delights her[1].)).

---

[1] Mosnad / Abi ᶜAwānah = vol. 3, page 70. Mosnad Fāṭimah al-Zahrā' / al-Soyōṭi = page 134. Nawādir al-Oṣōl / al-Termedhi = vol. 3, page 184. Ṣaḥēḥ / Moslem = vol. 4, page 1903. al-Sonan al-Kobrā / al-Bayhaqi = vol. 10, page 201.

[2] Faḍā'el al-Ṣaḥābah / Ibn Ḥanbal = vol. 2, page 755. al-Foṣōl al-Mohemmah / Ibn al-Ṣabbāgh = page 150. Kanz al-ᶜOmmāl / al-Hendi = vol. 13, page 96. Mosnad Fāṭimah al-Zahrā' / al-Soyōṭi = page 134. Nōr al-Abṣār / al-Shablanji = pages 45 and 52. Nozhat al-Majālis / al-Ṣafōri = vol. 2, page 228. al-Sonan al-Kobrā / al-Bayhaqi = vol. 10, page 201. Yanābēᶜ al-Mawaddah / al-Qandōzi = vol. 2, page 322.

[3] al-Foṣōl al-Mohemmah / Ibn al-Ṣabbāgh = page 139. Nōr al-Abṣār / al-Shablanji = pages 41 and 52. Nozhat al-Majālis / al-Ṣafōri = vol. 2, page 228.

[4] Fayḍ al-Qadēr / al-Monāwi = vol. 6, page 18. Montakhab Kanz al-ᶜOmmāl / al-Hendi = vol. 5, page 96.

[5] al-Āḥād wa al-Mathāni / al-Shaybāni = vol. 5, page 362. al-Moᶜjam al-Kabēr / al-Ṭabarāni = vol. 22, page 405.

((Fāṭimah is a part of me, so whoever makes her angry, he has surely made me angry[2].)).

((Verily, Fāṭimah is a part of me, enrages me what enrages her and annoys me what annoys her[3].)).

And such closeness to Rasōlollāh would not have been possible unless she was just as close to Allāh.

3- At war with your enemies and in peace with your friends

The above statements from Rasōlollāh about Fāṭimah, which were all narrated and recorded by the Bakris show how close to him she was and how much he loved and respected her. And because the reason for this much love and respect was Allāh and her closeness to Him, Rasōlollāh went further to give yet stronger declarations.

Bakri scholars narrate that Rasōlollāh said to ᶜAli, Fāṭimah, Hasan and Ḥosayn:

((I am at war with whoever you are at war, and I am in peace with whoever you are in peace[4].)).

---

[1] al-Jāmiᶜ al-Ṣaghēr / al-Soyōṭi = vol. 2, page 653. al-Ṣawāᶜeq al-Moḥreqah / al-Haythami = page 188.

[2] al-Āḥād wa al-Mathāni / al-Shaybāni = vol. 5, page 361. Esᶜāf al-Rāghibēn / Ibn al-Ṣabbān = page 188. al-Ferdaws / al-Hamadāni = vol. 3, page 145. al-Jāmiᶜ al-Ṣaghēr / al-Soyōṭi = vol. 2, page 653. Kanz al-ᶜOmmāl / al-Hendi = vol. 3, pages 93 and 97. al-Khaṣā'eṣ / al Nasā'i = pages 35 and 122. Maṣabeḥ al-Sonnah / al-Baghawi = vol. 4, page 185. Moṣannaf / Ibn Abi Shaybah = vol. 6, page 388. Mosnad Fāṭimah al Zahrā' / al-Soyōṭi = page 143. Ṣefat al-Ṣafwah / Ibn al-Jawzi = vol. 2, page 13. Ṣaḥēḥ / al-Bokhāri = vol. 3, pages 1361 and 1374; vol. 5, pages 21 and 29. Dhakhā'er al-ᶜOqbā / al-Ṭabari = page 37. Yanābēᶜ al-Mawaddah / al-Qandōzi = vol. 2, pages 52 and 79.

[3] Mosnad / al-Bazzār = vol. 6, page 150.

[4] al-Dorr al-Manthōr / al-Soyōṭi. Kanz al-ᶜOmmāl / al-Hendi. al-Moᶜjam al-Awsaṭ / al-Ṭabarāni = vol. 5, page 182; vol. 7, page 197. Moᶜjam al-Shoyokh / al-Ṣaydāwi = vol. 1, page 133. Mosnad / Aḥmad. al-Mostadrak /

They also narrate:

((I am at war with whoever fights you, and I am in peace with whoever is in peace with you[1].)).

They also narrate that Rasōlollāh said about cAli, Fāṭimah, Ḥasan and Ḥosayn:

((I am at war with whoever fights them, and I am in peace with whoever is in peace with them[2].)).

4- Sayyedat Nesā' al-cĀlamēn

As the third most complete person ever to be created after Rasōlollāh and Amēr al-Mo'menēn, Fāṭimah was the most important woman of her time, before her time and after her time.

And this is not what her friends say; it is what Allāh says, and her enemies narrate.

---

al-Naysābōri = vol. 3, page 161. Osd al-Ghābah / Ibn al-Athēr. al-Reyāḍ al-Naḍirah / al-Ṭabari. Ṣaḥēḥ / Ibn Mājah. Ṣaḥēḥ / al-Termedhi = vol. 5, page 699. Seyar Aclām al-Nobalā' / al-Dhahabi = vol. 10, page 432. Sonan / al-Termedhi = vol. 5, page 360. Tārēkh Baghdād / al-Baghdādi. Dhakhā'er al-cOqbā / al-Ṭabari.

Bakri scholars also narrate that Rasōlollāh said to cAli, Fāṭimah, Ḥasan and Ḥosayn:

> *((I am in peace with whoever you are in peace, and at war with whoever you are at war.)).* (al-Mocjam al-Kabēr / al-Ṭabarāni = vol. 3, page 40; vol. 5, page 184. Seyar Aclām al-Nobalā' / al-Dhahabi = vol. 2, page 125. Sonan / Ibn Mājah = vol. 1, page 52. Tahdhēb al-Kamāl / al-Mazzi = vol. 13, page 112)

[1] Amāli / al-Maḥāmili = vol. 1, page 447. Majmac al-Zawā'ed / al-Haythami = vol. 9, page 169. al-Mocjam al-Awsaṭ / al-Ṭabarāni = vol. 3, page 179. al-Mocjam al-Ṣaghēr / al-Ṭabarāni = vol. 2, page 53. Mocjam al-Shoyōkh / al-Ṣaydāwi = vol. 1, page 380. Seyar Aclām al-Nobalā' / al-Dhahabi = vol. 2, page 122. Tārēkh Baghdād / al-Baghdādi = vol. 7, page 137.

[2] al-Eṣābah / al-cAsqalāni = vol. 8, page 56. al-Mocjam al-Kabēr / al-Ṭabarāni = vol. 5, page 184.

Bakri scholars narrate from Hothayfah, one of the most respected companions of Rasōlollāh, who said:

((When Rasōlollāh finished his ṣalāt, he left and I followed him. While he was walking, someone came and spoke with him and then left. I continued following the Prophet, and as he heard me, he asked: Who is this?
I said: Hothayfah.
He said: What do you want?
So I told him what had happened between my mother and me.
And he said: May Allāh forgive you and your mother. Did you not see the person who just came to see me?
I said: Yes.
He said: He was an angel who had not descended to the earth before this night; he asked for permission from his God to come greet me and inform me that Ḥasan and Ḥosayn are the "Masters of the Youths of Heaven" and that Fāṭimah is the "Chief of the Women of the World"[1].)).

Bakri scholars also narrate from Rasōlollāh, who said:

((Verily, an angel from the sky who had never visited me before, asked for Allāh's permission to visit me; and he told me that Fāṭimah is the Chief of the Women of my nation[2].)).

---

[1] Faḍā'el al-Ṣaḥābah / al-Nasā'i = vol. 1, page 58. Mosnad / Aḥmad = vol. 5, page 391. Sonan / al-Termedhi = vol. 5, page 660. al-Sonan al-Kobrā / al-Bayhaqi = vol. 5, pages 80 and 95.

A shorter form of this ḥadēth has also been recorded in other Bakri references, such as:

Fatḥ al-Bāri / al-ᶜAsqalāni = vol. 6, page 471. Ḥelyat al-Awleyā' / Abō Noᶜaym = vol. 4, page 190. al-Mostadrak / al-Naysābōri = vol. 3, page 164. Seyar Aᶜlām al-Nobalā' / al-Dhahabi = vol. 2, page 123; vol. 3, page 252. al-Sonan al-Kobrā / al-Bayhaqi = vol. 5, page 80.

[2] Majmaᶜ al-Zawā'ed / al-Haythami = vol. 9, page 201. Mēzān al-Eᶜtedāl / al-Dhahabi = vol. 6, page 329. al-Moᶜjam al-Kabēr / al-Ṭabarāni = vol. 22,

Bakri scholars also narrate that Rasōlollāh gave Fāṭimah the following titles:

> *((Sayyedat Nesā' al-^{c}Ālamēn. Chief of the Women of the World[1].)).*

> *((Sayyedat Nesā' Hādheh al-Ommah. Chief of the Women of this Nation[2].)).*

---

page 403. Seyar A^{c}lām al-Nobalā' / al-Dhahabi = vol. 2, page 127. al-Sonan al-Kobrā / al-Bayhaqi = vol. 5, page 146. Tahdhēb al-Kamāl / al-Mazzi = vol. 26, page 391.

[1] Ansāb al-Ashrāf / al-Balādheri = page 552. al-Bedāyah wa al-Nehāyah / Ibn Kothayr = vol. 2, page 61. al-Eṣābah / al-^{c}Asqalāni = vol. 7, page 604; vol. 8, page 56. al-Este^{c}āb / Ibn ^{c}Abdelbarr = vol. 4, page 1895. Faḍā'el Sayyedat al-Nesā' / Ibn Shāhēn = page 5. Fatḥ al-Bāri / al-^{c}Asqalāni = vol. 9, page 324. al-Fatḥ al-Kabēr / al-Nabahāni = vol. 1, pages 28 and 249. al-Foṣōl al-Mohemmah / Ibn al-Ṣabbāgh = page 127. Ḥelyat al-Awleyā' / Abō No^{c}aym = vol. 2, pages 40 and 42. Jāmi^{c} al-Oṣōl / Ibn al-Athēr = vol. 3, page 317. al-Jāmi^{c} al-Ṣaghēr / al-Soyōṭi = page 177. al-Kāmil / al-Jorjāni = vol. 5, page 152. Kanz al-^{c}Ommāl / al-Hendi = vol. 13, page 95. al-Khaṣā'eṣ / al-Nasā'i = page 34. al-Khaṣā'eṣ al-Kobrā / al-Soyōṭi = vol. 2, page 265. Kefāyat al-Ṭālib / al-Kanji = page 275. Ketāb al-Wafāt / al-Nasā'i = vol. 1, page 23. Maṣābēḥ al-Sonnah / al-Baghawi = vol. 2, page 204. Mo^{c}tasar al-Mokhtaṣar / Abō al-Maḥāsin al-Ḥanafi = vol. 2, page 247. Moshkel al-Āthār / al-Ṭaḥāwi = vol. 1, page 48. Mosnad / Aḥmad = vol. 6, page 282. Mosnad / al-Ṭayālisi = vol. 1, page 196. al-Mostadrak / al-Naysābōri = vol. 3, page 170. Osd al-Ghābah / Ibn al-Athēr = vol. 5, page 523. Ṣaḥēḥ / al-Bokhāri = vol. 8, page 78. Ṣaḥēḥ / Moslem = vol. 7, page 143. Ṣaḥēḥ / al-Termedhi = vol. 5, page 660. al-Ṣawā^{c}eq al-Moḥreqah / al-Haythami = page 185. Seyar A^{c}lām al-Nobalā' / al-Dhahabi = vol. 2, pages 126 and 130. Sharh Nahj al-Balāghah / Ibn Abi al-Ḥadēd = vol. 9, page 193; vol. 16, page 457. Sonan / al-Dārimi = vol. 1, page 37. al-Sonan al-Kobrā / al-Bayhaqi = vol. 4, page 251. Tārēkh Demashq / Ibn ^{c}Asākir = vol. 1, page 298. Tārēkh al-Kholafā' / al-Soyōṭi = page 114. al-Ṭabaqāt al-Kobrā / Ibn Sa^{c}d = vol. 2, page 248; vol. 8, page 27. Dhakhā'er al-^{c}Oqbā / al-Ṭabari = page 42. al-Dhorreyyah al-Ṭāhirah / al-Dōlābi = vol. 1, page 102. Yanābē^{c} al-Mawaddah / al-Qandōzi = page 260.

[2] al-Bedāyah wa al-Nehāyah / Ibn Kothayr = vol. 5, page 226. al-E^{c}teqād / al-Bayhaqi = vol. 1, page 328. al-Este^{c}āb / Ibn ^{c}Abdelbarr = vol. 4, page

((Sayyedat Nesā' al-Mo'menēn. Chief of the Faithful Women[1].)).

((Sayyedat Nesā' al-Moslemeen. Chief of the Moslem Women[2].)).

((Sayyedat Nesā' Yawm al-Qeyāmah. Chief of the Women on the Day of Resurrection[3].)).

((Sayyedat Nesā' Ahl al-Jannah. Chief of the Women of the Heaven[1].)).

1894. Faḍā'el al-Ṣaḥābah / Ibn Ḥanbal = vol. 2, page 762. Faḍā'el al-Ṣaḥābah / al-Nasā'i = vol. 1, page 77. al-Mo^cjam al-Kabēr / al-Ṭabarāni = vol. 22, page 419. Ketāb al-Wafāt / al-Nasā'i = vol. 1, page 23. al-Mo[c]jam al-Kabēr / al-Ṭabarāni = vol. 22, page 418. Mo[c]tasar al-Mokhtaṣar / Abō al-Maḥāsin al-Ḥanafi = vol. 2, page 327. al-Montaẓam / Ibn al-Jawzi = vol. 4, page 36. Mosnad /Abi Ya[c]lā = vol. 12, page 112. Mosnad / Aḥmad = vol. 6, page 282. Ṣaḥēḥ / al-Bokhāri = vol. 5, page 2317. Ṣaḥēḥ / Moslem = vol. 4, page 1905. Ṣefat al-Ṣafwah / Ibn al-Jawzi = vol. 2, page 12. al-Sonan al-Kobrā / al-Bayhaqi = vol. 4, page 251; vol. 5, page 146. al-Ṭabaqāt al-Kobrā / Ibn Sa[c]d = vol. 2, page 248; vol. 8, page 27. Tahdhēb al-Kamāl / al-Mazzi = vol. 35, page 249. al-Dhorreyyah al-Ṭāhirah / al-Dōlābi = vol. 1, page 102.

[1] al-Bedāyah wa al-Nehāyah / Ibn Kothayr = vol. 5, page 226. al-E[c]teqād / al-Bayhaqi = vol. 1, page 328. al-Estē[o]āb / Ibn [c]Abdelbarr = vol. 4, page 1894. Faḍā'el al-Ṣaḥābah / Ibn Ḥanbal = vol. 2, page 762. Faḍā'el al-Ṣaḥābah / al-Nasā'i = vol. 1, page 77. al-Mo[c]jam al-Kabēr / al-Ṭabarāni = vol. 22, page 419. Mo[c]tasar al-Mokhtaṣar / Abō al-Maḥāsin al-Ḥanafi = vol. 2, page 327. al-Montaẓam / Ibn al-Jawzi = vol. 4, page 36. Mosnad / Abi Ya[c]lā = vol. 12, page 112. Mosnad / Aḥmad = vol. 6, page 282. Mosnad / Esḥāq ibn Rāhawayh = vol. 1, page 7. Mosnad / al-Ṭayālisi = vol. 1, page 196. al-Mostadrak / al-Naysābōri = vol. 3, page 170. Ṣefat al-Ṣafwah / Ibn al-Jawzi = vol. 2, page 12. Ṣaḥēḥ / al-Bokhāri = vol. 3, page 1326; vol. 5, page 2317. Ṣaḥēḥ / Moslem = vol. 4, page 1905. al-Sonan al-Kobrā / al-Bayhaqi = vol. 5, pages 96 and 146. Sonan / Ibn Mājah = vol. 1, page 518. Tahdhēb al-Kamāl / al-Mazzi = vol. 35, page 249.

[2] al-Mo[c]jam al-Kabēr / al-Ṭabarāni = vol. 22, page 418.

[3] Ḥelyat al-Awleyā' / Abō No[c]aym = vol. 2, page 42.

Bakri scholars also narrate from Rasōlollāh, who said:

((Allāh chose Fāṭimah over the women of the world[2].)).

They also narrate:

((Fāṭimah is the most favored woman in Heaven[3].)).

Bakri scholars also narrate from ᶜĀ'eshah, who said:

((I have never seen anyone more superior than Fāṭimah, except her father[4].)).

5- Human Houri

Besides Moslems, Bakris also believe that Fāṭimah was a human houri who was created from the produce of Heaven; and they narrate various aḥādēth[5] in this regard from Rasōlollāh, one of which is what ᶜĀ'eshah narrates:

---

[1] al-Bedāyah wa al-Nehāyah / Ibn Kothayr = vol. 6, page 201. Faḍā'el al-Ṣaḥābah / Ibn Ḥanbal = vol. 2, page 788. Faḍā'el al-Ṣaḥābah / al-Nasā'i = vol. 1, page 58. Fatḥ al-Bāri / al-ᶜAsqalāni = vol. 6, pages 447 and 471; vol. 7, pages 78 and 105. Fayḍ al-Qadēr / al-Monāwi = vol. 1, page 105. Ḥelyat al-Awleyā' / Abō Noᶜaym = vol. 4, page 190. Majmaᶜ al-Zawā'ed / al-Haythami = vol. 9, page 201. al-Moᶜjam al-Kabēr / al-Ṭabarāni = vol. 22, page 402. Moṣannaf / Ibn Abi Shaybah = vol. 6, page 388. Mosnad / Aḥmad = vol. 5, page 391. Mosnad / al-Bazzār = vol. 3, page 102. al-Mostadrak / al-Naysābōri = vol. 3, page 164. Ṣaḥēḥ / al-Bokhāri = vol. 3, pages 1326 and 1360. Ṣaḥēḥ / al-Termedhi = vol. 5, page 660. Seyar Aᶜlām al-Nobalā' / al-Dhahabi = vol. 2, page 123; vol. 3, page 252. al-Sonan al-Kobrā / al-Bayhaqi = vol. 5, pages 80 and 95. Tadrēb al-Rāwi / al-Soyōṭi = vol. 2, page 225. al-Dhorreyyah al-Ṭāhirah / al-Dōlābi = vol. 1, page 103. Waselat al-Ma'āl = page 176.

[2] Yanābēᶜ al-Mawaddah / al-Qandōzi = page 247.

[3] Mosnad / Aḥmad = vol. 1, page 293.

[4] al-Sērah al-Ḥalabiyyah / al-Ḥalabi = vol. 2, page 6.

[5] Plural of ḥadēth: a narration from one of the Fourteen Maᶜṣōmēn.

((I frequently saw Rasōlollāh kiss Fāṭimah; so one day I said: O Rasōlollāh! I see you do something I had not seen you do before.
So he told me: O Ḥomayrā'![1] Indeed, on the night during which I was taken to the sky, I entered Heaven and I stood by its most beautiful tree, with the whitest leaves, and the most delicious fruit. So I took from its fruit and ate...
And when I descended to the earth, I approached Khadējah; and she became pregnant with Fāṭimah from that produce.
So whenever I yearn for the scent of Heaven, I smell the scent of Fāṭimah. O Ḥomayrā'! Verily, Fāṭimah is not like the human women[2].)).

Bakri scholars also narrate from ᶜĀ'eshah, who said:

((Whenever the Prophet returned from a journey, he kissed Fāṭimah's throat and said: From her I smell the scent of Heaven[3].)).

Bakri scholars also narrate the following from Rasōlollāh:

((My daughter Fāṭimah is a Human Houri[4].)).

---

[1] A name by which the Prophet sometimes called ᶜĀ'eshah.
[2] Farā'ed al-Semṭayn / al-Ḥamō'i = vol. 2, page 61. Lesān al-Mēzān / al-ᶜAsqalāni = vol. 1, page 134; vol. 5, page 160. Majmaᶜ al-Zawā'ed / al-Haythami = vol. 9, page 202. al-Majrōḥēn / al-Bosti = vol. 2, pages 29 and 30. Mēzān al-Eᶜtedāl / al-Dhahabi = vol. 1, page 212; vol. 4, page 220. al-Moᶜjam al-Kabēr / al-Ṭabarāni = vol. 22, page 400. Tārēkh Baghdād / al-Baghdādi = vol. 5, page 87.
[3] Lesān al-Mēzān / al-ᶜAsqalāni = vol. 1, page 134.
[4] Esᶜāf al-Rāgheben / Ibn al-Ṣabbān = page 188. Fayḍ al-Qadēr / al-Monāwi = vol. 4, page 422. Kanz al-ᶜOmmāl / al-Hendi = vol. 13, page 94. Moᶜjam al-Shoyokh / al-Ṣaydāwi = vol. 1, page 359. al-Ṣawāᶜeq al-Moḥreqah / al-Haythami = page 160.

((Fāṭimah was created as a houri in the shape of a human[1].)).

((I smell the scent of Heaven from the throat of Fāṭimah[2].)).

((Whenever I yearn for the scent of Heaven, I smell Fāṭimah's neck[3].)).

((Whenever I yearn for the produce of Heaven, I kiss Fāṭimah[4].)).

---

[1] Manāqib ᶜAli ibn Abi Ṭālib / Ibn al-Maghāzili = page 296.
[2] Yanābēᶜ al-Mawaddah / al-Qandōzi.
[3] Manāqib ᶜAli ibn Abi Ṭālib / Ibn al-Maghāzili = page 360. Montakhab Kanz al-ᶜOmmāl / al-Hendi = vol. 5, page 97. Nōr al-Abṣār / al-Shablanji = page 51.
[4] Nōr al-Abṣār / al-Shablanji = page 51.

SAYYEDAT NESĀ' AL-ᶜĀLAMĒN'S KARĀMĀT AND MOᶜJEZĀT

Supernatural actions that are performed by or for Godly persons are either done in a challenge, etc. by which the Godly person tries to show his or her challenger the right path, in this case the supernatural action is called a moᶜjezah. Or they are done for other reasons, in which case the supernatural action is called a karāmah.

And like the other Fourteen Maᶜṣōmēn*(AmS)*[1], Sayyedat Nesā' al-ᶜĀlamēn performed some of the greatest karāmāt[2] and moᶜjezāt[3] ever recorded in history books.

A few examples of her karāmāt and moᶜjezāt are as follows:

1- The light of Fāṭimah's face

Bakri scholars narrate from ᶜĀ'eshah, who said:

((We used to sew and spin and put the thread through the needle-hole, at night, in the light of Fāṭimah's face[4].)).

---

[1] *ᶜAlayhemos Salām,* peace be upon them.

[2] Plural of karāmah.

[3] Plural of moᶜjezah.

[4] Mostadrakāt ᶜAwālim al-ᶜOlōm / al-Abṭaḥi = vol. 11, page 75, from: Akhbār al-Dowal wa Āthār al-Owal / al-Qermāni = page 87.

2- Fire does not burn Fāṭimah

Moslems narrate:

((One day ᶜĀ'eshah went to Fāṭimah's home while she was cooking a kind of pap for Ḥasan and Ḥosayn, with flour, milk and fat in a pot.
However, while the pot was boiling on the fire, Fāṭimah was stirring its contents with her finger.
So ᶜĀ'eshah left horrified and went to her father and told him: O Father! Indeed, I have seen of Fāṭimah Zahrā' a very surprising act. I saw her cooking and stirring the contents of a pot that was boiling on the fire with her hand.
So he told her: O Daughter! Keep this a secret, as this is very significant.
Later, Rasōlollāh ascended the menbar[1], praised Allāh and extolled Him, then he said: The people hold as significant, and regard as too much, what they have seen of the pot and the fire. By Him Who sent me with the Mission, and selected me for the Prophethood! Verily, Allāh, the Most High, has prohibited the fire from burning Fāṭimah's meat, and blood, and hair, and nerve, and bone, and has kept away her descendants and followers from Hell.
Verily, of the descendants of Fāṭimah is whom the fire, and the sun, and the moon, and the stars, and the mountains obey; and the Jinn fight for; and the prophets called their peoples to believe in him; and the earth shall surrender to him its treasures; and the sky shall bring down on him its blessings.
Woe unto him who doubts the superiority of Fāṭimah. May Allāh keep away from His Blessing he who hates her. May Allāh keep away from His Blessing

---

[1] A raised platform for a Moslem speaker in a mosque, Ḥosayneyyah, etc. where he/she would either stand or sit to give a speech.

he who hates her husband, and does not accept the imāmah[1] of her children.
Indeed, Fāṭimah will be asked [on the Day of Judgment by sinners to intervene], and she will accept, and she will intervene, and her intervention will be accepted by Allāh, despite those who do not like it[2].)).

3- The light of Fāṭimah's wrapper

It has been narrated:

((One day ᶜAli asked a Jew to loan him some barely, and the Jew demanded to hold something as security. So he gave him Fāṭimah's wrapper, which was made of wool, and the Jew took it to his house and put it in a room.
At night, when his wife entered that room, she saw a dazzling light illuminating the room; she went to her husband and told him what she had seen. The Jew was surprised.
He quickly jumped up and went to the room, and saw the light emitting rays as if it were coming from a shining full moon glowing at a close distance, so he was greatly amazed. When he looked closely at the source of the light, he saw it coming from Fāṭimah's wrapper.
Thus he ran to his relatives, and his wife ran to her relatives; and before long more than eighty Jews had gathered, and after seeing the light of Fāṭimah's wrapper they all converted to Islam[3].)).

---

[1] Successorship of Prophet Moḥammad. A person who has the imāmah is called an imām. There are only twelve a'emmah (plural of imām) all of whom have been chosen by Allāh, and appointed by the Prophet.
[2] ᶜAwālim al-ᶜOlōm / al-Baḥrāni = vol. 11, page 198.
[3] ᶜAwālim al-ᶜOlōm / al-Baḥrāni – vol. 11, page 228. Beḥār al-Anwār / al-Majlesi = vol. 43, page 30.

4- When Fāṭimah threatens to curse

Bakri and Moslem scholars narrate from Salmān, who said:

((When Amēr al-Mo'menēn was forcefully extracted from his home[1], Fāṭimah came out until she reached the grave [of Rasōlollāh], and said: Release my cousin. By Him Who sent Moḥammad with the Truth! If you do not release him, I will let loose my hair, and I will put Rasōlollāh's shirt on my head, and I will cry to Allāh; for surely Ṣāliḥ's she-camel[2] is not more precious to Allāh than me, and its young is not more precious to Allāh than my two sons[3].
[Salmān says:] I was close to her and, by Allāh! I suddenly saw the foundations of the mosque's walls come out from their places, so high that a man could pass from underneath them. So I went to her and said: O my Mistress! O my Lady! Allāh the Blessed, and the Most High, sent your father as a mercy [to the people], so do not bring them wrath.
Thus she returned, and the walls returned to their places and a lot of dust raised and went into our nostrils[4].)).

---

[1] To be taken to the mosque and be forced into pledging his allegiance to the Usurper of the Khelāfah, Abō Bakr.
[2] Allāh sent a very gigantic she-camel for Prophet Ṣāliḥ's people as a sign. However they killed it, and Allāh brought upon them a great calamity that destroyed them. The Holy Qor'ān refers to the Thamōd, Ṣāliḥ's people, and their actions in a number of āyāt, and mentions the she-camel in the following places: sōrah 7, āyah 73; sōrah 11, āyah 64; sōrah 17, āyah 59; sōrah 26, āyah 155; sōrah 91, āyah 13.
[3] al-Ekhteṣāṣ / al-Mofēd = page 185. al-Kāfi / al-Kolayni = vol. 8, page 238. Manāqib Āl Abi Ṭālib / Ibn Shahrāshōb = vol. 3, page 188. al-Rejāl / al-Ṭōsi. Tārēkh / al-Yaᶜqōbi = vol. 2, page 116. Tafsēr / al-ᶜAyyāshi = vol. 2, page 66. al-Wāfi / al-fayḍ = vol. 2, page 187.
[4] ᶜAwālim al-ᶜOlōm / al-Baḥrāni = vol. 11, page 231. Beḥār al-Anwār / al-Majlesi = vol. 28, page 206; vol. 43, page 47. al-Eḥtejāj / al-Ṭabarsi = vol. 1, page 86. Manāqib Āl Abi Ṭālib / Ibn Shahrāshōb = vol. 3, page 339. Nāsikh al-Tawārēkh = vol. 2, page 356.

It has also been narrated:

((When she was kept away from her rights, she took the jamb of Rasōlollāh's room, and said: Ṣāliḥ's she-camel is not dearer to Allāh than me. Then she pulled up the side of her veil to the sky and was about to pray, suddenly, the walls of the mosque raised from the ground, and calamity became imminent.
So Amēr al-Mo'menēn came and took her arm, and said: O Remainder of the Prophethood, and the Sun of the Messengerhood, and the Source of the ᶜEṣmah and Wisdom! Your father was a mercy for the people of the world, so do not be a wrath over them. I swear to you by the Most Compassionate, the Most Merciful. Thus she returned[1].)).

5- Angels serve Fāṭimah

It has been narrated from Omm Ayman, who said:

((One day I went to the home of my Lady Fāṭimah Zahrā' to visit her. It was a hot summer day. When I reached her home, I found the door locked; so I looked inside through the cracks of the door and saw Fāṭimah lying asleep next to the hand mill, and saw the hand mill grinding wheat, rotating without a hand turning it; and I also saw the cradle in which Ḥosayn was asleep next to her, rocking without someone moving it; and I saw a hand praising Allāh next to Fāṭimah's hand.
So I was surprised to see that, and went to my Master Rasōlollāh, greeted him and said: O Rasōlollāh! Indeed, I saw an amazing thing, the likes of which I had never seen before.
So he asked me: O Omm Ayman! What have you seen?

[1] Mostadrakāt ᶜAwālim al-ᶜOlōm / al-Abṭaḥi = vol. 11, page 232.

So I told him: I went to my Lady's home and found the door locked, and saw the hand mill grinding wheat, rotating without a hand turning it; and I saw Ḥosayn's cradle rocking without a hand moving it; and I saw a hand praising Allāh, the Most High, next to Fāṭimah's hand, and it was not attached to a person; so I was surprised to see that O my Master!
So he said: O Omm Ayman! Fāṭimah is fasting, and she is tired and hungry, and the day is very hot. So Allāh, the Most High, put her in drowsiness and she slept. So praise be to Him Who does not sleep. Then Allāh sent an angel to grind the food for her family; and He sent another angel to rock Ḥosayn's cradle, so that her sleep may not be disturbed; and He sent another angel to praise Him on behalf of Fāṭimah near her hand, with its reward going to Fāṭimah, as she had not been languorous in the invocation of Allāh. So whenever she sleeps, Allāh sends the reward of that angel's Praise of God to her.
So I said: O Rasōlollāh! Tell me who is the grinder, and who is the one who rocks Ḥosayn's cradle and talks tenderly to him, and who is the giver of Praise?
So the prophet smiled and said: The grinder is Jabra'ēl, and the one who rocks Ḥosayn's cradle is Mēkā'ēl[1], and the angel who praises is Esrāfēl[2].)).

---

[1] Also Michael.

[2] Mostadrakāt ᶜAwālim al-ᶜOlōm / al-Abṭaḥi = vol. 11, page 196. Beḥār al-Anwār / al-Majlesi = vol. 37, page 97.

SAYYEDAT NESĀ' AL-ᶜĀLAMĒN AND RASŌLOLLĀH'S MARTYRDOM

After ᶜĀ'eshah*(LAa)* and Ḥafṣah*(LAa)*[1] poisoned Rasōlollāh acting on the order of Abō Bakr and ᶜOmar[2], some very emotional and very important words were exchanged between the grief-stricken Fāṭimah and her beloved father on his deathbed.

In his last hours, Rasōlollāh gave his last instructions to Fāṭimah. In his last hours, Rasōlollāh gave his last prophecies about his descendants. In his last hours, Rasōlollāh showed, for one last time, his never ending worries about the future of a people who had the best ever chance to find eternal pleasure, yet they were about to sell all that for short term interests.

In these last hours, Rasōlollāh who was going to Heaven—to a place in which there is what no eye has ever seen, and no ear has ever heard, and no imagination has ever imagined—was saying goodbye to his only daughter, who was about to be subjected to the worst injustice and to face a most horrific death.

In these last hours, Fāṭimah was saying farewell to an affectionate, compassionate and warmhearted father, the most beloved person to her in the world, a person whom she had defended against the Idolaters when she was five, a person whom she had nursed whenever his enemies injured him, a person for whom she would have sacrificed herself.

---

[1] *Laᶜnatollāh ᶜAlayha,* may Allāh distance her from His Blessings and Mercy.

[2] For more detailed information about Rasōlollāh's martyrdom and his assassins, see: Rasōlollāh, the Messenger of Allāh / by the author = page 181.

So let us go back to those hours, and read some of what history records. It has been narrated:

> *((The Prophet called ᶜAli, Fāṭimah, Ḥasan and Ḥosayn, and said to those who where in the room: Leave me. And said to Omm Salamah: Stay at the door, and do not let anyone near it.*
>
> *Then he said to ᶜAli: Come near me. So he went nearer to him. And he took Fāṭimah's hand and put it on his chest and took ᶜAli's hand with his other hand. Then when Rasōlollāh wanted to speak, he was overcome with tears, so he could not talk.*
>
> *So Fāṭimah, ᶜAli, Ḥasan and Ḥosayn wept intensely, for Rasōlollāh's crying. Then Fāṭimah said: O Rasōlollāh! You have surely cut my heart, and set my liver on fire with your crying O Master of the Prophets! and O Trusty of his God! and O His friend and His Prophet! Who is left for my children after you?! And for the degradation that will descend upon me after you?! Who is left for ᶜAli, your Brother and the Defender of the Religion?! Who is left for Allāh's revelation?! Then she wept and fell on his face and kissed it, and ᶜAli and Ḥasan and Ḥosayn fell on him.*
>
> *He raised his head to them, and while Fāṭimah's hand was still in his hand, he placed it in ᶜAli's hand telling him: O Abā al-Ḥasan! Allāh's deposit, and His messenger's deposit is with you, so keep it safe; and I know that you will indeed do your duty.*
>
> *O ᶜAli! She is, by Allāh, the Chief of the Women of the Heaven. She is, by Allāh, the Great Maryam. Verily, I have asked Allāh for her and for you all, and He has granted me what I have asked of Him.*
>
> *O ᶜAli! Carry out what Fāṭimah tells you to do, for I have indeed told her what Jebra'il has told me. And know O ᶜAli! that I am satisfied from whom my daughter Fāṭimah is satisfied from, and also are my God and His angels.*

O ᶜAli! Woe unto him who does her injustice; woe unto him who extorts her rights from her; woe unto him who dishonors her sacredness[1].)).

Bakri scholars narrate from ᶜAli al-Helāli, who said:

((I went to the Prophet while he was on his deathbed, and found Fāṭimah sitting near his head. She wept heavily, so the Prophet looked at her and said: O my beloved Fāṭimah! What makes you cry?
So she said: I fear the loss after you.
So he said: O my beloved! Do you not know that Allāh, the Great and the Almighty, looked at the inhabitants of the earth and chose your father, and sent him with His message; then He looked once more and chose your husband, and revealed to me to give you to him in marriage?!
O Fāṭimah! We are a family to which, Allāh, the Great and the Almighty, has surely given seven gifts, that He had not given anyone before us and will not give anyone after us: I am the last of the Prophets, and the most honorable to Allāh. And my Waṣi[2] is the best of the awṣeyā'[3], and the most beloved to Allāh, the Great and the Almighty; and he is your husband. And our Martyr is the best of the martyrs, and the most beloved to Allāh; and he is Ḥamzah ibn ᶜAbdolmoṭṭalib, your father's uncle. And from us is he who has two green wings, who flies with the angels to whatever direction he wants; and he is your father's cousin, and your husband's brother. And from us are the two Grandsons of this nation, who are your sons Ḥasan and Ḥosayn, and they are the Masters of the Youths of Heaven; and their father, by Him Who sent me with the Truth, is better than them.

---

[1] Fāṭimah al-Zahrā' min al-Mahd elā al-Laḥd / al-Qazwēni = page 298.
[2] A successor of a prophet, chosen by Allāh and appointed by that prophet. A waṣi is not, himself, a prophet. Also khalēfah or caliph. Plural awṣeyā'.
[3] Plural of waṣi.

O Fāṭimah! By Him Who sent me with the Truth, from your sons is the Mahdi of this nation. When the world is reduced to commotion and turmoil, and when strife follows strife, and when the paths are broken, and when some people raid others, so that no old has mercy for a young, and no young has mercy for an old, then Allāh the Great and the Almighty shall send from your sons he who will conquer the fortresses of deviation, and the covered hearts; and he will rule according to the religion at the end of the time, as I ruled by the religion at the beginning of the time; and he will fill the world with justice just as it had been filled with oppression.

O Fāṭimah! Do not be sorrowful, and do not cry, for indeed Allāh, the Great and the Almighty, is more merciful and compassionate to you than I am, and that is because of your place and position in my heart. Indeed, Allāh gave you in marriage to your husband, and he is of the noblest pedigree, and with the most honorable position; and he is the most kind to the subjects, and the most just in equality, and the most knowledgeable in any field.

And I have surely asked my God, the Great and the Almighty, that you be the first of my family to join me.

And Fāṭimah died seventy-five days after Rasōlollāh's death[1].)).

A large number of Bakri scholars narrate from ᶜĀ'eshah who said:

((During his illness in which he died, Rasōlollāh summoned Fāṭimah, his daughter, and whispered in her ear, so she wept. Then he called her again and whispered in her ear, so she laughed.

[1] Majmaᶜ al-Zawā'ed / al-Haythami = vol. 9, page 165. al-Moᶜjam al-Awsaṭ / al-Ṭabarāni = vol. 6, page 327. al-Moᶜjam al-Kabēr / al-Ṭabarāni = vol. 3, page 57. Tārēkh Demashq / Ibn ᶜAsākir = vol. 42, page 130.

So I asked her: What was it that Rasōlollāh whispered in your ear so you wept, and then whispered in your ear again so you laughed?
She said: The Prophet told me that he will die in his illness, so I wept. Then he told me that I will be the first to join him from his family, so I laughed[1].)).

Some Bakri scholars have also narrated this ḥadēth in more detail:

((ᶜĀ'eshah used to say: During his illness in which he died, Rasōlollāh said to Fāṭimah: O daughter! come closer to me; then he whispered in her ear for a while, and she came back crying.
Moments later he told her again: O daughter! come closer to me; then he whispered in her ear for a while, and she came back laughing.
So ᶜĀ'eshah asked her: O daughter! Tell me what your father whispered in your ear.
And Fāṭimah said: You saw him whispering in my ear, and you thought I would tell you his secret while he is alive?!
It was very hard for ᶜĀ'eshah to be kept out of their secret. And when Rasōlollāh died, she once again asked Fāṭimah, and Fāṭimah said: Now I can tell you. He first whispered in my ear and told me that

---

[1] al-Āḥād wa al-Mathāni / al-Shaybāni = vol. 5, page 368. Dalā'el al-Nobowwah / Abō Noᶜaym = vol. 1, page 98. Faḍā'el al-Ṣaḥābah / Ibn Ḥanbal = vol. 2, page 754. Faḍā'el al-Ṣaḥābah / al-Nasā'i = vol. 1, page 77. al-Moᶜjam al-Kabēr / al-Ṭabarāni = vol. 22, pages 417, 419 and 420. Moᶜjam al-Moḥaddethēn / al-Dhahabi = vol. 1, page 14. Mosannaf / Ibn Abi Shaybah = vol. 6, page 388. Mosnad /Abi Yaᶜlā = vol. 12, page 122. Mosnad / Aḥmad = vol. 6, pages 77, 240 and 282. Ṣaḥēḥ / al-Bokhāri = vol. 3, pages 1327 and 1361; vol. 4, page 1612. Ṣaḥēḥ / Ibn Ḥabbān = vol. 15, page 402. Ṣaḥēḥ / Moslem = vol. 4, page 1904. Seyar Aᶜlām al-Nobalā' / al-Dhahabi = vol. 2, page 131. al-Sonan al-Kobrā / al-Bayhaqi = vol. 5, page 95. al-Ṭabaqāt al-Kobrā / Ibn Saᶜd = vol. 2, page 247. Tahdhēb al-Kamāl / al-Mazzi = vol. 35, page 253. al-Dhorreyyah al-Ṭāhirah / al-Dōlābi = vol. 1, page 100.

Jebra'il used to present to him the whole of the Qor'ān once every year, but he presented it to him twice this year...; and he said that he will shortly die, so I cried. And he told me: O daughter! Indeed, no Moslem woman is afflicted with more calamity than you, so do not be one with the least patience. Then, for the second time, he whispered in my ear and told me that I will be the first of his family members to join him, so I laughed[1].)).

Ibn ᶜAbbās narrates:

((Just before he died, Rasōlollāh cried so much that his tears soaked his beard.
Someone asked him: O Rasōlollāh! What makes you weep?
So he said: I weep for my descendants and what the evil of my nation will do to them after me. As if I can see my daughter Fāṭimah, having been subjected to injustice, cries out: O my father! But no member of my nation supports her.
So Fāṭimah heard that and cried. And Rasōlollāh told her: Do not cry O my daughter. So she said: I am not crying for what will be done to me after you, but I cry for leaving you O Rasōlollāh.
So he told her: Rejoice! O daughter of Moḥammad! with the quickness of joining me, for surely you are the first of my family to join me[2].)).

---

[1] al-Āḥād wa al-Mathāni / al-Shaybāni = vol. 5, page 369. Dalā'el al-Nobowwah / al-Bayhaqi = vol. 7, page 166. Fatḥ al-Bāri / al-ᶜAsqalāni = vol. 7, page 82. Kanz al-ᶜOmmāl / al-Hendi = vol. 16, page 281. al-Moᶜjam al-Kabēr / al-Ṭabarāni = vol. 22, page 417. Moshkel al-Āthār / al-Ṭaḥāwi = vol. 1, page 48. Dhakhā'er al-ᶜOqbā / al-Ṭabari = page 40. Tajhēz al-Jaysh / al-Dehlawi = page 98. al-Dhorreyyah al-Ṭāhirah / al-Dōlābi = vol. 1, page 105.

[2] Amāli / al-Ṭōsi = page 188. Beḥār al-Anwār / al-Majlesi = vol. 28, page 41; vol. 43, page 156.

Both Moslem and Bakri scholars narrate from Ibn ᶜAbbās who said that on his deathbed, Rasōlollāh said the following about Fāṭimah*(AaS)*[1]:

> *((...And when I saw her, I remembered what will be done to her after me. As if I can see the degradation enter her house, and her sacredness violated, and her rights usurped, and her inheritance kept away from her, and her ribs broken, and her fetus killed; while she cries: O my Moḥammad! But she will not be answered. And asks for help, but she will not be helped.*
>
> *Thus, she will remain after me sorrowful, grief-stricken and crying. Remembering the end of revelation from her home, at one time, and remembering my absence, at another time. She will feel desolated when the night falls, as she can no longer listen to me reciting the Qor'ān. Then she finds herself humiliated after having been respected at the time of her father; thus Allāh shall cheer her up and call on her with what He called on Maryam[2] the daughter of ᶜEmrān[3]/[4], so He would say: O Fāṭimah! Surely Allāh has chosen you and purified you and chosen you above the women of the world. O Fāṭimah! Keep to obedience to your Lord and perform sojōd[5] and perform rokōᶜ[6] with those who perform rokōᶜ.*

---

[1] *ᶜAlayhas Salām,* peace be upon her.

[2] Also Mary.

[3] Also Amran.

[4] Holy Qor'ān = sōrah 3, āyāt 42 and 43.

[5] A particular position in ṣalāt in which the forehead, the palms, the knees and the toes of both feet are placed on the ground. Sojōd is also performed on its own—not as part of a ṣalāt—for a number of reasons, some of which are mandatory whereas others are recommended.

[6] A particular position in ṣalāt in which a person bows down, placing the palms on the knees, whilst keeping the legs and the back in a straight position.

Then the pain will start, and she will fall ill; so Allāh, the Great, the Almighty, shall send Maryam the daughter of ᶜEmrān to her to nurse her and keep her company. She then shall say: O Lord! I have surely become bored with the life, and have been annoyed by the people; so join me with my father. And Allāh, the Great, the Almighty will join her with me; and she will be the first to join me from my family. Thus she will come to me sorrowful, anguished, grief-stricken, usurped, killed.
Rasōlollāh then added: O Allāh! Keep away from Your Mercy him who does her injustice, and punish him who usurps her, and humiliate him who humiliates her, and keep forever in Your Fire him who hits her side causing the miscarriage of her fetus.
And the angels said: Āmēn[1].)).

It has also been narrated:

((Then Ḥasan and Ḥosayn came [to Rasōlollāh], kissing his feet and weeping loudly. So ᶜAli wanted to move them, but the Prophet said: Let them smell me and I smell them, and see me for one last time and I see them for one last time, for they will encounter after me an earthquake, and a very difficult thing. So may Allāh distance from His Mercy those who wrong them. O Allāh! I surely entrust them to You and the righteous faithful[2].)).

Bakri scholars narrate that, during his last hours, Rasōlollāh told his daughter Fāṭimah:

---

[1] Amāli / al-Ṣadōq = page 112. Beḥār al-Anwār / al-Majlesi = vol. 28, page 38; vol. 43, page 172. Beshārat al-Moṣṭafa / al-Ṭabari = page 197. Ershād al-Qolōb / al-Daylami = vol. 2, page 295. al-Faḍā'el / Ibn Shādhān = page 8. Farā'ed al-Semṭayn / al-Ḥamō'i = vol. 2, page 35. Jalā' al-ᶜOyōn / al-Majlesi = vol. 1, page 186.
[2] Fāṭimah min al-Mahd elā al-Laḥd / al-Qazwēni = page 300.

((O daughter! Indeed, no Moslem woman is afflicted with more calamity than you, so do not be one with the least patience. You are surely the Chief of the Women of the Heaven[1]*.)).*

He also told her:

((Then he (Rasōlollāh) said: O daughter! You are the oppressed after me. And you are the week after me. So whomsoever annoys you, he has surely annoyed me; and whomsoever turns away from you, he has surely turned away from me; and whomsoever keeps

---

1 al-Āḥād wa al-Mathāni / al-Shaybāni = vol. 5, page 369. al-Bedāyah wa al-Nehāyah / Ibn Kothayr = vol. 3, page 206. Ansāb al-Ashrāf / al-Balādheri = page 405. al-Ecteqād / al-Maqrēzi = page 165. Ershād al-Sāri / al-Qasṭalāni = vol. 6, page 80. al-Eṣābah / al-cAsqalāni = vol. 4, page 367. Escāf al-Rāghebēn / Ibn al-Ṣabbān = page 128. al-Estēcāb / Ibn cAbdelbarr = vol. 2, page 750. al-Jāmic al-Ṣaghēr / al-Soyōṭi = vol. 1, page 7. Kanz al-cOmmāl / al-Hendi = vol. 13, page 95. al-Khaṣā'eṣ al-Kobrā / al-Soyōṭi = vol. 2, pages 226 and 265. Fatḥ al-Bāri / al-cAsqalāni = vol. 8, page 136. al-Foṣōl al-Mohemmah / Ibn al-Ṣabbāgh = page 127. Kanz al-cOmmāl / al-Hendi = vol. 7, page 111; vol. 16, page 281. Kefāyat al-Ṭālib / al-Kanji = page 275. al-Khaṣā'eṣ / al-Nasā'i = page 33. al-Maghāzi wa al-Seyar / al-Ḥaḍrami = page 286. Majmac al-Zawā'ed / al-Haythami = vol. 9, pages 23 and 201. Maqtal al-Ḥosayn / al-Khārazmi = page 55. Manāqib cAli ibn Abi Ṭālib / Ibn al-Maghāzili = page 5. al-Mocjam al-Kabēr / al-Ṭabarāni = vol. 22, page 417. Moshkel al-Āthār / al-Ṭaḥāwi = vol. 1, page 48. Mosnad / Aḥmad = vol. 3, page 64; vol. 5, page 391. Mosnad Fāṭimah / al-Soyōṭi = page 41, and a similar narration in pages 49, 51, 52, 78 and 79. al-Mostadrak / al-Naysabōri = vol. 3, pages 151 and 154. Osd al-Ghābah / Ibn al-Athēr = vol. 4, page 42. Ṣaḥēḥ / Bokhāri = vol. 4, page 203; vol. 5, page 20. Ṣaḥēḥ / Moslem = vol. 7, page 143. al-Ṣawācеq al-Mohreqah / al-Haythami = page 185. Seyar Aclām al-Nobala' / al-Dhahabi = vol. 3, page 168. Sharh al-Maqāṣid / al-Taftāzāni = vol. 2, page 221. Sonan / al-Termedhi = vol. 13, page 197. Tārēkh Demashq / Ibn cAsākir = vol. 4, page 95. al-Ṭabaqāt al-Kobrā = vol. 2, page 248. Tahdhēb al-Tahdhēb / al-cAsqalāni = vol. 12, page 441. Dhakhā'er al-cOqbā / al-Ṭabari = pages 39 and 136. al-Dhorreyyah al-Ṭāhirah / al-Dōlābi = vol. 1, page 105. Waselat al-Ma'āl / al-Ḥaḍrami = page 88. Yanābēc al-Mawaddah / al-Qandōzi = page 165.

ties with you, he has surely kept ties with me; and whomsoever breaks ties with you, he has surely broken ties with me; and whomsoever treats you fairly, he has surely treated me fairly. For surely you are from me and I am from you; and you are a part of me, and my soul that is between my sides. Then he said: To Allāh I complain of your oppressors[1].)).

And she addressed her father with these heartrending words just before his death:

((My soul be the sacrifice for your soul; my face be the shield for your face. O my father! Won't you speak to me a single word?! for surely I look at you and see you leaving this world, and I see the armies of death approaching you.
So he told her: My daughter! I am leaving you, so salām be upon you from me[2].)).

Sayyedat Nesā' al-ᶜĀlamēn was badly affected by Rasōlollāh's death. She had lost a dear father, and a great prophet whose death had been caused by poison at the hands of those who called themselves good Moslems, and were now claiming leadership.

She was grieving all the time, and crying most of her waking moments. Her great-grandson, Imām Bāqir(AS)[3], speaks of her sadness after Rasōlollāh's demise:

((Fāṭimah was not seen cheerful or laughing after Rasōlollāh's death, until she died[4].)).

---

[1] Fāṭimah min al-Mahd elā al-Laḥd / al-Qazwēni = page 301.
[2] Fāṭimah min al-Mahd elā al-Laḥd / al-Qazwēni = page 301.
[3] *ᶜAlayhes Salām,* peace be upon him.
[4] Kashf al-Ghommah / al-Erbelli = vol. 1, page 498.
Bakri scholars also narrate two similar aḥādēth from Imām Bāqir, which are:

> *((Fāṭimah was not seen laughing after Rasōlollāh, except once when she made a small smile.)).*
> *((...Except that she rarely made a short, small smile.)).* (Ḥelyat al-Awleyā' / Abō Noᶜaym = vol. 2, page 43. al-Ṭabaqāt al-Kobrā =

She was not even able to hear or see the things that reminded her of her father without losing consciousness, as the following two narrations show:

> *((When Rasōlollāh died, Belāl[1] refused to perform the adhān[2]. One day Fāṭimah said: I wish to hear the sound of my father's Mo'ath-then performing the adhān.*
> *So Belāl started to recite the adhān. When he said: "Allāho Akbar" (Allāh is greater), she remembered her father and his days, so she could not hold back her tears. And when he reached: "Ash-hado anna Moḥammadan Rasōlollāh" (I testify that Moḥammad is the Messenger of Allāh), Fāṭimah whooped and fell unconscious on her face.*
> *So people told Belāl: Stop O Belāl! for surely Rasōlollāh's daughter departed from this world, and they thought that she had died.*
> *So he stopped his adhān, and left it unfinished. And when Fāṭimah regained consciousness, she asked him to finish the adhān, but he refused and said: O Chief of the Women! I fear for you from what you will*

---

vol. 2, page 312. Tahdhēb al-Kamāl / al-Mazzi = vol. 35, page 253)

[1] Belāl was an Ethiopian slave who belonged to one of Makkah's Idolaters. He accepted Islam very early on, and thus suffered vicious tortures at the hands of his owner and his friends to renounce Islam and its prophet; but he bravely withstood the punishment and endured the pain, and instead of rejecting the One God, he reaffirmed his faith, under torture, by saying: One, One, One. Finally he escaped that terrifying excruciation when Rasōlollāh bought him from the Idolater and freed him.
After the migration to Madinah, the Prophet appointed him as the mo'adh-dhen (performer of the adhān: call to the daily wājib ṣalawāt.) in his mosque. He remained at that post until Rasōlollāh's martyrdom. However, when Abō Bakr usurped the khelāfah, Belāl refused to perform the adhān; and when the Bakri pressure mounted on him, he left Madinah for today's Syria, announcing that he no longer wanted to remain in Madinah.

[2] Call to the daily wājib ṣalawāt.

bring on yourself when you hear my voice reciting the adhān[1].)).

Bakri scholars narrate from Amēr al-Mo'menēn(AS)[2] who said:

((I washed Rasōlollāh (after his death) in his shirt. So Fāṭimah used to tell me: Show me the shirt. And whenever she smelled it, she lost consciousness. So seeing that, I hid the shirt[3].)).

---

[1] Fāṭimah min al-Mahd elā al-Laḥd / al-Qazwēni = page 312.
[2] *ᶜAlayhes Salām,* peace be upon him.
[3] Fāṭimah min al-Mahd elā al-Laḥd / al-Qazwēni = page 313, from Maqtal al-Ḥosayn / al-Khārazmi.

SAYYEDAT NESĀ' AL-ᶜĀLAMĒN AND THE BAKRI PARTY

On the 28th of Ṣafar, 11 years after the Hejrah[1], Rasōlollāh answered the call of Allāh after ᶜĀ'eshah and Ḥafṣah, who were implementing the order of Abō Bakr and ᶜOmar, forcefully poisoned him[2].

Rasōlollāh had already told ᶜĀ'eshah that he would die soon, and he had already performed the Farewell Pilgrimage[3], telling Moslems that his death was near; so the Bakri leaders knew that his death would come within a few months. But why did they have to poison him when he was going to die anyway?!

The decision to assassinate him, at this particular time, was made for two reasons:

Firstly: because Rasōlollāh had started a new method in appointing Amēr al-Mo'menēn*(AS)*[4] as his khalēfah. He would often give speeches to large crowds during which he would appoint Imām ᶜAli*(AS)*[5] as his successor, as he did so after the Farewell Pilgrimage to an audience of more than one hundred and twenty thousand; and then he would tell them to give their pledge of allegiance to Imām ᶜAli as

---

[1] Rasōlollāh's migration from Makkah to Madinah in the thirteenth year of his mission. Moslems start their lunar calendar from the year of the Hejrah.

[2] For more detailed information about the assassination of Rasōlollāh, and his assassins, see: Rasōlollāh, The Messenger of Allāh / by the author = page 181.

[3] For more detailed information about the Farewell Pilgrimage, see: Rasōlollāh, The Messenger of Allāh / by the author = page 171.

[4] *ᶜAlayhes Salām,* peace be upon him.

[5] *ᶜAlayhes Salām,* peace be upon him.

his Khalēfah, and call him by his God-given title: "Amēr al-Mo'menēn", Commander of the Faithful[1]. Therefore the Bakris desperately needed to stop these events, by quickly assassinating him, so that Abō Bakr(LA)[2] could still show some legitimacy after usurping the khelāfah.

And secondly: because he was evacuating all the Bakri leaders from Madinah, ordering them to join Osāmah's army which was going to face a much larger and stronger Roman army in today's Jordan; a mission that would take several months and have many casualties. And they knew that the Prophet would die while they were away and Amēr al-Mo'menēn would become his successor, and that would be the end of the Bakri ambition of coming to power.

And that is why the Bakri leaders obstinately insisted on staying in Madinah and brought desperate excuses for not marching with Osāmah. But the Prophet repeated his direct order, and prayed against those who disobeyed this order[3]. And as this shameless

---

[1] For more detailed information about the appointment of Amēr al-Mo'menēn as Rasōlollāh's khalēfah after the Farewell Pilgrimage, see: Rasōlollāh, the Messenger of Allāh / by the author = pages 171-180.

[2] *Laᶜnatollāh ᶜAlayh,* may Allāh distance him from His Blessings and Mercy.

[3] Bakri scholars admit that Abō Bakr and ᶜOmar were among the people who were ordered by Rasōlollāh to join Osāmah's army; and they all agree that Rasōlollāh's order for joining Osāmah's army was extraordinarily emphasized and stressed on, as he repeated it several times and on numerous occasions; and no Bakri scholar has ever claimed that Abō Bakr and ᶜOmar did actually march with Osāmah. Therefore Abō Bakr and ᶜOmar disobeyed the repeated direct orders of Rasōlollāh, and ignored his firm commands, and were among those against whom Rasōlollāh had prayed for disobeying his order.

But to make matters even worse, some Bakri scholars claim that Abō Bakr and ᶜOmar had two reasons for not joining Osāmah's army and staying in Madinah—disobeying Rasōlollāh:

First: That after Rasōlollāh's death, Madinah was in danger of a Bedouin raid, so they needed to stay in the city to protect it.

Second: That after Rasōlollāh's death, the people of Madinah were divided over the leadership, so they needed to stay to unite the people.

However, these lame excuses bring more problems for the Bakris:

1- Bakri scholars admit that Rasōlollāh had announced his death several months before he died, so at the time of ordering Abō Bakr and ᶜOmar to

join Osāmah's army, he knew that he would shortly die. Thus disobeying his order to march with Osāmah for the excuses of protecting Madinah against the two internal and external dangers means that Abō Bakr and ᶜOmar knew Moslems' interests better than Rasōlollāh, and cared about Moslems more than Rasōlollāh.

2- The imminent Bedouin raid on Madinah is yet to be proven; as the Bedouins around Madinah were all Moslems, and had been loyal Moslems for some time, and had not posed any danger on Madinah in the previous years. So why should they threaten to invade the city after the Prophet's death?! This external danger seems to be just another fictitious Bakri account of historic events, a product of the creative Bakri imagination by which revealing events are hid.

3- Supposing that the danger was real, how could Abō Bakr and ᶜOmar have defended the city?! They were not famous fighters, as they had not killed or even injured anyone in the numerous battles they had participated in during the life of Rasōlollāh. And they did not have a shred of bravery, as they were not killed when many others were, and they were not injured as were all the other Moslems who had taken part in those early wars, including Rasōlollāh. They often fled from the battlefield and left their positions.

4- If the Bakris claim that the role of Abō Bakr and ᶜOmar in the defense of Madinah was important in planning a good defense strategy; then they are overseeing the fact that neither of them had ever been known to be any good in that field.

5- And if they claim that Abō Bakr and ᶜOmar were competent military commanders, then the fact that each one of them commanded only one campaign during Rasōlollāh's life and completely failed in his command and had to be replaced by Amēr al-Mo'menēn, proves it wrong.

6- In almost every account of this event in Bakri references, Abō Bakri is quoted to have said that he does not care if Madinah is raided and its people are hurt and stripped of their positions, and that under no circumstances would he keep Osāmah's army in Madinah to protect the city, because he does not want to disobey Rasōlollāh's order in this regard. So if the protection of Madinah is not his aim, why did he and ᶜOmar stay behind?!

7- Is it conceivable that with such a danger so imminent, the men of Madinah would knowingly and willingly decide to march to today's Jordan, leaving their wives, children, and positions unprotected at the mercy of the Bedouin raiders?! Why did not, at least, half of them stay in Madinah?!

8- And if the Bakris claim that Rasōlollāh's order regarding Abō Bakr and ᶜOmar joining Osāmah's army was in force while he was alive, but it was no longer valid after his death; therefore Abō Bakr and ᶜOmar had to stay in

insubordination continued, Rasōlollāh summoned Qays ibn ᶜAbādah and Ḥabbāb ibn al-Mondher to round them up and escort them to Jorf, outside Madinah, where Osāmah was camping. However, when the escort returned to Madinah to report the completion of its

---

Madinah to unite the people who were having disagreements about the leadership after the Prophet; one could say:

1- Assuming that there was such a disagreement, what made Abō Bakr and ᶜOmar so capable in resolving it, especially when only the Bakris listened to them?!

2- And their claim that after Rasōlollāh's death Moslems were left without a leader and they had to choose a khalēfah to prevent internal disintegration, and that is why Abō Bakr and ᶜOmar stayed behind, is easily refuted by the fact that Rasōlollāh did indeed choose his successor before his death, as he had already appointed Amēr al-Mo'menēn as his khalēfah and had taken pledges of allegiance from the Moslems for him.

3- But supposing that Rasōlollāh had not appointed a khalēfah, and that the Moslems had to choose a leader for themselves, then why did only Abō Bakr and ᶜOmar return from Osāmah's army and ordered the others to leave?! Is it possible to have an election with only one candidate?! And why were not others in Osāmah's army given a chance to be chosen for the khelāfah?!

4- Further more, it could be said that there was no disagreement between the Moslems over the khelāfah, as they all wanted Amēr al-Mo'menēn as the Khalēfah; and that the trouble started when the Bakris began to show Abō Bakr as the Khalēfah. If we look at the facts, we see that the disagreements over the khelāfah were between three camps:

a: the Moslems who wanted Amēr al-Mo'menēn as the khalēfah, because Rasōlollāh had appointed him;

b: the Bakris who wanted Abō Bakr to be the khalēfah, because he had promised them wealth and power;

c: and the Anṣār who wanted one of them to be the khalēfah, because they knew that if the Bakris—who were among the Mohājirēn—usurp the khelāfah from Amēr al-Mo'menēn, the precedence would always be given to the Bakri Mohājirēn, and that at no time will any of the Anṣār be allowed to share some of the wealth and power.

After the above, one can say that Abō Bakr and ᶜOmar stubbornly disobeyed Rasōlollāh's repeated direct orders about joining Osāmah's army and stayed behind to usurp the khelāfah from Amēr al-Mo'menēn and become the first and the second khalēfah?!

mission, Rasōlollāh said that those people were not about to obey his order and stay with Osāmah[1].

Just as the Prophet had foretold, Abō Bakr along with his men slipped back into the city under the cover of darkness and hid, waiting for the right moment to appear and act as Rasōlollāh's representative before his death, which would automatically make him the khelāfah after his death. However, the Prophet immediately announced their return, describing it as: "A great evil that has come upon the city of Madinah". But regardless, they continued with their plot to pave the way for Abō Bakr's future position as the Khalēfah instead of Amēr al-Mo'menēn.

And as Rasōlollāh's denouncements and strong stances against them became clearer and more intense and as he went further to give public speeches against them for disobeying his order to march with Osāmah, all of which were making it harder for Abō Bakr to usurp the khelāfah, the Bakris decided to poison him to death, and bring his death nearer and prevent further damage.

After giving the order, Abō Bakr retreated to Sonh, a Madinah suburb, and most of his men hid in the city, waiting for the poison to take effect.

Therefore when Rasōlollāh[2] died, the Bakri party, with the exception of ᶜĀ'eshah and Ḥafṣah, was not present in public. And even ᶜĀ'eshah, herself, was not with Rasōlollāh at the time of his death, as many Bakri scholars narrate from her[3]; although Bakri references testify that she was present only moments before, when the Angel of Death came, and she even heard him[4]!!!

---

[1] For more detailed information, see: Rasōlollāh, the Messenger of Allāh / by the author = page 201.

[2] Messenger of Allāh; a title exclusively given to Prophet Moḥammad by Allāh.

[3] Bakri scholars narrate:

> *((Maᶜādh asked ᶜĀ'eshah: How did you find Rasōlollāh at the time of his illness and death?*
> *So she answered: O Maᶜādh! I was not with him at the time of his death; but go to Fāṭimah, his daughter, and ask her.)).* (al-Eṣābah / al-ᶜAsqalāni = vol. 8, page 41)

[4] Bakri scholars narrate:

> *((Then the Angel of Death descended and stood at the door, in the shape of a Bedouin, and said: Peace be upon you O*

So why would she leave just as the Prophet was about to die?! Is that not a time when people like to be close to their loved ones?!

The fact is that as soon as ᶜĀ'eshah heard ᶜEzrā'ēl[1] at the door, and heard Rasōlollāh telling Fāṭimah that ᶜEzrā'ēl was here to take his soul, she quickly left to send a courier to her father in Sonh and report Rasōlollāh's death to the other Bakris, so that they could quickly gather and make their move for the khelāfah.

Therefore, within minutes of Rasōlollāh's death, ᶜOmar[(LA)2], who was in hiding along with some other Bakris, came to stop the announcement of his death, allowing enough time for Abō Bakr to

---

Members of the Household of the Prophethood! and the Source of the Messengerhood, and the point of come and go for the angels. Do I have permission to enter?
So ᶜĀ'eshah said to Fāṭimah: Answer the man.
And Fāṭimah said: May Allāh reward you for coming here, O Servant of Allāh! Indeed, Rasōlollāh is ill.
The man repeated his request to enter for a second time. And ᶜĀ'eshah said to Fāṭimah: Answer the man.
So Fāṭimah said: May Allāh reward you for coming here, O Servant of Allāh! Indeed, Rasōlollāh is ill.
Then the man repeated for a third time: Peace be upon you O Members of the Household of the Prophethood! and the Source of the Messengerhood, and the point of come and go for the angels. Do I have permission to enter? As this is unavoidable.
Rasōlollāh said: O Fāṭimah! Who is at the door?
So she said: O Rasōlollāh! The man at the door is requesting permission to enter. We told him twice that you could not receive him; but for a third time he repeated his request with a voice that made me tremble.
The Prophet told her: O Fāṭimah! Do you know who is at the door? He is the destroyer of the pleasures; and the disperser of the groups; he is the one who makes the spouses widower and widow, and makes the children orphans; he is the demolisher of the homes, and the populator of the graves; he is the Angel of Death.
Enter, may Allāh be Merciful to you, O Angel of Death! So he entered.)). (Ḥelyat al-Awleyā' / Abō Noᶜaym = vol. 4, page 76. Majmaᶜ al-Zawā'ed / al-Haythami = vol. 9, page 29. al-Moᶜjam al-Kabēr / al-Ṭabarāni = vol. 3, page 62)

[1] The Angel of Death.

[2] *Laᶜnatollāh ᶜAlayh,* may Allāh distance him from His Blessings and Mercy.

return. And to do this successfully, ᶜOmar denied that Rasōlollāh had died, saying that he was alive and threatened to kill anyone who said otherwise[1].

And as soon as Abō Bakr appeared in Madinah, the Bakri leaders headed for the Bani Sāᶜedah's gethering place[2]; and while Amēr al-Mo'menēn and the other Moslems were busy with Rasōlollāh's burial ceremonies, the Bakris won over their Anṣār[3] rivals and appointed Abō Bakr as Rasōlollāh's Khalēfah. Therefore no Bakri party member was present in any of the burial ceremonies!!!

Now, with the support of a number of influential Mohājirēn[4] and Anṣār, through promises of wealth and power and also threats, Abō Bakr had the backing of numerous tribes which provided him with a very large number of fighters. With all this force, the Bakris went to the mosque and asked the Moslems for their pledge of allegiance to Abō Bakr.

Meanwhile, a number of Moslems who had not followed the tribal rule of blind obedience to their chiefs, and were not tempted by the promises of wealth and power and did not give in to the threats, stayed with Amēr al-Mo'menēn and refused to give their pledge of allegiance to Abō Bakr the False Khalēfah.

---

[1] Ibn Abi al-Ḥadēd, one of the most famous Bakri scholars, writes in his highly respected encyclopedia:

> *((All Islamic historians narrate that when Rasōlollāh died, Abō Bakr was in his home in Sonh, so ᶜOmar ibn al-Khaṭṭāb said: Rasōlollāh has not died, and will not die until he makes his religion prevail over all religions; and that he will, most assuredly, return and will, most certainly, cut the arms and the legs of those who were shocked with his apparent death. I will strike anyone who says Rasōlollāh has died with my sword.)).* (Sharh Nahj al-Balāghah / Ibn Abi al-Ḥadēd = vol. 2, page 40)

For more detailed information, see: Rasōlollāh, the Messenger of Allāh / by the author = page 219.

[2] For more detailed information, see: Rasōlollāh, the Messenger of Allāh / by the author = page 222.

[3] Plural of Anṣāri: a citizen of Madinah who converted to Islam before the liberation of Makkah.

[4] Plural of Mohājir: a Moslem who migrated from Makkah to Madinah to escape Idolater suppression, before the liberation of Makkah.

At this crucial time, a refusal of this magnitude was very dangerous for Abō Bakr, and he could not afford to have Amēr al-Mo'menēn and a number of influential Moslems oppose his khelāfah. Therefore he ordered ᶜOmar to crush this resistance at all costs.

ᶜAli and Fāṭimah's options

After Abō Bakr usurped the khelāfah through promises of wealth and power and intimidation and threats, Amēr al-Mo'menēn and Sayyedat Nesā' al-ᶜĀlamēn had several options:

1- To publicly and actively support Abō Bakr, and give up all claim for the khelāfah, thus protect their personal interests and share the wealth and power. And it is very clear why the likes of Amēr al-Mo'menēn and Sayyedat Nesā' al-ᶜĀlamēn could never have chosen with this option.

2- To give their pledge of allegiance to Abō Bakr like everyone else, without any sort of opposition, thus protect themselves from the Bakri wrath. If they had done so, then the whole world would have believed that Abō Bakr and his successors represented Islam, and see their goals, hopes, values, teachings, etc. as that of Islam, and so there would be nothing called real Islam. And it is quite clear why they could not have taken this option.

3- To take up arms against the Bakri party and try to topple their regime, and replace Abō Bakr, the False Khalēfah, with Amēr al-Mo'menēn, the True Khalēfah. If they had chosen the armed opposition, then countless people would have been killed, and the right path would have been severed completely and forever. And it is obvious why they could not have selected this option.

4- To stay in the middle, thus non-violent resistance. As non-violent actions attract a limited violent reaction, therefore a non-violent opposition is usually suppressed to a certain extent, which allows it to be known to others and live on however thinly. And this was the only feasible option for Amēr al-Mo'menēn and Sayyedat Nesā' al-ᶜĀlamēn and the rest of the Rightful Kholafā', which allowed their opposition to the Bakri party be known to the peoples of their times and live on to our time without being severed completely.

However, as it was an opposition, and as it posed a great danger to the Bakri regime, it was suppressed violently throughout the ages. It started by the violent attacks on Amēr al-Mo'menēn and Sayyedat Nesā' al-ᶜĀlamēn, causing her death and the miscarriage of her fetus that was named Moḥassin by Rasōlollāh, and it continued by the assassination, vicious killing, long imprisonment and torture of every single khalēfah, not to mention their families and supporters, by the successive Bakri regimes.

Therefore after burying Rasōlollāh, when Amēr al-Mo'menēn saw that Abō Bakr had usurped the khelāfah and had gathered a number of tribes in his corner, he went to his home and stayed there.

And as the Bakri party desperately needed his pledge of allegiance to complete its mission, it started a campaign of pressure that rapidly increased its force and violence.

Fāṭimah's role in the defense of ᶜAli

During this crucial time, Sayyedat Nesā' al-ᶜĀlamēn played a very important role:

1- She strongly supported Amēr al-Mo'menēn in his claim for the khelāfah.

2- She strongly opposed Abō Bakr in his claim for the khelāfah.

3- By standing with Amēr al-Mo'menēn, she prevented the Bakri party from forcefully extracting his pledge of allegiance.

4- By supporting Amēr al-Mo'menēn, she helped his opposition to the Bakri party continue during those first crucial days, and become widely known.

5- By defending Amēr al-Mo'menēn, she prevented the Bakri party from eliminating this perilous obstacle from its path. Thus she became a shield for ᶜAli from the most serious wrath of the Bakri regime; and she effectively attracted the sharpness of the Bakri hatred during those early days to herself, averting it from ᶜAli, sacrificing herself to prevent the Bakri regime from killing him.

The more the Bakri regime struggled to force Amēr al-Mo'menēn into submission, the more she supported him and opposed them; and the harder the Bakri regime tried to draw him into a conflict which would result in his death, the harder she worked to attract the sharp edge of the sword to herself and to keep it as far away as possible from Amēr al-Mo'menēn. So that he neither be coerced into swearing allegiance to Abō Bakr and nor be killed.

Therefore when ᶜOmar and three hundred Bakri ruffians converged on her home, in their worst attack, to forcefully take Amēr al-Mo'menēn to Abō Bakr and end his opposition either by his allegiance to Abō Bakr or by a summary execution, we see how she stands in their way, and tries to prevent them from entering her home; and we see how insistent she remains despite the various injuries that they inflict upon her. We see how she stands her ground behind that burning door, despite the fire and that hot jagged nail piercing her chest, and how she struggles to keep them out under those vicious whips, and against those punches and kicks.

ᶜOmar and the other Bakri ruffians could only enter the house when Fāṭimah was unconscious. But as soon as she regained consciousness she ignored all the unbearable pains and life-threatening injuries and hurried after Abō Bakr's ruffians who were pulling Amēr al-Mo'menēn by his neck to Abō Bakr.

The following narration shows just how insistent she was in preventing the Bakris from extracting a pledge of allegiance from ᶜAli, and from executing him if he continued his refusal:

> *((When they dragged Amēr al-Mo'menēn [towards the mosque] with a saddlecloth, Fāṭimah held on to one side of it despite all the pain that she was suffering, pulling it, and the others were pulling to the other direction. Then ᶜOmar took a sword from Khālid ibn al-Walēd and began to hit Fāṭimah on her shoulder with its sheath until she was wounded[1].)).*

Finally, she threatened to pray to Allāh to send a calamity to destroy them, and the Bakris released ᶜAli when they saw the foundations of the mosque rise from its place[2].

---

[1] Mostadrakāt ᶜAwālim al-ᶜOlōm / al-Abṭaḥi = vol. 11, page 581

[2] See page 214 of this book.

Several attacks on Fāṭimah's home

To coerce Amēr al-Mo'menēn who was staying in his home to give his pledge of allegiance, Abō Bakr ordered the Bakris to fetch him to the mosque. But he refused to go with them, and Sayyedat Nesā' al-ᶜĀlamēn prevented them from forcing their way into her home.

So these house calls repeated, each time with more terror and viciousness. And a large number of Bakri references have recorded them, but as usual, they have failed to mention some of the more damaging details. Nevertheless, what they have narrated, however incomplete, short, and heavily censured, remains highly troublesome for the Bakri faith.

Below are a few examples of such Bakri narrations about a number of these attacks:

> *((Abō Bakr sought after a group of people who had not given [him] their pledge of allegiance, and had gathered in ᶜAli's home; so he sent ᶜOmar to them, and he came and called them out, but they refused to come out. Then ᶜOmar asked for some wood and said: By Him in Whose hand is ᶜOmar's life! Either you come out now, or I will most certainly put the house on fire with whoever is inside.*
> *Someone said to him: O Abā Ḥafṣ[1]! Indeed, Fāṭimah is inside.*
> *ᶜOmar said: Even so.*
> *So the people came out and gave Abō Bakr their pledge of allegiance, except ᶜAli, who said: I have sworn not to leave, and not to put my robe on my shoulder, until I compile the Holy Qur'ān.*
> *Then Fāṭimah came and stood at the door and said: I have never seen a people gathered on a worst thing than you. You left the body of Rasōlollāh with us and determined the leadership between yourselves; you did not give us the leadership and did not allow us our right.*

---

[1] ᶜOmar was also known as Abā Ḥafṣ.

So ᶜOmar went to Abō Bakr and told him: Will you not force this rejecter to pledge his allegiance to you?!
So Abō Bakr said to Qonfodh: Go and summon ᶜAli to me. So he went to ᶜAli.
Ali asked him: What do you want?
Qonfodh said: Rasōlollāh's Khalēfah calls for you.
So ᶜAli astonishingly said: Indeed, how soon you fabricated lies against Rasōlollāh's wishes!!
Qonfodh returned and conveyed the message, and Abō Bakr wept for a long time.
So, for a second time, ᶜOmar said: Do not allow this rejecter any time for giving his pledge of allegiance.
So Abō Bakr said to Qonfodh: Return to him and tell him: Amēr al-Mo'menēn[1] *calls you to give your pledge of allegiance.*
So Qonfodh went to ᶜAli and gave him the message.
And ᶜAli raised his voice saying: Allāh is far above! Abō Bakr has surely claimed what is not his.
Qonfodh returned and conveyed the message, so Abō Bakr cried again for a long time.
Then ᶜOmar stood up and walked with his group to Fāṭimah's door, and they knocked on the door. When Fāṭimah heard their voices, she called out, with all her voice: O my father! O Rasōlollāh! What have we suffered after you from the son of al-Khaṭṭāb[2] *and the son of Abi Qoḥāfah*[3]*?!*
So when the group heard her voice and her crying, they left weeping, and their hearts nearly stopped and their livers nearly cracked. But ᶜOmar stayed there along with a few men, and they extracted ᶜAli from his home and took him to Abō Bakr.
So they said to him: Give your pledge of allegiance.
Ali: What if I do not?

---

[1] Commander of the Faithful; a title exclusively given to Imām ᶜAli by Allāh. Although its use by others is prohibited, but Bakri rulers have always used it for themselves.

[2] al-Khaṭṭāb was said to be ᶜOmar's father.

[3] Abō Bakr's father.

ᶜOmar and his men: Then, by Allāh besides Whom there is no God, we will behead you.
Ali: Then you will have killed the Servant of Allāh and the Brother of His Messenger[1].
ᶜOmar said: The Servant of Allāh, yes, but the Brother of His Messenger, no[2].
And during all of this, Abō Bakr was not talking and was keeping silent. So ᶜOmar said to him: Will you not give your order about him?
Abō Bakr: I will not force him to do anything as long as Fāṭimah is on his side.
So [after being released] ᶜAli went to Rasōlollāh's grave, screaming and weeping, saying: "SON OF MY MOTHER! SURELY THE PEOPLE RECKONED ME WEAK AND HAD WELL-NIGH SLAIN ME[3]"[4].)).

Bakri scholars also narrate:

((Abō Bakr and ᶜOmar heard that a group of Mohājirēn and Anṣār had refused to give their pledge of allegiance, and were gathering in ᶜAli's home. So they came with a large group of people to raid the home...
And they entered the house, so Fāṭimah came out and said: By Allāh! Either you leave right now, or I

---

[1] There are countless aḥādēth in Bakri references, some of which were narrated by ᶜOmar himself, that Rasōlollāh chose Amēr al-Mo'menēn as his brother, on the Day of Brotherhood, after he migrated to Madinah. All Bakri and Moslem scholars agree on this fact.

[2] This is the only time in history that a person has denied the brotherhood of Rasōlollāh and Amēr al-Mo'menēn. And the fact that this very person is one of the people who had narrated many aḥādēth about this brotherhood, shows the falsehood of his latter statement. However, this assertive denial after that expressive proclamation is not so surprising from a personality such as ᶜOmar.

[3] Holy Qor'ān = sōrah 7, āyah 150.

[4] al-Imāmah wa al-Seyāsah / Ibn Qotaybah = vol. 1, page 18. A shorter form of this narration is also mentioned in: Aᶜlām al-Nesā' / Kaḥḥālah = vol. 4, page 114.

will most certainly cry to Allāh. So those who had entered the house came out, and those who had gathered outside left[1].)).

Bakri scholars also narrate:

((Abō Bakr sent ᶜOmar ibn al-Khaṭṭāb to ᶜAli, when he refused to give his pledge of allegiance, and told him: Bring him to me with the utmost violence[2].)).

Bakri scholars also narrate:

((ᶜOmar ibn al-Khaṭṭāb came to ᶜAli's home, when Ṭalḥah and Zobayr and a number of Mohājirēn were inside, and said: By Allāh! I will most certainly burn down the house on you unless you come out for allegiance right now[3].)).

Bakri scholars also narrate:

((When Abō Bakr was given pledge of allegiance after Rasōlollāh's death, ᶜAli and Zobayr often went to Fāṭimah, the Daughter of Rasōlollāh, to consult with her.
When the news reached ᶜOmar, he went to Fāṭimah and said: O Daughter of Rasōlollāh! There is no one more beloved to me than your father, and there is no

---

[1] Tārēkh / al-Yaᶜqōbi = vol. 2, page 126.

[2] Ansāb al-Ashrāf / al-Balādheri = vol. 1, page 587.

[3] al-ᶜEqd al-Farēd / Ibn ᶜAbderabbeh = vol. 5, page 12. Tārēkh / al-Ṭabari = vol. 3, page 198.
Some Bakri scholars record a similar narration:

> *((ᶜOmar came to Fāṭimah's home along with many Anṣār and a few Mohājirēn, and said: By Him in Whose hand is ᶜOmar's life! Either you come out for allegiance right now, or I will most certainly burn down the house on you...*
> *Then he pulled them out by their collars, dragging them [in the streets] violently.)).* (Sharh Nahj al-Balāghah / Ibn Abi al-Ḥadēd = vol. 1, page 134)

one more beloved to us, after your father, than you. But I swear by Allāh that this will not stop me from ordering to set fire to your house if these people come to you again[1].)).

Bakri scholars also narrate:

((And there was a large group of people with Khālid outside the house, all of whom Abō Bakr had sent for support. Then ᶜOmar entered and said to ᶜAli: Stand up and pledge your allegiance.
But he (Ali) did not.
So ᶜOmar took his hand and said to him: Stand up and pledge your allegiance.
But he refused to stand up.
So ᶜOmar pulled him up and pushed him, just as he had pushed Zobayr, and Khālid took them both.
Then ᶜOmar and his company dragged them violently, and a lot of people gathered to watch, and the streets of Madinah became crowded with men.
And when Fāṭimah saw what ᶜOmar had done, she screamed and wailed and a large number of women gathered with her; so she stood at the door of her room [inside the mosque] and called out: O Abā Bakr! How soon you attacked the members of the

---

[1] al-Esteᶜāb / Ibn ᶜAbdelbarr = vol. 3, page 975. Ezālat al-Khafā' / al-Dehlawi = vol. 2, pages 29 and 179. Jamᶜ al-Jawāmiᶜ / al-Soyōṭi = vol. 1, page 233. Kanz al-ᶜOmmāl / al-Hendi = vol. 5, page 651. al-Moghni / ᶜAbdoljabbār = vol. 20, page 335. Moṣannaf / Ibn Abi Shaybah = vol. 7, page 432; vol. 14, page 567. Mosnad Fāṭimah / al-Soyōṭi = page 20. Nehāyat al-Erab / al-Nowayri = vol. 19, page 39. Qorrat al-Aynayn / al-Dehlawi = page 78. al-Saqēfah wa Fadak / al-Jawhari = pages 38, 50 and 51. al-Wāfi fi al-Wafayāt / al-Ṣafdi = vol. 17, page 311.
Ibn Abi al-Ḥadēd, the famous Bakri scholar, also records this narration but with a difference in its beginning:

> *((When pledges of allegiance were taken for Abō Bakr, Zobayr, Meqdād and a number of other people often came to ᶜAli, who was in Fāṭimah's home, to consult with him...)).* (Sharh Nahj al-Balāghah / Ibn Abi al-Ḥadēd = vol. 2, page 45)

Household of Rasōlollāh!! By Allāh, I will not speak with ᶜOmar until I meet Allāh[1].)).

Bakri scholars also narrate:

((Then Abō Bakr sent ᶜOmar ibn al-Khaṭṭāb to ᶜAli and those who were with him, to extract them from Fāṭimah's home, and told him: If they disobey you, so fight them.
Then ᶜOmar took some fire and went to Fāṭimah's home to set it, along with those inside, on fire. Fāṭimah saw him and said: To where O Ibn al-Khaṭṭāb[2]?! Have you come to set fire to our home?!
ᶜOmar said: Yes, unless you accept what the people have accepted (Abō Bakr's khelāfah)[3].)).

Bakri scholars also narrate:

((And ᶜOmar used the same harshness with Ahl al-Bayt, so he surrounded them with the wood and set it on fire. And when the group entered Fāṭimah's home, Qonfodh pushed the door against Fāṭimah, breaking her rib, so she miscarried her fetus; and she remained bedridden until she died. And it is said that the person who hit her was ᶜOmar[4].)).

---

[1] Sharh Nahj al-Balāghah / Ibn Abi al-Ḥadēd = vol. 2, page 26; vol. 6, page 49.

[2] Son of al-Khaṭṭāb.

[3] Aᶜlām al-Nesā' / Kaḥḥālah = vol. 3, page 1207. al-ᶜEqd al-Farēd / Ibn ᶜAbderabbeh = vol. 2, page 250; vol. 4, page 259; vol. 5, page 12. al-Mokhtaṣar fi Akhbār al-Bashar / Abō al-Fedā' = vol. 1, page 156. Tārēkh / al-Ṭabari = vol. 3, page 198.
Bakri scholars also narrate:

> *((Abō Bakr summoned ᶜAli, wanting his pledge of allegiance, but he refused. So ᶜOmar came with fire, and Fāṭimah saw him at the door and said: O Ibn al-Khaṭṭāb?! Do you intend to put fire to my door?! ᶜOmar said: Yes.)).* (Ansāb al-Ashrāf / al-Balādheri = vol. 1, page 586)

[4] The footnotes of: al-Melal wa al-Neḥal / al-Shahrestāni = vol. 1, page 53; and al-Wāfi fi al-Wafayāt / al-Ṣafdi = vol. 6, page 17.

Bakri scholars also narrate from Zayd ibn Aslam, who said:

((I was among those who carried the wood with ᶜOmar to Fāṭimah's door, when ᶜAli and his supporters refused to give Abō Bakr their pledge of allegiance.
So ᶜOmar said to Fāṭimah: Bring out those who are in the house, or I will most certainly burn it down on them. And there were ᶜAli, Fāṭimah, Ḥasan, Ḥosayn and a number of Rasōlollāh's Companions in the house.
Then Fāṭimah astonishingly asked: You will set me and my two sons on fire?!
So ᶜOmar replied: Yes, by Allāh, unless they come out to give their pledge of allegiance[1].)).

Aside from these Bakri references, the Moslem scholar Solaym ibn al-Qays narrates in his book from Salmān, who said:

((...Then ᶜOmar said to Abō Bakr: What is stopping you from summoning him (Ali) for giving his allegiance?! for surely all the people have sworn their allegiance to you except him and those four (Salmān, Abō Dharr, Meqdād and Zobayr).
Abō Bakr was the softer of the two (Abō Bakr and ᶜOmar), the gentler, the more cunning and the more farsighted. And the other (Omar) was the cruder of the two, the harsher and the rougher.
Abō Bakr asked: Who should we send?
ᶜOmar replied: We should send Qonfodh. He is a rough, harsh and crude man from the Ṭolaqā'[2], from the Bani Oday tribe.

---

[1] al-Ghorar / Ibn Khayzorānah.

[2] Plural of Ṭalēq, a captive freed by the Moslems. This term is especially used to refer to the Idolater leaders in Makkah who were forgiven by Prophet Moḥammad after the liberation of Makkah.

Thus Abō Bakr sent him with a number of helpers, and they came and asked ᶜAli permission for entering. But he refused.
So Qonfodh's men went back to Abō Bakr and ᶜOmar, who were sitting in the mosque among the people, and said: He did not permit us to enter.
ᶜOmar ordered them: Go back, and if he gave you permission, so be it; and if not, then enter without his permission.
They went back and asked for permission to enter. Fāṭimah answered them: I strongly prohibit you from entering without permission.
Thus they returned and the accursed Qonfodh remained, and they reported what Fāṭimah had said.
ᶜOmar suddenly became angry and said: What have we to do with women?! Then he ordered some of those who were around him to carry the firewood, so they carried the firewood and ᶜOmar carried with them, and they placed it around the home of ᶜAli, Fāṭimah and their two sons. Then ᶜOmar called out so that ᶜAli and Fāṭimah could hear: By Allāh, indeed you must come out O ᶜAli! And you must give your allegiance to Rasōlollāh's Khalēfah, or I will burn down the house on you.
Fāṭimah said: O ᶜOmar! What have we to do with you? So he said: Open the door or I will burn down the house on you.
She said: O ᶜOmar! Do you not fear Allāh in entering my house?! But ᶜOmar refused to leave.
Then ᶜOmar called for the fire and set the door alight, and he pushed it open and entered. So Fāṭimah came forward to stop him and cried out: O my father! O Rasōlollāh!
Omar, then, raised the sword in its sheath and struck her side, so she cried out: O my father! And he raised the whip and lashed her forearm, so she called out: O Rasōlollāh! How bad have Abō Bakr and ᶜOmar acted after you!
Suddenly ᶜAli leaped and grabbed ᶜOmar by his collar, pulled him hard and threw him to the ground,

hitting him on the nose and the neck, and wanted to kill him, but he remembered what Rasōlollāh had told him; so he said: By Him Who honored Moḥammad with the Prophethood, O son of Ṣahhāk[1]! Were it not for a command from Allāh and an order from Rasōlollāh, you will have surely known that you could not enter my house.

There, ᶜOmar sent for help, and the people converged on the house. By this time, Qonfodh had returned to Abō Bakr and told him of his fears should ᶜAli come out with his sword, knowing his bravery and power.

So Abō Bakr told him: Return, and if he came out, so be it; and if not storm into his house; and if he resisted, then burn down their house on them.

So the accursed Qonfodh set out and stormed the house with his men, and some used their swords, and they took ᶜAli and put a rope around his neck.

At the door, Fāṭimah came between them and between ᶜAli, so the accursed Qonfodh lashed her with the whip...

I asked Salmān: Did they really enter Fāṭimah's home without permission?!

He answered: Yes by Allāh, and she was not wearing a veil. So she cried out: O my father! O Rasōlollāh! How bad have Abō Bakr and ᶜOmar acted after you!! She called out with all her voice.

And indeed I saw Abō Bakr and those around him crying, and there was not anyone who was not shedding tears except ᶜOmar and Khālid ibn al-Walēd and Moghayrah ibn al-Shoᶜbah. And ᶜOmar was continuously saying: We have nothing to do with women and their views[2].)).

---

[1] ᶜOmar's mother; she was known as a vile woman. In such cases, a person was called by his mother's name if people wanted to remind him of his corrupt past and illegitimate conception, etc.

[2] Ketāb Solaym ibn al-Qays = vol. 2, page 584. This narration has also been recoded with an addition on page 865 of the same reference, the addition is:

> *((Khālid ibn al-Walēd unsheathed his sword to strike Fāṭimah, so ᶜAli attacked him with his sword; but Khālid swore to ᶜAli in Allāh's name that he does not kill him, and ᶜAli refrained.*

Moslem scholars also narrate:

((After the events, Fāṭimah grabbed ᶜOmar's collar, pulled him and said: By Allāh, O son of Khaṭṭāb! If I did not hate to see the calamity come to the innocent, you will have surely seen me pray to Allāh and then find Him quick to respond[1].)).

MOḤASSIN, THE MARTYRED FETUS

Both Moslem and Bakri scholars who have recorded the names of the children of Amēr al-Mo'menēn and Sayyedat Nesā' al-ᶜĀlamēn, also mention the name of Moḥassin as their third son.

And a large number of these scholars also mention that it was Rasōlollāh^(SAA)[2] who named this third son, when he was a fetus in Fāṭimah's womb, as Moḥassin.

And all Moslem scholars unanimously agree on the martyrdom of Moḥassin^(AS)[3], the fetus that was killed in its sixth month in the most serious of the Bakri attacks on Amēr al-Mo'menēn's home. And as such, Moḥassin becomes Islam's first martyr after the assassination of Rasōlollāh.

But, understandably, Bakri scholars do not have this unanimous agreement on the martyrdom of Moḥassin, or at least they do not show it. And how could they?! How can a Godly person (Omar) kill two other Godly persons (Moḥassin and Fāṭimah)?!

And Meqdād, Salmān, Abō Dharr, ᶜAmmār and Boraydah al-Aslami entered the house, supporting ᶜAli... Saying [to the Bakris]: How soon you betrayed Rasōlollāh, and let out the rancor that was in your chests!!

And Boraydah said: O ᶜOmar! Do you leap against the Brother of Rasōlollāh and his Waṣi, and against his daughter and hit her?! And you are the one whom the Qoraysh knows by which it knows.)).

[1] Beḥār al-Anwār / al-Majlesi = vol. 28, page 250. al-Kāfi / al-Kolayni = vol. 1, page 460.

[2] *Ṣallallāh ᶜAlayh wa Ālih,* Allāh's Blessings be upon him and his descendants.

[3] *ᶜAlayhes Salām,* peace be upon him.

However, many Bakri scholars have recorded this vicious crime just as they recorded many other Bakri crimes. Below are a few examples:

> *((Indeed, ᶜOmar kicked Fāṭimah's stomach, so she miscarried Moḥassin[1].)).*

> *((Indeed, ᶜOmar hit Fāṭimah's stomach on the Day of Allegiance, so she miscarried the fetus. And he was shouting: Put her house of fire with all those inside; and there was no one inside other than ᶜAli, Fāṭimah, Ḥasan and Ḥosayn[2].)).*

> *((Indeed, he (Omar) hit Fāṭimah, the Daughter of Rasōlollāh, and he took away the inheritance of Rasōlollāh's descendants[3].)).*

A revealing comparison

The famous Bakri scholar Ibn Abi al-Ḥadēd records a conversation on this subject between him and one of his teachers, in his highly respected encyclopedia, which hits at the core of the Bakri faith:

> *((...Then the Chief, Abō Jaᶜfar, said: If Rasōlollāh had ordered the execution of Habbār ibn al-Aswad for frightening Zaynab[4] and causing the miscarriage of*

---

[1] Lesān al-Mēzān / al-ᶜAsqalāni = vol. 1, page 405. Mēzān al-Eᶜtedāl / al-Dhahabi = vol. 1, page 139. Seyar Aᶜlām al-Nobalā' / al-Dhahabi = vol. 15, page 578.

[2] Ansāb al-Ashrāf / al-Balādheri = vol. 1, page 404. al-Melal wa al-Neḥal / al-Shahrestāni = vol. 1, page 83. al-Wāfi fi al-Wafayāt / al-Ṣafdi = vol. 5, page 347.

[3] al-Khoṭaṭ / al-Maqrēzi = vol. 2, page 346. al-Farq bayn al-Feraq / al-Esfarā'ēni = page 148.

[4] Historians narrate that when Rasōlollāh and the Moslems migrated from Makkah to Madinah, Rasōlollāh asked his stepdaughter Zaynab to join him. On her way to Madinah, a group of Idolaters followed her with the intention of forcing her to return to Makkah; and Habbār ibn al-Aswad hit her

her fetus, then it is quite clear that if he was alive, he would have ordered the execution of those who frightened Fāṭimah causing the miscarriage of her fetus!![1]*)).*

Who took part in the attacks?

Since the opposition of ᶜAli and Fāṭimah and their supporters to the khelāfah of Abō Bakr was very strong and very serious, it needed a lot of force to crush it. But since ᶜAli had not taken up arms against Abō Bakr, the Bakri party could not march an army to his home to eliminate him. They had to somehow coerce him into pledging his allegiance, or to behead him for refusing.

And since ᶜAli was not an ordinary person, they had to use their best people for this job.

Historians record that in one of these attacks, Abō Bakr*(LA)*[2] had dispatched more than three hundred Bakri ruffians to force Amēr al-Mo'menēn[3] to accept his khelāfah.

They also record that besides ᶜOmar, some very big names took part in these raids. People such as:

1- ᶜOthmān[4] (the Third Usurper of the Khelāfah, and the first Amawi ruler). He is the murderer of two of Rasōlollāh's stepdaughters; he was also among those who took part in an attempt on Rasōlollāh's life, on his way back to Madinah from the Farewell Pilgrimage, after appointing Amēr al-Mo'menēn as his Khalēfah[5].

2- Moᶜāwiyah[6] (the Governor of Damascus, the Forth Usurper of the Khelāfah, and the second Amawi ruler). He is the son

---

howdah with his spear, so she fell down on a rock, and miscarried her fetus. She later died in Madinah from her injuries.

[1] Sharh Nahj al-Balāghah / Ibn Abi al-Ḥadēd = vol. 14, page 193.

[2] *Laᶜnatollāh ᶜAlayh,* may Allāh distance him from His Blessings and Mercy.

[3] Commander of the Faithful; a title given exclusively to Imām ᶜAli by Allāh.

[4] al-Ekhteṣāṣ / al-Mofēd = pages 184 and 187.

[5] For more detailed information, see: Rasōlollāh, the Messenger of Allāh / by the author = page 189.

[6] Wāqiᶜat Ṣeffēn / al-Menqari = page 163.

of the Idolater leader Abō Sofyān, who marched several armies against the Moslems, and Hend, who mutilated the bodies of Moslems in the battle of Oḥod particularly the body of Rasōlollāh's uncle Ḥamzah and put his liver in her mouth to eat it. Moᶜāwiyah was also among those who took part in the attempt on Rasōlollāh's life, after appointing Amēr al-Mo'menēn as his Khalēfah[1].

3- ᶜAmr ibn al-ᶜĀs (the Governor of Palestine, Moᶜāwiyah's right hand, and the Governor of Egypt). He was also among those who took part in the attempt on Rasōlollāh's life, after appointing Amēr al-Mo'menēn as his Khalēfah.

4- ᶜAbdorraḥmān ibn al-ᶜAwf[2] (an influential Bakri leader, and one of ᶜOmar's six nominees to succeed him). He was also among those who took part in the attempt on Rasōlollāh's life, after appointing Amēr al-Mo'menēn as his Khalēfah.

5- Moghayrah ibn al- Shoᶜbah[3] (the Governor of Bahrain, Basrah-Iraq and Koofah-Iraq). He was known as: "The Biggest Arab Adulterer; he was also among those who took part in the attempt on Rasōlollāh's life, after appointing Amēr al-Mo'menēn as his Khalēfah.

6- Abō ᶜObaydah ibn al-Jarrāḥ[4] (the Governor of Hems-Syria). He was also among those who took part in the attempt on Rasōlollāh's life, after appointing Amēr al-Mo'menēn as his Khalēfah.

7- Khālid ibn al-Walēd[5]. A General in the Idolater armies that fought with Moslems. After Abō Bakr usurped the khelāfah, he appointed Khālid as the highest commander in charge of Shām's entire army, in today's Syria, Lebanon, Palestine and Jordan. He also

---

[1] A God-appointed successor of Rasōlollah. Also caliph. Bakris wrongfully use this title for the leaders of the Bakri party who usurped the Rightful Khelāfah from the a'emmah. Plural Kholafā'.

[2] al-Bedāyah wa al-Nehāyah / Ibn Kothayr = vol. 5, page 250. Seyar Aᶜlām al-Nobalā' / al-Dhahabi = page 26. Sharh Nahj al-Balāghah / Ibn Abi al-Ḥadēd = vol. 6, page 48.

[3] al-Eḥtejāj / al-Ṭabarsi = vol. 1, page 414. al-Ekhteṣāṣ / al-Mofēd = page 185.

[4] al-Ekhteṣāṣ / al-Mofēd = page 185.

[5] Sharh Nahj al-Balāghah / Ibn Abi al-Ḥadēd = vol. 6, page 48.

appointed him as the Governor of Iraq, but Abō Bakr died before Khālid could become the governor.

8- Qonfodh (the Governor of Makkah). Bakri scholars record that one year ᶜOmar asked for half of all the wealth from all of his governors accept Qonfodh.

And in this regard it has been narrated:

> *((When ᶜAbbās asked Amēr al-Mo'menēn: What stopped ᶜOmar from fining Qonfodh, just as he fined all of his governors?*
> *Ali looked at those who were with him as tears filled his eyes, then he said: ᶜOmar thanked him for lashing Fāṭimah with the whip; so when she died, the effect of the whip was like an armlet on her upper arm[1].)).*

Abō Bakr orders the attacks

Some people like to acquit Abō Bakr of these hideous crimes, and keep him well clear and clean of such barbaric acts of aggression against the Household of the Prophethood. Therefore they create a nice image for Abō Bakr, and say how kind and gentle he was and how diplomatically and wisely he acted. And claim that such a personality could never have played any role in such horrible crimes.

On the other hand, they say how rough and harsh ᶜOmar was in his nature, and how impatient and restless he could become when it came to God's work!! And claim that he was the one who ordered and oversaw the suppression and elimination of ᶜAli and Fāṭimah's opposition to the Bakri rule.

---

[1] Ketāb Solaym ibn al-Qays = vol. 2, page 675. It has also been narrated from Solaym, who said:

> *((I met with ᶜAli and asked him about what ᶜOmar had done. So he said: Do you know why ᶜOmar did not fine Qonfodh?*
> *I answered: No.*
> *He said: Because he lashed Fāṭimah with the whip when she came to stand between them and me. So when she died, the effect of the whip was like an armband on her upper arm.)).*
> (Ketāb Solaym ibn al-Qays = vol. 2, page 674)

And as such, they would exonerate the Khalēfah from any blame and place the responsibility on ᶜOmar's shoulder, who was not a khalēfah at the time; then they would use a thousand and one excuses and lies to remove this stain from ᶜOmar's record; absurdities such as: He made a judgment and Allāh will reward him two rewards if he was right and one reward if he was wrong?! It was his nature to be severe, not his intention?!...

However, even the Bakri historic records contradict the above.

Firstly, Bakri narrations clearly name Abō Bakr as the person who ordered these attacks. Some examples are as follows:

> *((Abō Bakr sought after a group of people who had not given [him] their pledge of allegiance... So he sent ᶜOmar to them[1].)).*

> *((Abō Bakr sent ᶜOmar ibn al-Khaṭṭāb to ᶜAli when he refused to give his pledge of allegiance, and told him: Bring him to me with the utmost violence[2].)).*

> *((Then Abō Bakr sent ᶜOmar ibn al-Khaṭṭāb to ᶜAli and those who were with him, to extract them from Fāṭimah's home, and told him: If they disobey you, so fight them[3].)).*

Secondly, Bakri records go further to show that Abō Bakr witnessed these events and, actually, gave orders on the spot. One instance is as follows:

> *((Then Zobayr came out with his sword unsheathed, so a man from the Anṣār and Zeyād ibn Lobayd held on to him and the sword fell from his hand. So Abō*

---

[1] al-Imāmah wa al-Seyāsah / Ibn Qotaybah = vol. 1, page 18. Aᶜlām al-Nesā' / Kaḥḥālah = vol. 4, page 114.

[2] Ansāb al-Ashrāf / al-Balādheri = vol. 1, page 587.

[3] Aᶜlām al-Nesā' / Kaḥḥālah = vol. 3, page 1207. al-ᶜEqd al-Farēd / Ibn ᶜAbderabbeh = vol. 2, page 250; vol. 4, page 259; vol. 5, page 12. al-Mokhtaṣar fi Akhbār al-Bashar / Abō al-Fedā' = vol. 1, page 156. Tārēkh / al-Ṭabari = vol. 3, page 198.

Bakr, while sitting on the menbar[1]*, shouted: Strike it at the rock. And it was broken*[2]*.))*.

Thirdly, Bakri records go even further to show that Abō Bakr, personally, took part in some of these raids. One example is as follows:

((Abō Bakr and ᶜOmar heard that a group of Mohājirēn and Anṣār had refused to give their pledge of allegiance, and were gathering in ᶜAli's home. So they came with a large group of people to raid the home[3]*.))*.

Fourthly, how was it possible for Abō Bakr not to have witnessed those acts of aggression and not to have heard those heartrending screams, when he was sitting in the mosque, and ᶜAli and Fāṭimah's home was next to the mosque and had a door inside the mosque?!

Historic records also show that in some of those attacks, the people of Madinah had gathered in that area to witness what was happening, so how is it possible for the Khalēfah, who was sitting in the mosque next to that home, not to have seen or heard anything?!

Some Bakri narrations even show that at the time of some of the attacks, Fāṭimah[*(AaS)*4] called out to Abō Bakr. For instance:

((So she stood at the door of her room [inside the mosque] and called out: O Abā Bakr! How soon you attacked the members of the Household of

---

[1] A raised platform for a Moslem speaker in a mosque, Ḥosayneyyah, etc. where he/she would either stand or sit to give a speech.

[2] Sharh Nahj al-Balāghah / Ibn Abi al-Ḥadēd = vol. 2, page 56. It has also been narrated:

> *((Then Zobayr came out with his sword, and Abō Bakr shouted: Restrain the dog!!... Then Abō Bakr said: Strike it at the rock.))*. (Amāli / al-Mofēd = page 246)

[3] Tārēkh / al-Yaᶜqōbi = vol. 2, page 126.

[4] *ᶜAlayhas Salām,* peace be upon her.

Rasōlollāh!! By Allāh, I will not speak with ᶜOmar until I meet Allāh[1].)).

Fifthly, Abō Bakr admitted, on his deathbed, that he had ordered the raids.

Rasōlollāh prophesizes Fāṭimah's sufferings

Years before they happened, Rasōlollāh prophesized Fāṭimah's sufferings in detail. These prophecies were made so often and on so many occasions, that despite their threat to the Bakri faith, they found their way into well-known Bakri references.

Bakri scholars narrate from Rasōlollāh, who said the following:

((Heaven has been made forbidden to him who does injustice to my Ahl al-Bayt, and annoys me in my lineage[2].)).

((And if someone worshiped Allāh between the Rokn[3] and the Maqām[4] until he became like an old skin, but he met Allāh whilst hating the family of Moḥammad, then Allāh shall throw him from his nose into the fire of Hell[5].)).

((Whomsoever curses my Ahl al-Bayt, he has surely apostatized from Allāh and Islam; and whomsoever annoys me in my descendants, may Allāh distance

---

[1] Sharh Nahj al-Balāghah / Ibn Abi al-Ḥadēd / vol. 2, page 26; vol. 6, page 49.

[2] al-Jāmiᶜ le Aḥkām al-Qor'ān / al-Qorṭobi = vol. 16, page 22.

[3] One of the four corners of the Kaᶜbah, in which Ḥajar al-Aswad, the Black Stone is placed.

[4] Maqām Ebrāhēm is the stone on which Prophet Ebrāhēm stood to build the Kaᶜbah. Later, the pre-Islamic Arabs moved it away from the Kaᶜbah; and after the liberation of Makkah, Rasōlollāh returned it to its correct place next to the Kaᶜbah. But during his rule, ᶜOmar moved it back to the place in which the pre-Islamic Arabs had placed it!!

[5] Tārēkh Baghdād / al-Baghdādi = vol. 3, page 122.

him from His Blessings and Mercy; and whomsoever annoys me in my descendants, he has surely annoyed Allāh.
Allāh has indeed made Heaven forbidden to him who does injustice to my Ahl al-Bayt, or kills them, or supports their enemy, or curses them[1].)).

((By Him in Whose Hand is my life, whoever hates us Ahl al-Bayt, Allāh shall take him to the Fire[2].)).

((...And when I saw her, I remembered what will be done to her after me. As if I can see the degradation enter her house, and her sacredness violated, and her rights usurped, and her inheritance kept away from her, and her ribs broken, and her fetus killed, while she cries: O my Moḥammad! But she will not be answered. And asks for help, but she will not be helped...
Thus she will come to me sorrowful, anguished, grief-stricken, usurped, killed.
Rasōlollāh then added: O Allāh! Keep away from Your Mercy him who does her injustice, and punish him who usurps her, and humiliate him who humiliates her, and keep forever in Your Fire him who hits her side causing the miscarriage of her fetus.
And the angels said: Āmēn[3].)).

((O daughter! Indeed, no Moslem woman is afflicted with more calamity than you, so do not be one with

---

[1] al-Ṣawāᶜeq al-Moḥreqah / Ibn Ḥajar = page 143.
[2] al-Mostadrak / al-Naysābōri = vol. 3, page 150.
[3] Amāli / al-Ṣadōq = page 112. Beḥār al-Anwār / al-Majlesi = vol. 28, page 38; vol. 43, page 172. Beshārat al-Moṣṭafa / al-Ṭabari = page 197. Ershād al-Qolōb / al-Daylami = vol. 2, page 295. al-Faḍā'el / Ibn Shādhān = page 8. Farā'ed al-Semṭayn / al-Ḥamō'i = vol. 2, page 35. Jalā' al-ᶜOyōn / al-Majlesi = vol. 1, page 186.

the least patience. You are surely the Chief of the Women of the Heaven[1].)).

Aside from the above Bakri narrations, Moslem scholars also narrate from Rasōlollāh who said the following:

((O my daughter! You are the oppressed after me. And you are the week after me... To Allāh I complain of your oppressors[2].)).

((...Then he (Rasōlollāh) looked at Fāṭimah and said: You are surely the first to join me from my Ahl al-

---

[1] al-Āḥād wa al-Mathāni / al-Shaybāni = vol. 5, page 369. al-Bedāyah wa al-Nehāyah / Ibn Kothayr = vol. 3, page 206. Ansāb al-Ashrāf / al-Balādheri = page 405. al-E[c]teqād / al-Maqrēzi = page 165. Ershād al-Sāri / al-Qasṭalāni = vol. 6, page 80. al-Eṣābah / al-[c]Asqalāni = vol. 4, page 367. Es[c]āf al-Rāghebēn / Ibn al-Ṣabbān = page 128. al-Estē[c]āb / Ibn [c]Abdelbarr = vol. 2, page 750. Fatḥ al-Bāri / al-[c]Asqalāni = vol. 8, page 136. al-Foṣōl al-Mohemmah / Ibn al-Ṣabbāgh = page 127. al-Jāmi[c] al-Ṣaghēr / al-Soyōṭi = vol. 1, page 7. Kanz al-[c]Ommāl / al-Hendi = vol. 7, page 111; vol. 13, page 95; vol. 16, page 281. Kefāyat al-Ṭālib / al-Kanji = page 275. al-Khaṣā'eṣ / al-Nasā'i = page 33. al-Khaṣā'eṣ al-Kobrā / al-Soyōṭi = vol. 2, pages 226 and 265. al-Maghāzi wa al-Seyar / al-Ḥaḍrami = page 286. Majma[c] al-Zawā'ed / al-Haythami = vol. 9, pages 23 and 201. Manāqib [c]Ali ibn Abi Ṭālib / Ibn al-Maghāzili = page 5. Maqtal al-Ḥosayn / al-Khārazmi = page 55. al-Mo[c]jam al-Kabēr / al-Ṭabarāni = vol. 22, page 417. Moshkel al-Āthār / al-Ṭaḥāwi = vol. 1, page 48. Mosnad / Aḥmad = vol. 3, page 64; vol. 5, page 391. Mosnad Fāṭimah / al-Soyōṭi = page 41, and a similar narration in pages 49, 51, 52, 78 and 79. al-Mostadrak / al-Naysābōri = vol. 3, pages 151 and 154. Osd al-Ghābah / Ibn al-Athēr = vol. 4, page 42. Ṣaḥēḥ / Bokhāri = vol. 4, page 203; vol. 5, page 20. Ṣaḥēḥ / Moslem = vol. 7, page 143. al-Ṣawā[c]eq al-Moḥreqah / al-Haythami = page 185. Seyar A[c]lām al-Nobalā' / al-Dhahabi = vol. 3, page 168. Sharh al-Maqāṣid / al-Taftāzāni = vol. 2, page 221. Sonan / al-Termedhi = vol. 13, page 197. Tārēkh Demashq / Ibn [c]Asākir = vol. 4, page 95. al-Ṭabaqāt al-Kobrā = vol. 2, page 248. Tahdhēb al-Tahdhēb / al-[c]Asqalāni = vol. 12, page 441. Dhakhā'er al-[c]Oqbā / al-Ṭabari = pages 39 and 136. al-Dhorreyyah al-Ṭāhirah / al-Dōlābi = vol. 1, page 105. Wasēlat al-Ma'āl / al-Ḥaḍrami = page 88. Yanābē[c] al-Mawaddah / al-Qandōzi = page 165.

[2] Fāṭimah min al-Mahd elā al-Laḥd / al-Qazwēni = page 301.

Bayt. And you are the "Chief of the Women of the Heaven". And you will suffer, after my death, a great injustice and rage, until you are beaten up, and your rib breaks. May Allāh keep away from His Mercy your killer, and keep away from His Mercy the one who orders your killing, and those who agree and support, and those who are against you, and do injustice to your husband and your two sons[1].))

((He is kept away from Allāh's Mercy, he is kept away from Allāh's Mercy[2] who does injustice to Fāṭimah after my death, and usurps her right and kills her[3].)).

((One day the Prophet went to Fāṭimah's home and she prepared a meal from bread, date and fat. Then ᶜAli, Fāṭimah, Ḥasan and Ḥosayn came to eat with Rasōlollāh. When Rasōlollāh finished eating, he made a very long sojōd[4], then he laughed, then he cried, then he sat.
Ali said: O Rasōlollāh! We saw from you what we had not seen before?1
So Rasōlollāh said: When I ate with you, I became happy for your good health and for your gathering here, so I performed a sojōd thanking Allāh the Almighty.
But Jabra'ēl descended and said: Do you perform sojōd because of your happiness for your family?
I answered: Yes.
He said: Do you want me to tell you what will happen to them after your death?
I answered: Yes, O my brother! O Jabra'ēl!

---

[1] Ketāb Solaym ibn al-Qays = vol. 2, page 907.
[2] Rasōlollāh repeated this twice.
[3] Kanz al-Fawā'ed / al-Karājaki = vol. 1, page 149.
[4] A particular position in ṣalāt in which the forehead, the palms, the knees and the toes of both feet are placed on the ground. Sojōd is also performed on its own—not as part of a ṣalāt—for a number of reasons, some of which are mandatory whereas others are recommended.

So he told me: Your daughter will be the first to join you from your family after suffering injustice, and after her right is usurped, and her inheritance is kept away from her, and her rib is broken. And your cousin; he will suffer injustice, and his right will be usurped, and he will be killed. And Ḥasan; he will suffer injustice, and his right will be usurped, and he will be murdered by poison. And Ḥosayn; he will suffer injustice, and his right will be usurped, and his family will be killed, and horses will trample his body, and his caravan will be plundered, and his women and children will be enslaved, and his body will be buried while soaked in blood and covered by sand...[1])).

Moslems also narrate from Amēr al-Mo'menēn, who said:

((Whilst Fāṭimah, Ḥasan, Ḥosayn and I were sitting with Rasōlollāh, he looked at us and cried. So I asked: O Rasōlollāh! What makes you cry?
He said: I cry for what will be done to you.
So I said: And what is that O Rasōlollāh?
He said: I weep for the strike on your upper head; and the slap on Fāṭimah's face; and the stabbing of Ḥasan's thigh, and the poison which he will drink; and the killing of Ḥosayn.
So all of us the Ahl al-Bayt cried, and I said: O Rasōlollāh! Our Lord has not created us except for calamity?!
He said: Rejoice O ᶜAli! For surely Allāh, the Great, the Almighty, has revealed to me that no one will like you except a Mo'men[2] and that no one will hate you except a Monāfiq[3]/[4].)).

---

[1] Beḥār al-Anwār / al-Majlesi = vol. 98, page 44.
[2] Moslem, Shēᶜah, a follower of Rasōlollāh and Amēr al-Mo'menēn.
[3] A person who shams Islam but in fact is not a Moslem.
[4] Amāli / al-Ṣadōq = page 118. Beḥār al-Anwār / al-Majlesi = vol. 28, page 51; vol. 44, page 149. Manāqib Āl Abi Ṭālib / Ibn Shahrāshōb = vol. 2, page 209.

Moslems also narrate from Imām Ṣādiq(AS)[1], who said:

((When the Prophet was taken to the skies, it was said to him: ...And your daughter will suffer injustice, and her right will be usurped, and she will be beaten up whilst pregnant, and her home will be raided, and she will be humiliated and degraded; but she will not find any supporters. She will miscarry what is in her womb because of the beating, and she will die because of that beating[2].)).

AHL AL-BAYT SPEAK ABOUT FĀṬIMAH'S SUFFERING

Fāṭimah speaks about her suffering

It has been narrated that Sayyedat Nesā' al-ᶜĀlamēn[3] briefly explained some of what she suffered at the hands of the Bakri ruffians as the following:

((...Then Qonfodh, ᶜOmar ibn al-Khaṭṭāb and Khālid ibn al-Walēd were sent to our home to take out my cousin ᶜAli to Bani Sāᶜedah's gethering place, for the hopeless allegiance; but he refused to go with them, as he was busy carrying out what Rasōlollāh had asked of him in his will...
So they gathered plenty of wood and put it at our door, and brought fire to light it, to burn us all. Thus I stood behind the door and beseeched them in Allāh's name and my father's name to leave us and support us.

---

[1] *ᶜAlayhes Salām,* peace be upon him.
[2] Beḥār al-Anwār / al-Majlesi = vol. 28, page 62; vol. 53, page 23. Jalā' al-ᶜOyōn / al-Majlesi = vol. 1, page 184.
[3] Chief of the Women of the World; a title given exclusively to Fāṭimah, the Daughter of Rasōlollāh, by Allāh.

But ʿOmar took the whip from Qonfodh's hand and lashed my upper arm so hard that it left a welt like an armlet, and kicked the door and pushed it against me although I was pregnant; so I fell down forward, and the fire was burning my face. Then he slapped me so hard that my earring tore apart from ear. Then I went into labor and miscarried Moḥassin, murdered without guilt.
So is this the nation that solutes me?! Indeed, Allāh and His Messenger have renounced it, and so have I[1].)).

Fāṭimah also composed a number of poems, mourning her father and pointing to her suffering. And both Moslem and Bakri scholars narrate them; some of these poems are as follows:

((And Islam cried for you as it became a stranger between people, like other strangers.
If you see the menbar[2] on which you used to rise, darkness has risen on it after light.
O My Lord! make my death very near, as life has indeed become embittered[3].)).

((Say! to the one hidden under levels of the earth: If you can hear my scream and my call,
calamities have poured on me that if were to pour on the days, they will have become nights.
Indeed I had protection in the shade of Moḥammad; I did not fear injustice, and he was my protector.
But today I am humble for the lowly, and cautious of injustice; and I ward off my oppressor with my robe.
So if a turtledove weeps in her night from sadness on a branch, I weep in my day.
I shall make sadness my friend after you, and I shall make the tear for you my scarf[1].)).

---

[1] Beḥār al-Anwār / al-Majlesi = vol. 30, page 347.
[2] A raised platform for a Moslem speaker in a mosque, Ḥosayneyyah, etc. where he/she would either stand or sit to give a speech.
[3] Beḥār al-Anwār / al-Majlesi = vol. 43, page 177.

((Indeed, there were news and many difficulties after you; if you had witnessed them, there would not be much talk.
We surely missed you, as the earth misses her downpour; and your people became disordered, so witness them and do not be absent...
Some people showed us the animosities they had hidden in their chests when you left, and the earth shielded you.
Some people frowned on us and disparaged us when you became absent, and all the earth is usurped[2].)).

((The person who embarks on inflicting injustice upon us shall know on the Day of Judgment to what turning he shall turn.
Indeed we suffered [after you O Rasōlollāh!] what no Arab or non-Arab has ever suffered.
So we shall weep on you as long as we live, and as long as we have eyes that can shed tears[3].)).

ᶜAli speaks about Fāṭimah's sufferings

After one of the raids when the Bakri ruffians extracted ᶜAli from his home, he stood between the people and raised his voice with a most damaging statement against the Bakris, parts of which are as follows:

((...Your evil-commanding selves abstained from the everlasting Hereafter, and our selves craved after what you abstained from.

---

[1] Fāṭimah al-Zahrā' Min Qabl al-Mēlād elā Baᶜd al-Estesh-hād / al-Hāshimi = page 219. al-Fotōḥāt al-Rabbāneyyah / Ibn al-ᶜAllān = vol. 3, page 160.
[2] al-Abdāl / al-Ḥalabi = vol. 1, page 164. al-Eḥtejāj / al-Ṭabarsi = vol. 1, page 145. Fāṭimah al-Zahrā' Min Qabl al-Mēlād elā Baᶜd al-Estesh-hād / al-Hāshimi = page 289. Gharēb al-Ḥadēth / Ibn Qotaybah = page 590.
[3] ᶜAwālim al-ᶜOlōm / al-Baḥrāni = vol. 11, page 832.

And the appointment is near, and the Lord is the best judge; so prepare your answers for the questioning, and prepare your accounts for your injustice towards us Ahl al-Bayt.

Is Zahrā' beaten up in suppression?! And our rights are forcefully usurped?! And there is no supporter and no defender, and no helper and no rescuer?!

I wish the son of Abō Ṭālib (Ali) had died before today, so he would not see the evil-doer infidels rallied for doing injustice to the Pure, the Pious (Fāṭimah).

So Destruction! Destruction! And Ruination! Ruination! This is something that returns to Allāh, and is taken to Rasōlollāh.

It has surely been excruciating for the son of Abō Ṭālib [to see] the blackening of Fāṭimah's back by the lashing.

His [brave] position has been known and his [victorious] days have been seen, but he does not erupt to protect his wife and does not firmly stand in front of his spouse; as patience is more suitable and appropriate, and accepting what Allāh wants is better, so that the truth does not lose its gravity, and the falsehood does not emerge from its den; until I meet with my Lord, when I shall complain to Him what you have committed...[1])).

It has been narrated from Ibn ᶜAbbās, who said that Amēr al-Mo'menēn used to recite the doᶜā' of Sanamay Qoraysh, the Two Idols of Qoraysh, in the qonōt[2] of his ṣalāt. Some parts of this doᶜā'[3] are as follows:

---

[1] Bahjat Qalb al-Moṣṭafa / al-Raḥmānı = page 531.

[2] A particular position in ṣalāt in which the palms are brought up in line with the face, whilst the palms are placed adjacent side by side and facing upwards.

[3] [3] Praying to Allāh, asking Him for something for oneself and/or for others... Doᶜā' can be positive or negative, and has many forms and many uses and effects. Some adᶜeyah (plural of doᶜā') should only be recited in specific times and/or places, whereas other adᶜeyah are not bound to any

((O Allāh! Keep away from Your Mercy the Two Idols of Qoraysh...
for surely they have demolished the House of the Prophethood, and blocked up its door...
and exterminated its residents, and annihilated its supporters, and killed its children...
and [for] the blood that they spilled...
and the inheritance that they usurped...
and the Khoms[1] that they took-over...
and the stomach that they ruptured, and the fetus that they killed, and the rib that they broke...[2])).

Imām Ḥasan speaks about Fāṭimah's suffering

It has been narrated that Imām Ḥasan*(AS)*[3], ᶜAli and Fāṭimah's first son, spoke these words in a heated encounter in the presence of the Second Amawi ruler, Moᶜāwiyah*(LA)*[4], who had called his aids and a number of high-ranking Bakri leaders for the one purpose of crushing Imām Ḥasan in that famous debate:

---

time or place restrictions. There is a huge number of set formal adᶜeyah narrated from the Fourteen Maᶜṣōmēn, the recitation of which is highly recommended, but it is also possible for any Moslem to compose his own doᶜā', in any language format, provided that he has a considerable knowledge of Islam.

[1] An Islamic tax of 20% levied, among other things, on the annual superfluous income. Khoms is given to the Prophet or one of his kholafā' or one of the representatives of the final khalēfah—Marājiᶜ[1], who then give it to its legal recipients accordingly. It could also be directly given to the legal recipients under the supervision or with the permission of the Marāji`. Once Khoms is deducted from a certain amount, it will no longer be subject to Khoms in the coming years.

[2] Beḥār al-Anwār / al-Majlesi = vol. 85, page 260.

[3] *ᶜAlayhes Salām,* peace be upon him.

[4] *Laᶜnatollāh ᶜAlayh,* may Allāh distance him from His Blessings and Mercy.

((...And you O Moghayrah! You are indeed an enemy of Allāh, and a discarder of His Book, and an accuser of His Prophet; and you are the Adulterer...
And you are the one who beat Fāṭimah, the Daughter of Rasōlollāh, until she bled, and she miscarried her fetus.
You did this as a mark of degradation towards Rasōlollāh, and as a sign for disobeying his order, and violating his sacredness; when Rasōlollāh had told her: O Fāṭimah! You are the Chief of the Women of the Heaven[1].)).

Imām Sajjād refers to Fāṭimah's suffering

Imām Ṣādiq has narrated from his fathers a zeyārah[2] about Fāṭimah, a part of which is as follows:

((...Peace be upon you O oppressed! The one whose right was taken from her...[3])).

Imām Bāqir points to Fāṭimah's suffering

Ali ibn Ḥamzah narrates that one day he went to Imām Kāẓim[(AS)4] and said:

((I be your sacrifice. If you permit me, I will narrate to you a ḥadēth from Abi Baseer about your grandfather [Imām Bāqir].

---

[1] Ṣaḥēḥ / al-Bokhāri = vol. 13, page 197.
[2] Zeyārah means visiting; it also means the collection of words and sentences which the zā'er (visitor) recites when visiting the shrine of a prophet or a waṣi or a Godly person. There is a large number of set formal zeyārāt (plural of zeyārah) narrated from the Fourteen Maᶜṣōmēn, the recitation of which is highly recommended. Some of these zeyārāt should only be recited in specific times and/or places, whereas other zeyārāt are not bound to any time or place restrictions.
[3] Beḥār al-Anwār / al-Majlesi = vol. 100, page 199.
[4] *ᶜAlayhes Salām,* peace be upon him.

Whenever he (Imām Bāqir) fell ill, he used cold water to bring down his fever; so he would use two clothes, one in the cold water and one on his body, and he would alternate between them. Then he would scream loudly so that the people outside his house could hear him: "O Fāṭimah daughter of Moḥammad!"[1])).

The Moslem scholar Shaykh ᶜAbbās Qommi writes in his book "Bayt al-Aḥzān", that it is very likely that these fevers were caused by the Imām's continuous hiding of his grief and sadness for what had happened to his oppressed mother Fāṭimah; so just as he tries to reduce his fever with called water, he also tries to ease the pain of that tormenting grief by calling out her name.

Imām Ṣādiq speaks about Fāṭimah's suffering

In a lengthy conversation between Mofaḍḍal ibn ᶜOmar and Imām Ṣādiq[(AS)2], during which Mofaḍḍal asked a number of questions evolving around Imām Mahdi[(AS)3], Imām Ṣādiq pointed to some of Fāṭimah's sufferings. Some related excerpts are as follows:

((...And setting fire to the door of Amēr al-Mo'menēn, Fāṭimah, Ḥasan and Ḥosayn to burn them, and lashing the hand of the Great Seddeeqah Fāṭimah with the whip, and kicking her stomach causing the miscarriage of Moḥassin...
Then Fāṭimah complains [to Rasōlollāh] about what came to her from Abō Bakr and ᶜOmar, and about the usurpation of Fadak...
And he (Abō Bakr) says that the prophets do not leave inheritance... And ᶜOmar says: Bring out your document which you mentioned your father had written for you, and then he takes it from her, spits

---

[1] Fāṭimah al-Zahrā' min Qabl al-Mēlād elā Baᶜd al-Estesh-hād / al-Hāshimi = page 450.

[2] *ᶜAlayhes Salām,* peace be upon him.

[3] *ᶜAlayhes Salām,* peace be upon him.

on it and tears it in the presence of witnesses from the Qoraysh and the Mohājirēn and the Anṣār...
And she tells him (Rasōlollāh) about Abō Bakr and his ordering Khālid ibn al-Walēd, Qonfodh and ᶜOmar ibn al-Khaṭṭāb along with a large number of people to forcefully extract Amēr al-Mo'menēn from his home to giving his allegiance in the gathering place of Bani Sāᶜedah tribe...
And what ᶜOmar says: Come out O ᶜAli! and accept what the groups of Moslems have accepted, or we will kill you...
And their gathering firewood to burn the house of Amēr al-Mo'menēn, Fāṭimah, Ḥasan, Ḥosayn, Zaynab, Omm Kolthoom[1] *and Feḍḍah*[2]*, and putting fire to the door. And Fāṭimah coming behind the door to speak with them, saying: Woe unto you O ᶜOmar! What is this boldness towards Allāh and His Messenger?! Do you intend to severe his lineage from this world, and vanish him and extinguish the Light of Allāh?!...*
And ᶜOmar saying: That is enough O Fāṭimah! Moḥammad is no longer present, and the angels are no longer bringing commands and prohibitions from Allāh, and ᶜAli is none other than just another Moslem; so either he pledges allegiance to Abō Bakr or you will all burn.
So she says crying: O Allāh! To You we complain about the loss of Your Prophet and Your Messenger and Your Sincere Friend, and about the turning of his nation against us, and their usurping of our right which You had given us in Your Book that was revealed to Your Prophet.
Then ᶜOmar says to her: Keep away O Fāṭimah! from the stupidity of women, for surely Allāh was not to choose for you the prophecy and the khelāfah. And so the fire was burns the door...

---

[1] Zaynab and Omm Kolthōm were the two daughters of ᶜAli and Fāṭimah.
[2] Feḍḍah was Fāṭimah's student and housemaid.

And ᶜOmar lashes her upper arm with the whip until it leaves a black mark like an armlet, and kicks the door until it hits her stomach when she is six month pregnant with Moḥassin, and his miscarriage.

And ᶜOmar's attack along with Qonfodh and Khālid, and slapping her face so hard that her earring is torn from her ear, while she weeps loudly and says: O my father! O Rasōlollāh! Your daughter Fāṭimah is being accused of lying, and is being beaten and the fetus in her womb is being killed.

And Amēr al-Mo'menēn comes out, bareheaded with red eyes, spreads his wrap over her, holds her to his chest, and says to her: O Daughter of Rasōlollāh! You have surely known that your father was sent by Allāh to be a mercy for the creatures; so I swear to you in the name of Allāh, I swear to you in the name of Allāh not to move back your veil and raise your forehead [to pray to Allāh to send a calamity on the people], so by Allāh O Fāṭimah! If you do this, Allāh won't keep on the earth anyone who bares witness that Moḥammad is the Messenger of Allāh and nor Mōsā, ᶜĒsā, Ebrāhēm, Nōh and Ādam, and no animal will walk the earth and no bird will fly in the sky.

Then he (Ali) says: O son of al-Khaṭṭāb! Woe unto you, leave here before I unsheathe my sword and kill. So ᶜOmar, Khālid, Qonfodh and ᶜAbdorraḥmān ibn Abi Bakr leave and stay outside the house.

So ᶜAli calls out to Feḍḍah: O Feḍḍah! Your mistress, come to her, as she has gone into labor because of the kick and the pushing of the door. Thus she miscarries Moḥassin, and Amēr al-Mo'menēn says: He is joining his grandfather Rasōlollāh, and will complain to him[1].)).

Imām Kāẓim speaks about Fāṭimah's suffering

[1] Beḥār al-Anwār / al-Majlesi = vol. 53, excerpts from pages 14 to 19.

Moslem historians record that one day Imām Kāẓim*(AS)*[1] was narrating a ḥadēth[2] from his fathers that just before he died, Rasōlollāh summoned the Anṣār and spoke to them for one last time, explaining the importance of the Holy Qor'ān and the Ahl al-Bayt*(AmS)*[3], and that the two will never separate from one another and will ever remain together until the Day of Judgment; and the Imām[4] continued narrating that ḥadēth until he reached this part of Rasōlollāh's speech:

> *((Beware! that Fāṭimah's door is my door, and her home is my home; so whomsoever attacks it, he has surely attacked Allāh's representative.)).*

Then the Imām cried for a long time, cutting the rest of his speech, and then he repeated three times:

> *((By Allāh, Allāh's representative was attacked; by Allāh, Allāh's representative was attacked; by Allāh, Allāh's representative was attacked. O mother! Allāh's Blessing be upon you[5].)).*

Imām Reḍa mentions some of Fāṭimah's suffering

It has been narrated from Moḥammad ibn Esmācēl ibn Bazee' and Solaymān ibn Jacfar who said:

---

[1] *ʿAlayhes Salām,* peace be upon him.
[2] A narration from one of the Fourteen Maʿṣomēn. Plural aḥādēth.
[3] *ʿAlayhemos Salām,* peace be upon them.
[4] Leader, good or bad, religious or otherwise. This title has been used for any person with a religious leading role, such as a public prayer leader or leader of a religious group or movement. But in this book it is only used as a title for one of the twelve God-appointed successors of the Prophet Moḥammad. Plural a'emmah.
[5] Beḥār al-Anwār / al-Majlesi = vol. 22, page 477.

((We went to Imām Reḍa while he performing the Sojōd of Shokr[1], and he extended his sojōd. So when he raised his head we asked him: You extended your sojōd?
So he said: Whoever recites this doᶜā' in the Sojōd of Shokr will be rewarded as much as a Moslem who shot arrows with Rasōlollāh in the battle of Badr[2].
So we asked: Can we write it?
He said: Write: When you are in the Sojōd of Shokr, recite: O Allāh! Keep away from Your Mercy the two who altered Your religion...
And killed the son of Your Prophet [Moḥassin]...[3])).

Imām Jawād refers to Fāṭimah's suffering

Zakariyyā ibn Ādam narrates:

((I was with Imām Reḍa when Abō Jaᶜfar [Imām Jawād], who had less than four years of age, was brought in. He put his hand on the ground and raised his head towards the sky and became lost in thought. So Imām Reḍa asked him: I be your sacrifice, what made you become lost in thought?

---

[1] A sojōd especially performed for the purpose of thanking Allāh.

[2] In another narration, recorded immediately after this one in this reference, it is mentioned that the Imām said:

> *((He will be rewarded as much as a soldier who shot a million arrows with Rasōlollāh in the battles of Badr, Oḥod and Ḥonayn)).*

Participating in battles with Rasōlollāh has a great reward, and its reward dramatically increases according to the importance, etc. of that battle; and the battles of Badr, Oḥod and Ḥonayn were three of the most decisive battles. And shooting every arrow with Rasōlollāh has a great reward, and its reward dramatically increases according to the importance, etc. of that battle.
Here the Imām says that the reward of reciting this doᶜā' in the Sojōd of Shokr is as much as shooting one million arrows with Rasọlollāh in these three most important battles.

[3] Beḥār al-Anwār / al-Majlesi = vol. 86, page 223.

He said: What happened to my mother Fāṭimah...[1])).

Imām ᶜAskari refers to Fāṭimah's suffering

It has been narrated from ᶜAbdollāh ibn Moḥammad who said:

((I asked my master Abā Moḥammad Ḥasan ibn ᶜAli [Imām ᶜAskari] in Sāmirrā'[2], in the year 255 AH, to dictate to me a ṣalawāt[3] to be recited for the Prophet and his Awṣeyā'. And I had taken with me a large sheet of paper. So he dictated to me:
...The ṣalāt for Lady Fāṭimah:
...O Allāh! You be her claimant from those who did her injustice, and usurped her right. O Allāh! You be her avenger for the blood of her children...[4])).

BAKRI LEADERS CONFESS TO THEIR CRIMES AGAINST FĀṬIMAH

Abō Bakr's confession

Bakri[5] scholars narrate from Abō Bakr^(LA)[1] who, after the attacks on ᶜAli and Fāṭimah's home, said to his men:

---

[1] Beḥār al-Anwār / al-Majlesi = vol. 50, page 59.
[2] The city in which he and his father (Imām Hādi) were held prisoner and were killed and were buried, in today's Northern Iraq.
[3] Plural of ṣalāt. Here, ṣalat means doᶜā' for Allāh's Blessings and Mercy for someone. There is a large number of set formal ṣalawāt narrated from some of the Fourteen Maᶜṣōmēn to be recited for other maᶜṣōmēn; however any Moslem can compose his own ṣalāt for one or more of the Fourteen Maᶜṣōmēn, in any language format, provided that he has a considerable knowledge of Islam.
[4] Beḥar al-Anwār / al-Majlesi = vol. 94, page 74.
[5] A Bakri is a follower of Abō Bakr. Opposite Moslem, Shēᶜah, follower of Rasōlollāh. Some people unknowingly call the followers of Abō Bakr

((Every man sleeps at night hugging his wife, happy with his family; but you left me alone with this problem. I do not need your allegiance, discharge me[2].)).

A large number of Bakri scholars also narrate that when Abō Bakr was on his deathbed, a number of people went to visit him, including ᶜAbdorraḥmān ibn ᶜAwf, an influential high-ranking Bakri leader. And in the conversation that followed, Abō Bakr told ᶜAbdorraḥmān:

((Indeed, I do not feel sorry about anything I did in this world, except three things which I did, and wish that I had not done: ...I wish I had not attacked Fāṭimah's home[3].)).

ᶜOmar's confession

Moslem scholars narrate:

((When Ḥosayn ibn ᶜAli [Imām Ḥosayn] was killed, and the news that his head had been cut and carried

---

"Sonnis". Sonni means a follower of the tradition of Rasōlollāh; and since the followers of Abō Bakr follow him and not Rasōlollāh, it is wrong to call them Sonnis.

[1] *Laᶜnatollāh ᶜAlayh,* may Allāh distance him from His Blessings and Mercy.

[2] al-Imāmah wa al-Seyāsah / Ibn Qotaybah = vol. 1, page 14.

[3] al-ᶜEqd al-Farēd / Ibn ᶜAbderabbeh = vol. 4, page 268. al-Imāmah wa al-Seyāsah / Ibn Qotaybah = vol. 1, page 18. Kanz al-ᶜOmmāl / al-Hendi = vol. 5, page 631. Lesān al-Mēzān / al-ᶜAsqalāni = vol. 4, page 219. Mēzān al-Eᶜtedāl / al-Dhahabi = vol. 2, page 215. al-Moᶜjam al-Kabēr / al-Ṭabarāni = vol. 1, page 62. Mosnad Fāṭimah / al-Soyōṭi = page 34. Sharh Nahj al-Balāghah / Ibn Abi al-Ḥadēd = vol. 2, page 46; vol. 6, page 51; vol. 17, page 164. Tārēkh al-Islam / al-Dhahabi = page 117. Tārēkh al-Omam wa al-Molōk / al-Ṭabari = vol. 2, page 619. Tārēkh / al-Yaᶜqōbi = vol. 2, page 137.

to Yazēd ibn Moᶜāwiyah[1] *reached Madinah... mourning ceremonies were held in the home of Rasōlollāh's wife, Omm Salamah, and the homes of the Mohājirēn and the Anṣār.*
Suddenly, ᶜAbdollāh ibn ᶜOmar ibn al-Khaṭṭāb came out of his home, with his collar torn[2]*, slapping his face, and screaming: O crowd of Bani Hāshim*[3]*, and Qoraysh, and Mohājirēn and Anṣār! Is it assumed permissible to do this to the family and the lineage of Rasōlollāh while you are alive?! Yazēd must be dethroned.*
That night he left Madinah traveling towards Damascus, and in every city he called the people to rise against Yazēd. And reports of his activities were constantly sent to Yazēd.
And the people listened to him and cursed Yazēd, saying: This is ᶜAbdollāh son of ᶜOmar, Rasōlollāh's khalēfah, and he is denouncing what Yazēd has done to Ahl al-Bayt, and is calling the people against him; so whoever does not answer his call is not a Moslem. Thus a great unrest hit Damascus.
Finally, he entered the capital and came to Yazēd's castle with a large crowd...
He was given permission to enter the castle alone, so he entered screaming at Yazēd: You have done what the Turks and the Romans would not have done; move aside so that the Moslems choose someone more suitable for this position.
However, Yazēd received him politely, hugged him, and respected him greatly. Then he said: O Aba Moḥammad! [ᶜAbdollāh] calm down...

---

[1] The fifth Usurper of the Khelāfah, and the third Amawi ruler. His paternal grandparents were Abō Sofyān, the Idolater leader, and Hend, the Liver Eater.

[2] It was a custom to tear open one's collar in the mourning of a very important and much beloved deceased.

[3] The tribe of Rasolollāh and the Ahl al-Bayt.

Did your father appoint my father as the Governor of Shām[1]*, or did my father appoint your father as Rasōlollāh's Khalēfah?*
ᶜAbdollāh: My father appointed your father.
Yazēd: O Abā Moḥammad! Do you accept your father and his advice to my father?
ᶜAbdollāh: Yes I accept.
Then Yazēd held ᶜAbdollāh's hand, saying: Stand up O Abā Moḥammad! and read it (Omar's advice to Moᶜāwiyah). So they walked into one of the safes where Yazēd asked for a specific box, opened it and took out a smaller box which was sealed and locked, he then took out a thin scroll wrapped in a black silk cloth and gave it to ᶜAbdollāh, saying: O Abā Moḥammad! is this not your father's hand writing?
ᶜAbdollāh: Yes, by Allāh; and he kissed it.
Yazēd: Read.
And ᶜAbdollāh read it. [Only some excerpts of ᶜOmar's letter to Moᶜāwiyah are mentioned here):
...So I swear by the Hobal and the Idols and the Lāt and the ᶜOzzā[2] *that ᶜOmar never renounced them since he first worshiped them, and that he never worshiped the God of the Kaᶜbah, and that he never believed Moḥammad. And that he never saluted him accept for becoming powerful enough to work against him and suppress him, for he (Rasōlollāh) had indeed come to us with a great sorcery, and added to that of the Israelites with Mōsā, Hārōn, Dāwōd, Solaymān and ᶜĒsā; he brought us all of their sorcery and added to it so much that if they had seen him, they would have testified that he is the Master of the Sorcerers.*
So hold on O son of Abi Sofyān! to the tradition of your people, and follow their religion, and continue the mission of your fathers in denouncing this structure (Kaᶜbah) which they say has a God whom

---

[1] Today's Syria, Lebanon, Jordan and Palestine.
[2] Hobal, Lāt and ᶜOzzā where the three most respected idols to the Idolaters.

ordered them to come to it and circumambulate around it...

And thank the Lāt and the ᶜOzzā for the rule of the Wise Master ᶜAtēq ibn ᶜAbdolᶜozzā [Abō Bakr] on the nation of Moḥammad, and his authority in their finances, bloods, faiths, souls, permissibles, prohibitions, taxes... so he would rule leniently in public and harshly in secret...

And indeed, I made a magnificent leap on the shining star of Bani Hāshim[1]*, and its luminous summit... the one named Ḥaydarah*[2]*, Moḥammad's son-in-law, husband of the woman they appointed as Sayyedat Nesā' al-ᶜĀlamēn, calling her Fāṭimah. I came to the home of ᶜAli, Fāṭimah and their two sons Ḥasan and Ḥosayn, and their two daughters Zaynab and Omm Kolthoom, and their housemaid Feḍḍah, along with Khālid ibn al-Walēd, Qonfodh and a number of our most loyal men. So I knocked on the door very hard and the housemaid answered me. I told her: Tell ᶜAli: Forget this nonsense and do not think about the khelāfah, for surely it is not yours; it is for whom has been chosen by the Moslems...*

Again I went to ᶜAli's home and told Feḍḍah: Tell ᶜAli to come out and pledge allegiance to Abō Bakr. But she said: Indeed, Amēr al-Mo'menēn is busy. So I said: Tell him to come out, or we will come in and extract him by force.

Then Fāṭimah came and stood behind the door, saying: O you straying liars! What are you saying? And what do you want?

So I said: O Fāṭimah!

Fāṭimah: What do you want O ᶜOmar?

I said: Why did your cousin send you to answer me and he chose to sit behind the cover?!

Fāṭimah: Your tyranny O scoundrel! Brought me out.

I said: Forget the women's nonsense and myths and tell ᶜAli to come out.

---

[1] Rasōlollāh's tribe.

[2] One of the names of Amēr al-Mo'menēn.

Fāṭimah: Do you threaten me with the party of the Shayṭān[1] O ᶜOmar?!...

I said: If he does not come out, I will bring a lot of firewood and will burn down this house on whoever is inside; and I took the whip from Qonfodh and lashed her, and told Khālid: You and the men gather the wood, for surely I am burning it down.

Fāṭimah: O enemy of Allāh and the enemy of His Messenger and the enemy of Amēr al-Mo'menēn!

She then put her hands on the door, trying to stop me from entering; so I lashed her hands with the whip which hurt her, and I heard her sighs and cries; and I nearly went soft and was about to return, but I remembered my despise of ᶜAli and his passion for the blood of the stouthearted Arabs, and the cunning of Moḥammad and his sorcery, so I kicked the door against her while she was behind it, and I heard her scream: O my father! This is what is done to your beloved daughter! Ah O Feḍḍah! Hold me, for indeed, by Allāh, my fetus has been killed.

I heard her go into labor, leaning on the wall, so I pushed the door and entered the house. She came towards me and I slapped her face so hard that her earring tore from her ear, and she fell down.

Then ᶜAli came, and when I sensed him I quickly went out and said to Khālid and Qonfodh: I escaped from a great danger; indeed, I have committed a serious crime and I fear for my life. This is ᶜAli coming out, and none of us can handle him.

So ᶜAli reached her just as she was about to pray to Allāh against us and complain of what had happened to her, so he spread a wrap on her, telling her: O Daughter of Rasōlollāh! indeed Allāh sent your father as a mercy to the creatures. I swear by Allāh, that if you uncovered your forehead and prayed to your Lord, He will most definitely destroy these people; as you and your father are dearer to Allāh than Nōḥ, for whom He drowned the people who

[1] Also Satan.

were not on his ship... So be O Chief of the Women! a mercy to these inverted people, and do not be a punishment.
Her pain then increased, and she entered her room and miscarried a dead fetus that was called Moḥassin...
So when ᶜAbdollāh read the letter, he stood up and kissed Yazēd's head, saying: Praise be to God O Amēr al-Mo'menēn! for your killing the enemy, son of the enemy!! I swear that my father did not tell me what he had told your father...[1])).

FĀṬIMAH REJECTS ABŌ BAKR AND ᶜOMAR

A large number of Bakri scholars narrate the following three aḥādēth from Fāṭimah's archenemy, ᶜĀ'eshah(LAa)[2]:

((So Fāṭimah rejected Abō Bakr, and did not speak with him until she died. And ᶜAli buried her at night, and did not inform Abō Bakr[3].)).

((So Fāṭimah became angry at Abō Bakr and rejected him, and did not speak with him until she died... And when she died, her husband ᶜAli buried her at night, and did not inform Abō Bakr[4].)).

---

[1] Beḥār al-Anwār / al-Majlesi = vol. 30, page 287.

[2] *Laᶜnatollāh ᶜAlayha,* may Allāh distance her from His Blessings and Mercy.

[3] Moshkel al-Athār / al-Ṭaḥāwi = vol. 1, page 47. Sharh Nahj al-Balāghah / Ibn Abi al-Ḥadēd = vol. 6, page 46. al-Sonan al-Kobrā / al-Bayhaqi = vol. 6, page 300. Tārēkh al-Omam wa al-Molōk / al-Ṭabari = vol. 3, page 208. Taysēr al-Woṣōl / al-Shaybāni = vol. 2, page 46. Wafā' al-Wafa / al-Samhōdi = vol. 2, page 995.

[4] Ṣaḥēḥ / al-Bokhāri = vol. 5, page 177. Sharh Nahj al-Balāghah / Ibn Abi al-Ḥadēd = vol. 16, page 217. Tārēkh al-Khamēs / al-Deyārbakri = vol. 2, page 173.

((So Fāṭimah became angry and rejected Abō Bakr; and continued her rejection until she died[1].)).

Bakri scholars also narrate:

((ᶜOmar told Abō Bakr: Let us go to Fāṭimah, as we have made her angry. So they went together and asked for permission to see Fāṭimah, but she refused to permit them.
Thus they asked ᶜAli for permission, so he took them to her.
When they entered her room and sat in front of her, she turned her face towards the wall. They greeted her, but she did not return their greeting.
Abō Bakr then started to speak, saying: O the beloved of Rasōlollāh! We exasperated you...
She said: Do you think that if I narrate to you a ḥadēth from Rasōlollāh that you have already heard, you would admit that you had heard it?
They said: Yes.
So she said: I ask you in Allāh's name, did not you hear Rasōlollāh say: Fāṭimah's satisfaction is my satisfaction, and Fāṭimah's exasperation is my exasperation; so whomsoever loves my daughter Fāṭimah, he has surely loved me; and whomsoever satisfies Fāṭimah, he has surely satisfied me; and whomsoever exasperates Fāṭimah, he has surely exasperated me?
They said: Yes, we have heard that from Rasōlollāh.
Fāṭimah said: I hold Allāh and His angels as my witnesses that you indeed exasperated me and did not satisfy me. And when I meet the Prophet, I will most definitely complain you to him.

---

[1] al-Bedāyah wa al-Nehāyah / Ibn Kothayr = vol. 5, page 285. Jāmiᶜ al-Oṣōl / Ibn al-Athēr = vol. 10, page 386. Mosnad / Aḥmad = vol. 1, page 9. Ṣaḥēḥ / al-Bokhāri = vol. 4, page 96. Ṣaḥēḥ / Moslem = vol. 5, page 25. al-Sērah al-Nabawiyyah / Ibn Kothayr = vol. 4, page 496. Tārēkh al-Islam / al-Dhahabi = page 21. Taysēr al-Woṣōl / al-Shaybāni = vol. 4, page 11.

So Abō Bakr said: I ask Allāh for refuge from his (Rasōlollāh) exasperation and your exasperation O Fāṭimah! Then Abō Bakr cried lamenting, until he nearly lost consciousness, while Fāṭimah repeated: By Allāh! I will most definitely pray to Allāh against you in every ṣalāt I perform.
Then Abō Bakr left weeping, and the people gathered around him; So he told them: Every man sleeps at night hugging his wife, happy with his family; but you left me alone with this problem. I do not need your allegiance, discharge me[1].)).

Some scholars record this narration with more details:

((When Fāṭimah fell ill, Abō Bakr and ᶜOmar went to visit her, but she refused to accept them... Thus ᶜOmar went to ᶜAli and said: We have gone to Fāṭimah several times asking for permission to see her, but she has repeatedly refused to receive us and to hear our apology; so could you prepare a meeting for us?
He said: Yes. And he went to Fāṭimah and said: O Daughter of Rasōlollāh! You have seen what you have seen from these two men; and they have come to see you several times but you have refused to receive them; now they have asked me to ask you for permission.
Fāṭimah: By Allāh, I will not give them permission, and will not speak with them a single work until I meet Allāh and complain to Him what they had done to me.
Ali: I have said yes to them.
Fāṭimah: If you have said yes, then the home is yours, and the women follow the men, and I will not disagree with you over anything; so you may give permission to anyone you like. Thus ᶜAli went out and gave them permission to come and see her.

---

[1] al-Imāmah wa al-Seyāsah / Ibn Qotaybah = vol. 1, page 13.

When they saw Fāṭimah [who was lying], they greeted her, but she did not answer their greeting and turned her face towards the wall. So they came and sat in front of her. So she said to ᶜAli: Cover me with a thick cloth; and told the women who were there: Turn my face. So she repeatedly turned her face to the opposite direction as they repeatedly changed their places to sit in front of her.

Then Abō Bakr said: O Daughter of Rasōlollāh! indeed we have come to you to seek your satisfaction, and avoid your exasperation; we ask you to forgive us and pardon us for what we have done to you.

Fāṭimah: I will not speak to you a single world until I meet my father and complain to him what you have done to me.

She then looked at ᶜAli and said: Indeed, I will not speak with them until I ask them about something they had heard from my father, so if they admitted hearing it, then I will see.

They said: Let her ask, and we shall not say other than the truth, and will not testify except truthfully.

So she said: I ask you in Allāh's name, do you remember that Rasōlollāh once summoned you at night about something regarding ᶜAli?

They said: Yes.

Fāṭimah: I ask you in Allāh's name, did you hear the Prophet say: Fāṭimah is a part of me, and I am a part of her. Whomsoever annoys her, he has surely annoyed me; and whomsoever annoys me, he has surely annoyed Allāh. And whomsoever annoys her after my death, is as if he had annoyed her during my life; and whomsoever annoys her during my life is as if he has annoyed her after my death?

They said: Yes.

Fāṭimah: Praise be to Allāh. O Allāh! I hold You as my witness; and so bare witness you who are present [in the room], that these two have indeed annoyed me during my life and at my death. By Allāh, I will not speak with you a single word until I

meet my Lord and complain what you have done to me.
Thus Abō Bakr said: Woe unto me, I wish my mother had not given birth to me.
So ᶜOmar said: What a surprise! How did the people chose you to rule them, when you are a old man who has gone senile?! You become anxious by a woman's anger, and happy by her satisfaction?! And what guilt does a man carry for exasperating a woman?!
So they left[1].)).

Were Abō Bakr and ᶜOmar truthful in their apology?

It is not ambiguous for a fair-minded person who reads the above narrations, that Abō Bakr and ᶜOmar were not truthful in their apology to Fāṭimah. Had they at all been sincere, they would have put things right, instead of continuing their suppression. But we see that nothing changed, and the Bakri leaders continued on their path.

Abō Bakr screamed to his men: "discharge me", as if it were up to them to dethrone him. And even if they could, then what is the meaning of his apology when he wants one of his men to replace him, instead of the Rightful Khalēfah?!

The fact is that Abō Bakr wanted to rule and had no intention of stepping aside, whether for Amēr al-Mo'menēn or for anyone else. But at the same time, he wanted erase the black mark that attacking Fāṭimah had brought him.

And ᶜAli and Fāṭimah were cleverer than to be tricked by Abō Bakr and ᶜOmar, and could not be fooled by crocodile tears into forgiving and forgetting and announcing to the people that all was well between them.

Therefore Fāṭimah turned their public show against them by insistently refusing to meet with them, and by her unwavering unwillingness to accept their apology, and by her severe tone... Telling the whole world that Sayyedat Nesā' al-ᶜĀlamēn, whose

---

[1] Fāṭimah min al-Mahd elā al-Laḥd / al-Qazwēni = page 596 from ᶜElal al-Sharā'eᶜ / al-Ṣadōq.

anger and satisfaction are that of Allāh and Rasōlollāh, was angry with Abō Bakr and ᶜOmar.

Whoever dies without knowing his imām...

A very large number of Bakri scholars narrate from Rasōlollāh who said:

> *((Whoever dies while having no allegiance to the imām, he has died the death of the ignorance[1].)).*

They also narrate that Sayyedat Nesā' al-ᶜĀlamēn never accepted Abō Bakr as her imām until she died.

Ṣaḥēḥ al-Bokhāri and Ṣaḥēḥ Moslem, the two most respectable and authentic references to the Bakris after the Holy Qor'ān, record that she died rejecting Abō Bakr.

---

[1] This ḥadēth has been recorded with different forms, through various Bakri chains of narrators, in many Bakri references, some of which are as follows: al-Aḥādēth al-Mokhtārah / al-Maqdesi = vol. 8, pages 194 and 198. Fatḥ al-Bāri / al-ᶜAsqalāni = vol. 13, page 7. Ḥelyat al-Awleyā' / Abō Noᶜaym = vol. 3, page 224. Majmaᶜ al-Zawā'ed / al-Haythami = vol. 1, page 324; vol. 5, pages 218 and 223. al-Moᶜjam al-Awsaṭ / al-Ṭabarāni = vol. 1, page 79; vol. 6, page 70. al-Moᶜjam al-Kabēr / al-Ṭabarāni = vol. 12, page 160; vol. 19, pages 334 and 388. Moṣannaf / ᶜAbdorrazzāq = vol. 2, page 379. Moṣannaf / Ibn Abi Shaybah = vol. 7, page 457. Mosnad / Abi ᶜAwānah = vol. 4, pages 416, 422 and 423. Mosnad / Abi Yaᶜlā = vol. 4, page 234; vol. 13, page 366. Mosnad ᶜAbdollāh ibn ᶜOmar / al-Tarsōsi = vol. 1, page 28. Mosnad / Aḥmad = vol. 1, pages 297 and 310; vol. 3, pages 445 and 446; vol. 4, page 96. Mosnad al-Shāmiyyēn / al-Ṭabarāni = vol. 2, page 437. Mosnad al-Shahāb / al-Qoḍāᶜi = vol. 1, page 277. Mosnad / al-Ṭayālisi = vol. 1, page 259. Ṣaḥēḥ / Bokhāri = vol. 6, pages 2588 and 2612. Ṣaḥēḥ / Ibn Ḥabbān = vol. 10, page 434. Ṣaḥēḥ / Moslem = vol. 3, pages 1476, 1477 and 1478. Shoᶜab al-Ēmān / al-Bayhaqi = vol. 6, page 60. Sonan / al-Dārimi = vol. 2, page 214. Sonan / Ibn Abi ᶜĀsim = vol. 2, page 503. al-Sonan al-Kobrā / al-Bayhaqi = vol. 2, page 314; vol. 6, page 300; vol. 8, page 157. al-Tārēkh al-Kabēr / al-Bokhāri = vol. 6, page 445. al-Ṭabaqāt al-Kobrā = vol. 5, page 144. Tafsēr al-Qor'ān al-ᶜAẓēm / Ibn Kothayr = vol. 1, page 518. al-Jāmiᶜ le Aḥkām al-Qor'ān / al-Qorṭobi = vol. 14, page 56. Tahdhēb al-Kamāl / al-Mazzi = vol. 9, page 463.

So did she die while having no allegiance to her imām?! Are the Bakris bold enough to say that Fāṭimah died as a non-Moslem?!

This is another contradiction which crushes what is left of the Bakri conscience. On the one hand they cannot abandon their beloved Ṣaḥēḥ al-Bokhāri and Ṣaḥēḥ Moslem and deny the authenticity of this ḥadēth which almost all of their references have recorded, and on the other hand they do not dare claim that Fāṭimah died the death of the ignorance.

However, the answer is simple and clear. Sayyedat Nesā' al-ᶜĀlamēn died in the allegiance of Amēr al-Mo'menēn, who was chosen by Allāh and appointed by His Messenger as the first khalēfah.

But the Bakris cannot say this either, as it would mean that Abō Bakr and ᶜOmar and the rest of their leaders had usurped the khelāfah[1]; and what greater crime?!

---

[1] Successorship of Rasōlollāh. Also caliphate.

THE BAKRI PARTY USURPS SAYYEDAT NESĀ' AL-ᶜĀLAMĒN'S POSITIONS

After the attacks on the home of ᶜAli and Fāṭimah, Abō Bakr ordered the usurpation of Fāṭimah's positions.

WHAT WERE THESE POSITIONS?

Fadak

Fadak was a vast expanse of fertile land in the Arabian Peninsula that produced crops, especially dates. It is also said that it included several villages, and it is said that it included a town. Its owners gave it to Rasōlollāh as part of a deal, and it is said that it was given to him as a gift[1].

It has been narrated that the annual profits of Fadak, during those years, was as much as seventy thousand Dēnārs[2].

Many Bakri scholars narrate that Rasōlollāh gave Fadak to Fāṭimah during his life, thus it was her property when he died.

One such Bakri narration is as follows:

> *((When "AND GIVE TO THE NEAR OF KIN HIS DUE[1]" was revealed, the Prophet asked for Fāṭimah, and gave her Fadak[2].)).*

---

[1] Dar Maktab Fāṭimah = page 225.

[2] Fāṭimah min al-Mahd elā al-Laḥd / al-Qazwēni = page 354.

Moslems also narrate from Rasōlollāh who said:

((...And your father gives it (Fadak) to you as a gift, for you and your children after you. Then he (Rasōlollāh) asked for a skin and told ᶜAli ibn Abi Ṭālib: Write, that Fadak belongs to Fāṭimah, a gift from Rasōlollāh[3].)).

The Seven Farms

When Mokhayrēq, a wealthy influential Jewish scholar from the Bani al-Naḍēr tribe, converted to Islam, he gave these farms around Madinah to Rasōlollāh as a gift[4].

And Rasōlollāh gave them to Fāṭimah as *waqf*[5], and used some of their income for his needs[6]. So at the time of his death, they were Fāṭimah's property.

---

[1] Holy Qor'ān = sōrah 17, āyah 26.

[2] al-Bedāyah wa al-Nehāyah / Ibn Kothayr = vol. 3, page 36. al-Dorr al-Manthōr / al-Soyōṭi = vol. 2, page 158; vol. 5, page 273. Kanz al-ᶜOmmāl / al-Hendi = vol. 2, page 158; vol. 3, page 767. Majmaᶜ al-Zawā'ed / al-Haythami = vol. 7, page 49. Maqtal al-Ḥosayn / al-Khārazmi = vol. 1, page 70. Mēzān al Eᶜtedāl / al-Dhahabi = vol. 5, page 164. Mosnad / Abi Yaᶜlā = vol. 2, pages 334 and 534. Rōḥ al-Maᶜāni / al-Ālōsi = vol. 5, page 58. Shawāhid al-Tanzēl / al-Ḥasakāni = vol. 1, pages 438, 439, 441 and 442. Tafser al-Qor'ān al-ᶜAẓēm / Ibn Kothayr = vol. 3, page 37.

[3] Beḥār al-Anwār / al-Majlesi = vol. 17, page 378

[4] Fāṭimah min Qabl al-Mēlād elā Baᶜd al-Estesh-hād / al-Hāshimi = page 249.

[5] An Islamic form of endowment.

[6] Fāṭimah min Qabl al-Mēlād elā Baᶜd al-Estesh-hād / al-Hāshimi= page 249.

The Khoms[1] of Khaybar

Khaybar was a series of forts, a most important Jewish center in the Arabian Peninsula.

After the Arab Jews turned against the newly established Moslem rule, broke their numerous agreements with the Moslems, made a pact with the Idolaters, participated with the Idolaters in some of their battles against the Moslems, and independently waged a number of wars against the Moslems, Rasōlollāh finally marched an army to their most important stronghold in the Arabia—Khaybar.

There, a large number of Jews converted to Islam when they saw the miracles performed by Rasōlollāh and Amēr al-Mo'menēn; and the remaining Jews made a new agreement with Rasōlollāh.

After the liberation of Khaybar, four-fifth of its assets were divided between the Moslems, and one fifth of it which was the Khoms went to Allāh, Rasōlollāh, Dhawi al-Qorbā[2], and the orphans, and the poor and the travelers in need of financial help among the larger family of Rasōlollāh.

And after Rasōlollāh's martyrdom, the remainder of the Khoms of Khaybar should have come to ᶜAli and Fāṭimah as the representatives of Rasōlollāh and his Dhawi al-Qorbā.

Rasōlollāh's inheritance

After his martyrdom, Rasōlollāh left a huge inheritance, all of which were usurped by Abō Bakr.

---

[1] An Islamic tax of 20% levied, among other things, on the annual superfluous income. Khoms is given to the Prophet or one of his kholafā' or one of the representatives of the final khalēfah—Marājiᶜ[1], who then give it to its legal recipients accordingly. It could also be directly given to the legal recipients under the supervision or with the permission of the Marājiᶜ. Once Khoms is deducted from a certain amount, it will no longer be subject to Khoms in the coming years.

[2] Sayyedat Nesā' al-ᶜĀlamēn, and the twelve God-appointed successors of Rasōlollāh.

Khoms

Khoms is an Islamic tax of 20% levied, among other things, on the annual superfluous income. Khoms is given to the Prophet or one of his kholafā' or one of the representatives of the final khalēfah—Marājic[1], who then give it to its legal recipients accordingly.

However, when Abō Bakr usurped the khelāfah, he withheld the Khoms from cAli and Fāṭimah; and the other Usurpers of the Khelāfah followed suit.

The portion of Dhawi al-Qorbā

Khoms has six portions: that of Allāh, Rasōlollāh, Dhawi al-Qorbā, and the orphans, and the poor and the travelers in need of financial help among the larger family of Rasōlollāh.

All Bakri and Moslem scholars agree that the during the life of Rasōlollāh, the portion of Allāh was to be given to Rasōlollāh to be spent in His way; and they all agree that after the martyrdom of Rasōlollāh, the portions of Allāh and Rasōlollāh were to be given to his khalēfah, who according to the Moslems was Amēr al-Mo'menēn. But after the usurpation of the khelāfah, these two portions, like the rest of the Khoms, were withheld from Amēr al-Mo'menēn as the Bakri party refused to recognize his khelāfah.

However, according to the Holy Qor'ān, the portion of Dhawi al-Qorba should have been given to Amēr al-Mo'menēn and Sayyedat Nesā' al-cĀlamēn irrespective of who was considered to be the legitimate khalēfah, where Allāh says:

> ﴾*AND KNOW THAT WHATEVER THING YOU GAIN, A FIFTH OF IT IS FOR ALLĀH AND FOR THE APOSTLE AND FOR THE NEAR OF KIN (DHAWI AL-QORBĀ) AND THE ORPHANS AND THE NEEDY AND THE WAYFARER, IF YOU BELIEVE IN ALLĀH AND IN THAT WHICH WE REVEALED TO OUR SERVANT*[2].﴿

---

[1] Plural of Marjec: a highest religious authority.

[2] Holy Qor'ān = sōrah 8, āyah 41.

But regardless, Abō Bakr and the other usurpers refused to even allow the portion of Dhawi al-Qorbā, one-sixth of the Khoms, to go to ᶜAli and Fāṭimah.

Usurpation of Fāṭimah's positions and her demand for them in Bakri and Moslem references

Fāṭimah's usurped positions were of three categories:

1- The property that she owned during the life of Rasōlollāh.
2- Her inheritance from her father.
3- The Khoms.

When Abō Bakr usurped the first and withheld the other two, she sat out to demand them publicly.

First she demanded Fadak as her property, but when Abō Bakr asked for witnesses who testified that Rasōlollāh had given it to her during his life, and then rejected all of her witnesses, she demanded it as her inheritance from Rasōlollāh; but Abō Bakr was well prepared for this!!

And as this subject is highly sensitive and very revealing, Bakri scholars have been extremely cautious in narrating it. Therefore, one thing that these narrations have in common is their lack of detail and the usual censorship. Some instances are:

Bakri scholars narrate from ᶜOmar*(LA)*[1], who said:

((Fāṭimah came to Abō Bakr along with ᶜAli, and said: I want my inheritance from my father Rasōlollāh... Fadak and Khaybar and his assets in Madinah. I inherit them just as your daughters will inherit you when you die.
Abō Bakr said: ...Indeed Rasōlollāh had said: We [the prophets] do not leave inheritance[1]*.)).*

---

[1] *Laᶜnatollāh ᶜAlayh,* may Allāh distance him from His Blessings and Mercy.

Bakri scholars narrate from ᶜĀ'eshah who said:

((Indeed, Fāṭimah asked Abō Bakr for her inheritance from Rasōlollāh (in Madinah and Fadak, and the remaining Khoms of Khaybar[2]).
But Abō Bakr said: Indeed, Rasōlollāh has said: We [the prophets] do not leave inheritance.
Thus Fāṭimah became angry and rejected Abō Bakr, and continued her rejection until she died[3].)).

Bakri scholars also narrate from ᶜĀ'eshah who said:

((Indeed, Fāṭimah and ᶜAbbās came to Abō Bakr, asking for their inheritance from Rasōlollāh, demanding Fadak and his share of Khaybar.
Abō Bakr said to them: I have heard Rasōlollāh say: We [the prophets] do not leave inheritance[4].)).

However a number of Bakri scholars have, to some extent, resisted the temptation to censor, and have narrated a little bit more detail. A few instances are as follows:

((...Thus Fāṭimah rejected him and did not speak with him until she died[5]; so ᶜAli buried her at night, and did not inform Abō Bakr[6].)).

---

[1] Kanz al-ᶜOmmāl / al-Hendi = vol. 5, page 622. Mosnad Fāṭimah / al-Soyōṭi = page 15. al-Ṭabaqāt al-Kobrā / Ibn Saᶜd = vol. 2, page 315.
[2] Ṣaḥēḥ / al-Bokhari = vol. 5, page 177.
[3] Jāmiᶜ al-Oṣōl / Ibn al-Athēr = vol. 10, page 386. Ṣaḥēḥ / al-Bokhāri = vol. 4, page 96. Ṣaḥēḥ / Moslem = vol. 5, page 25.
[4] Mosnad / Aḥmad = vol. 1, pages 4 and 10. al-Reyāḍ al-Naḍirah / al-Ṭabari = vol. 2, page 124. Ṣaḥēḥ / al-Bokhāri = vol. 4, page 1481. Ṣaḥēḥ / Moslem = vol. 3, page 1381. Tarakat al-Nabi / al-Baghdādi = vol. 1, page 82.
[5] Ṣaḥēḥ / al-Bokhāri = vol. 6, page 2474. al-Theqāt / Ibn Ḥabbān = vol. 2, page 164.
[6] Jāmiᶜ al-Oṣōl / Ibn al-Athēr = vol. 4, page 482. Moṣannaf / ᶜAbdorrazzāq = vol. 5, page 472. Mosnad / Abi ᶜAwānah = vol. 4, page 251. Sharh Nahj

((Fāṭimah said to Abō Bakr: Who inherits you when you die?
Abō Bakr: My children and my family.
Fāṭimah: So why cannot we inherit the Prophet?![1])).

((Fāṭimah came to Abō Bakr and demanded Fadak. But Abō Bakr said: Rasōlollāh has said: We [the prophets] do not leave inheritance.
Fāṭimah: O Abā Bakr! Do your daughters inherit you, and Rasōlollāh's daughter does not inherit him?!
Abō Bakr: It is exactly as you said[2].)).

((After Rasōlollāh's death, Fāṭimah came to Abō Bakr and said: Indeed, Fadak was a gift from my father that he gave me during his life.
But Abō Bakr denied this and told her: I want witnesses for your claim.
Thus ᶜAli stood as her witness. Abō Bakr then asked for another witness, and Omm Ayman stood as the second witness.
So Abō Bakr said to Fāṭimah: Do you demand Fadak from me with one male and one female witnesses?![3])).

((Fāṭimah said to Abō Bakr: Give me Fadak, for surely it was given to me by Rasōlollāh.
He asked her for witnesses, and she brought Omm Ayman and Rebāḥ, the Prophet's servant; and they testified.
Abō Bakr then said: In this matter the minimum required witnesses are one man and two women[1].)).

---

al-Balāghah / Ibn Abi al-Ḥadēd = vol. 6, page 46. al-Sonan al-Kobrā / al-Bayhaqi = vol. 6, page 300.

[1] Jāmiᶜ al-Oṣōl / Ibn al-Athēr = vol. 10, page 388. Mosnad / Aḥmad = vol. 1, page 13. Sharh Nahj al-Balāghah / Ibn Abi al-Ḥadēd = vol. 16, page 232. Tārēkh al-Khamēs / al-Deyārbakri = vol. 2, page 173.

[2] Tārēkh al-Madinah al-Monawwarah / Ibn Shobbah = vol. 1, page 198.

[3] al-Sērah al-Ḥalabiyyah / al-Ḥalabi = vol. 3, page 39.

((Fāṭimah said to Abō Bakr: Indeed, Omm Ayman testifies that Rasōlollāh gave Fadak to me.
Abō Bakr: This property did not belong to Rasōlollāh!!?
Fāṭimah: By Allāh, I shall never speak to you again.
She also said: I will surely pray to Allāh against you[2].)).

((Fāṭimah and ᶜAbbās came to Abō Bakr asking for their inheritance, and ᶜAli came along with them.
Abō Bakr said: Rasōlollāh has said: We [the prophets] do not leave inheritance.
So ᶜAli said: "AND SOLAYMĀN INHERITED DĀWŌD[3]"; and Zakariyyā said: "WHO SHOULD INHERIT ME AND INHERIT FROM THE CHILDREN OF YAᶜQŌB[4]"...
Ali then said: This is the Book of Allāh speaking[5].)).

((ᶜAbdorraḥmān ibn Abi Laylā narrates: I met ᶜAli and asked him: My parents be your sacrifice, what did Abō Bakr and ᶜOmar do with the right of Ahl al-Bayt to Khoms?
Ali: ...Indeed, ᶜOmar said: You have the right to the Khoms, but I do not think that you can have it all if it is a large amount; so if you like, I will give you some of it.
Thus we rejected anything less that all of the Khoms, and he refused to give us all of it[6].)).

((Fāṭimah came to Abō Bakr to demand the portion of Dhawi al-Qorbā. But Abō Bakr told her: I heard Rasōlollāh say: The portion of Dhawi al-Qorbā is

---

[1] Fotōḥ al-Boldān / al-Balādheri = page 38.
[2] Sharh Nahj al-Balāghah / Ibn Abi al-Ḥadēd = vol. 16, page 214.
[3] Holy Qor'ān = sōrah 27, āyah 16.
[4] Holy Qor'ān = sōrah 19, āyah 6.
[5] Kanz al-ᶜOmmāl / al-Hendi = vol. 5, page 625.
[6] Mosnad / al-Shāfeᶜi = page 187. al-Sonan al-Kobrā / al-Bayhaqi = vol. 6, page 344.

given to them during my life and not after my death!![1])).

((Ibn ᶜAbbās said: ᶜOmar wanted to give us some of the Khoms, but we rejected it and said: The portion of Dhawi al-Qorbā is one-fifth of the Khoms[2].)).

Moslems scholars narrate from Imām Ṣādiq[(AS)3] who said:

((When Abō Bakr started his rule, ᶜOmar told him: Indeed, people are the slaves of money, they do not see any other thing; so withhold the Khoms and Fadak from ᶜAli and his family, for surely his followers will leave him as soon as they find out, and will come to you wanting some of that money.
And Abō Bakr acted as ᶜOmar had suggested...
(When Fāṭimah went to claim her legal positions, ᶜOmar said to her in that heated argument): Then all of the Khoms, etc. belong to you and your followers?!
Then ᶜOmar asked her for proof, and she said: You believed Jābir and Jorayr without asking them for proof, and my proof is in the Qor'ān.
Omar: Jābir and Jorayr asked for a small thing, but you are asking for a large thing[4].)).

Moslems also narrate:

((Then Omm Ayman said: Fāṭimah who is the Chief of the Women of the Heaven claims to own what does not belong to her?! And I as an inhabitant of Heaven do not testify to what I have not heard.

---

[1] Mosnad Fāṭimah / al-Soyōṭi = page 17. Tahdhēb al-Tahdhēb / al-ᶜAsqalāni = vol. 12, page 48.
[2] Kanz al-ᶜOmmāl / al-Hendi = vol. 2, page 305. And a similar narration in: Lesān al-Mēzān / al-ᶜAsqalāni = vol. 6, page 148. Mosnad / Aḥmad = vol. 1, page 320. Ṣaḥēḥ / Moslem = vol. 5, page 198. al-Sonan al-Kobrā / al-Bayhaqi = vol. 6, page 344. Sonan / al-Nasā'i = page 177.
[3] *ᶜAlayhes Salām,* peace be upon him.
[4] Beḥār al-Anwār / al-Majlesi = vol. 29 , page 194.

Omar: O Omm Ayman! Forget these stories!! What is your testimony?
Omm Ayman: I was sitting in Fāṭimah's home when Rasōlollāh gave her Fadak. And then he said: O Omm Ayman! Witness this, and O ᶜAli! Witness this.
Omar: You are a woman and we do not accept the single testimony of one woman. And ᶜAli is biased...[1])).

((Fāṭimah came to Abō Bakr and said: Why have you withheld my inheritance from my father Rasōlollāh, and forced out my trustee from Fadak, despite the fact that Rasōlollāh had given it to me by Allāh the Almighty's command?!
Abō Bakr: Bring me witnesses.
So she brought Omm Ayman. And Omm Ayman said: I will not testify O Abō Bakr! until I ask you about what Rasōlollāh had said. I ask you in Allāh's name, do you not know that Rasōlollāh said: Omm Ayman is a woman from the inhabitants of Heaven?!
Abō Bakr: Yes.
Omm Ayman: Now I stand witness that Allāh, the Great, the Almighty, revealed to Rasōlollāh: "AND GIVE TO THE NEAR OF KIN HIS DUE[2]", and he gave Fadak to Fāṭimah by the order of the Almighty Allāh.
Then ᶜAli came and testified to that.
Thus Abō Bakr wrote a deed giving Fadak to Fāṭimah.
Suddenly ᶜOmar entered and said: What is this document?
Abō Bakr: Indeed, Fāṭimah claimed Fadak and Omm Ayman and ᶜAli testified to her ownership, so I wrote this deed for her.
ᶜOmar then took the deed, spited on it and tore it.
So Fāṭimah went out crying.
Later ᶜAli went to Abō Bakr in the mosque, when the Mohājirēn and the Anṣār were sitting around him,

---

[1] Beḥār al-Anwār / al-Majlesi = vol. 29, page 189.
[2] Holy Qor'ān = sōrah 17, āyah 26.

and said: O Abā Bakr! Why do you withhold Fāṭimah's inheritance from Rasōlollāh [Fadak], even though she owned it during his life?!
Abō Bakr: It belongs to the Moslems. And if she does not bring witnesses that Rasōlollāh had given it to her, then she does not have any claim to it.
Ali: O Abā Bakr! You judge against Allāh's rule?!
Abō Bakr: No.
Ali: So if the Moslems had something in their hands, and I claimed that it belonged to me, who will you ask to bring witnesses?
Abō Bakr: I will ask you.
Ali: So why did you ask Fāṭimah to bring witnesses for what she had in her hands, even though she owned it during Rasōlollāh's life and after his death?!
Abō Bakr stayed silent for a while, then he said: O ᶜAli, let us forget what you just said, as we cannot refute your argument. If you cannot bring acceptable witnesses, then Fadak belongs to the Moslems, and neither you nor Fāṭimah have any right to it.
Ali: O Abā Bakr! do you read Allāh's Book?
Abō Bakr: Yes.
Ali: Tell me about: "ALLĀH ONLY DESIRES TO KEEP AWAY THE UNCLEANNESS FROM YOU, O PEOPLE OF THE HOUSE! AND TO PURIFY YOU A (THOROUGH) PURIFYING[1]". About whom was it revealed? About us or others?
Abō Bakr: About you.
Ali: So if some witnesses came forward and testified that Fāṭimah the Daughter of Rasōlollāh had committed adultery, what will you do to her?
Abō Bakr: I would punish her just as I would punish any other Moslem woman.
Ali: Then you would be an infidel!!
Abō Bakr: And for what reason?
Ali: Because you reject the testimony of Allāh to her cleanness and accept people's testimony, just as you rejected the rule of Allāh and His Messenger when

[1] Holy Qor'ān = sōrah 33, āyah 33.

they gave her Fadak, and claimed that it belonged to the Moslems, although Rasōllollāh had said: The burden of proof lies on the claimant, and the oath is for the respondent.
So people began to murmur their disapproval, and said: By Allāh, ᶜAli is right[1].)).

Moslems scholars also narrate a lengthy ḥadēth from Imām Ṣādiq on this subject, a shortened version of which is as follows:

((When Abō Bakr's rule became stable, he ordered his herald to announce: Whoever had loaned Rasōlollāh money or any other thing, come to me to repay him.
Thus Jābir ibn ᶜAbdollāh and Jorayr ibn ᶜAbdollāh al-Bajli went to him and each of them made a claim; and Abō Bakr repaid them.
So Fāṭimah also went to Abō Bakr and protested, reading some verses of the Holy Qor'ān, and said: You believed Jābir and Jorayr and did not ask them to bring proof, and my proof is in the Book of Allāh.
Then they asked her to bring witnesses, so she sent for ᶜAli, Ḥasan, Ḥosayn, Omm Ayman and Asmā' bint ᶜOmays, Abō Bakr's wife, all of whom testified for her.
Abō Bakr said: ᶜAli is her husband, and Ḥasan and Ḥosayn are her sons, and Omm Ayman is her housemaid, and Asmā' bint ᶜOmays was previously married to Jaᶜfar ibn Abi Ṭālib, so she tends to be bios towards Bani Hāshim; so all of these people are biased witnesses!!
Ali said: Fāṭimah is a part of Rasōlollāh, whomsoever annoys her, he has surely annoyed Rasōlollāh; and whomsoever accuses her of lying, he has surely accused Rasōlollāh of lying. And Ḥasan and Ḥosayn are the Two Sons of Rasōlollāh, and the Masters of the Youths of Heaven; whoever accuses them of lying, he has surely accused Rasōlollah of lying, as the inhabitants of Heaven are all truthful. And

---

[1] Beḥār al-Anwār / al-Majlesi = vol. 29, page 127.

Rasōlollāh has said about me: You are from me and I am from you, and you are my Brother in this world and the Hereafter, and your denier is my denier; whomsoever obeys you, he has surely obeyed me; and whomsoever disobeys you, he has surely disobeyed me. And Rasōlollāh promised Omm Ayman the Heaven. And he prayed for Asmā' bint ᶜOmays and for her lineage.

Omar: You are as you explained yourselves, but the testimony of the biased cannot be accepted.

Ali: If we are as you know and do not deny, yet our testimonies are not acceptable, and neither is the testimony of Rasōlollāh, thus "Surely we are Allāh's and to Him we shall surely return[1]".

When we claim something you ask us for proof, and there is no supporter to support!!... "And they who act unjustly shall know to what final place of turning they shall turn back[2]".

Then he said to Fāṭimah: Leave, until Allāh rules between us, and He is the best of the judges[3].)).

When Abō Bakr is cornered

As Abō Bakr claimed that the Moslems had chosen him as Rasōlollāh's khalēfah, he could not always act as harsh as he wanted to. That is when his top ruffian, ᶜOmar, made himself useful.

One such instance was when Abō Bakr*(LA)*[4] ran out of argument and had no civil way to escape from Fāṭimah's reasoning. Thus he resorted to his preferred tactic, as Bakri scholars narrate:

((Fāṭimah the Daughter of Rasōlollāh came to Abō Bakr whilst he was on the menbar, and she said: O Abā Bakr! Is it in the Book of Allāh that your

---

[1] Holy Qor'ān = sōrah 2, ayah 156.

[2] Holy Qor'ān = sōrah 26, ayah 227.

[3] Fāṭimah min al-Mahd elā al-Laḥd / al-Qazwēni = page 346.

[4] *Laᶜnatollāh ᶜAlayh,* may Allāh distance him from His Blessings and Mercy.

daughters can inherit you, but I cannot inherit my father?!...
So Abō Bakr descended from the menbar weeping, and wrote a deed, returning Fadak to Fāṭimah.
Suddenly, ᶜOmar came and said: What is this?
Abō Bakr: A document that I wrote, allowing Fāṭimah her inheritance from her father...
ᶜOmar then took the document and tore it[1].)).

The famous Bakri scholar Ibn Abi al-Ḥadēd writes in his acclaimed encyclopedia after recording the above event:

((And indeed, this meaning has been narrated through different chains of narrators in different forms[2].)).

Moslem scholars narrate:

((...Thus he (Abō Bakr) called for a paper, and he wrote that Fadak be returned to her.
So when she left, ᶜOmar met her [in the street] and said: O daughter of Moḥammad! what is that document you are holding?
Fāṭimah: Abō Bakr has written that Fadak be returned to me.
Omar: Let me have it. But she refused to give it to him; so he hit her and took the document and tore it[3].))

Fāṭimah's public speeches

---

[1] Fāṭimah min Qabl al Mēlād elā Baᶜd al-Estesh-had / al-Hāshimi = page 252 from: Fotōḥ al-Boldān / al-Balādheri; Moᶜjam al-Boldān / al-Ḥamawi; Sharh Nahj al-Balāghah / Ibn Abi al-Ḥadēd; Tārēkh al-Madinah / Ibn Shobbah. A shorter version of this ḥadēth has also been recorded in: al-Sērah al-Ḥalabiyyah / al-Ḥalabi = vol. 3, page 362.
[2] Sharh Nahj al-Balāghah / Ibn Abi al-Ḥadēd = vol. 16, page 274.
[3] al-Ekhteṣāṣ / al-Mofēd = page 183. And a similar narration in: Beḥār al-Anwār / al-Majlesi = vol. 29, page 157.

When Abō Bakr repeatedly refused to return Fāṭimah's positions to her, she went to the mosque and gave a most damaging public speech against the Bakri rule, which went beyond the usurpation of her positions[1]; and later in her home, she gave another public speech to the women of Mohājirēn and Anṣār who had come to visit her, against the Bakri regime[2].

When people heard her speech in the mosque, they started to murmur; so attempting to contain the damage, Abō Bakr spoke and brought excuses for his actions; but Fāṭimah[(AaS)3] immediately refuted him. And his second attempt encountered another strong reaction from Fāṭimah, creating uproar in the crowds.

After the gathering ended in disorder and confusion, and the people dispersed, voices were raised and the city went into shock.

It has been narrated that Abō Bakr and ᶜOmar had the following discussion:

> *((Abō Bakr said to ᶜOmar: Dirt be on your hands! Why could not leave me?! Maybe things would have turned out our way without violence. Would not that have been best?!*
>
> *Omar: It would have weaken your authority...*
>
> *Abō Bakr: Woe unto you, and what about the daughter of Moḥammad?! People have indeed learned what she is calling for, and know what treachery we are committing.*
>
> *Omar: Was it but a trouble that ended, and a difficult hour that passed?! It is now as though nothing had happened...*
>
> *Perform the ṣalāt; pay the Zakāt[4] to its recipients; command to the good deeds; prohibit the bad deeds... for indeed Allāh says: "*SURELY GOOD DEEDS

---

[1] You can read excerpts of her speech in the Prophet's Mosque, in page 96 to 101 of this book.

[2] You can read her speech for the women of the Mohājirēn and the Anṣār in her home in page 92 to 95 of this book.

[3] *ᶜAlayhas Salām,* peace be upon her.

[4] An Islamic tax of different rates levied on a number of items beyond a certain limit.

TAKE AWAY EVIL DEEDS[1]". A single crime in a number of good deeds. Follow me on this.
Then Abō Bakr tapped ᶜOmar on the shoulder and said: How many agonies you have removed O ᶜOmar!
Then he called people to the mosque, and they gathered[2].)).

When the people gathered in the mosque, Abō Bakr ascended the menbar and gave a short public speech against Amēr al-Mo'menēn[3], in which he also threatened his opposition, especially the Anṣār.

Ibn Abi al-Ḥadēd, the famous Bakri scholar, narrates:

((When Abō Bakr heard her (Fāṭimah) speech, and saw the dissension and the angry murmurs among the people, he feared an uprising; so he ascended the menbar and said:
O you people! Why do you listen to everything that is said?!...
Indeed, he (Ali) is but a fox whose witness is his tail!! He accompanies every disturbance...
They (Ali and Fāṭimah) ask for help from the weak, and ask for support from the women!! Just like Omm Ṭaḥāl to whom the prostitute is her favorite family member[4]!!...
Then he looked at the Anṣār and said: O crowd of the Anṣār! I have surely heard the words of your fools!... Beware of the fact that I will indeed not extend my hand and tongue to anyone who does not deserve it!!...
Ibn Abi al-Ḥadēd continues to say: I read this speech to the chief Abō Yaḥyā al-Baṣri [one of my teachers], and asked him: To whom is Abō Bakr pointing?

---

[1] Holy Qor'ān = sōrah 11, āyah 114.
[2] Dalā'el al-Imāmah / al-Ṭabari = page 39.
[3] Commander of the Faithful; a title given exclusively to Imām ᶜAli by Allāh.
[4] An Arabic proverb. Omm Ṭaḥāl was a known Arab prostitute in the pre-Islamic era who became an example of prostitution.

Abō Yaḥyā: His statement is rather undisguised.
I said: If it were, I would not have asked you.
So he laughed and said: ᶜAli ibn Abi Ṭālib.
So I said: He is saying all of this about ᶜAli?!
Abō Yaḥyā: Yes, O my son! It is the reign!!...[1])).

Omm Salamah objects to Abō Bakr

It has been narrated that after Abō Bakr's response to Fāṭimah's speech in the mosque, Omm Salamah (Rasōlollāh's wife) stood up and said:

((To the likes of Fāṭimah, the Daughter of Rasōlollāh, is this said?!
She is, by Allāh, the Human Houri, and Rasōlollāh's soul; she has been brought up on the laps of God-fearing men, and has grown on the laps of pious women, and has been touched by the hands of the angels...
Do you think that Rasōlollāh prohibited her from his inheritance and did not inform her, when the Almighty Allāh says: "And warn your nearest relations[2]"?!
Or did he warn her but she ignored his warning?!
She is the best of the women and the mother of the Masters of the Youths of Heaven. With her father, Allāh completed His missions. By Allāh, he always protected her from the heat and the cold, and cushioned her with his right hand and covered her with his left hand.
Slowly! Rasōlollāh is watching you, and to Allāh you will return, and then you will learn.
As a result, her dues were withheld that year[3].)).

---

[1] Sharh Nahj al-Balāghah / Ibn Abi al-Ḥadēd = vol. 16, page 214.
[2] Holy Qor'ān = sōrah 26, āyah 214.
[3] Dalā'el al-Imāmah / al-Ṭabari = page 39.

Do the prophets leave inheritance?!

After Rasōlollāh's death, Abō Bakr usurped Fāṭimah's positions and rejected her witnesses who testified that she owned them during Rasōlollāh's life.

Fāṭimah then demanded them, in addition to new assets, as her inheritance from her father. But Abō Bakr who was well prepared, claimed that he had heard Rasōlollāh say: "We the prophets do not leave inheritance"; and said that his daughter ᶜĀ'eshah testifies that she had also heard Rasōlollāh make that statement.

Now, did Fāṭimah own those assets during the life of her father; or was Abō Bakr right in usurping them? And did Rasōlollāh really say that he does not leave inheritance; or was it just another Bakri falsification?

The following notes should give some irrefutable answers:

1- Abō Bakr rejected Fāṭimah's six witnesses: ᶜAli, Ḥasan, Ḥosayn, Omm Ayman, Rebāḥ (Rasōlollāh's servant) and Asmā' bint ᶜOmays (Abō Bakr's wife), who testified to Fāṭimah's ownership of those positions during Rasōlollāh's life, when he had only one witness, ᶜĀ'eshah (his daughter), who claimed that she had also heard Rasōlollāh say: "We the prophets do not leave inheritance"!!

2- It was much to Abō Bakr's benefit if Rasōlollāh were not to leave any inheritance, as he would have received a good portion of all that wealth when it was divided between the Moslems. More importantly, none of that huge financial support would go to his strongest and most dangerous opposition, but instead it will all come to him to be spent under his supervision. And ᶜĀ'eshah, as Abō Bakr's daughter, would equally benefit.

3- The kinds of ᶜAli, Fāṭimah, Ḥasan, Ḥosayn, Omm Ayman and Asmā' bint ᶜOmays have a property in them which makes them unreliable in anything they claim, no matter how many they are; whereas the kinds of ᶜĀ'eshah have a property in them which makes them reliable in anything they say, no matter how few they are!! Contrasts can be made, as an instance, in the question of the khelāfah, when the testimony of a large number of witnesses who testified to the fact that Amēr al-Mo'menēn(AS)[1] was Rasōlollāh's God-Appointed successor was shamelessly rejected, whereas the claim of ᶜĀ'eshah, on her own, that Rasōlollāh had said: "Tell Abō Bakr to lead the Moslems in the ṣalāt" was eagerly accepted!!

4- When Abō Bakr claimed that he had heard Rasōlollāh make that statement, only his daughter testified that she had also heard him; but no other person came forward to support his claim. This means that no one else had heard Rasōlollāh. But how is that possible?! Why would the Prophet only tell these two that the prophets do not leave inheritance, and not tell others, especially when he was always with people and among them, and could easily have told them?!

5- Why would Rasōlollāh tell a stranger such as Abō Bakr that what he leaves behind can not be inherited, and not tell his closest family—his heir?! If Rasōlollāh was not to leave any inheritance, should not he, by the Islamic law, have informed his family—his heir, so that they would not take his positions as inheritance?! This is when Islam so much encourages writing a will, and renewing it regularly; and very strongly discourages leaving anything, no matter how little, out of the will; and warns against not having a will, even for very small and inconsiderable things.

6- Could it be that Rasōlollāh in fact told his family—his heir, that they can not inherit him; but after his death, they lied and demanded his inheritance?! Not even a blind-hearted, prejudiced, bigot Bakri has ever claimed that.

7- The Holy Qor'ān tells many stories about the people of the past and their Messengers, and Rasōlollāh spoke much about the prophets, their lives, missions, characteristics, personalities, etc. So why would not he or the Holy Qor'ān tell the Moslems about this very distinctive and special law that only the prophets were subject to?!

---

[1] *ᶜAlayhes Salām,* peace be upon him.

8- According to Bakri references, when Fāṭimah demanded the portion of Dhawi al-Qorbā[1] from Abō Bakr, he told her that he had heard Rasōlollāh say: "The portion of Dhawi al-Qorbā is given to them during my life and not after my death". But as with the statement regarding the inheritance of the prophets, no one else did ever claim to have heard Rasōlollāh make this statement. So Abō Bakr is the only person to have heard Rasōlollāh make these two very important announcements both of which happened to be most crucial for him after the Prophet's demise!?

9- If Rasōlollāh's positions were to automatically become ṣadaqah[2] after his death, as Abō Bakr claimed to have heard it from him, then the late prophet should have appointed a trustee to manage and supervise it, as is the case with all large ṣadaqāt[3]. But after his martyrdom, no one claimed to have been appointed as his trustee, and no one came forward with any knowledge of any appointed trustee; and even Abō Bakr did not claim to be his trustee. So could it be that this great prophet who saw to every large and small thing had forgotten or ignored his own teachings and not chosen a trustee for his large ṣadaqāt?! Or like everyone else, his positions should have been inherited by his heirs, but were usurped by the Bakri party?!

10- But supposing, for the sake of argument, that the first possibility was the case, then, according to Islamic law, these *ṣadaqāt* should have been surrendered to the guardianship of his closest relative, his daughter Fāṭimah. And under no circumstances could they legally be usurped by Abō Bakr, as according to the Bakris, Abō Bakr was chosen by the people to be their leader; and as a leader who had been appointed by the people, his authority was not extensive enough to allow

---

[1] Sayyedat Nesā' al-ᶜĀlamēn, and the twelve God-appointed successors of Rasōlollah.

[2] Charity, or helping those in need of anything, financial or otherwise; even giving directions can be a ṣadaqah, even removing rubbish, etc. from walkways can be a ṣadaqah. Ṣadaqah has different forms and different effects. Plural ṣadaqāt.

[3] Plural of ṣadaqah.

him to interfere in people's financial affairs. So on what basis did he takeover the positions of Fāṭimah?!

11- Abō Bakr's actions contradict his claim that the prophets do not leave inheritance. As the Bakris narrate that he gave Rasōlollāh's turban, sword and mule to Amēr al-Mo'menēn as his inheritance from Rasōlollāh!! He also gave Rasōlollāh's room to ᶜĀ'eshah as her inheritance from Rasōlollāh. He also gave Zobayr ibn al-ᶜAwām and Moḥammad ibn Moslemah some of Rasōlollāh's patrimony.

12- The claims of Jābir and Jorayr that Rasōlollāh owed them were accepted without asking them for proof or witnesses, whereas Fāṭimah's claim to which she had both proof and witnesses was rejected.

13- ᶜĀ'eshah's testimony is not acceptable, as her claiming her inheritance from Rasōlollāh, from ᶜOthmān, rejects "We the prophets do not leave inheritance"!!

14- ᶜOthmān, the first Amawi ruler and the Third Usurper of the Khalēfah, gave Fadak during his rule to Marwān ibn al-Ḥakam, the only Idolater sent into exile by Rasōlollāh!! And after ᶜOthmān, almost every usurper of the khelāfah gave it to one or a number of people during his rule. So why could not Abō Bakr give Fadak to Rasōlollāh's only daughter, Fāṭimah?! Was he wrong, or were they wrong?!

15- Why must Fāṭimah bring several witnesses (a minimum of two men or one man and two women) who should meet strange conditions such as not being related to her tribe, not even once married to a member of her tribe, when Abō Bakr brings only his daughter as his witness in the very important claim that the prophets do not leave inheritance?!

16- Abō Bakr had never been known as a knowledgeable person, and had not narrated many aḥādēth[1]; so what are the chances of authenticity in a ḥadēth that only such a person narrates?!

17- Among all the Moslems, Allāh chose only ᶜAli, Fāṭimah, Ḥasan and Ḥosayn to go to the Mobāhalah with Rasōlollāh; and He revealed the Āyah of Taṭ-hēr about them, testifying

[1] Plural of ḥadēth: a narration from one of the Fourteen Maᶜṣōmēn.

to their ᶜEṣmah[1]; and He chose ᶜAli as the Commander of the Faithful; and He chose Fāṭimah as the Chief of the Women of the Heaven, and He chose Ḥasan and Ḥosayn as the Masters of the Youths of Heaven; and the Bakri leaders themselves have narrated countless praises from Rasōlollāh for these people, for instance ᶜĀ'eshah narrated from Rasōlollāh who said: *"ᶜAli is with the Truth, and the Truth is with ᶜAli; and they will never separate until they come to me in the Hereafter"*. These commendations and statements from Allāh and Rasōlollāh mean that ᶜAli, Fāṭimah, Ḥasan and Ḥosayn do not lie, but nevertheless the Bakri party refused their testimony!!!

18- Abō Bakr's claim that the prophets do not leave inheritance contradicts the Holy Qor'ān where it says: *"AND WOMEN SHALL HAVE A PORTION OF WHAT THE PARENTS AND THE NEAR RELATIVES LEAVE[2]"; "ALLĀH ENJOINS YOU CONCERNING YOUR CHILDREN: THE MALE SHALL HAVE THE EQUAL OF THE PORTION OF TWO FEMALES[3]"; "THEREFORE GRANT ME FROM THYSELF AN HEIR * WHO SHOULD INHERIT ME AND INHERIT FROM THE CHILDREN OF YAᶜQŌB[4]"; "AND SOLAYMĀN WAS DĀWŌD'S HEIR[5]".*

19- How can the Bakris particularize and restrict the generality and the generalization of the above āyāt, and make wild and far-fetched interpretations of its clear literal and the connotative meanings; all for the sake of one suspiciously isolated atypical narration?! And is the word of a single man, supported only by his daughter, adequate enough for all of this?! Especially when both of them are fallible, and subject to the enticement of Shayṭān, and susceptible to their evil-commanding selves, and impressible by bad friends, thus

---

[1] The state of immunity from committing sins, making mistakes, or any act of forgetfulness, etc. whilst the choice to commit sin remains open to the individual. Prophets and their awṣeyā' have this attribute and are called maᶜṣōm.

[2] Holy Qor'ān = sōrah 4, āyah 7.

[3] Holy Qor'ān = sōrah 4, āyah 11.

[4] Holy Qor'ān = sōrah 19, āyāt 5 and 6.

[5] Holy Qor'ān = sōrah 27, āyah 16.

liable to lie and relate lies!! Abō Bakr himself admitted to this by saying: "I have a Shayṭān who comes upon me...[1]"
20- Beside all of the above, a large part of these positions were in the hands of Fāṭimah during the life of Rasōlollāh; and even the Bakris admit that she had a trustee in Fadak who managed it on her behalf before the martyrdom of Rasōlollāh. And according to Islamic law, Abō Bakr should have proven that these positions did not belong to her, and could not legally ask her for proof of ownership for something that was already in her hands. Moreover, under the Islamic law, the burden of proof always lies with the claimant, and the defendant only has to swear to Allāh against the claim. But was Abō Bakr a Moslem to rule according to the Islamic law?!

An interesting Bakri explanation!

When reading about the usurpation of Fāṭimah's positions and her demand for them, a series of questions come to the Bakri mind; primarily: was Fāṭimah truthful in her claims? And if she was, why did Abō Bakr and ᶜOmar so stubbornly refuse to return her positions?!

A great Bakri scholar gives the answer:

((I [Ibn Abi al-Ḥadēd] asked ᶜAli ibn al-Fāriqi: Was Fāṭimah truthful [in her claims]?
He said: Yes.
I asked: So why did Abō Bakr not give her Fadak when he knew she was telling the truth?
He smiled and gave me a very interesting answer: If today Abō Bakr gave her Fadak relying only on her word, she would come back tomorrow and claim the khelāfah for her husband, and would overthrow Abō Bakr from his position; and he will not be able to argue against her for the fact that he had already admitted to her truthfulness in any claim she makes

[1] See page 185 of this book

without the need to look for proof or listen to witnesses[1].)).

FADAK BETWEEN USURPING AND RETURNING

Fadak, one of Fāṭimah's legal positions, remains to this day a richly fertile land; and throughout these centuries it has always been under usurpation. The land that they said belonged to the Moslems, was taken into position by countless usurpers and their staunch supporters.

The fact is that Fadak's owners could not have it, as it was said that it did not belong to any one person; and the Moslems could not claim it, as they were not close enough to the ruler. But some lucky ones earned it for their unquestionable loyalty to the usurpers, and some gained it through their deep animosity towards its legal owners.

However, and because of special circumstances, some rulers returned Fadak to some of the descendants of Fāṭimah, only to be usurped again within a short period of time.

And this give and take tells another revealing story from the book of the never ending Bakri contradictions.

Some of these exchanges are as follows:

* During his rule, ᶜOmar returned Fadak to ᶜAli and ᶜAbbās.

* During his rule, ᶜOthmān gave Fadak to Marwān ibn al-Ḥakam.

* During his rule, Moᶜāwiyah gave one-third of Fadak to Marwān ibn al-Ḥakam, and one-third to Amr ibn al-ᶜOthmān, and one-third to his son Yazēd.

* During his rule, Marwān ibn al-Ḥakam gave Fadak to his son ᶜAbdolᶜazēz. And he gave it to his son ᶜOmar ibn ᶜAbdolᶜazēz.

* During his rule, ᶜOmar ibn ᶜAbdolᶜazēz gave Fadak to some of Fāṭimah's children.

---

[1] Sharh Nahj al-Balāghah / Ibn Abi al-Ḥaded = vol. 16, page 284.

* During his rule, Yazēd ibn ᶜAbdolmalik usurped Fadak, and it went from hand to hand between the rulers of Bani Marwān until the end of their rule.

* During his rule, Saffāḥ gave Fadak to ᶜAbdollāh ibn al-Ḥasan.

* During his rule, Mansoor usurped Fadak.

* During his rule, Mahdi ibn al-Mansoor gave Fadak to some of Fāṭimah's children.

* During his rule, Mōsā ibn al-Mahdi usurped Fadak, and it went from hand to hand between the rulers of Bani al-ᶜAbbās until Ma'mōn's rule.

* During his rule, Ma'mōn gave Fadak to some of Fāṭimah's children.

* During his rule, Motawakkil usurped Fadak, and it went from hand to hand between the rulers of Bani al-ᶜAbbās[1].

---

[1] Eḥrāq Bayt al-Zahrā' / al-Sajjād = page 136 from many Bakri references including Ṣaḥēḥ / al-Bokhāri and Ṣaḥēḥ / Moslem.

SAYYEDAT NESĀ' AL-ᶜĀLAMĒN'S MARTYRDOM

Fāṭimah's wish to be buried secretly at night

Moslem scholars narrate that before her death, Fāṭimah[(AaS)1] said to ᶜAli[(AS)2]:

> *((O cousin! I see myself nearing death, and know that I will shortly join my father; and I want to tell you about things in my heart.*
> *Ali: Tell me what you like O Daughter of Rasōlollāh! And he sat near her head, and told everyone else to leave the room.*
> *Then she said: O cousin! You have never known me to be a liar nor treacherous, and I have not disagreed with you since you have been with me.*
> *Ali: God forbid. You are more learned, by Allāh, and better, and more pious and nobler, and more God-fearing to commit reproachable acts. And your separation from me and your loss, is indeed hard for me; but it is something unavoidable. By Allāh, you surely renewed the calamity of Rasōlollāh's death for me, and your death and your loss is definitely received very painfully. So "SURELY WE ARE ALLĀH'S AND TO HIM WE SHALL SURELY RETURN[3]". A calamity,*

---

[1] *ᶜAlayhes Salām,* peace be upon him.
[2] *ᶜAlayhes Salām,* peace be upon him.
[3] Holy Qor'ān = sōrah 2, āyah 156.

> *how painful, and how hurtful, and how bitter and how sorrowful. This is a loss that has no consolation, and it is a disaster that has no end.*
> *Then they cried for a while, and the Imām held her head to his chest and said: Entrust me with your will, for surely you will find me loyal; I will carry out all your orders, and choose your wish over mine.*
> *Fāṭimah: May Allāh reward you for [what you have done for] me the best reward...*
> *O cousin! I ask you not to allow those who did me injustice come to my funeral, for surely they are my enemies and the enemies of Rasōlollāh; and that you do not allow any one of them or their followers to perform the Deceased Prayer on me; and that you burry me at night, when the eyes rest and go to sleep[1].)).*

Many Bakri scholars also record in their references various aḥādēth, narrated through different chains of narrators, that Fāṭimah stipulated in her will to ᶜAli not to let Abō Bakr and ᶜOmar take part in her funeral. These aḥādēth also state that Fāṭimah was buried at night without their knowledge; or that ᶜAli buried her at night and did not inform Abō Bakr and ᶜOmar; or that she was secretly buried at night[2].

---

[1] Fāṭimah al-Zahrā' min al-Mahd elā al-Laḥd / al-Qazwēni = page 609.

[2] Some Bakri references are: Ansāb al-Ashrāf / al-Balādheri = page 405. al-Bedāyah wa al-Nehāyah / Ibn Kothayr = vol. 5, page 285. Fotōḥ al-Boldān / al-Balādheri = page 45. Jāmiᶜ al-Oṣōl / Ibn al-Athēr = vol. 4, page 482. Majmaᶜ al-Zawā'ed / al-Haythami = page 211. Maqtal al-Ḥosayn / al-Khārazmi = page 82. al-Moṣannaf / Ibn Abi Shaybah = vol. 4, page 141. Moshkel al-Athār / al-Ṭaḥāwi = vol. 1, page 47. Ṣaḥēḥ / al-Bokhāri = vol. 5, page 177. al-Sērah al-Ḥalabiyyah / al-Ḥalabi = vol. 3, page 361. Seyar Aᶜlām al-Nobalā' / al-Dhahabi = vol. 2, page 128. Sharh Nahj al-Balāghah / Ibn Abi al-Ḥadēd = vol. 6, page 46; vol. 16, page 214. al-Sonan al-Kobrā / al-Bayhaqi = vol. 4, page 29; vol. 6, page 300. Tārēkh al-Khamēs / al-Deyārbakri = vol. 2, page 173. Tārēkh al-Omam wa al-Molōk / al-Ṭabari = vol. 2, page 448; vol. 3, page 208. Tārēkh / al-Yaᶜqōbi = vol. 2, page 115. al-Ṭabaqāt al-Kobrā / Ibn Saᶜd = vol. 8, page 30. Tahdhēb al-Asmā' / al-Nawawi = vol. 2, page 353. Talkhēṣ al-Mostadrak / al-Dhahabi (printed in

One instance of such Bakri narrations is the following:

((Fāṭimah stipulated in her will to be buried at night, and her wish was carried out. And therefore the exact place of her grave is secret and not known. Some people think that she was buried in her home, and some people think that she was buried in the Baqēᶜ[1], and others think that she was buried in the mosque...[2])).

Fāṭimah prepares for death

Bakri scholars narrate:

((Fāṭimah said to Asmā' bint ᶜOmays (her student, and Abō Bakr's wife): I hate what is done with the body of a dead woman—they spread a cloth over her, and it shows her body.
Asmā': O Daughter of Rasōlollāh! Do you want me to show you what I had seen in Ethiopia? Then she asked for some fresh palm branches striped of their leaves, she curved them and covered them with a cloth.
Fāṭimah said: How great and nice this is! It dose not distinguish a woman from a man! So when I die, you and ᶜAli wash me; and do not let anyone else enter the house.
And when she died, ᶜĀ'eshah wanted to enter, but Asmā told her: Do not come in.
So she went to Abō Bakr, complaining: This Khathᶜami[3] woman stands between us and Rasōlollāh's daughter, and she has made for her something like a bride's howdah.

---

the footnotes of al-Mostadrak / al-Naysābōri) = vol. 3, page 154. Taysēr al-Woṣōl / al-Shaybāni = vol. 2, page 46. al-Thoghōr al-Bāsimah = al-Soyōṭi = page 15. Wafā' al-Wafā / al-Samhōdi = vol. 2, page 995.

[1] A cemetery in Madinah.

[2] Tahdhēb al-Asmā' / al-Nawawi = vol. 2, page 353.

[3] An Arab tribe.

Abō Bakr came and stood at the door, and said: O Asmā'! what made you stop the Prophet's wives from entering Fāṭimah's home?! And why have you made a bride's howdah for her?!
Asmā': She ordered me not to let anyone inside. And when she was alive, I showed her this, and she ordered me to make one for her[1].)).

Bakri scholars also narrate a most important and remarkable ḥadēth from Salmā, one of Fāṭimah's students, without actually realizing its significance:

((In her illness, one morning Fāṭimah woke up in the best state we had ever seen her during her infirmity; and when ᶜAli ibn Abi Ṭālib went out, she said: O woman! Pour some water for me to perform a ghosl[2]. Thus she performed the best ghosl I had ever seen her perform.
She then said: Give me my new clothes, so I gave them to her.
She then came to the room, and said: Spread my mattress in the middle of the room; and she lied down, putting her right hand under her right cheek, facing the Qeblah (direction of the Kaᶜbah).
She then said: O woman! I will shortly die. No one should uncover me, and no one should perform the Ghosl of the Deceased[3] on me.
So she died where she was lying, and I told ᶜAli what she had ordered me, and he said: By Allāh! No one

---

[1] al-Estēᶜāb / Ibn ᶜAbdelbarr = vol. 4, page 1897. Dhakhā'er al-ᶜOqbā / al-Ṭabari = page 53.
[2] Islamic ritual washing of the body with plain water. It has two forms, and is performed for a number of reasons some of which are mandatory, whereas others are recommended.
[3] Islamic ritual washing of the body of a deceased. Ghosl of the Deceased is a wājib (mandatory) ghosl.

will uncover her. He then carried her and buried her without performing the ghosl on her[1].)).

This is a very extraordinary ḥadēth that the Bakris have narrated in some of their most respected references without appreciating its implications. It clearly shows that Fāṭimah died a martyr's death.

Only a martyr—who has been killed in the way of Allāh—is exempt from the mandatory Ghosl of the Deceased. And only a martyr is exempt from the mandatory enshrouding in the Kafan[2].

Fāṭimah asks not to be washed and not to be uncovered (it is necessary to take off a deceased's clothes before the shrouding); and ᶜAli does not object to her wishes as contrary to Islamic law. This can only mean that she died a martyr's death.

And there is no contradiction between this ḥadēth and the ḥadēth that says she asked ᶜAli to wash her, and it is quite possible to put them together.

Here, she tells Salmā that no one should wash her or uncover her, to tell her and the world through her Bakri enemies, that she died a martyr's death. And ᶜAli does not object to her wish for the very same reason.

But for the same reason for which her father asked ᶜAli to wash him, even though he died a martyr's death, she also asked to be washed.

This theatrical method of broadcasting was commonly used, and its instances in the holy ḥadēth are countless. And this is just another example of its effectiveness, which has efficiently fooled these censor-happy Bakris into transmitting it through their most respected works such as Mosnad / Ahmad.

ᶜAli and Fāṭimah just before her death

It has been narrated from Feḍḍah who said:

---

[1] Dhakhā'er al-ᶜOqbā / al-Ṭabari = page 53. Mosnad / Aḥmad = vol. 6, page 461. Osd al-Ghābah / Ibn al-Athēr = vol. 5, page 590. al-Ṭabaqāt al-Kobrā / Ibn Saᶜd = vol. 8, page 27.

[2] A series of cloths in which a deceased is wrapped before burial.

((Amēr al-Mo'menēn performed his noon ṣalāt [in the mosque] and was about to return home, when some women came to him crying.
So he asked them: What has happened?! Why do I see you with such changed faces?!
They said: O Amēr al-Mo'menēn! catch up with your cousin Zahrā' (Fāṭimah), and we do not think that you will reach her in time!
Amēr al-Mo'menēn hurried home, and saw her lying, in great agony. He threw down his robe from his shoulders, and his turban from his head, and took her head and put it in his lap, calling her: O Zahrā'! But she did not speak.
He called her again: O daughter of him who carried the Zakāt in his robe and gave it to the poor! But she did not speak.
He called her again: O daughter of him who led the angels in ṣalāt in the sky! But she did speak.
He called her again: O Fāṭimah! Speak to me, for surely it is I your cousin ᶜAli ibn Abi Ṭālib.
So she opened her eyes to his face, looked at him and cried; and he also cried.
He asked her: What are you feeling? It is I your cousin ᶜAli ibn Abi Ṭālib.
Fāṭimah: O cousin! I feel the death that is unavoidable...
O cousin! If you marry after me, allow a day and night for your wife, and allow a day and night for my two sons. O Abā al-Ḥasan! they will shortly become two broken orphans. Yesterday they lost their grandfather, and today they will lose their mother; so woe unto the nation that kills them and hates them.
She then composed a poem:
"Cry for me O Best Guide! and shed tears, for surely this is the day of separation.
O husband of Batool! (Fāṭimah) I entrust you with the sons, for surely they have became allies of yearning.
Cry for me, and cry for the orphans; and do not forget the slain of the enemies in the Ṭaff (Karbala) of Iraq."

I saw my beloved Rasōlollāh in a dream, and he said: Come to me O daughter! for surely I yearn for you.
And I said to him: By Allāh, indeed I yearn to meet you even more.
So he said: You are with me tonight. And he is truthful in what he promises.
By the time you recite the Yāsēn (the 36th sōrah), I will have died. So wash me without uncovering my body; and perform the Deceased Prayer on me along with the closest family members, secretly not openly; and hide my grave; and do not allow those who did me injustice attend my funeral[1].)).

It has also been narrated:

((Before her death, Fāṭimah cried. So Amēr al-Mo'menēn asked her: O my Lady! What makes you cry?
Fāṭimah: I cry for what you will encounter after my death.
Ali: Do not cry; by Allāh, that is so small to me in Allāh's cause[2].)).

Fāṭimah in her last minutes

Asmā' bint ᶜOmays talks about the last minutes of Fāṭimah just before her death, she narrates:

((Then she (Fāṭimah) told me: ...Leave [the room] and wait [outside] for a while, because I want to talk to my Lord, the Great, the Almighty.
So I left and heard her talking to her Lord, so I entered the room [quietly] without her knowing, and saw her with her hands raised to the sky, saying: O Allāh! I ask You in Moḥammad the Moṣṭafa's name,

[1] Beḥār al-Anwār / al-Majlesi = vol. 43, page 178.
[2] Beḥār al-Anwār / al-Majlesi = vol. 43, page 218.

and his yearning for me; and in my husband ᶜAli the Mortaḍā's name, and his grief for me; and in Ḥasan the Mojtaba's name, and his crying for me; and in Ḥosayn the Martyr's name, and his sorrow for me; and in my daughters' names, and their heartbreak for me; that You have Mercy upon the sinners of the followers of Moḥammad, and take them to Heaven. You are indeed the Most Noble, and the Most Merciful[1].)).

Fāṭimah dies

Asmā' bint ᶜOmays narrates:

((Fāṭimah told me: Wait for a while and then call me. If I answer you so be it, and if not, then it means that I have joined my father.
So Asmā' waited for a while, and she called her, but Fāṭimah did not respond. Then Asmā' said: O daughter of Moḥammad the Moṣṭafa! O daughter of the best person ever born! O daughter of the best person ever to walk the earth! O daughter of him who "WAS AT A DISTANCE OF TWO BOWS' LENGTH OR (EVEN) CLOSER[2]". But she did not respond to her calls. So Asmā' removed the cloth from Fāṭimah's face to find that she had left this world. So she fell on her kissing her, saying: O Fāṭimah! when you see your father Rasōlollāh convey to him my greetings...
As she left the room, Ḥasan and Ḥosayn entered the house and asked her: Where is our mother?
She remained silent; so they entered that room and saw her lying. Ḥosayn moved her and found her dead. So he said: O brother! May Allāh reward you for [losing] the mother.
Then Ḥasan fell on her kissing her, saying: O mother! Talk to me before my soul leaves my body. And

---

[1] Bahjat Qalb al-Moṣṭafa / al-Raḥmāni = page 576.
[2] Holy Qor'ān = sōrah 53, āyah 9.

Ḥosayn fell on her feat kissing them, saying: O mother! I am your son Ḥosayn; talk to me before my heart stops and I die.
Asmā' then told them: Go to your father ᶜAli and inform him of your mother's death. Thus they left their home, screaming: O Moḥammad! O Aḥmad! Today we relive your death, as our mother has died. Then they gave ᶜAli the news in the mosque, and he lost consciousness and fell on his face. Water was poured on him until he regained consciousness; then he repeated over and over: Who is the consolation after you O daughter of Moḥammad?! You used to be my consolation, so who shall be the consolation after you?![1])).

Abō Bakr and ᶜOmar want to attend Fāṭimah's burial ceremonies

Moslems narrate from ᶜAmmār ibn Yāsir, who said:

((...And he (ᶜAbbās, ᶜAli's uncle) sent his messenger to ᶜAli and told him: Tell ᶜAli, O nephew! Your uncle sends you greetings, and says: I was unexpectedly overtaken by sorrow for the illness of the beloved of Rasōlollāh and the delight of his eye and my eyes, Fāṭimah. And I think she is the first of us to join Rasōlollāh...
So if she died, gather the Mohājirēn and the Anṣār so that they gain the reward of attending her burial ceremonies.
While I was there, ᶜAli said to his messenger: Convey my greetings to my uncle, and tell him: May your compassion never cease; I have heard your advice, and your opinion has its respect.
Indeed, Fāṭimah the Daughter of Rasōlollāh remains oppressed; and her right remains usurped; and her inheritance remains withheld; and Rasōlollāh's

[1] Bahjat Qalb al-Moṣṭafa / al-Raḥmāni = page 576.

wishes about her were not carried out... And Allāh is All-Sufficient as a judge and Avenger from the oppressors.
And I ask you O uncle! to permit me to disregard your advice, as she has indeed stipulated in her will to me to conduct her burial ceremonies in secret[1].)).

It has also been narrated:

((When Fāṭimah died, Abō Bakr and ᶜOmar came to ᶜAli to console him!! and to say: O Abā al-Ḥasan! Do not precede us in the Prayer [of the Deceased] on the Daughter of Rasōlollāh!![2])).

Fāṭimah's burial ceremonies

Both Bakri and Moslem scholars narrate that all of Fāṭimah's burial ceremonies were conducted secretly at night, with the presence of only a few men and women who were close relatives or loyal followers.

And finally, the only daughter of Rasōlollāh[3], the last Messenger and the ruler of nine countries in today's geography, was laid to rest in a way not suitable for even the least important and unknown person of that day: at night, in secrecy, in an unmarked grave!!...

All of this, to prevent Abō Bakr and ᶜOmar from participating in and leading the ceremonies in an attempt to cover up the cause of her death and what they had done to her. Therefore Fāṭimah preferred to have an unmarked grave, so that as long as her grave remains unknown, her enemies remain exposed; and so that the unprejudiced hearts know that Rasōlollāh's only daughter was beaten to death, and her life was brought to an end at the young age of eighteen by Abō Bakr and ᶜOmar.

---

[1] Amāli / al-Ṭōsi = page 289.
[2] Beḥār al-Anwār / al-Majlesi = vol. 43, page 199.
[3] Messenger of Allāh; a title exclusively given to Prophet Moḥammad by Allāh.

Moslems narrate from Amēr al-Mo'menēn[1] who responded when asked about the reason for which Fāṭimah was buried at night:

> *((Indeed she was angry with a group of people, and did not like their presence during her burial ceremonies.*
> *And it is forbidden for those who follow them to participate in the burial ceremonies of any of her children[2].)).*

Moslems also narrate:

> *((When Fāṭimah died, all the people of Madinah screamed, and the Bani Hāshim women gathered in her home, screaming: O my Lady! O Daughter of Rasōlollāh! And the men came to ᶜAli who was sitting with Hasan and Ḥosayn and were all crying.*
> *So people gathered, shedding tears and waiting for the funeral ceremonies to start.*
> *Abō Dharr came out and said: Leave; there has been a delay in the ceremonies, and it will not be tonight. Thus the people left.*
> *Later when the eyes calmed, and a part of the night passed, ᶜAli, Ḥasan, Ḥosayn, ᶜAmmār, Meqdād, ᶜAqēl, Zobayr, Abō Dharr, Salmān, Boraydah and some of the Bani Hāshim brought her out, performed the Prayer of the Deceased and buried her under the darkness of the night.*
> *Then, ᶜAli made some fake graves, so that her grave cannot be distinguished; and he leveled her grave with the ground and flattened the dirt on and around it in a way that it could not be recognized[3].)).*

---

[1] Commander of the Faithful; a title given exclusively to Imām ᶜAli by Allāh.

[2] Fāṭimah min Qabl al-Mēlād elā Baᶜd al-Estesh-hād / al-Hāshimi = page 362.

[3] Beḥār al-Anwār / al-Majlesi = vol. 43, page 192.

ᶜAli on Fāṭimah's grave

Bakri and Moslem scholars narrate:

((When Fāṭimah died, ᶜAli composed the following poem:
My soul is the captive of my sighs, I wish it left [my body] along with the sighs.
There is nothing good in life after you [r death], and indeed I weep fearing that my life becomes long.
And when he shook the dust off his hand after burring Fāṭimah, a new wave of grief erupted inside him, and while tears streamed down his cheeks he turned his face towards Rasōlollāh's grave and said:
Peace be upon you O Rasōlollāh! from me, and from your daughter who just descended to your proximity, and who joined you so soon.
O Rasōlollāh! my patience in the absence of your true friend has reduced, and my endurance has thinned; except that your great separation and grave calamity (Rasōlollāh's death) is my only consolation, for surely I was the one who laid you in your grave, and between my throat and my chest your soul left your body; "SURELY WE ARE ALLĀH'S AND TO HIM WE SHALL SURELY RETURN[1]".
The deposit[2] has surely been returned, and the pledge has been taken back!
As for my sorrow, it is eternal; and as for my night, it is sleepless; until Allāh chooses for me your home in which you reside.
And your daughter shall inform you of your nation assisting each other in her oppression; so ply her with questions, and ask her about it (for surely

---

[1] Holy Qor'ān = sōrah 2, ayah 156.

[2] Before his death, when Rasōlollāh called for ᶜAli and Fāṭimah, he placed Fāṭimah's hand in ᶜAli's hand telling him: O Abā al-Ḥasan! Allāh's deposit, and His messenger's deposit is with you, so keep it safe.

numerous burnings are agitating in her chest about which she could not find a way to speak[1]).
And peace be upon you O Rasōlollāh from one who says farewell, who is neither bored nor hateful. So if I leave, it is not because of weariness; and if I stay, it is not because I doubt what Allāh has promised the patient.
(And patience is more favorable and more graceful. And if it were not for the dominance of the usurpers over us, I would have certainly stayed next to your grave; and I would have surely wailed the wailing of a woman bereaved of her son, because of the graveness of the disaster.
So in the eyes of Allāh, your daughter is secretly buried?!! And her right is forcefully usurped?!! And her inheritance is openly withheld?!![2]) [3])).

Abō Bakr and ᶜOmar attempt to exhume Fāṭimah's body!!

Understanding the meaning and the consequences of ᶜAli's actions, Abō Bakr and ᶜOmar wanted to exhume Fāṭimah's body to perform the *Prayer of the Deceased* on her.

Only days before, when they assassinated her father Rasōlollāh*(SAA)*[4], they also did not participate in his burial ceremonies. But this time, their absence would cost them much more.

Therefore they had to some how compensate. But how?! It has been narrated:

((In the morning, Abō Bakr and ᶜOmar and the people came [to ᶜAli's home], wanting to perform the Prayer

---

[1] Beḥār al-Anwār / al-Majlesi = vol. 43, page 193.
[2] Beḥār al-Anwār / al-Majlesi = vol. 43, page 193.
[3] Aᶜlām al-Nesā' / Kaḥḥālah = vol. 4, page 310. Sharh Nahj al-Balāghah / Ibn Abi al-Ḥadēd – vol. 10, page 265.
[4] *Ṣallallāh ᶜAlayh wa Ālih,* Allāh's Blessings be upon him and his descendants.

of the Deceased on Fāṭimah. Meqdād came forward and said: Indeed, we buried Fāṭimah last night.
ᶜOmar looked at Abō Bakr and said: Did I not tell you that they would do it.
ᶜAbbās said: Indeed, she had stipulated in her will that you do not pray on her.
Omar: You Bani Hāshim never forget your old jealousy of us!! Indeed all of this grudge in your hearts will never fade away!! By Allāh, I have decided to exhume her body and pray on her.
Ali said: By Allāh, if you crave after that O son of Ṣahhāk! I will return to you your right arm[1]. If I unsheathe my sword, I will not return it to its sheath before killing you[2].
So ᶜOmar broke down and stayed silent, knowing that ᶜAli always honors his oath[3].)).

It has also been narrated:

((When Meqdād told ᶜOmar that they had buried Fāṭimah in the previous night, ᶜOmar started to beat him.
Then Meqdād said: Indeed, the Daughter of Rasōlollāh went from this world, while blood was coming out of her back and her side as a result of your beating her with the sword and the whip[4].)).

It has also been narrated:

---

[1] An Arabic proverb.

[2] It has also been narrated that Amēr al-Mo'menēn responded to ᶜOmar, by saying:

> *((Beware! By Allāh, as long as my heart is in my chest, and Dhol-Faqār [the name of his sword] is in my hand, you will most definitely not be able to exhume her body.)).* (al-Ekhteṣāṣ / al-Mofēd = page 185.)

[3] Beḥār al-Anwār / al-Majlesi = vol. 43, page 199. Ketāb Solaym ibn al-Qays = vol. 2, page 870.

[4] al-Kāmil / al-Ṭabari = vol. 1, page 312.

((When the Moslems heard about her burial, they came to Baqē^c and found forty new graves. So they could not distinguish her grave from the others.

Thus they came to a boil, some of them blaming the others saying: Your Prophet did not leave among you but one daughter, and she dies and gets shrouded in the Kafan, and you do not attend her burial ceremonies, and do not know the place of her grave!!

The leaders said: Bring some Moslem women to dig up these graves, and find her body, so that we can pray on her and visit her grave.

When Amēr al-Mo'menēn heard the news, he came out of his home angry, his eyes had turned red, and his jugular veins had become swollen, wearing his yellow Qabā'[1] which he only wore in very hard battles, leaning on his sword Dhol Faqār. He entered the Baqē^c, and the people said: This is ^{c}Ali in the way you see him; he swears to Allāh that if a single stone on any of these graves are moved, he will put the sword to the last of us.

Then ^{c}Omar, accompanied by his men, came to ^{c}Ali and said: What is with you O Abā al-Ḥasan! By Allāh, I will most certainly exhume her body and will surely pray on her!!

So ^{c}Ali grabbed him by his clothes, shook him and hit him to the ground, saying: O son of Ṣahhāk! As for my right, I am not pursuing it fearing that people turn back from their religion; but as for Fāṭimah's grave, so by Him in Whose hand is ^{c}Ali's life, if you and your men seek to dig it up, I will most definitely irrigate the earth from your blood.

Abō Bakr took ^{c}Ali and said: O Abā al-Ḥasan! I plead with you in Rasōlollāh's name and in Allāh's name to let go off ^{c}Omar, for surely we will not do anything you hate.

Thus ^{c}Ali released ^{c}Omar, and the people dispersed and did not repeat that[2].)).

---

[1] An Arabic outer garment.

[2] Beḥār al-Anwār / al-Majlesi = vol. 43, page 171.

ᶜĀ'eshah and Fāṭimah's death

Ibn Abi al-Ḥadēd, the famous Bakri scholar, narrates from his teacher Abō Yaᶜqōb:

> *((...And since Rasōlollāh's death, until Fāṭimah's death, ᶜAli and Fāṭimah repeatedly received hurtful news from ᶜĀ'eshah; but despite the great pain and anger they remained patient.*
>
> *And ᶜAli and Fāṭimah were let down and vanquished; and Fadak was usurped; and although Fāṭimah argued several times for its return, but it was not returned. And regarding that, she heard many hurtful things from ᶜĀ'eshah.*
>
> *And when she died, all of Rasōlollāh's wives came to console Bani Hāshim, except ᶜĀ'eshah who did not come and pretended illness; and ᶜAli heard something from her indicating her happiness [for Fāṭimah's death]!!*[1]*)).*

Moṣṭafa ibn Mojtaba ibn Mahdi al-Ḥosayni al-Shērāzi
9 Rabiᶜ al-Awwal 1424

[1] Sharh Nahj al-Balāghah / Ibn Abi al-Ḥadēd = vol. 9, page 198.

GLOSSARY

Adhān Call to the daily wājib salawāt.

Ahl al-Bayt The Fourteen Maʿsōmēn, who are Rasōlollāh, Sayyedat Nesā' al-ʿĀlamēn, and the twelve God-appointed successors of Rasōlollāh.

Ahl Bayt al-Nobowwah
  Ahl al-Bayt, the Fourteen Maʿsōmēn.

Ahl al-Dhekr The Fourteen Maʿsōmēn.

ʿAlayhas Salām (AaS)
  Peace be upon her. Used after mentioning the name of a female descendant of Rasōlollāh.

ʿAlayhemos Salām (AmS)
  Peace be upon them. Used after mentioning the names of three or more descendants of Rasōlollāh.

ʿAlayhes Salām (AS)
  Peace be upon him. Used after mentioning the name of a male descendant of Rasōlollāh.

Amēr al-Moʾmenēn
  Commander of the Faithful, a title given exclusively to Imām ʿAli by Allāh.

Anṣāri A citizen of Madinah who converted to Islam before the liberation of Makkah. Plural Anṣār.

Āyah A verse from the Holy Qor'ān. Plural āyāt.

Bakri A follower of Abō Bakr. Opposite Moslem, Shēᶜah, follower of Rasōlollāh. Some people unknowingly call the followers of Abō Bakr "sonni". Sonni means a follower of the tradition of Rasōlollāh; and since the followers of Abō Bakr follow him and not Rasōlollāh, it is wrong to call them sonnis.

Dhawi al-Qorbā Sayyedat Nesā' al-ᶜĀlamēn, and the twelve God-appointed successors of Rasōlollāh.

Dhekr A word or a number of words which one is encouraged to repeat many times to be reminded of Allāh and His attributes, etc. There is a huge number of adhkār (plural of dhekr) with different spiritual and material effects. Some adhkār should only be repeated in specific times and/or places, whereas other adhkār are not bound to any time or place restrictions.

Doᶜā' Praying to Allāh, asking Him for something for oneself and/or for others… Doᶜā' can be positive or negative, and has many forms and many uses and effects. Some adᶜeyah (plural of doᶜā') should only be recited in specific times and/or places, whereas other adᶜeyah are not bound to any time or place restrictions. There is a huge number of set formal adᶜeyah narrated from the Fourteen Maᶜṣōmēn, the recitation of which is highly recommended, but it is also possible for any Moslem to compose his own doᶜā', in any language format, provided that he has a considerable knowledge of Islam.

ᶜElm al-Ghayb Knowledge-of-the-Unseen. An all-encompassing knowledge granted by Allāh to a person without the usual methods of learning; a knowledge that covers everything and everyone, and is not limited by time or space, neither is it crippled by what plagues the knowledge gained through education, such as inaccuracy, forgetfulness, etc. ᶜElm al-Ghayb includes the Unseen-World just as it includes the Seen-World; and it has various levels. Prophets and their awṣeyā' have ᶜElm al-Ghayb.

ᶜEṣmah — The state of immunity from committing sins, making mistakes, or any act of forgetfulness, etc. whilst the choice to commit sin remains open to the individual. Prophets and their awṣeyā' have this attribute and are called maᶜṣōm.

ᶜEtrah — Sayyedat Nesā' al-ᶜĀlamēn, and the twelve God-appointed successors of Rasōlollāh.

Fajr — Fajr is one to two hours before sunrise, depending on the time of the year and geographical location.

Ghosl — Islamic ritual washing of the body with plain water. It has two forms, and is performed for a number of reasons some of which are mandatory, whereas others are recommended.

Ḥadēth — A narration from one of the Fourteen Maᶜṣōmēn. Plural aḥādēth.

Ḥalāl — Permissible actions, foods, etc.

Ḥarām — Prohibited actions, foods, etc.

Hejrah — Rasololläh's migration from Makkah to Madinah in the thirteenth year of his mission.

Hejri calendar — The Moslem lunar calendar. It has 12 months and 355 days in a year; it starts from the year of Rasōlollāh's migration to Madinah. AH: after the Hejrah, BH: before the Hejrah.

Imām Leader, good or bad, religious or otherwise. This title has been used for any person with a religious leading role, such as a public prayer leader or leader of a religious group or movement. But in this book it is only used as a title for one of the twelve God-appointed successors of the Prophet Moḥammad. Plural a'emmah.

Imāmah Successorship of Rasōlollāh. Also imamate.

Jehād Linguistically jehād means struggle, religious or otherwise. But as an Islamic term, jehād is only used for religious struggle. Religious struggle in Islam is unlimited, in the sense that it can be in the field of worship, education, economics, politics, society, self training, etc. Therefore the meaning of jehād is determined by the context in which it is used. Here, martial jehād is meant.

Karāmah A supernatural action, etc. performed by or for a Godly person, not as part of a challenge and not to prove that he or she is a Godly person. Plural karāmāt.

Khalēfah A God-appointed successor of Rasōlollāh. Also caliph. Bakris wrongfully use this title for the leaders of the Bakri party who usurped the Rightful Khelāfah from the a'emmah. Plural Kholafā'.

Khelāfah Successorship of Rasōlollāh. Also caliphate.

Khoms An Islamic tax of 20% levied, among other things, on the annual superfluous income. Khoms is given to the Prophet or one of his kholafā' or one of the representatives of the final khalēfah—Marājiᶜ[1], who then give it to its legal recipients accordingly. It

[1] Plural of Marjeᶜ: a highest religious authority.

could also be directly given to the legal recipients under the supervision or with the permission of the Marāji`. Once Khoms is deducted from a certain amount, it will no longer be subject to Khoms in the coming years.

La^c^natollāh ^c^Alayh (LA)

May Allāh distance him from His Blessings and Mercy. Used after mentioning the name of a male enemy of the Fourteen Ma^c^ṣōmēn.

La^c^natollāh ^c^Alayha (LAa)

May Allāh distance her from His Blessings and Mercy. Used after mentioning the name of a female enemy of the Fourteen Ma^c^ṣōmēn.

La^c^natollāh ^c^Alayhem (LAm)

May Allāh distance them from His Blessings and Mercy. Used after mentioning the names of three or more enemies of the Fourteen Ma^c^ṣōmēn.

Maghreb Maghreb is ten to twenty minutes after sunset, depending on the time of the year and geographical location.

*Marje^c^* A highest religious authority.

Ma^c^ṣōm A person who does not commit sins, does not make mistakes, does not forget, etc. although he/she has the choice to commit sins. Prophets and their awṣeyā' are ma^c^ṣōm. Plural: ma^c^ṣōmen. The Fourteen Ma^c^ṣōmen are the Prophet Moḥammad, his daughter Fāṭimah, and his twelve God-appointed successors.

Meḥrāb Place of worship, where a Moslem worships Allāh. Meḥrāb also means a place, especially in a mosque, where the public prayer leader performs the ṣalāt.

Menbar	A raised platform for a Moslem speaker in a mosque, Ḥosayneyyah, etc. where he/she would either stand or sit to give a speech.
Mohājir	A Moslem who migrated from Makkah to Madinah to escape Idolater suppression, before the liberation of Makkah. Plural Mohājirēn.
Moᶜjezah	A supernatural action, etc. performed by or for a Godly person to show others the right path. Plural moᶜjezāt.
Mo'men	Moslem, Shēᶜah, a follower of Rasōlollāh and Amēr al-Mo'menēn.
Monāfiq	A person who shams Islam but in fact is not a Moslem.
Mostaḥab	Recommended.
Qonōt	A particular position in ṣalāt in which the palms are brought up in line with the face, whilst the palms are placed adjacent side by side and facing upwards.
Rasōlollāh	Messenger of Allāh, a title given exclusively to Prophet Moḥammad by Allāh.
Rokōᶜ	A particular position in ṣalāt in which a person bows down, placing the palms on the knees, whilst keeping the legs and the back in a straight position.
Ṣadaqah	Charity, or helping those in need of anything, financial or otherwise; even giving directions can be a ṣadaqah, even removing rubbish, etc. from walkways can be a ṣadaqah. Ṣadaqah has different forms and different effects. Plural ṣadaqāt.
Ṣaḥābi	A companion of the Prophet Moḥammad. Plural Ṣaḥābah.

Ṣalāt 1- Certain connected movements during which parts of the Holy Qor'ān, as well as several adhkār (plural of dhekr) and ad[c]eyah (plural of do[c]ā') are recited. There are many different forms of ṣalāt for different reasons and with different effects; some of which are wājib, whereas others are mostaḥab. Some of these ṣalawāt (plural of ṣalāt) should only be performed in specific times and/or places, whereas other ṣalawāt are not bound to any time or place restrictions.
2- Ṣalāt also means do[c]ā' for Allāh's Blessings and Mercy for someone. There is a large number of set formal ṣalawāt (plural of ṣalāt) narrated from some of the Fourteen Ma[c]ṣōmēn to be recited for other ma[c]ṣōmēn; however any Moslem can compose his own ṣalāt for one or more of the Fourteen Ma[c]ṣōmēn, in any language format, provided that he has a considerable knowledge of Islam.

Ṣallallāh [c]Alayh wa Ālih (SAA)
Allāh's Blessings be upon him and his descendants. Used only after mentioning the name of Rasōlollāh.

Ṣawm Moslem fasting—refraining from eating, drinking, smoking, inhaling steam and thick vapor, sexual intercourse, etc. from fajr to maghreb.

Sayyedat Nesā' al-[c]Ālamēn
Chief of the Women of the World, a title given exclusively to Fāṭimah, the Daughter of Rasōlollāh, by Allāh.

Shē[c]ah Moslem: a follower of Rasōlollāh and Amēr al-Mo'menēn. Opposite Bakri: a follower of Abō Bakr. Shē[c]ah is used as singular and as plural.

Sojōd A particular position in ṣalāt in which the forehead, the palms, the knees and the toes of both feet are

	placed on the ground. Sojōd is also performed on its own—not as part of a ṣalāt—for a number of reasons, some of which are mandatory whereas others are recommended.
Sōrah	A chapter from the Holy Qor’ān. Plural sowar.
Ṭolaqā’	Plural of Ṭalēq, a captive freed by the Moslems. This term is especially used to refer to the Idolater leaders in Makkah who were forgiven by Prophet Moḥammad after the liberation of Makkah.
Wājib	Mandatory acts of worship. Plural wājibāt.
Waṣi	A successor of a prophet, chosen by Allāh and appointed by that prophet. A waṣi is not, himself, a prophet. Also khalēfah or caliph. Plural awṣeyā’.
Zāhid	A person who practices zohd.
Zakāt	An Islamic tax of different rates levied on a number of items beyond a certain limit.
Zeyārah	Zeyārah means visiting, but technically it means the collection of words and sentences which the zā’er (visitor) recites when visiting the shrine of a prophet or a waṣi or a Godly person. There is a large number of set formal zeyārāt (plural of zeyārah) narrated from the Fourteen Maᶜṣōmēn, the recitation of which is highly recommended. Some of these zeyārāt should only be recited in specific times and/or places, whereas other zeyārāt are not bound to any time or place restrictions.
Zohd	Non-attachment to material things.

MOSLEM REFERENCES

1- The Holy Qor'ān

2- Amāli / al-Mofēd
3- Amāli / al-Ṣadōq
4- Amāli / al-Ṭōsi
5- ᶜAwālim al-ᶜOlōm / al-Baḥrāni

6- Bahjat Qalb al-Moṣṭafa / al-Raḥmāni
7- Beḥār al-Anwār / al-Majlesi
8- Beshārat al-Moṣṭafa / al-Ṭabari

9- Dalā'el al-Imāmah / al-Ṭabari
10- Dar Maktab Fāṭimah
11- al-Doᶜā' wa al-Zeyārah / The Martyr, Āyatollāh al-ᶜOẓmā Sayyed Moḥammad Shērazi

12- Eḥqāq al-Ḥaqq / al-Tostari
13- Eḥrāq Bayt al-Zahrā' / al-Sajjād
14- al-Eḥtejāj / al-Ṭabarsi
15- al-Ekhteṣāṣ / al-Mofēd
16- ᶜElal al-Sharā'eᶜ / al-Ṣadōq
17- Eᶜlamō Anni Fāṭimah / al-Mohājir
18- Ershād al-Qolōb / al-Daylami

19- al-Faḍā'el / Ibn Shādhān
20- Fāṭimah al-Zahrā' fi al-Qor'ān / Āyatollāh al-ᶜOẓmā Sayyed Ṣādiq Shērazi
21- Fāṭimah al-Zahrā' min al-Mahd ela al-Laḥd / al-Qazwēni

22- Fāṭimah al-Zahrā' min Qabl al-Mēlād elā Baᶜd al-Estesh-hād / al-Hāshimi

23- al-Ghadēr / al-Amēni
24- Ghāyat al-Marām / al-Sayyed al-Baḥrāni

25- al-Ḥosayn wa Baṭalat Karbala / al-Moghneyah

26- Jalā' al-ᶜOyōn / al-Majlesi
27- Jāmiᶜ al-Saᶜādāt / al-Narāqi

28- al-Kāfi / al-Kolayni
29- Kalimatollāh / The Martyr Āyatollāh Sayyed Ḥasan Shērāzi
30- Kanz al-Fawā'ed / al-Karājaki
31- Kashf al-Ghommah / al-Erbelli
32- al-Kawthar / al-Mōsawi
33- Ketāb Solaym ibn al-Qays
34- al-Konā wa al-Alqāb / al-Qommi

35- Manāqib Āl Abi Ṭālib / Ibn Shahrāshōb
36- Man Lā Yaḥḍoroh al-Faqēh / al-Ṣadōq
37- Min Feqh al-Zahrā' / The Martyr Āyatollāh al-ᶜOẓmā Sayyed Moḥammad Shērāzi
38- Montahā al-Āmāl / al-Qommi (Arabic translation)
39- Mostadrak al-Wasā'el / al-Nōri
40- Mostadrakāt ᶜAwālim al-ᶜOlōm / al-Abṭaḥi

41- Nafaḥāt al-Lāhōt fi Laᶜn al-Jebt wa al-Ṭāghōt / al-Karaki
42- Nahj al-Ḥayāt / al-Dashti
43- Nāsikh al-Tawārēkh / Sepehr
44- Naẓariyyāt al-Khalēfatayn / al-Ṭā'i

45- ᶜOyōn Akhbār al-Reḍā / al-Ṣadōq

46- Pāidāri tā Pāye Dār / Mondhir

47- al-Rejāl / al-Ṭōsi

48- al-Ṣaḥēfah al-Fāṭimeyyah / al-Abṭaḥi

49- Tafsēr / Forāt al-Kōfi
50- Toḥfat al-Aḥbāb fi Nawādir Āthār al-Aṣḥāb / al-Qommi

51- al-Wāfi / al-fayḍ
52- Wasā'el al-Shēᶜah / al-Ḥorr al-ᶜĀmili

BAKRI REFERENCES

1- al-Abdāl / al-Ḥalabi
2- al-Āḥād wa al-Mathāni / al-Shaybāni
3- al-Aḥādēth al-Mokhtārah / al-Maqdesi
4- Aḥkām al-Qor'ān / al-Jaṣṣāṣ
5- Akhbār al-Dowal wa Āthār al-Owal / al-Qermāni
6- A^{c}lām al-Nesā' / Kaḥḥālah
7- Amāli / al-Maḥāmili
8- al-Ansāb / al-Sam^{c}āni
9- Ansāb al-Ashrāf / al-Balādheri
10- Anwār al-Tanzēl / al-Bayḍāwi
11- Arba^{c}ēn / al-Rāzi
12- Asnā al-Maṭālib / Ibn Darwēsh
13- Asnā al-Maṭālib fi Manāqib ^{c}Ali ibn Abi Ṭālib / Ibn al-Jazari
14- Āthār al-Belād wa Akhbār al-^{c}Ebād / al-Qazwēni

15- al-Badr al-Ṭāli^{c} / al-Shawkāni
16- Bahjat al-Nofōs / al-Ḥāfiẓ al-Azdi
17- Balāghāt al-Nesā' / Ibn Ṭayfōr
18- al-Bedāyah wa al-Nehāyah / Ibn Kothayr

19- Dalā'el al-Nobowwah / al-Bayhaqi
20- Dalā'el al-Nobowwah / Abō No^{c}aym
21- al-Ḍaw' al-Lāmi^{c} / al-Sakhāwi
22- Dhakhā'er al-^{c}Oqbā / al-Ṭabari
23- al-Dhorreyyah al-Ṭāhirah / al-Dōlābi
24- al-Dorar al-Montathirah / al-Soyōṭi
25- Dorar al-Semṭayn / al-Zarandi

26- al-Dorr al-Manthōr / al-Soyōṭi

27- Eḥyā' ^{c}Olōm al-Dēn / al-Ghazāli
28- E^{c}jāz al-Qor'ān / al-Bāqillāni
29- al-^{c}Enāyah / Shahābboddēn
30- al-^{c}Eqd al-Farēd / Ibn ^{c}Abderabbeh
31- Ershād al-Sāri / al-Qasṭalāni
32- al-Eṣābah / al-^{c}Asqalāni
33- Es^{c}āf al-Rāghibēn / Ibn al-Ṣabbān
34- al-Estē^{c}āb / Ibn ^{c}Abdelbarr
35- al-E^{c}teqād / al-Bayhaqi
36- al-Etqān / al-Soyōṭi
37- Ezālat al-Khafā' / al-Dehlawi

38- Faḍā'el al-Ṣaḥābah / Ibn Ḥanbal
39- Faḍā'el al-Ṣaḥābah / al-Nasā'i
40- Faḍā'el Sayyedat al-Nesā' / Ibn Shāhēn
41- al-Fā'eq / al-Zamakhshari
42- Farā'ed al-Semṭayn / al-Ḥamō'i
43- al-Farq bayn al-Feraq / al-Esfarā'ēni
44- Fatḥ al-Bāri / al-^{c}Asqalāni
45- al-Fatḥ al-Kabēr / al-Nabahāni
46- Fatḥ al-Qadēr / al-Shawkāni
47- al-Fawā'ed / al-Ḥāfiẓ al-Azdi
48- al-Fawā'ed al-Majmō^{c}ah / al-Shawkāni
49- Fayḍ al-Qadēr / al-Monāwi
50- al-Ferdaws / al-Hamadāni
51- al-Foṣōl al-Mohemmah / Ibn al-Ṣabbāgh
52- Fotōḥ al-Boldān / al-Balādheri
53- al-Fotōḥāt al-Rabbāniyyah / Ibn al-^{c}Allān

54- Gharā'eb al-Qor'ān / al-Naysābōri
55- Gharēb al-Ḥadēth / Ibn Qotaybah
56- al-Ghorar / Ibn Khayzorānah

57- Ḥāshiyat al-Shaykh-zādeh ^{c}alā Tafsēr al-Bayḍāwi
58- Ḥelyat al-Awleyā' / Abō No^{c}aym

59- al-Imāmah wa al-Seyāsah / Ibn Qotaybah

60- Jamᶜ al-Jawāmiᶜ / al-Soyōṭi
61- Jāmiᶜ Bayān al-Elm / Ibn ᶜAbdelbarr
62- Jāmiᶜ al-Bayān fi Tafsēr al-Qor'ān / al-Ṭabari
63- al-Jāmiᶜ al-Kabēr / al-Soyōṭi
64- al-Jāmiᶜ le Aḥkām al-Qor'ān / al-Qorṭobi
65- Jāmiᶜ al-Oṣōl / Ibn al-Athēr
66- al-Jāmiᶜ al-Ṣaghēr / al-Soyōṭi
67- Jawāhir al-ᶜEqdayn / al-Samhōdi

68- al-Kāmil / Ibn ᶜOday
69- al-Kāmil / al-Jorjāni
70- al-Kāmil / al-Ṭabari
71- Kanz al-ᶜOmmāl / al-Hendi
72- Kashf al-Khafā' / al-ᶜAjlōni
73- al-Kashf wa al-Bayān / al-Thaᶜlabi
74- al-Kash-shāf / al-Zamakhshari
75- Kefāyat al-Ṭālib / al-Kanji
76- Ketāb al-Wafāt / al-Nasā'i
77- al-Khaṣā'eṣ / al-Nasā'i
78- al-Khaṣā'eṣ al-Kobrā / al-Soyōṭi
79- al-Khoṭaṭ / al-Maqrēzi
80- al-Konā / al-Bokhāri

81- La'āli al-Akhbār / al-Soyōṭi
82- Lesān al-ᶜArab / Ibn Manẓōr
83- Lesān al-Mēzān / al-ᶜAsqalāni
84- Lobāb al-Ta'wēl fi Maᶜāni al-Tanzēl / al-Khāzin

85- Maᶜālim al-Tanzēl / al-Baghawi
86- Mafāteḥ al-Ghayb / al-Rāzi
87- al-Maghāzi wa al-Seyar / al-Ḥaḍrami
88- al-Majālis / Kōseh-zādeh
89- Majmaᶜ al-Zawā'ed / al-Haythami
90- al-Majrōḥēn / al-Bosti
91- al-Majrōḥēn / Ibn Ḥabbān
92- Manāl al-Ṭālib / Ibn al-Athēr

93- al-Manāqib / al-Khārazmi
94- Manāqib ^{c}Ali ibn Abi Ṭālib / Ibn al-Maghāzili
95- Manāqib Fāṭimah / al-Naysābōri
96- Maqātil al-Ṭālibeyyēn / al-Eṣbahāni
97- Maqtal al-Ḥosayn / al-Khārazmi
98- Ma^{c}refat ^{c}Olōm al-Ḥadēth / al-Naysābōri
99- Ma^{c}refat al-Ṣaḥābah / Abō No^{c}aym
100- Maṣābēḥ al-Sonnah / al-Baghawi
101- Maṭālib al-Sa'ōl / Abō Sālim al-Shāfe^{c}i
102- Mawārid al-Ẓam'ān
103- al-Melal wa al-Neḥal / al-Shahrestāni
104- Mēzān al-E^{c}tedāl / al-Dhahabi
105- al-Moghni / ^{c}Abdoljabbār
106- Mo^{c}jam / Ibn al-Mothanna
107- al-Mo^{c}jam al-Awsaṭ / al-Ṭabarāni
108- Mo^{c}jam al-Boldān / al-Ḥamawi
109- al-Mo^{c}jam al-Kabēr / al-Ṭabarāni
110- Mo^{c}jam al-Moḥaddethēn / al-Dhahabi
111- al-Mo^{c}jam al-Ṣaghēr / al-Ṭabarāni
112- Mo^{c}jam al-Shoyōkh / al-Ṣaydāwi
113- al-Mojtaba / Ibn Dorayd
114- Mokhtaṣar Dhakhā'er al-^{c}Oqbā
115- al-Mokhtaṣar fi Akhbār al-Bashar / Abō al-Fedā'
116- Mokhtaṣar Jāmi^{c} al-Elm
117- Mokhtaṣar al-Maḥāsin al-Mojtami^{c}ah
118- Mokhtaṣar Tārēkh Demashq
119- Montakhab Kanz al-^{c}Ommāl
120- al-Montaẓam / Ibn al-Jawzi
121- Moṣannaf / ^{c}Abdorrazzāq
122- Moṣannaf / Ibn Abi Shaybah
123- Moshkel al-Athār / al-Ṭaḥāwi
124- Mosnad / Abi ^{c}Awānah
125- Mosnad / Abi Dāwōd
126- Mosnad / Abi Ya^{c}la
127- Mosnad / Aḥmad
128- Mosnad / al-Bazzār
129- Mosnad / Eshāq ibn Rāhawayh
130- Mosnad / al-Ḥomaydi

131- Mosnad / al-Shāfeᶜi
132- Mosnad / al-Ṭayālisi
133- Mosnad ᶜAbdollāh ibn ᶜOmar / al-Tarsōsi
134- Mosnad Fāṭimah al-Zahrā' / al-Soyōṭi
135- Mosnad ᶜOmar / al-Sadōsi
136- Mosnad al-Shahāb / al-Qoḍāᶜi
137- Mosnad al-Shāmiyyēn / al-Ṭabarāni
138- al-Mostadrak / al-Ḥākim
139- al-Mostadrak / al-Naysābōri
140- al-Mostaṭraf / al-Ebshēhi
141- Moᶜtasar al-Mokhtaṣar / Abō al-Maḥāsin al-Ḥanafi

142- Nawādir al-Oṣōl / al-Termedhi
143- al-Nehāyah / Ibn al-Athēr
144- Nehāyat al-Erab / al-Nowayri
145- Nōr al-Abṣār / al-Shablanji
146- Nozhat al-Majālis / al-Ṣafōri

147- ᶜOmdat al-Qāri' / al-ᶜAyni
148- Osd al-Ghābah / Ibn al-Athēr
149- Oṣōl al-Tafsēr / Ibn Taymeyyah
150- ᶜOyōn al-Akhbār / Ibn Qotaybah

151- al-Qawl al-Fasl / al-Ḥaḍrami
152- Qorrat al-Aynayn / al-Dehlawi

153- Rashfat al-Ṣādi / al-Ḥaḍrami
154- Rasōlollāh, the Messenger of Allāh / by the author
155- al-Rawḍ al-Fā'eq / al-Meṣri
156- al-Reyāḍ al-Naḍirah / al-Ṭabari
157- Rōḥ al-Bayān / al-Borōsawi
158- Rōḥ al-Maᶜāni / al-Ālōsi

159- Ṣefat al-Ṣafwah / Ibn al-Jawzi
160- Ṣaḥēḥ / Ibn Ḥabbān
161- Ṣaḥēḥ / Ibn Mājah
162- Ṣaḥēḥ / Moslem
163- al-Saqēfah wa Fadak / al-Jawhari

164- al-Ṣawā^{c}iq al-Moḥreqah / Ibn Ḥajar
165- Sērah / Ibn Hoshām
166- al-Sērah al-Ḥalabiyyah / al-Ḥalibi
167- al-Sērah al-Nabawiyyah / Ibn Kothayr
168- Sērat ^{c}Omar / Ibn al-Jawzi
169- Seyar A^{c}lām al-Nobalā' / al-Dhahabi
170- Sharaf al-Nobowwah / Abō Sa^{c}d
171- Sharh al-Maqāṣid / al-Taftāzāni
172- Sharh Nahj al-Balāghah / Ibn Abi al-Ḥadēd
173- Shawāhid al-Tanzēl / al-Ḥasakāni
174- Sho^{c}ab al-Ēmān / al-Bayhaqi
175- Sonan / Abi Dāwōd
176- Sonan / al-Dārimi
177- Sonan / Ibn Abi ^{c}Āsim
178- Sonan / Ibn Mājah
179- Sonan / Sa^{c}ēd ibn Manṣōr
180- Sonan / al-Termedhi
181- al-Sonan al-Kobrā / al-Bayhaqi
182- al-Sonan al-Kobrā / al-Nasā'i
183- al-Sonnah / Ibn Abi ^{c}Āsim

184- al-Ṭabaqāt al-Kobrā / Ibn Sa^{c}d
185- Ṭabaqāt al-Moḥaddethēn be-Eṣbahān
186- Tadhkerat Khawāṣ al-Ommah / Ibn al-Jawzi
187- Tadrēb al-Rāwi / al-Soyōṭi
188- al-Tadwēn fi Akhbār al-Qazwēn / al-Rāfi^{c}i al-Qazwēni
189- Tafsēr / al-^{c}Ayyāshi
190- Tafsēr / al-Bayḍāwi
191- Tafsēr / al-Ḥāfiẓ al-Eṣbahāni
192- Tafsēr / Ibn Kothayr
193- Tafsēr / al-Jalālayn
194- Tafser al-Kash-shāf / al-Zamakhshari
195- Tafsēr al Khāzin / al-Baghdadi
196- Tafsēr al-Qor'ān al-^{c}Aẓēm / Ibn Kothayr
197- Tahdhēb al-Asmā' / al-Nawawi
198- Tahdhēb al-Kamāl / al-Mazzi
199- Tahdhēb al-Tahdhēb / al-^{c}Asqalāni
200- Taḥdhēr al-Khawāṣ / al-Soyōṭi

201- Tāj al-[c]Arōs / al-Zabēdi
202- Tajhēz al-Jaysh / al-Dehlawi
203- Talkhēṣ al-Mostadrak / al-Dhahabi
204- al-Tamhēd / al-Bāqillāni
205- Tarakat al-Nabi / al-Baghdādi
206- Tārēkh / al-Ṭabari
207- Tārēkh / al-Ya[c]qōbi
208- Tārēkh Baghdād / al-Baghdādi
219- Tārēkh Demashq / Ibn [c]Asākir
210- Tārēkh al-Islam / al-Dhahabi
211- al-Tārēkh al-Kabēr / al-Bokhāri
212- Tārēkh al-Khamēs / al-Deyārbakri
213- Tārēkh al-Kholafā’ / al-Soyōṭi
214- Tārēkh al-Madinah / Ibn Shobbah
215- Tārēkh al-Omam wa al-Molōk / al-Ṭabari
216- al-Tashēl le-[c]Olōm al-Tanzēl / al-Kalbi
217- Taysēr al-Woṣōl / al-Shaybāni
218- al-Theqāt / Ibn Ḥabbān
219- al-Thoghōr al-Bāsimah = al-Soyōṭi
220- Toḥfah / al-Āḥōdhi

221- Wafā’ al-Wafā / al-Samhōdi
222- al-Wāfi fi al-Wafayāt / al-Ṣafdi
223- Wāqi[c]at Ṣeffēn / al-Menqari
224- Wasēlat al-Ma’āl / al-Ḥaḍrami
225- Wasēlat al-Mota[c]abbedēn / Omar ibn Moḥammad

226- Yanābē[c] al-Mawaddah / al-Qandōzi

227- Zayn al-Fata fi Tafsēr Sōrat Hal Atā / al-Ḥāfiẓ al-[c]Āsimi